Migration Models

MIGRATION MODELS: MACRO AND MICRO APPROACHES

Edited by
John Stillwell and Peter Congdon

Belhaven Press
London and New York

© The Editors and Contributors, 1991

First published in Great Britain in 1991 by
Belhaven Press (a division of Pinter Publishers),
25 Floral Street, London WC2E 9DS

British Library Cataloguing in Publication Data

A CIP catalogue record for this book is available from the
British Library

ISBN 1–85293–148–5

Library of Congress Cataloging in Publication Data

Migration models: macro and micro approaches/edited by John
    Stillwell and Peter Congdon.
        p. cm.
    Includes bibliographical references and index.
    ISBN 1–85293–148–5
    1. Migration, Internal – Great Britain – Econometric models.
2. Migration, Internal – Mathematical models.   I. Stillwell, John.
II. Congdon, P.
HB2043.M55   1991
304.8′0941–dc20
                                                                    91-14335
                                                                    CIP

Typeset by Mayhew Typesetting, Bristol, England
Printed and bound in Great Britain by Biddles Ltd of Guildford and Kings Lynn

Contents

List of Figures

List of Tables

List of contributors

Ursula Bilger, Institut fur Volkswirtschaftslehre, Universitat Hohenheim, 7000 Stuttgart 70, Germany.

Peter Boden, School of Geography, University of Leeds, Leeds LS2 9JT, United Kingdom.

Peter D. Congdon, London Research Centre, Parliament House, 81 Black Prince Road, London SE1 7SZ, United Kingdom.

Richard B. Davies, Centre for Applied Statistics, School of Engineering, Computing and Mathematical Sciences, Lancaster University, Lancaster LA1 4YF, United Kingdom.

Christopher J. Duley, School of Geography, University of Leeds, Leeds LS2 9JT, United Kingdom.

Robin Flowerdew, Department of Geography, University of Lancaster, Lancaster LA1 4YR, United Kingdom.

A. Stewart Fotheringham, Department of Geography, Faculty of Social Science, Wilkeson Quad, Buffalo, New York 14261, United States.

Joachim Genosko, Institut fur Volkswirtschaftslehre, Universitat Hohenheim (S20), 7000 Stuttgart 70, Germany.

Ian R. Gordon, Department of Geography, University of Reading, Whiteknights, P.O. Box 227, Reading RG6 2AB, United Kingdom.

Georg Hirte, Institut fur Volkswirtschaftslehre, Universitat Hohenheim, 7000 Stuttgart 70, Germany.

Donald R. Haurin, Department of Economics, Ohio State University, 1945 N. High St, Columbus, Ohio 43210, United States.

R. Jean Haurin, Center for Human Research, Ohio State University, 921 Chatham Lane Suite 200, Columbus, Ohio 43221, United States.

George Kephart, Department of Sociology, Pennsylvania State University, University Park, PA 16802, United States.

Gunther Maier, Institute for Urban and Regional Studies, University of Economics and Business Administration, A-1090 Wien, Augasse 2-6, Austria.

William Milne, Institute for Policy Analysis, University of Toronto, 140 St. George Street Suite 707, Toronto, Canada.

Philip H. Rees, School of Geography, University of Leeds, Leeds LS2 9JT, United Kingdom.

Gary D. Sandefur, Institute for Research on Poverty and Center for Demography and Ecology, University of Wisconsin-Madison, Madison, Wisconsin 53711, United States.

Lasse S. Stambøl, Central Bureau of Statistics, Oslo, Norway.

John C.H. Stillwell, School of Geography, University of Leeds, Leeds LS2 9JT, United Kingdom.

Nancy B. Tuma, Department of Sociology, Stanford University, California 94305, United States.

Peter Weiss, Institute for Urban and Regional Studies, University of Economics and Business Administration, A-1090 Wien, Augasse 2-6, Austria.

Preface

Migration is an experience with which most of us are familiar. For some it is associated with excitement and challenge; for others, sadness and failure. It has a special relevance in the current economic climate when individual solutions to economic problems, such as 'getting on your bike', are stressed, and when a classless society is defined in terms of unhindered social and geographic mobility.

1981 Census statistics suggest that, on average, British people change their place of usual residence at least six times during the course of their lives. Each time an individual contemplates moving home, there is likely to be a unique set of forces shaping the decision of whether to move or to remain *in situ* and influencing the choice of destination from among possible alternatives.

The processes which confront the migration analyst trying to understand human behaviour in this context are therefore very complicated. Research has tended to be undertaken either at the individual (micro) level primarily using life history information or at a more aggregate (macro) level based on data from published sources. In both these contexts, migration models have been constructed as tools with which to investigate functional relationships or to generate predictions. This book contains a collection of some of the macro and micro approaches that migration modellers have developed and used in their investigations during the last decade. The intention has been to produce a volume accessible to relative newcomers to migration analysis as well as containing some of the most up-to-date methodology in the field. Some of the chapters are therefore intentionally more pedagogic than others. In most cases, methodologies are exemplified and results are discussed.

Contributors to a volume such as this are frequently subjected to a certain amount of editorial 'encouragement'. We recognise the time and effort that authors have committed to preparing chapters for this project and wish to thank those concerned for responding positively to our suggested revisions. In addition, we are very grateful for the cartographic help received from Tim Hadwin and John Dixon in the Drawing Office in the School of Geography at the University of Leeds.

John Stillwell and Peter Congdon
February 1991

Chapter 1

Migration modelling: concepts and contents

John Stillwell and Peter Congdon

1.1 Introduction

Migration models are typically designed to provide either explanations of the historical processes of population redistribution or frameworks for generating projections of migration activity in the future. Thus, the calibration of multiple regression models, for example, enables quantification of the influences of independent variables on migration behaviour purely to clarify the processes involved. By contrast, spatial interaction models or model migration schedules seek to achieve parsimony by concentrating on the reduction of large amounts of data to a relatively small number of parameters so as to facilitate secondary applications such as forecasting. Explanatory models may also be applied with a secondary purpose in mind but are frequently constructed as an end in themselves. They include, for example, logit models of the individual migration decision-making process, as well as simultaneous discrete choice models expressing the interaction between different types of mobility at the micro level, or at the macro level, models of the relationship between migration flows and labour or housing market change. When used in demographic forecasting, migration models often have a simplified explanatory structure as, for example, in the case of housing stock-led forecasts of the migration component of population change and forecasts linked to labour force change.

However, the form of the migration model is defined as much by the nature of the available data as it is by the purpose (e.g. explanation or forecasting) for which the model is intended. Surveys such as the Labour Force Survey (LFS) in Europe or the Current Population Survey (CPS) in the United States generate data at the micro or individual level based on a comparison of place of residence at time t and time t-1. More complex surveys, such as the Longitudinal Study (LS) in Britain or the Panel Survey of Income Dynamics (PSID) in the United States, provide a continuous record of migrant residences and (sometimes also) lengths of stay plus the ability to track other socio-demographic changes of both the migrant and the non-migrant populations over time. Generally speaking, the richer the detail that is provided from the data source, the more sophisticated (and more rigorous) the models that can be fitted. For example, data limitations mean that relatively simple logit models of either whether to move or not, or which particular destination to move to, generally ignore any influence that the length of residence at one address has on the migration decision.

Whilst survey data on internal migration is available in most of the world's more developed countries (Nam *et al.* 1990), enabling analysts to tackle questions about motivation at the micro or individual level, the basic sources of macro or aggregate migration data are censuses and registration systems. Censuses employ questions about a person's place of previous residence at some earlier date whereas registration systems record changes of address on an ongoing basis. In some countries such as Sweden or the Netherlands, population registration systems provide detailed and accurate information on changes of residence. In other countries such as the United Kingdom where no population registration system exists, less reliable and less comprehensive data can be extracted from sources such as the National Health Service Central Register of patient re-registrations or the Electoral Register. The macro data available from censuses and registers is the most suitable for evaluating the relationship between migration and changes in labour and housing markets or for the purposes of migration forecasting.

The availability of different types of data from alternative sources emphasises in a practical way the distinction between micro and macro levels of investigation. In a more conceptual sense, it is evident that neither level provides a complete picture of the migration process. Micro-level models do not provide a comprehensive treatment of origin or destination area influences on migration or of the interdependence between migration and other socioeconomic processes, while macro-level models can only allow relatively crudely for the influence of life-cycle characteristics or individual job skills. In this sense, all migration models are partial models.

There are three further initial points of importance before we introduce some of the theoretical concepts underlying migration modelling that will appear in more detail in later chapters. First, the nature of the migration model will also depend on the context of its application. A model designed to describe counterurbanisation movements in developed societies is likely to be distinctly different from a model of urbanisation in less developed societies, for example. Second, there are fundamental questions about which theory of migration behaviour should be used to underpin the model and which statistical or modelling technique should be used to calibrate the model. Finally, whilst it is convenient to draw attention to the pressures which influence model form — the purpose of the model, the nature of the data that is available, the scale and type of migration involved and the theoretical context — there is no unique way to model a particular set of data of a given degree of complexity. There is no necessarily correct or incorrect method of modelling migration and this is undoubtedly one of the reasons for the bewildering plethora of model structures and applications which is to be found in the literature. Neither is debate confined to the selection of variables for inclusion in the model equation. It goes much beyond that to issues that relate to the way in which the whole process of migration is conceived, exemplified by the contrasting approaches of nested choice and simultaneous choice models as applied to a matrix of migration flows between a set of regions. The nested choice approach assumes that the migrant's choice of destination follows the decision of whether or not to migrate at all, whereas the simultaneous choice approach assumes that both movers and stayers are involved in evaluating potential destinations with a view to possible migration. Choice of modelling technique may therefore be crucial in the validation or otherwise of migration theory.

1.2 Migration definition and measurement

There are certain issues of migration definition and measurement which it is necessary to confront by way of introduction. As a simple concept, the definition of migration is straightforward. It involves a change of usual residence by a person, family or household. The concept of migration is inherently geographical because a change of residence necessitates movement from one location to another. This geographical interaction may occur over very short distances (e.g. to a different residence in the same apartment block) or across much longer distances (e.g. between continents). The focus of this book is on 'internal' migration — changes of residence between origins and destinations that are located within the same national territorial boundary.

The actual movements of individuals from one dwelling to another only form one very small subset of the total movements of population across the surface of the globe. Consequently, the concept of population 'mobility' is useful in distinguishing residential migration from the other movements such as journeys to work, shopping trips, recreation excursions or holiday outings (Zelinsky 1971). There are, however, situations in which it becomes difficult to decide what constitutes a migration. These circumstances are commonly associated with vagrants or persons of no fixed abode, temporary workers employed perhaps on a seasonal basis or on short-term contracts, or students of higher education who move back and forth between parental home and college or university three or four times a year. Another anomaly is presented by those who own more than one property and who may move from one home to another on a regular or more random basis. These examples demonstrate that in order to measure migration it may be necessary to sharpen the definition by including a temporal dimension to distinguish permanent changes of dwelling place from temporary changes of address. Moreover, White and Woods (1980, p. 3) have indicated that 'the reason for the difference between the conceptual and the operational definitions lies in the nature of the sources available for the study of any migrational phenomenon'.

Details of the variety of sources of internal migration data in different countries of the developed and less developed world can be obtained from the recently published *International Handbook on Internal Migration* (Nam *et al*. 1990). The basic sources of data upon which migration models are calibrated and tested include censuses, registration systems and regular or special surveys. In the context of migration measurement, a very important distinction was drawn by Courgeau (1973; 1980) between the concept of 'migration', the event that takes place through which a person, family or household changes residence, and the concept of the 'migrant', the individual person involved in making the move. The first concept of 'movements' (Ledent 1980) involves measuring migration from counts of moves registered by a population registration system, whereas the second concept of 'transitions' is based on retrospective questions in population censuses or surveys. Typically, in the case of the latter, migration is measured by comparing locations at two points in time. The 1966 Census of Population (10% sample) in England and Wales, for example, defined a migrant as anyone resident in one location on census night whose usual residence was different from that one year or five years beforehand. Rees (1986) indicates that transitions over a time period are classifications of the population by initial and final locations. Any intermediate locations at which a person may have been resident are unknown. Moves, on the other hand, are events in which both the immediately preceding and following locations are known.

The distinction between transition and movement data is exemplified by comparison of the two primary sources of internal migration data in Britain — the Census of Population and the National Health Service Central Register (NHSCR). The NHSCR provides information on Health Service patients transferring between doctors in different NHS administrative areas. Thus, for example, an individual who undertakes several re-registrations within a given period of observation (say, the twelve months prior to the 1981 Census) will have each transfer recorded in the NHSCR, but will only be classified as a single migrant in the census. If that individual returns to the same address occupied initially before the period of observation ends, that person would be classified as a non-migrant. Consequently, the conceptual difference between the two types of data is highlighted by the way in which multiple and return movements are handled. This distinction, together with differences in the populations covered by the two sources and additional operational measurement differences, is clarified in Boden *et al*. (1991), where the results of a systematic comparison of migration data from the NHSCR and from the 1981 Census for 1980–81 are described. Confusion over the distinction between moves and transitions led Ledent and Rees (1980) to suggest that several of population projections undertaken as part of the Migration and Settlement Study (Rogers and Willekens 1986) were hybrid in character because census-based transition data were used in movement-based population models. Rees (1983) shows that it really does matter which type of migration data is used in a population model.

1.3 Some theoretical underpinnings

The micro–macro distinction taken from economics provides a central criterion in the formulation of alternative migration models and conditions the way that migration is linked to the wider operations of housing and labour markets. White (1980) refers to the distinction between the two approaches as a philosophical dichotomy which also has parallels in psychology.

Micro theory essentially relates to the processes underlying the 'decision' by a potential migrant to remain in a current residence or to migrate to another one. However, it also takes into consideration those influences bearing on this decision and on the 'choice' of destination if a move is made, as well as the interrelation between the change of residence and other changes of status that relate to an individual.

A central theoretical issue underpinning much analysis of migration behaviour has been the distinction between, on the one hand, the individual's decision to move and, on the other, the nature and direction of the move itself, once the decision to migrate has been made. The factors bearing on these decisions include both the characteristics of individual persons (such as their age, marital status, household status) or individual housing units (such as their size, structure) and the wider characteristics of areas and markets (such as the regional relativities of wages and house prices) which provide the context for the migration. In the words of Greenwood (1985, p. 527), 'given an individual's personal characteristics, general labour market conditions and employment composition will help determine the probability of gaining employment (at the destination)'. The interdependence between an individual's migration and other state changes will tend to vary according to the distance over which the migration takes place. When a change of residence involves a move within one locality, this will often not be associated with a change of workplace or with any alteration in commuting pattern, but it may involve a change of house type as the individual moves from one life course state to another. In this situation migration is interacting with the housing career of the individual. Longer-distance migrations, on the other hand, will usually be accompanied by changes in workplace and often in other labour market attributes (such as income or occupational status), reflecting migration interactions with job careers. The interrelation between migration behaviour and the changes which individuals experience as a consequence of progress through their life courses has been examined by various researchers since Thomas's early study (1938) of age differentials of interstate migration in the United States. It has been in the context of intra-urban residential mobility that much of the seminal work on choice behaviour and the social psychology of the decision-making process with respect to migration has been achieved (Rossi 1955; Abu-Lughod *et al*. 1960).

Macro theory, on the other hand, relates to aggregate moves and is more appropriate for setting migration in its labour market context in order to deal with questions such as whether people migrate into subnational areas where new jobs are available or whether jobs result after an initial influx of population. The 'people-first' versus 'jobs-first' debate has been important in attempts to explain counterurbanisation processes in different parts of the world (see, for example, Robinson 1981). Macro approaches are therefore concerned with investigating the relationships between migration and objectively determined macro variables such as changing job provision, unemployment rates, wage rates or environmental conditions. The central questions here have focused on the role of migration in the labour and housing markets and in particular on the impact of migration on receiving and exporting regions in terms of their demand for homes and jobs.

In connection with the labour market, the question can be formulated in terms of whether rates of outmigration are higher from areas with high unemployment characteristics and whether rates of inmigration are correspondingly lower to these regions. If so, then migration would appear to be reducing unemployment differentials and is said to act as an 'equilibrating' mechanism, evening out regional disparities in labour market indicators such as unemployment or wages. This type of perspective has its roots in classical theory of regional self-balance through inter-regional adjustment. Classical models of migration which postulate a negative feedback role for migration have been challenged by arguments that both gross outmigration and inmigration flows are higher for growth regions (Gleave and Cordey-Hayes 1977) and that the selective nature of migration enhances differentials in regional incomes and job growth. This theoretical perspective therefore recognises migration as being disequilibrating (Myrdal 1957). A more recent school of thought associated with the American analyst Graves (1983), for example, challenges labour market equilibrium-seeking models of migration and argues that location-specific amenities, measured by property rents, are a major determinant of inmigration.

The distinction between micro and macro approaches to migration modelling provides a useful broad classification framework, but it must be recognised that migration flows that occur in reality are the summation of decisions made by individuals and that theories that underpin the determination of individual migration decisions also bear on the validation of macro models. Molho (1986, p. 406) indicates that 'whilst microeconomic theories of migration start at the level of the individual, most such models will clearly generate some form of gravity [macro] formulation when aggregated over homogeneous population groups'.

The need to integrate micro and macro analyses was emphasised by Morrison (1973) and a conceptual framework has been proposed more recently by Cadwallader (1989) which comprises four sets of relationships. Firstly, there is the link between aggregate migration and the set of regional variables which has traditionally been investigated using macro models. Secondly, there are the links between the regional variables defined objectively and the subjective perceptions of those indicators by each individual potential migrant. The third set of relations involves the integration of these perceptions about places into aggregate utility functions which, in the final set of relations, are translated into migration flows. The requirement for aggregation of individual perceptions of utility over homogeneous groups is often difficult in practice and micro-economic relationships may not aggregate linearly. However, some form of partial aggregation, retaining a classification by the crucial individual variables such as age or household type (e.g. migration by five-year age groups or by social class) provides a method of testing micro theories at the macro level. Furthermore, theoretical concepts such as equilibrium or disequilibrium apply equally to macro and micro analysis. Micro models of residential mobility (Onaka and Clarke 1983, for example) interpret the housing 'stress' which precedes changes in residence in terms of macro theoretical disequilibrium concepts.

However, the reality is that much of the theory that has been delivered has tended to strengthen the dichotomy as much as to encourage synthesis between the two approaches. This may in part be due to the particular interest in different aspects of the whole migration process by researchers from different disciplines. Sociologists and social psychologists have been influential in formulating behavioural theories that specify the nature of migration choice (Wolpert 1973). A good deal of theory about the nature of the decision process itself was formulated on the basis of the distinction between the decision to move and the choice of destination (Speare *et al.* 1975). However, the validity of this separation has been challenged more recently by those who advocate the indivisible nature of the decisions about whether to move and where to move to (see Maier and Weiss in Chapter 2).

The former decomposition has provided a theoretical platform for macro migration modelling, including work on identifying temporal stability in migration patterns. Baydar (1983) for example, decomposes the flow of migrants from one region to another into three components: (i) a level component, representing the total number of migrations occurring in the time period, (ii) a generation component which measures the probability that a migration in the system of interest originates from region i, and (iii) a distribution component that measures the probability that a migrant to region j given he or she originates from region i.

Whilst population geographers have been preoccupied with aggregate theories of spatial interaction and gravity model representations of migration flows in particular, economists and econometricians have made use of the micro–macro categorisation which characterises their discipline. Theories have been articulated which formally specify the role of macro and micro variables relating to employment, housing and the environment. The human capital approach (Sjaastad 1962), for example, emphasises the income returns to migration which can accrue over the remainder of the migrant's working life. Thus, an individual's age and human capital skills (such as education and training) have a formalised role in assessing the validity of the human capital model of migration. At the micro level, there exists a plethora of theoretical perspectives relating to the influences on migration set within a push–pull framework (Lee 1966) and a long tradition of statistical models for testing the explanatory significance of sets of explanatory variables. One classic example is that of Lowry (1966) whose model of migration flows between Standard Metropolitan Statistical Areas in the United States incorporated measures of economic opportunity at origin and destination as well as traditional gravity variables measuring the sizes of places and the distance between them.

In macro models of this type, data have to be collected to measure the dependent or response variable and the independent variables which are used to predict migration. Typically, linear regression techniques have been adopted to generate coefficients (or parameters) for each of the independent variables using log transformed data values. The shortcomings of this form of regression have stimulated subsequent experimentation with different structural forms, resulting in more satisfactory operational expressions (Flowerdew and Lovett 1989). It has also been suggested that single equation models (both micro and macro) are unsatisfactory since they suffer from simultaneity bias (Willis 1974; Greenwood 1985). The implicit assumption of single equation models is that while certain factors influence migration, migration does not in turn influence these factors. If this assumption does not hold, then the parameter estimates of single equation models will be vitiated. At the macro level, an example is the relation between job growth, inmigration and changes in local labour force participation. A strong local economy will attract high levels of inmigration, *ceteris paribus*. However, it is also likely to stimulate an increase in labour participation in formally inactive groups in the local labour force. This competition for the available jobs will affect the job growth–migration relationship. At the micro level, it is likely that factors influencing migration (e.g. age) are also influences on career and housing choices, so that part of the migration–age relationship is in fact a relationship between housing or career change and age. The problem of simultaneity has resulted in the development of systems of simultaneous equations for modelling both interregional migration (Greenwood 1975) and residential mobility (Cadwallader 1985).

Migration models with explanatory variables whose significance is calibrated using statistical procedures can be distinguished from mathematical models of spatial interaction calibrated using iterative proportional fitting routines or balancing factor methods which allow constraints to be introduced so that the origin–destination flows add up to known origin outmigration and destination inmigration totals (Wilson 1970). However, the underlying theory of migration conforming to gravitational pressures is assumed in both these types of approach.

Probability theory provides the basis for a wide variety of migration models. At the micro scale, utility maximization theory is formalised using probabilistic models. Hagerstrand (1957), for example, used Monte Carlo simulation techniques to simulate migration fields in which moves occur at random within a frame of probability distributions. Household and individual attribute lists based on conditional probabilities obtained from published sources are at the heart of migration specifications in microsimulation models used for household and population forecasting (Clarke 1986). The original formulation of the Markov chain transition model uses a single period matrix of probabilities of moving from origin i to destination j and, assuming that these probabilities are fixed, makes predictions of migration over more than one time unit. This type of model has been developed in both discrete and continuous time to reflect the non-constancy of mobility behaviour with respect to time indicators such as age, duration of stay and calendar time.

1.4 Model operationalisation

Once theoretical assumptions and propositions have been formulated, it is necessary to construct hypotheses which can be tested for their significance. Migration models are the conceptual, mathematical or statistical expressions of the hypotheses under question, which frequently involve attempting to identify the factors which explain certain types of migration behaviour. Typically, a model is made operational by selecting a specific measure of migration as the dependent or predicted variable; choosing a mathematical or statistical function with which to relate the migration variable to one or more independent variables; and adopting a suitable method of calibrating the model equation and a set of statistics with which to assess how close the predictions generated by the model are to the observed information. In this section of the chapter, we focus briefly on the ways in which migration is represented in modelling, exemplify the types of effect that are built into different models, and re-emphasise certain of the problems associated with modelling the phenomenon.

1.4.1 Model frameworks

A review of the migration modelling literature would throw up a very wide-ranging set of different forms and measures of the migration variable. This serves to complicate comparative analysis of different studies. Variations occur in the nature of the migration variable for conceptual reasons associated with the type of data that is collected in censuses, surveys and registers, as indicated in the discussion of transitions versus movements in Section 1.2. Variations also occur in the spatial, temporal and sectoral levels of resolution associated with migration. In Britain, aggregate studies of migration have tended to use data for census-based time periods to examine migration at regional, county, district, labour market area and ward scales, for example. In some cases, systems of spatial units have been utilised that fail to exhaust national territories and therefore imply models that are not comprehensive. Given the paucity of data on migration which is cross-classified by other variables, age, gender and social class represent the most familiar disaggregation dimensions. This allows the separate modelling of migration of those in the economically active or retirement age groups, for example, but does not enable motivation-specific streams to be identified. Attempts have been made to define regionalizations in which 'home-based' migrations are distinguished from 'job-based' moves (Johnson *et al*. 1974), to disaggregate census data on the basis on independent survey information about reasons for moving (Stillwell 1978), or to identify distance cut-off points either side of which either employment-related or housing-related predominate (Gordon 1982).

The object of analysis in macro migration models varies from the overall volume of interaction (M) taking place in a system of interest to the individual flows of migrants occurring between origins and destinations (M_{ij}, where i varies from 1 to n origin zones and j varies from 1 to m destination zones). Some models are constructed for gross flows of outmigration or of inmigration; others for the net balance between either the generation and attraction components or the directional gross flows. It has been argued that on theoretical grounds (Rogers 1990), gross migration models are to be preferred to net migration models, but no choice is permitted where the only estimates of migration available are the residuals generated from other vital statistics (Siegel and Hamilton 1952).

Frequently, the migration variable is represented as a rate in which the denominator should be the appropriate population at risk. In the case of gross outmigration, transition rates for areas can usually be calculated with 'start-of-the-period' populations without difficulty. It is less easy to conceive of the most suitable rate for gross inmigration to an area given the uncertainty of the population outside of the zone that is at risk. 'Admission' rates can be calculated for inmigrants using 'end-of-period' populations or 'mid-period' population estimates in their destination areas. Interaction flows between zones are sometimes divided by respective origin and destination populations, thereby normalising the effects of zone size.

Standardisation is also common practice in models of the migration age schedule. In this context, the 'gross migraproduction rate', the sum of the age-specific migration rates, is used to standardise each of the age-specific rates so that the area under the model schedule sums to the value one. Transformations of migration counts into probabilities are equally commonplace as, for example, in Willekens and Baydar (1986), where the generation component is defined by dividing the gross outmigration flow from one area by the total volume of migration during the time period, and the distribution component is calculated as a probability derived by dividing the origin–destination flow by the gross outmigration total.

Models in continuous time at micro level use longitudinal histories of migration. Such histories give a sequence of residences year by year so that durations of residence before moving to a new location can be derived. Ideally, times of moving are given to a high degree of accuracy so that a 'discrete time approximation' to the continuous process is not necessary. Two important functions are the 'hazard rate' of moving, the probability of moving in a short time interval, and the 'survivor function' which gives the probability of not moving (of surviving or staying) at different locations. Continuous time models accommodate an enlarged conception of migration behaviour by seeking to relate 'lengths of sojourn' to the characteristics of places and individuals (Bailey 1989), a contrast with analysis based on relative frequencies of migration events. One important influence on migration histories is the life-cycle stage of the individual, and continuous models are best for studying life-cycle effects (Greenwood 1985, p. 529). They throw light on a problem often treated in terms of labour market factors but which can be seen as a statistical artefact — the correlation between inmigration and outmigration rates arising from short durations of stay among 'chronic' migrants (Odland and Bailey 1990; Mueser and White 1989).

1.4.2 Independent variables

An immense variety of factors have been shown to exert influences of differing emphasis on potential migrants and consequently deterministic migration models endeavour to capture the most important of these variables linked to migration through appropriate functions. Thus explanatory variables reflect a host of economic (e.g. unemployment, earnings, house prices), social (e.g. welfare conditions, amenity levels, housing, education), political (e.g. government expenditure, legislation, fiscal benefits), physical (e.g. climate, quality of the environment) and other causal influences. Measured accordingly, they can be incorporated in isolation or in combination to represent the characteristics of the origin areas which generate migrants (push factors) or features of the destination areas which attract migrants (pull factors). In some cases, measures of the difference between the origin and destination (e.g.

unemployment rate differentials) are used, whilst in other cases, lagged variables (e.g. unemployment rates in the previous period) are introduced.

In addition to the measures which describe regional attributes, migration analysts from the time of Ravenstein (1885, 1889) have been interested in the frictional effect of distance on movement. Migration modellers have had to contend with the questions relating to the measurement and functional representation of distance in gravity model equations. In transport modelling, generalised trip costs are used with little hesitation, whereas in migration modelling, it might be argued that the cost function should include search and removal costs as well as social costs brought about by the disruption of making a move. In practice, physical road or airline distances between regional centroids are frequently adopted, although there are notable studies in which the less conventional measures of distance have been used. Somermeyer (1971), for example, introduced the difference between the religious composition of regions as a measure of social distance, whereas Stouffer (1940, 1960) preferred to measure the number of opportunities intervening between the origin and the destination and the number of competing migrants.

Much of the development and use of migration models for projection and forecasting has been undertaken in the context of multiregional population projection (Rees and Wilson 1977; Rees and Stillwell 1984) and is perhaps less well advanced in terms of relating migration to predicted changes in regional economic development. Time-series studies of migration in the Netherlands (Willekens and Baydar 1986) have shown regularities in certain components of the migration stream which reinforce the idea of 'historical dependence' and models based on historical conditional probabilities or growth factors have proved effective in distributing projected gross flows in the United Kingdom (Stillwell 1986). The need to combine spatial interaction models and econometric models to generate migration forecasts has encouraged the development of procedures in which the parameters of spatial interaction models calibrated on time series data are linked to exogenous variables (Ledent 1986a).

Given the wide variety of influences that determine destination choice, it is not possible to introduce independent variables into macro models of migration that fully explain patterns of movement. A random component must therefore be included in regression equations. Correct error specification is as important in statistical modelling as is the correct specification of the regression function. Regression models also suffer from multicollinearity problems such that a simple first-order association between migration and, say, job growth may be changed in direction and/or statistical significance if several other predictors are included in the model. Various approaches (e.g. stepwise regression) can be adopted which ensure parsimony in the model, resulting in only the most important predictors being included and the avoidance of overlap between predictors measuring essentially the same dimension (e.g. job growth and vacancy rates as indicators of labour demand).

The specification of a migration model in both its regression and error aspects may also be vitiated if the nature of the migration decision and its interrelation with other labour or housing market processes is not properly specified. Thus, at the micro level, choices about residence and occupation may be interdependent so that single regression equation estimates of the influence of age or education on migration are in fact partially due to age and education effects on career choice. At the macro level, if it is assumed that migration depends on job and housing growth but not vice versa, a simultaneity bias will be induced if in fact migration does have a reciprocal effect on job and housing markets, i.e. if, for example, migration is selective and takes highly skilled workers from low-growth regions and so further depresses growth prospects there.

Finally, it is worth reiterating that if the migration decision is treated as a two-stage process (choice to move followed by choice of destination), then characteristics of alternative destinations do not enter directly into the initial decision to move. This decomposition is at variance with the microeconomic theories (e.g. human capital and reservation wage approaches) which posit a comparison of origin and destination characteristics. The often cited 'Lowry effect' of insignificant or wrongly signed effects of economic factors at origin on outmigration may therefore be due to inappropriate decomposition (Ginsberg 1978; Congdon 1989b; Cushing 1989). Decompositions which adopt an intermediate solution and represent origin–destination simultaneity by an 'inclusive value' (e.g. Hughes and McCormick 1989) may not actually measure the totality of influence on migrant choices of different characteristics in different potential locations.

1.5 Book contents

Broad distinctions can be drawn between different types of migration model. We have chosen the macro–micro classification as a guiding principle in this chapter and in the book as a whole. There are, of course, other broad model categorisations: probabilistic–deterministic, statistical–mathematical, spatial–aspatial, static–dynamic, historical–forecasting, and various researchers (such as Courgeau 1970 or Weeden 1973) have proposed slightly more refined typologies. However, we believe that any classification more detailed than those based on the broadest of generalisations is limited because of the conceptual and operational overlap which exists between different types of model, i.e. mutually exclusive migration model categories are almost impossible to establish. For this reason, the editors have decided not to force chapters of the book into discrete parts, but to establish a continuity in the ordering as far as this is possible.

The scene is set initially in Chapter 2 by Maier and Weiss who explain how the behaviour of the individual migrant conforms to a process of maximising utility by choosing to reside in a particular location. This allows the individual's decision to migrate to be formalised into a model of the probability that an individual will migrate to another location. The general framework for modelling is referred to as the discrete choice approach and the chapter reviews modelling applications on the basis of two important criteria: the level of aggregation of the data and the type of migration decision. The chapter raises issues concerning the definition of regional characteristics and clarifies the distinction between static and dynamic aspects of migration modelling.

The next three chapters deal essentially with macro models in that they are concerned with the flow of migration between regions using mathematical expressions known as spatial interaction models. In Chapter 3, Stillwell sets out the structural characteristics of the family of spatial interaction models of migration flows between zones, explains how they are calibrated and exemplifies the use of doubly constrained models for examining spatial and temporal variations in the propensity to migrate over distance in the United Kingdom. The value of spatial interaction models for migration estimation and projection is illustrated with an example of a recent application in the context of local authority population and housing projection. Migration projections generated by spatial interactions models are also compared against other sets of projections. Fotheringham argues in Chapter 4 that conventional destination choice (spatial interaction) models are misspecified because of the limiting assumptions that migrants evaluate all possible alternatives, whereas their choice will actually be influenced by the location of the origin. He suggests that migrants really select particular areas hierarchically and that there is competition between destinations in area clusters — hence the derivation of a competing destinations model. Data from a study of migration between Dutch housing market areas is used for exemplification. In Chapter 5, Gordon draws attention to the deficiencies relating to the calibration of conventional aggregate models which arise because of the different types of migration stream that constitute aggregate flows. In particular, an important distinction is made between longer-distance, labour-related migration and shorter-distance, home-based migration, and Gordon establishes the theoretical basis for multistream modelling. A calibration methodology for distinguishing three streams is proposed and exemplified with British data.

The focus then moves to statistical models of migration flows between zones using aggregate data sets. Chapter 6 by Flowerdew contains a comparison between the constrained interaction modelling approach adopted in the previous three chapters and statistical approaches grouped together as generalised linear models. The advantages of adopting the assumption of a Poisson distribution for the error term of a log-linear model for categorical data are explained. The methods of calibration (with and without constraints), the assessment of goodness-of-fit, the analysis of dispersion and the interpretation of model results are considered and exemplified using data for the largest functional regions in the United Kingdom. Problems associated with fitting Poisson regression models are also discussed. In Chapter 7, Congdon emphasises the importance of correct specification of the structure of general linear regression models and of the error component in particular. A set of independent variables measuring population, employment and housing at the origin and destination are assembled and fits of log normal models are compared with those of Poisson models for three different migration data sets in London and South East England. Models with alternative error specifications are compared and the results indicate that migration does appear to play an equilibrating role in the labour and housing markets of the South East.

The following four chapters are concerned specifically with modelling labour migration. In Chapter 8, Milne provides an economist's overview of the human capital approach in which migration is viewed as an investment through which income can be generated, and which implies that individuals will move to the areas with the highest incomes. The chapter discusses the econometric estimation of the human capital model, and reviews previous studies in this field which use cross-sectional or time-series macro data sets for Canada or the United States. In Chapter 9, Bilger, Genosko and Hirte investigate the relationship between migration and the way in which labour markets operate in West Germany using a simultaneous equations approach. Hypotheses about the relationships between the rate of net migration, the unemployment rate, the employment change rate, the labour force participation rate and the earnings change rate are tested and evidence is provided to support the theory that migration is important as an adjustment mechanism for bringing labour demand into line with labour supply, although changes in participation rates are also significant.

Chapters 10 and 11 provide examples of micro model-based research from North America. Haurin and Haurin focus on one specific subgroup of the population — that of youths aged 14–21 — and two particular streams of migration — those moving out and those returning to the Midwest region of the United States. This is a micro study which aims to determine the influence of factors on the costs and benefits of individual migration, but it also helps to clarify the different contributions of studies which use macro data. The data are drawn from a longitudinal survey and therefore it is possible to incorporate time-varying explanatory factors measuring benefits and gains into the analysis and to model the time spent in the region until the first outmigration. Sandefur, Tuma and Kephart also use longitudinal data and logistic regression with categorical data to investigate the relationships between race, county unemployment rates and intercounty migration in the United States for 18–64-year-old male household heads during the period 1975–84. The results reported in this chapter indicate that, on average, blacks more than whites, and individuals who did not complete high school more than those with some college education, resided in counties with relatively high unemployment rates. Blacks and those who did not complete high school were less likely to change counties of residence than whites and those with some college education. Furthermore, among migrants, a higher unemployment rate in the county of origin was associated with a higher unemployment rate in the destination county. This combination of factors means that poorly educated black men were not easily adapting to changes in local economies during this period. Migration appears to be less effective as an 'equilibrating' mechanism for blacks, so they tend to become trapped in counties with unfavourable labour markets.

Chapters 12 and 13 both contain descriptions of micro modelling approaches. Davies, in Chapter 12, outlines the role of continuous time models in clarifying the degree to which long-term housing and migration careers govern changes of residence. Such a focus contrasts with the short-term approach which sees migration as an equilibrating mechanism with successive decisions forming a sequence of independent decisions. A proportional hazard, competing risk model is applied to a variety of data sets, and an extension is made to allow for residual heterogeneity. Chapter 13 provides the link between micro analysis and migration projection. Duley and Rees describe how migration processes can be incorporated in a microsimulation model of small area populations that can be used to update census statistics. A new conceptual framework for handling the migration of households and independent individuals is developed. The probabilities input to the microsimulation model involve eclectic use of a wide variety of data sources and familiar models of migration. Steps in the modelling algorithm are illustrated with flow diagrams and computations exemplified using data for Leeds.

The final two chapters of the book describe national level macro models. In Chapter 14, Boden, Stillwell and Rees outline the equations relating to each stage of the migration submodel used by the Office of Population Censuses and Surveys for generating migration assumptions that feed into the model for projecting the populations of subnational administrative areas in England. Three features of the modelling exercise are examined using register data more recent than the 1981 Census, and recommendations for new procedures are made. The final chapter by Stambøl represents a framework for the integrating models which forecast population and economic activity in Norway. The migration submodel of DREM (Demographic Regional Economic Model) involves the use of regression techniques to link migration rates with a labour market indicator which reflects the difference between the tightness of the regional and the national labour markets.

Chapter 2

The discrete choice approach to migration modelling

Gunther Maier and Peter Weiss

2.1 Introduction: a general framework for analysing internal migration

Despite the many different approaches to the analysis of migration there is consensus about one point: all researchers seem to agree that people or households migrate to improve their situation, or, more precisely, to be better off in the new location in the future than they would be in the old. Rothenberg (1977, p. 185) argues that

each member of the population performs the following calculation: at each point of time he (she) perceives that a choice has to be made between remaining a resident of his (her) current region and moving to another region. Each region, including the current place of residence, is perceived as possessing a set of opportunities and constraints relevant to the calculation; in addition, if he (she) were to move, a set of costs would be incurred. By evaluating each of the regions as an alternative prospect in utility terms and subtracting the cost of moving to it in utility terms, the subject forms a utility level for each hypothetical course of action. If a move to any new region yields an expected utility level greater than that associated with remaining in the current region, the subject will become a migrant. He (she) will migrate to that region that promises the highest expected utility level.

Migration theory has stressed different aspects of this general framework (see e.g. De Jong and Fawcett 1981); economic (wages, vacancies, unemployment), social (social mobility, social status), environmental (residential satisfaction), etc. Numerous studies have tried to break down migration motives into various categories (see e.g. Shaw 1975; Bogue 1977; De Jong and Fawcett 1981).

Rothenberg's statement also illustrates the basic problems of behavioural migration theory. It is people's expectations about their own prospects in various locations which guide migration decisions. These expectations are based on their past experience, knowledge, contacts, etc. (Goodman 1981; Maier 1990a). This calls for a modelling strategy which is based on the maximization of some goal function and allows us to take into account regional as well as individual characteristics.

In a closed system of regions migration is characterized by a set of simple constraints such as 'gross migration flows can only be non-negative', or 'the number of out-migrants from a region cannot exceed the original population'. The most important behavioural constraint is that in a migration decision regions cannot be chosen in continuous quantities. A migrant cannot combine, for instance, a quarter of region A and three-quarters of region B. Rather, the option is to choose either region A or region B. Discrete choice models allow us to formulate behavioural models which take into account these constraints. They are therefore particularly well suited for migration modelling.

In Section 2.2 of this contribution we discuss the behavioural background of discrete choice models and random utility theory in particular. Section 2.3 is devoted to standard static discrete choice models. Section 2.4 discusses some migration-specific issues of model design and focuses particularly on the problem of defining the adequate regional characteristics. Among other aspects we discuss migration and job search and the relationship between migration and wage formation. In Section 2.5 we move from static to dynamic models and their significance for migration modelling. The contribution closes with some summarizing statements.

2.2 Behavioural background: random utility theory

The discrete choice approach to migration roots firmly in the axiom of utility maximization. The utility that region i provides for individual n may be described by the utility function:

$$U_{in} = U_n(R_{in}, p_i, y_{in}, \beta_i) \tag{2.1}$$

The vector of regional attributes, R_{in}, determines the individual utility directly. Although the perception and evaluation of these attributes (regional characteristics) may vary between individuals, they are essentially fixed for a specific individual and cannot be altered. For the moment we will ignore the possibility that these attributes might vary within the region. We will turn to this problem in Section 2.4. Examples are weather conditions, environmental quality, local amenities, cultural infrastructure, etc. Additionally, there are goods (market goods), the consumption level of which can be determined by the individual. The specific level of consumption will, of course, depend on the prevailing prices and the income of the individual which may again differ across regions. Thus, the regional utility index of an individual will be related to the constraints imposed by income possibilities, y_{in}, and prevailing prices, p_i. The vector β_i contains a set of parameters determining the shape of the utility function. Since this shape may differ across regions it has to be provided with a regional index.

In economic terms the function U_n represents an indirect utility function. It results from utility maximization over market goods for given prices and income, conditional on the regional attributes R_{in}. The concept of conditional utility maximization is discussed by Varian (1984) and Maier and Weiss (1990a). Note that all variables are defined region-specifically, so conforming to the idea that regional attributes, prices and individual income opportunities differ between regions.

The individual will choose the region offering the highest utility. Thus, region i will be chosen if and only if $U_{in} > U_{jn}$ for all $j \neq i$. In constructing a model of this decision the researcher will be facing two fundamental problems. First, as indicated by the index n in the utility function, individuals will differ in their evaluation of regional attributes, prices and income. We can try to account for this heterogeneity by supplementing the utility function with a vector of variables which describes the socioeconomic status of the individual. Second, we will not be able to observe all the factors which influence an individual's migration decision. A portion of the variation in utility will remain unexplained and must be attributed to idiosyncrasies and situational factors unknown to the researcher.

If we combine these unknowns into a single random variable ϵ_{in} we can formally partition the utility function into two additive components:

$$U_{in} = V(R_{in}, p_i, y_{in}, C_n, \beta_i) + \epsilon_{in}. \tag{2.2}$$

The first component, the deterministic part, is derived from the utility function above by adding to its arguments a vector of individual-specific characteristics, C_n. The second component, the stochastic part, represents all unobserved differences in utility for otherwise comparable individuals. The function V no longer depends on n since differences in evaluation and unobserved factors are captured partly by C_n and partly by ϵ_{in}. The model of equation (2.2) is called a random utility model. It does not necessarily imply that utility is a random variable for the consumer — although uncertainty on the part of the consumer could be incorporated — but that unknown factors contributing to utility give rise to partly stochastic behaviour from the view of the observer.

2.3 Static models of migration

2.3.1 Model structure

Using the random utility concept we can formalize the migration decision. Since utility is stochastic, the probability that individual n will choose region i in preference to $I-1$ alternative regions is:

$$
\begin{aligned}
P_{in} &= \mathrm{Prob}(U_{in} \geqslant U_{jn}, \ j = 1, \ldots, I) \\
&= \mathrm{Prob}(V_{in} + \epsilon_{in} \geqslant V_{jn} + \epsilon_{jn}, \ j = 1, \ldots, I) \\
&= \mathrm{Prob}(V_{in} - V_{jn} \geqslant \epsilon_{jn} - \epsilon_{in}, \ j = 1, \ldots, I) \tag{2.3}
\end{aligned}
$$

where V_{in} and V_{jn} are shorthand for $V(R_{in}, p_i, y_{in}, C_n, \beta_i)$ and

$V(R_{jn}, p_j, y_{jn}, C_n, \beta_i)$ respectively. This is the fundamental equation underlying any random utility model of discrete choice and any discrete choice model of migration in particular. It corresponds closely to the demand function of traditional microeconomic theory.

In order to deduce an empirically tractable model, we usually assume a specific joint distribution for ϵ_{in}. Assuming all ϵ_{in} to be independent and identically (extreme value type I) distributed yields the 'multinomial logit' model. The name of the model derives from the logistic-type functional form of its choice probabilities:

$$P_{in} = \frac{\exp(V_{in})}{\sum_j \exp(V_{jn})} \tag{2.4}$$

It can easily be verified from this expression that $0 \leqslant P_{in} \leqslant 1$ and that $\sum_i P_{in} = 1$. Hence the classical axioms of probability are fulfilled for the choice probabilities. This implies that predicted migration flows will be non-negative and cannot exceed the population of the region of origin. Furthermore, choice probabilities will be unaffected by the addition or multiplication of a constant to the region-specific utilities U_{in}. This implies that only relative utility levels of regions rather than absolute ones can be determined, which is in line with ordinal utility theory.

With a sample of individuals whose migration decisions are observed the unknown parameter vector β_i can be estimated by some appropriate method. When the individuals can be identified in the data the maximum likelihood method needs to be employed; with aggregate data, a weighted least-squares procedure is applicable as well.

The logit model's particularly simple expression for the choice probabilities is responsible for its wide popularity in applied work. Yet the model's analytical and computational tractability is not without cost. The most obvious drawback is its inability to account for correlation in the ϵ_{in} across regions. Formally, this implies the 'independence of irrelevant alternatives' (IIA) property of the multinomial logit model which states that the relative choice probability of two alternatives is unaffected by the presence of other alternatives (see e.g. Ben-Akiva and Lerman 1985; Maier and Weiss 1990a):

$$\frac{P_{in}}{P_{jn}} = \frac{\exp(V_{in})}{\exp(V_{jn})} \tag{2.5}$$

Taking the logarithm of equation (2.5) yields a function which is often used with aggregate data:

$$\ln\left[\frac{P_{in}}{P_{jn}}\right] = V_{in} - V_{jn} \tag{2.6}$$

Although it is sometimes argued that the IIA-property is a desirable property of a model of discrete choice there are situations where the independence assumption is quite implausible (see Section 2.4). In these cases we need a model type which is able to account for correlation in the utilities of alternatives. Such a model is the 'multinomial probit' model. This model is derived from the assumption that the $\epsilon_{1n},\ldots,\epsilon_{In}$ are distributed according to an I-dimensional multivariate normal distribution with expectation vector 0 and variance–covariance matrix Σ_n. Since Σ_n can be parametrized in very flexible ways, the probit model can account for various types of correlation between the utilities of different regions.

Yet use of the probit model in applied work is impeded by the fact that the choice probabilities involve multiple integrals, making parameter estimation very cumbersome. Although approximation procedures for these integrals have been developed they are only applicable in situations with a moderate number of alternatives. In the context of migration, where individuals usually face a large set of alternatives, the multinomial probit model is very rarely used in practice.

2.3.2 Applications of discrete choice models: a typology and review of migration studies

Although empirical discrete choice studies of migration could be differentiated along several lines, there are two features which are of particular relevance, namely the aggregation level of the analysis and the type of migration decision considered. Considering the first aspect — which is strongly connected with the type of data available — we have to distinguish studies using sample survey data on individuals at risk (disaggregate studies) from studies based on aggregate flow data for regions (aggregate studies). The distinction between aggregate and disaggregate studies is important since the potential questions addressed by these two kinds of studies differ sharply. With aggregate data it is usually impossible to disentangle the effects on the probability of migration of the individual presence of a certain characteristic (e.g. personal unemployment) from those of an aggregate measure of the same characteristic (e.g. regional unemployment rate).

The second aspect is related to the definition of the choice set. Again, two different approaches can be distinguished. The first approach takes into account only two alternatives, namely (i) to stay in the region of residence and (ii) to migrate to some other region (studies of outmigration). Obviously, the interest centres on factors which encourage migration out of a region ('push factors'). The second approach resembles more closely the theoretical model presented above with the choice set consisting of various different regions and the attractiveness of regions guiding the choice of individuals. The question addressed by these studies concerns those factors that determine the choice of a specific region ('pull factors') in preference to the current one (studies of regional choice).

Cross-classifying the two types of aggregation (aggregate versus disaggregate) with the two different definitions of the choice set (outmigration versus regional choice) yields four different categories of model. However, studying outmigration with aggregate data will usually be impracticable due to the limited number of degrees of freedom (equalling the number of regions). Our concern is, therefore, mainly with the remaining three categories. In disaggregate regional choice studies one might directly apply the model structure discussed in the previous subsection (see e.g. the residential choice model in Evers 1989). Almost all of the recent literature, however, uses the nested logit model for modelling disaggregate regional choice. Since this type of model is discussed in the next section, this subsection will review aggregate regional choice studies and disaggregate studies of outmigration, and the role of different independent variables in representing theoretical utility comparisons.

Examples of aggregate regional choice studies are Schultz (1982) and Gabriel *et al*. (1987). Schultz uses census data on lifetime migration (defined as a difference in the region of birth from the region of residence at the time of the census) between Venezuelan states; Gabriel *et al*. investigate migration between Israeli regions within a two-year period. Both studies use ordinary least squares regression with the dependent variable M_{ij}/M_{ii} as an approximation of P_{ij}/P_{ii} (see equation (2.6) where M_{ij} is the number of persons moving from region i to j and M_{ii} the number of persons staying in i.

Explanatory variables used in both studies are the expected regional nominal wage rate (defined as the average wage rate multiplied by the employment rate of the region) in the origin i and destination j regions; the distance between the origin and the destination region as a measure of migration costs; the percentage of urban population to account for unmeasured differences in real wages and local amenities between rural and urban regions; the population size in both regions; and a measure of the age structure of the population. The age selectivity of migration is one of the best-documented results in migration analysis and it is also implicit in the choice theoretic model presented above: younger persons will enjoy the potential benefits from migration for a longer period of time than older ones. Thus, even moderate differences in wage levels of two regions may induce younger people to migrate, while for older people the costs might well surpass the benefits.

Explanatory variables are transformed to logs in both studies, presumably because of a better fit of the estimated functions and to ensure that predicted migration is non-negative. Schultz prefers to introduce the characteristics of the origin and destination region as separate variables into the regression equation thus allowing for an asymmetric reaction pattern of origin and destination ('push/pull') factors on the migration propensity. By entering generally origin and destination variables in ratio form Gabriel *et al.* restrict the influence of these variables to being symmetrically opposite. Although the concept of symmetry is theoretically appealing (implying that a change of a variable in two regions by the same percentage leaves the propensity of migration between the two regions unaffected), it is preferable to test its validity (as in Schultz) rather than to postulate it without inspection.

The empirical results of both studies are generally in accordance with the expectations deriving from the theoretical model above. Thus an increase in the average expected wage level of a region discourages outmigration and encourages inmigration. Increasing distance between regions is a major factor deterring migration between these regions. Furthermore, a younger population has a significantly higher propensity to migrate. In both studies the population size of the destination region exerts a significant attraction for inmigration (for a rationalization of the population size in the destination region, see Section 2.4), while the influence of the population size of the origin region remains insignificant.

Further study-specific variables reflecting non-economic and economic characteristics of regions are the similarity of the industrial job structure, and the security hazard confronted in Israeli regions in proximity to the northern border in the study of Gabriel *et al.* or the percentage of children enrolled in school in Schultz. The latter variable is interesting because it illustrates the problem of aggregate economic measures in migration studies. This variable could be viewed as a socioeconomic indicator of the educational level of the population at risk (because parents with higher education lay more emphasis on the education of their children), but it could also reflect a regional variable, namely the availability of public services in the region. Thus the estimated coefficient is difficult to interpret because it may reflect the compound influence of two possibly opposite effects. It is therefore unclear in Schultz's study why the school enrolment rate of the origin region in general exerts a positive effect on migration while school enrolment in the destination region exhibits a negative impact. Note that the two effects could in principle be disentangled if data on individuals rather than on regions were available. The first effect could be captured by the individual educational attainment, the second by the aggregate enrolment rate.

Disaggregate studies of outmigration concentrate on people's decision to leave their region of residence. Examples can be found in Shields and Shields (1989), Harkman (1989), Goss and Schoening (1984), McDevitt *et al.* (1986), and van Dijk *et al.* (1989). All these studies attempt to find factors determining the decision to leave a region but differ in some important details. McDevitt *et al.*, for example, estimate an ordered probit model and find that age and education are important factors determining mobility. While higher education generally increases mobility, the age variable reveals the well-known inverse U-shaped relationship. These factors are important in other studies as well. Only Shields and Shields (1989) find a negative relationship between migration and education by looking at family migration in Costa Rica. The reason might be that they use a narrowly defined segment of the population: families with a five-year-old child.

There is more disagreement about the role of economic variables. The influence of unemployment rates in particular has been puzzling researchers for years. Many studies (e.g. Lowry 1966; Kau and Sirmans 1977) have found that migration flows were not closely related to regional unemployment rates. Van Dijk *et al.* (1989) differentiate between regional unemployment rates and the respondent being unemployed. Using data from the Netherlands and the north-eastern United States, they find that unemployed respondents are more likely to migrate in both countries. A high local unemployment rate, however, has a significant positive impact on mobility in the United States and a significant negative impact in the Netherlands. Van Dijk *et al.* attribute this difference to institutional differences in the two labour markets.

Goss and Schoening (1984) include a variable measuring the length of time an unemployed respondent has been searching for a job. This variable yields a significantly negative coefficient, implying that the longer a respondent is unemployed the lower is his propensity to move. Harkman (1989), on the other hand, derives a positive but insignificant coefficient for an explanatory variable measuring unemployment duration. A major problem with this type of explanatory variable is duration bias. It is likely that there are unobserved characteristics which lead to positive correlation between migration propensity and the probability of leaving unemployment. This generates a negative coefficient for unemployment duration even when the two variables are behaviourally unrelated. Harkman provides a weak test for duration bias and concludes that it is no serious problem in his model. His data set, however, also suffers from the defect that it contains only unemployed persons and the results are likely to be distorted by sample selection bias. Since unemployment status is necessary for inclusion into the sample, long-term unemployed and people with unfavourable unobserved labour market characteristics have a higher probability of entering the sample.

All disaggregate studies of outmigration, however, suffer from the drawback of looking only at one aspect of migration. In the tradition of distinguishing push and pull factors these studies concentrate on push factors only. From the discussion of the behavioural background we know that it is the relative performance of the regions which matters (see equation (2.3)) and that therefore push and pull factors cannot be separated. The bad performance of one region will lead to outmigration only when other regions are doing better. The latter component is ignored in all the outmigration studies.

2.4 Migration and related decisions

The intrinsic structure of the migration problem questions some of the basic assumptions of the models in Section 2.3. Regions are by no means homogeneous points in space. They exhibit considerable heterogeneity in various characteristics. They offer residential locations of different environmental quality and at different prices, different access to schools, shopping facilities, recreational facilities, public transport, etc. Regions supply different numbers of potential jobs for an individual with certain qualifications. Jobs may differ in numerous characteristics such as the wage level. These characteristics not only differ at one point in time but are also likely to change over time at different trajectories. The decision-maker has to take into account career possibilities and lifetime income rather than just the current wage level. Some of these questions are discussed in the rest of this section.

2.4.1 Correlated random utilities: the nested logit model

In their migration decision, people have to choose between their current region of residence and one from a set of alternative regions. Whatever the destination, migration requires considerable effort and an individual's willingness to migrate might be influenced by some unobserved individual characteristics. Also, some potential destinations might be evaluated similarly because of preferences for certain types of area. All this might lead to correlation in the random component of utility functions, which contradicts the assumptions of the multinomial logit model. The probit model, which allows for correlated error components, is hardly applicable in migration applications because of the large number of alternatives. Therefore the nested logit model, which allows for some correlation and is almost as practical as the logit model (McFadden 1978; Börsch-Supan 1987; Maier and Weiss 1990a, p. 152), is used frequently in migration modelling.

In the nested logit model, the migration decision is subdivided into two or more interdependent decisions. The choice probabilities are factored into conditional and marginal probabilities. By grouping similar alternatives into one subset we can avoid the problem of correlation and apply a logit model. From this conditional decision we can derive an inclusive value which serves as an aggregate characteristic of the respective subset of the migration problem. It is used to model the choice between the subsets where again a logit model can be used. The parameter of the inclusive value provides a measure for the correlation in the error components.

Liaw and Ledent (1987) used a nested logit model in a migration context (and similarly Hughes and McCormick 1989). We will use their specific application to illustrate the structure of the nested logit model.

Liaw and Ledent suspect that people's evaluations of regions other than their current region are correlated and that this correlation shows up in the error terms of random utility. Therefore they subdivide the migration decision into (i) the decision whether to migrate or not, and, conditional on that, (ii) the choice between the competing regions. It is important to note that in the nested logit model the migration decision is subdivided only conceptually. It does not mean that we assume there are actually two decisions.

If we denote the two alternatives of the upper-level decision — whether to migrate or not — by m (= move) and s (= stay) and the available regions by i, we can write the conditional probability that individual n selects region i provided he/she moves at all as:

$$P_n(i|m) = \frac{\exp(V_{in})}{\sum_{j \in A_n} \exp(V_{jn})}$$
(2.7)

where A_n is the set of all regions except the individual's home region. We can estimate this component of the model like a standard logit model and derive the inclusive value therefrom as:

$$I_n(m) = \ln \sum_{j \in A_n} \exp(V_{jn})$$
(2.8)

This is the expected maximum return of the lower-level decision, the choice between the competing regions. It serves as deterministic utility of the alternative m in the upper-level decision. So, we can model this part of the migration decision as:

$$P_n(m) = \frac{\exp(\delta I_n)}{\exp(\delta I_n) + \exp(V_{sn})}$$
(2.9)

$$P_n(s) = \frac{\exp(V_{sn})}{\exp(\delta I_n) + \exp(V_{sn})}$$
(2.10)

The parameter δ will be estimated probably along with some other parameters in V_{sn}. Its value needs to be between zero and one for the model to be compatible with utility maximization. It is directly related to the correlation in the error terms. Liaw and Ledent yield a parameter value of about 0.35, implying that the unobserved utilities at the lower level are highly correlated (corr $\approx$ 0.88). This sequential estimation technique produces consistent but not fully efficient parameter estimates as does the full information maximum likelihood procedure (McFadden 1981; Börsch-Supan 1987). However, the latter is computationally much more cumbersome.

There are more elaborate nested logit structures to be found in the migration literature. Evers and van der Veen (1985), for example, consider people's place of residence and place of work decisions and formulate a nested logit model for migration, labour market participation, and commuting (see also Maier and Fischer 1985). A similar model is estimated by Evers (1989) who concludes that interdependencies between participation, commuting and migration 'exist and should be incorporated because of their importance' (p. 194).

2.4.2 Regions as grouped alternatives

As mentioned above, people usually choose a location and/or workplace within a region rather than a region *per se*. So we can view regions as 'grouped alternatives' which consist of a number of 'elementary alternatives'. Usually regions differ by the number of elementary alternatives they contain. However, since people choose elementary alternatives (locations) rather than grouped alternatives (regions), a region which contains more elementary alternatives is more likely to be the destination of a migrant than a smaller one even when all elementary alternatives are identical.

If we have detailed information about the elementary alternatives we can easily apply a nested logit model where the lower level is the choice between locations in a region and the upper level the choice between regions. However, even without information about the lower level, we can use the nested logit concept to derive an adequate specification.

Suppose the elementary alternatives in region i, which we denote by the index w, differ only by a (extreme value distributed) random component. In this case all the W_i elementary alternatives in region i are equally likely to be chosen:

$$P_n(w) = \frac{\exp(V_{wn})}{\sum_{w'} \exp(V_{w'n})} = \frac{1}{W_i} \qquad (2.11)$$

The inclusive value of region i can be derived therefrom as:

$$I_n(i) = \ln \sum_{w'} \exp(V_{w'n}) = V_{w'n} + \ln W_i \qquad (2.12)$$

The deterministic utility of region i therefore consists of the (identical) deterministic utility of its elementary alternatives plus the logarithm of their number. The latter term corrects for the size effect in the migration decision. We can derive a similar expression for the case where the elementary alternatives differ systematically (e.g. Ben-Akiva and Lerman 1985, p. 255; Maier and Weiss 1990a, p. 206). In this case we have to add another term measuring the heterogeneity of the elementary alternatives in the region.

This model also illustrates the problem of adequately defining regional characteristics. Even when the elementary alternatives differ only randomly, the mean value of the characteristic is not adequate. Because of the individual's active role in selecting from the elementary alternatives, the number of alternatives and higher moments of their distribution are of importance. Together they define regional characteristics which are considerably more complex than average regional characteristics.

Despite that problem and the obvious fact that omitting these terms will yield biased parameter estimates, only a few empirical applications in a migration context correct for the size of grouped alternatives. Because of the obvious data problem, correction for heterogeneity can rarely be found. In Gabriel *et al.* (1987), the log of population in the destination region appears to be the most significant variable of all. Hughes and McCormick (1989) motivate the inclusion of a variable 'total employment' by attempting to correct for regions of different size, but use the absolute figure rather than its log. In the light of the discussion above, this appears to be a misspecification which questions the validity of the empirical results.

2.4.3 Migration and search

When deriving the corrections in the previous subsection, we implicitly assumed that the decision between elementary alternatives is a simultaneous one. According to random utility theory we assume that the migrant knows the value of all elementary alternatives in all regions and will choose the best one. The contingency in the model arises from the limited capability of the researcher.

In many situations the assumption of simultaneity of the decision is inadequate. Rather people investigate one alternative after the other and decide about each one in turn without particular knowledge of the other. This sequential type of decision-making corresponds to the logical structure of search models (Lippman and McCall 1976, 1979; McKenna 1987). In search models the decision-maker investigates one alternative at a time and decides about accepting it on the basis of the expected return of investigating all other available alternatives. The expected return is a function of search cost and the distribution of the values of alternatives. In the standard version of the search model these elements are assumed to be known to the decision-maker (for a critique of this assumption in a migration context see Maier 1985, 1990a; Molho 1986).

If the individual chooses sequentially from the elementary alternatives of a region the expected return of this search strategy is an important element for deciding about the regions as well. In this context, however it is necessary to assume that each regional labour market consists of only a finite number of potential employers, particularly when taking into account that an individual with his specific characteristics — schooling, work experience, training, etc. — usually qualifies only for a rather narrow segment of the labour market. With a finite number of wage offers the decision-maker will take into account that with each offer rejected he reduces the pool of wage offers and therefore will lower his aspiration level through the search process.

Moreover, in a spatial context, search costs are likely to be influenced by the distribution of alternatives (jobs) within the region. In the most general form the cost of going to a specific alternative in a search sequence depends upon the searcher's current location, implying that search costs are a function of the sequence in which alternatives are investigated. Therefore, in a spatial context the decision-maker not only has to decide about the acceptability of jobs but also about the optimal sequence in which to investigate them. In this general form the spatial search problem is highly complex and can be solved only for special cases (Maier 1990b).

Under some additional assumptions which, a priori, determine the sequencing of alternatives, it can be shown that the expected return of search (i.e. the attractivity of the region) is influenced by the spatial arrangement of alternatives within the region (Maier 1986, 1987). Because of the lower search costs, a region where the alternatives are concentrated around the individual's potential location is more attractive to a migrant than a region where the same number of alternatives is more dispersed.

In general, however, the theoretical treatment of intraregional search in a migration context is unsatisfactory. Many references to job search in the migration literature apply *ad hoc* formulations and practically none takes into account the spatial dimension of the problem. Nevertheless, the fact that so many migration studies refer to search processes and job search in particular (see, e.g. Van Dijk *et al.* 1989) supports the idea that people's prospective activities within the region are an important factor in the migration decision. It is rather unsatisfactory to treat regions as black boxes in migration modelling which possess specific characteristics on the one hand and absorb migrants on the other.

2.4.5 Migration and wage formation

Two of the most important questions in migration analysis are (i) whether people gain from migration in terms of wages and (ii) whether migration contributes to wage equilibration between regions. Interestingly, the two questions do not necessarily lead to the same answer. Maier and Weiss (1990b), for example, construct a dual labour market model where migration in pursuit of higher income does not narrow down regional income disparities. Thus the answer to the relationship between these two questions has to be passed on to empirical research. Unfortunately, the problem is complicated by the fact that even if individual data were available, the individual wage is usually observed only for the selected region. We do not know how much an individual would have earned had she or he chosen region i instead of j. The models discussed so far circumvent the problem by using aggregate regional (average) wages instead of individual wages. But in theory, discrete choice models of migration see utility as a function of the expected individual wage level rather than the expected regional wage level.

A possible procedure for imputing individual wages is to estimate wage functions for each region from the sample of the regional population and use individual and region-specific variables to predict wages for each individual. The standard OLS-estimate of this wage function suffers, however, from selectivity bias since people in different regions do not represent random samples from the population but have selected themselves *inter alia* on the basis of differences in expected individual wages.

This can be seen more clearly if we differentiate only between migrants and non-migrants in the population. The wage for an individual n conditional on his or her migrating is assumed to be linearly dependent on a vector of regional and individual-specific characteristics, X_n:

$$y_{mn} = X_n \gamma_n + \eta_{mn} \tag{2.13}$$

where η_{mn} is a normally distributed random variable with zero mean. Similarly, for the same individual staying in the origin region the wage level would be:

$$y_{sn} = X_n \gamma_{cs} + \eta_{sn} \tag{2.14}$$

Individual n migrates if the utility from migration exceeds the utility from staying. If we abstract from other differences in regional and individual-specific variables influencing utility, as well as from migration costs, the utility difference for a potential migrant would be:

$$U_n^* = U_{mn} - U_{sn} = (y_{mn} - y_{sn})\beta + \epsilon_n \tag{2.15}$$

where ϵ is again assumed to be normally distributed and represents all unobserved differences in utility between a person before and after migration. The probability of migration is equal to the probability that $U_n^* > 0$. In order to estimate this probability we face two problems: first, if ϵ_n is correlated with η_{mn} or η_{sn} an element of simultaneity is introduced into equation (2.15). Second, we usually observe either y_{mn} or y_{sn} but not both. Obviously, the solution for these problems consists of replacing y_{mn} and y_{sn} by an appropriate estimate. Unfortunately, basing this estimate on the regression equations of the two subsamples of migrants and non-migrants suffers from selectivity bias. To see this, for example for equation (2.13), we build the expectation of y_{mn} conditional on observing it:

$$E(y_{mn}|U_n^* > 0) = X_n \gamma_m + E(\eta_{mn}|U_n^* > 0) \qquad (2.16)$$

Since η_{mn} and X_n are contained in the condition $E(\eta_{nm}|U_n^* > 0)$, ordinary least squares regression with the sample of migrants would yield biased estimates. A similar result can be deduced for non-migrants.

A method developed by Heckman (1976) and Lee (1976) corrects for this 'selectivity' bias. The idea is to estimate first the reduced form migration equation, i.e. to estimate a binary probit model of (2.15) after substituting equations (2.13) and (2.14) for y_{mn} and y_{sn}. With this estimate it is possible to construct auxiliary variables which added to the right-hand side of (2.13) and (2.14) correct for selectivity bias of the ordinary least squares estimate of the wage equations. The (now consistent) numeric estimates for y_{mn} and y_{sn} resulting from this second-step estimation are in turn reinserted into equation (2.15) yielding in a third step consistent estimates of the structural migration equation by binary probit estimation.

The framework sketched above has been applied in a slightly more general form by Nakosteen and Zimmer (1980). Tunali (1986) considers a generalized version of the model to analyse the problem of self-selection in a model of migration and remigration. Falaris (1987, 1989) adapts the model to the case of migration into various regions. A nested logit model of regional choice is estimated after correction for selectivity bias. The results of all these studies point to the fact that selectivity is an important factor in migration. Moreover, higher expected individual income is an important incentive to migrate.

2.5 Dynamic aspects of migration modelling

The migration literature is full of arguments concerning the temporal aspects of migration. Numerous studies have demonstrated the influence the life cycle (age, marital status, etc.) has upon migration probabilities (for an overview, see Greenwood 1985). Return migration, i.e. migration back to the migrant's original location has received considerable attention (Vanderkamp 1972a, 1972b; Davanzo and Morrison 1981). So also has the fact that some people seem to be 'chronic migrants' (Morrison 1971), who move repeatedly while others remain in their original location (Goldstein 1964). Molho (1986) argues that there are likely to be response lags in migration. He mentions time lags attributable to the diffusion of information, to the formation of expectations, and to the time between the decision to migrate and the final enaction.

None of these effects can adequately be modelled with cross-section data. Moreover, macro-economic influences like the business cycle (Hart 1975; Gordon 1985a) are identical for all decision-makers and therefore cannot be identified from cross-section data. What is needed is a sequence of cross-sections or even panel-data where individuals are followed through time. The latter allow for more sophisticated analyses but pose specific problems as well.

The central problem of all longitudinal studies of individual behaviour is to separate state dependence from unobserved heterogeneity. Both effects produce very similar behavioural patterns but differ considerably in terms of political implications. By state dependence in a migration context we mean the hypothesis that people's migration behaviour is influenced by their past migration experience. By migrating, they accumulate information and experience and become more aware of opportunities and will therefore be more likely to move again (positive state dependence). Unobserved heterogeneity, on the other hand, means that some people are migrants because of (unobserved) personal characteristics (chronic migrants) and will therefore move more often than others. To illustrate the political implications, consider a policy which for some period of time encourages migration. When there is unobserved heterogeneity but no state dependence after termination of the policy migration rates will immediately drop to normal levels. With (positive) state dependence, however, they will remain at a high level because of the now larger number of people with migration experience.

Longitudinal models of migration behaviour can be formulated either in discrete time or in continuous time (Maier and Weiss 1990a, pp. 245ff). Discrete time models are a straightforward generalization of static models applied to cross-section data. The utility individual n derives from alternative i at time period t can be written as (e.g. Heckman 1981):

$$U_{int} = V_{int} + \epsilon_{in} + \epsilon_{int} \tag{2.17}$$

The error component ϵ_{in} represents unobserved heterogeneity. It varies over alternatives and individuals but not over time, thus leading to correlation in the random utilities. Because we are usually dealing with a small number of time periods, the heterogeneity component cannot be estimated consistently as individual specific dummy variables. Unfortunately, this inconsistency carries over into the structural parameters as well (Hsiao 1986, p. 159).

Continuous time (duration) models focus on the duration of states; in a migration context, on the interval an individual remains in one region. Migration is viewed as a transition from one state (residence in i) to another (residence in j), which terminates an episode. The length of episodes is of central importance to the analysis. An important concept in duration analysis is the hazard function. It is defined as the conditional probability of migration from region i at time t given residence at i at this time:

$$h(t) = \lim_{\Delta t \to 0} \frac{1}{\Delta t} P(t \leqslant T < t + \Delta t | T \geqslant t) \tag{2.18}$$

The hazard function can be formulated to depend upon exogenous variables (besides time) and used as basis for modelling. Again, separate unobserved heterogeneity and the impact of migration history (in duration models this relationship is usually formulated as duration dependence) is an important but difficult task (Heckman and Singer 1982). Bailey (1989) uses hazard (and survivor) functions for describing the dynamics of migration and speculating about the importance of migration history. Davies and Pickles (1985a) develop a dynamic model of residential mobility based on the discrete choice concept. Estimating the model with data from the Michigan Panel Study of Income Dynamics they find that, other things being equal, the probability for migration declines with increasing length of stay.

2.6 Concluding remarks

This chapter has discussed various aspects of the discrete choice approach to migration modelling. The technique which was developed in the early 1970s mainly in context with transportation research (e.g. Domencich and McFadden 1975) proved to be useful in the context of migration. The logit model in particular is closely related to some of the more traditional migration models (see Anas 1982; Maier and Rogerson 1986). In contrast to gravity models and intervening opportunities models, the discrete choice model has a sound behavioural basis and rests solidly in microeconomic theory.

The increasing emphasis on behavioural aspects of migration which accompanied the growing acceptance of the discrete choice approach in this field also raised a number of new research questions. As discussed in this chapter, the problem of adequately defining the variables influencing migration behaviour is far from solved. In particular the close relationship between migration and the labour market creates potential interdependencies which need to be taken into account when modelling migration. The discrete choice approach provides an adequate instrument for this effort but more conceptual and empirical work seems to be required. A similar statement can be made about the dynamic aspects of migration modelling. There too the discrete choice approach provides valuable guidelines but many of the details have remained unresolved as yet.

Chapter 3

Spatial interaction models and the propensity to migrate over distance*

John Stillwell

3.1 Introduction

The theoretical framework of spatial interaction modelling was established over twenty years ago (Wilson 1967). Since its original application for predicting daily commuting trips between places of usual residence and places of work, there have been a multitude of applications of this style of modelling in various fields where human interaction across space occurs. Population migration represents a classic example of a phenomenon influenced positively by push and pull factors associated with origins and destinations respectively, and related inversely to the distance separating the origins from the destinations. Migration models based on these gravitational features were first developed in the 1940s, although in the nineteenth century Ravenstein recognized the importance of the migration–distance relationship, stating that 'migrants enumerated in a certain centre of absorption will consequently grow less with distance proportionately to the native population which furnishes them' (Ravenstein 1885).

Modifications were made to these early Newtonian gravity models by introducing parameters to weight the influence of origin and destination factors and by experimenting with alternative regression model structures and distance functions. One of the shortcomings of the Newtonian model — its inability to predict interaction consistent with the number of flows from origins or to destinations — was remedied by the introduction of balancing factors to ensure consistency. This led to the emergence of the so-called constrained gravity model. However, the late 1960s also saw the independent derivation of the same model by Wilson (1970) using entropy-maximising techniques, which enabled interaction flows to be predicted that were consistent with known information, but that were also as unbiased as possible about the unknown details of where individuals moved from and to.

In this chapter, Section 3.2 is designed to outline the specification of the different models which constitute the spatial interaction model

*Many thanks to Philip Rees and Ian Gordon for their helpful comments on an earlier draft of this chapter.

family, and to explain a calibration methodology in common use which generates a parameter representing the frictional effect of distance on migration or the propensity for migrants to move over distance. The variation in the parameter by age group and by origin or destination is examined in Section 3.3, where examples of doubly constrained models applied to historical migration matrices in the United Kingdom are presented. Section 3.4 demonstrates how this modelling framework can be adopted to estimate unknown migration information in both historical and projection contexts, and a recent example of its application in population projection at the local scale is summarized. An attempt is made in Section 3.5 to compare short-term migration projections generated by a set of selected models, and conclusions are drawn in Section 3.6.

3.2 Model structure and calibration

Most of the early gravity model formulations (e.g. Zipf 1946) were log-transformed and calibrated using linear regression techniques. Spatial interaction models based on entropy-maximizing techniques were developed which overcame the limitations of unconstrained Ordinary Least Squares (OLS) models, as explained by Senior (1979), and have subsequently been applied in migration studies at a variety of different scales (intraurban, interurban, interregion) in a number of different countries (see, for example, Stillwell 1978; Willekens 1983; or Fotheringham 1983).

The general form of the spatial interaction model can be expressed verbally as follows:

Migration from area i to area j = Scaling constant or
Balancing factors
× Origin outmigration or
Attractiveness factor
× Destination inmigration or
Attractiveness factor
× Distance function   (3.1)

and different versions of the model are defined according to the information that is known about migration in a specified historical or projection period. The scaling constant or balancing factors operate to ensure that migration flow predictions are consistent with known information. The simplest form of spatial interaction model is defined in the situation where the only available data on migration in the prediction period is the total number of migrants in the system or the number of migrations taking place:

$$M_{..} = \sum_i \sum_j M_{ij} \qquad\qquad (3.2)$$

where

M_{ij} = the migration flow from origin area i to destination area j: and

   * represents summation over the subscript i which varies from 1 to n, and the subscript j which varies from 1 to m.

The so-called unconstrained model has the form:

$$M_{ij} = k \; W_i W_j \; f(d_{ij}) \tag{3.3}$$

where

k = a factor for scaling the total predicted flows to the total observed flows and thereby ensuring the overall constraint is satisfied:

$$k = M_{..}/\sum_i \sum_j \; W_i W_j \; f(d_{ij}) \tag{3.4}$$

W_i = a term representing the attractiveness of the origin area i as a generator of outmigrants;

W_j = a term representing the attractiveness of the destination area j as a recipient of inmigrants; and

$f(d_{ij})$ = a distance impedance function between area i and area j which is inversely related to migration.

Substituting for k in equation (3.3), the model can be written as a nonlinear equation:

$$M_{ij} = M_{..} \; \{(W_i W_j \; f(d_{ij}))/(\sum_i \sum_j \; W_i W_j \; f(d_{ij}))\} \tag{3.5}$$

where the { } bracketed terms are probabilities that sum to one.

Origin and destination attractiveness factors can be represented by a single variable (such as population size, number of dwellings, unemployment rates or relative wage rates) which reflect particular attributes or characteristics of the areas concerned which exhibit a functional relationship with outmigration or inmigration. Alternatively, variables may be combined into some form of composite measure prior to their inclusion in the distribution model. If population size is used to represent attractiveness, for example, parameter values may be attached to the factors which indicate the returns to scale: i.e. a parameter value below 1 on the origin attractiveness term shows declining outmigration rates for areas with larger populations; a value above 1 indicates increasing outmigration from areas with larger populations.

In certain circumstances, data may be available on outmigration from each origin area. In this situation, a production constrained model can be formulated as:

$$M_{ij} = A_i \ O_i \ W_j \ f(d_{ij}) \qquad (3.6)$$

where O_i = the total outmigration from origin area i;

$$A_i = 1/\sum_j W_j \ f(d_{ij}) \qquad (3.7)$$

> = a balancing factor derived endogenously to ensure that the total migration from origin area i is equal to the sum of migrations arriving at all destinations from area i:

$$O_i = M_{i\bullet} = \sum_j M_{ij} \qquad (3.8)$$

Thus:

$$M_{ij} = O_i\{(W_j \ f(d_{ij})) \ / \ (\sum_j W_j \ f(d_{ij}))\} \qquad (3.9)$$

where the { } bracketed terms are probabilities which must sum to one. The attractiveness of each destination and its distance from the origin are therefore evaluated against all other destinations.

The third relative in the family of spatial interaction models is one where observed data on totals of inmigration to each destination area are available. The attraction constrained spatial interaction model can be written as:

$$M_{ij} = B_j \ W_i \ D_j \ f(d_{ij}) \qquad (3.10)$$

where D_j = total inmigration to destination area j; and

$$B_j = 1 \ / \ \sum_i W_i \ f(d_{ij}) \qquad (3.11)$$

> = the balancing factor to ensure that:

$$D_j = M_{\bullet j} = \sum_i M_{ij} \qquad (3.12)$$

Finally, whenever a matrix of observed flows is available, a migration model can be fitted which is both production- and attraction-constrained. A doubly constrained spatial interaction model predicts migration flows which are constrained to known origin area outmigration totals and known destination area inmigration totals:

$$M_{ij} = A_i \ B_j \ O_i \ D_j \ f(d_{ij}) \qquad (3.13)$$

where:

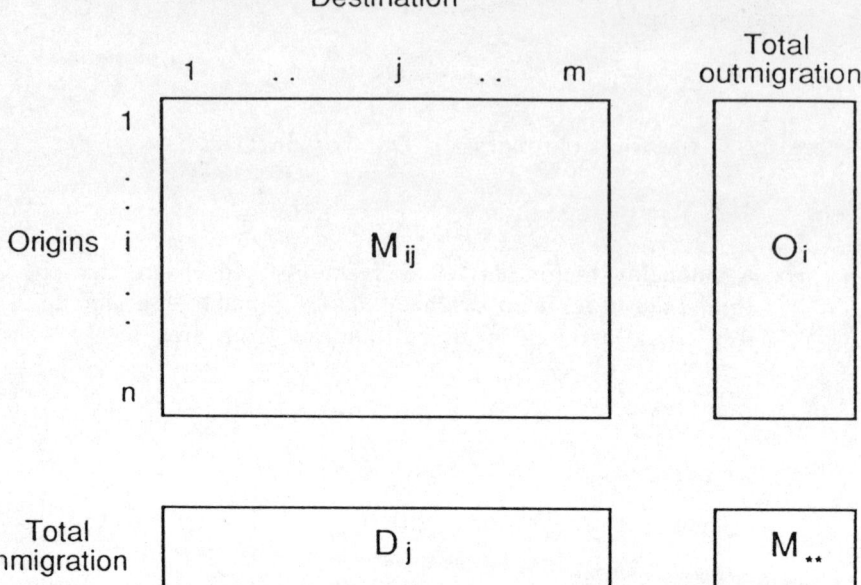

Figure 3.1   Constraint information in spatial interaction modelling

$$A_i = 1/ \sum_j B_j D_j \ f(d_{ij}) \tag{3.14}$$

and

$$B_j = 1 / \sum_i A_i O_i \ f(d_{ij}) \tag{3.15}$$

Thus, in each of these four cases, the spatial interaction model is predicting a matrix of migration flows (Figure 3.1), subject to the availability of different sets of information. At the least constrained level, only a single value of total movement is available; on the other hand, the volume of outmigration from each origin area and of inmigration to each destination area is available in the doubly constrained model.

How is the functional relationship between distance and migration specified in each of these models? A series of functions have been classified by Goux (1962) and tested on Swedish movement data by Taylor (1975). The most familiar of the double log set is the negative power or Pareto function in which:

$$M_{ij} = k \ d_{ij}^{-\beta} = k \ \exp \ (-\beta \ \ln \ d_{ij}) \tag{3.16}$$

where k and β are empirically derived parameters. This function, which assumes that migrants behave as though distance is logarithmic, is typical of that used in the calibration of log-linear regression models of the pre-entropy era. The decay function specified initially in the entropy-maximization derivation of the model is the negative exponential function:

$$M_{ij} = k \exp (-\beta \, d_{ij}) \tag{3.17}$$

which is the most common of the single log functions. These functions are two selected from a wide range of alternatives. Whichever function is selected, the inclusion of a distance term necessitates the provision of a matrix of distance values. The question of what measurement of distance is appropriate is a difficult one. Inevitably there are social as well as financial costs involved in migration and both should, in theory, be used. In practice, the measure of distance included in models is usually of a physical nature — the airline or road distance between two areas. In the case of the latter, area centroids must be distinguished as centres of gravity and inter-centroid distances measured from road maps. Alternatively, inter-area distances can be calculated using grid references for centroids as follows:

$$d_{ij} = \sqrt{ (e_i - e_j)^2 - (n_i - n_j)^2 } \tag{3.18}$$

where e_i, e_j, n_i and n_j are easting and northing coordinates of origin i and destination j. This method has been applied in the United Kingdom (Stillwell *et al*. 1988) using grid references for centres of local authority districts, counties and regions (OPCS 1984b).

The model equations set out above imply that the estimation of migration flows occurring within areas are included, i.e. modelling of the diagonal element of the matrix. In many situations, this data may not be available, but when intra-zonal migration is modelled, intra-zonal distances must be estimated. Duley (1989), for example, computes intra-zonal distance as the radius of a circle of the same area as the zone in question.

A range of alternative techniques exists for calibrating spatial interaction models (Batty and Mackie 1972; Wilson 1974) and Figure 3.2 indicates the general procedure for calibration in a program called IMP (Stillwell 1984), which adopts a Newton Raphson automatic search routine. The first task is to calculate an array of distance function values based on an initial beta parameter value. The computation of the balancing factors is complicated because, in a doubly constrained model, the A_i factor includes the B_j term and vice versa, so the factors can only be solved iteratively. The value of A_i is calculated initially on the assumption that B_j equals 1.0 and the computed A_i value is then used in the calculation of B_j. The balancing factors are recalculated until the difference between values on successive iterations falls below a certain level (0.001, for example). Once convergence has been achieved, the model equation is used to predict a flow between each origin and

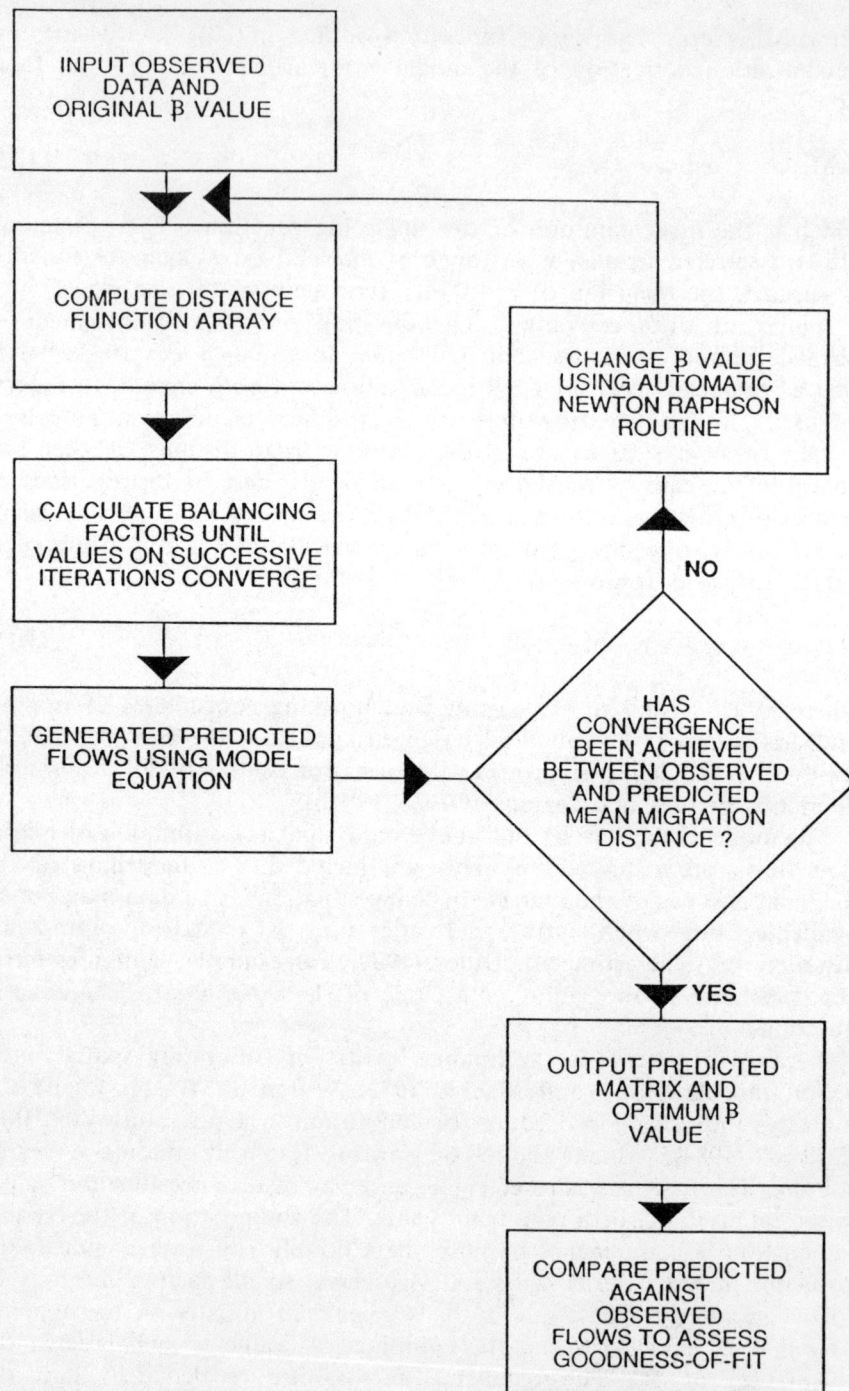

Figure 3.2   General procedure for calibrating spatial interaction models using
          IMP

destination. Comparison between the observed and predicted mean migration distance indicates whether or not the beta value is optimum, i.e. if the following condition is satisfied:

$$|(\sum_i \sum_j M^o_{ij} d_{ij} \ / \ \sum_i \sum_j M^o_{ij}) - (\sum_i \sum_j M^p_{ij} d_{ij} \ / \ \sum_i \sum_j M^p_{ij})| < 0.001 \qquad (3.19)$$

then the model has been calibrated with the optimum parameter value. If the criterion is not satisfied, the beta value is altered, the balancing factors recalculated and a new set of model predictions is generated. Due to its efficiency in relation to other search routines, a Newton Raphson iterative procedure is incorporated to alter the parameter. This involves incrementing the initial and alternate values by a constant (Inc = 0.001) which is replaced on second and alternate iterations by a value (Eps) defined as:

$$Eps \ = \ Inc \ ((ObsD - PredD^n) \ / \ (PredD^n - PredD^{n-1})) \qquad (3.20)$$

where ObsD   = observed mean migration distance;

PredD^n = predicted mean migration distance on nth iteration; and

PredD^{n-1} = predicted mean migration distance on n − 1th iteration.

The same methodology is employed to calibrate unconstrained and singly constrained models with appropriate revision of the balancing factor routine.

The results of calibration can be exemplified using 1981 Census data on migration between the ten standard regions of Britain during the twelve-month period before the census (OPCS, RGS 1983a). The distance matrix contains road distances between regional centroids and usually resident population estimates from the 1981 Census (OPCS, RGS 1983b) are used to represent origin and destination attractiveness. The ability of different models to predict the pattern of observed flows is assessed using selected goodness-of-fit statistics (Table 3.1) computed by IMP. The Sum of Squared Deviations (SSD) is a measure of the total difference between observed and predicted migration flows, whilst the Mean Absolute Difference (MAD) is the sum of the absolute deviations divided by the sum of the observed flows and expressed as a percentage. The Index Of Dissimilarity (IOD) compares the observed and predicted distributions by calculating the sum of the deviations between the observed and predicted proportions of total migration in each cell of the matrix. The final statistic is the correlation coefficient (R), the ratio of the covariation to the square root of the product of the variation in observed migration and in predicted migration. A fuller discussion of goodness-of-fit statistics can be found in Knudsen and Fotheringham (1986).

Table 3.1 Parameters and goodness-of-fit statistics for spatial interaction
models fitted to aggregate interregion flows, Great Britain, 1980–81

Model	Decay parameter (β_*)	SSD ('000)	MAD (%)	IOD	R
			Interregion flows		
		(Total flows = 611213; mean distance = 238 km)			
Unconstrained	0.6329	1 778 870	32.7	16.4	0.8245
Production constrained	0.7076	1 509 284	30.4	15.2	0.8535
Attraction constrained	0.6202	835 666	23.7	11.9	0.9232
Doubly constrained	0.7692	378 699	18.2	9.1	0.9661
			Inter + intraregion flows		
		(Total flows = 4 745 025; mean distance = 48 km)			
Doubly constrained	1.5736	18 504 306	15.6	7.8	0.9965

As one might expect, the goodness-of-fit of the models improves as additional constraints are incorporated. In this example of interregional migration, the MAD falls by 2.3 per cent when gross outmigration information is utilized, by 9 per cent when an inmigration constraint is imposed, and by 14.5 per cent when a doubly constrained model is calibrated. The R coefficient rises from 0.8245 in the unconstrained model to 0.9661 in the doubly constrained version. When intraregion flows are included in the model calibration, and a uniform intraregion distance of 20 km is assumed with a negative power function, the overall fit of the doubly constrained model is improved further (e.g. R = 0.9965). The distance decay parameter rises from 0.7 to 1.5 as the mean migration distance falls from 238 km to 48 km. The decay parameter can be interpreted as the propensity to migrate over distance. A high negative value suggests that distance has a stronger frictional effect on migration, whilst a low negative parameter suggests that migrants are less impeded by the distance over which they move. A positive beta value, which may occur in some situations, indicates that migration flows increase as the distance between the origin and the destination lengthens. The next section of the chapter demonstrates the application of doubly constrained spatial interaction models for exploring historical migration in the United Kingdom.

3.3 Historical applications of the doubly constrained model

The selective nature of migration has stimulated research on the variation in migrant behaviour according to age, sex, education, occupation and marital status. Only patterns of age selectivity (Rogers and Castro 1981) appear to have gained universal acceptance by population analysts and demographers in the developed world. Young adults have the highest propensities to migrate for reasons associated with that stage in their life cycle (Rossi 1955). Infants and children tend to move with their parents and have higher rates of migration than adolescents whose parents are older on average and therefore less mobile. Migration propensities generally fall to around the age of retirement, when a post-labour force peak may occur in some situations. Given these variations, it is logical to ask whether all migrants have the same propensity to migrate over distance.

This propensity and the distance over which migration occurs does vary by age. Figure 3.3 illustrates the distance decay parameters and the mean migration distances for National Health Service (NHS) patients in sixteen age groups (0–4 . . . 70–74, 75+) moving between the eighteen zones of a system of metropolitan and nonmetropolitan areas in the United Kingdom defined in Stillwell *et al.* (1988). The profiles, which conform with results based on migration flows occurring in other systems of interest (Stillwell 1978, 1990), reflect some of the characteristics of individuals in particular life groups. In the early age groups, distance exerts most influence on migrants aged 10–14 and least influence on those aged 20–24. Thereafter, the frictional effect of distance increases steadily to around retirement age before levelling off. Mean distances tend to decline with age, but there are three peaks in the profile associated with movers aged 10–14, 20–24 and 35–44. The presentation of the values for two different time periods indicates how the model can be used for examining changes taking place over time. In this case, the comparison of figures for 1983–84 with those of 1985-86 suggests that the effect of distance becomes less important for all ages up to 55–59, but more important for those aged 60 and over. This has not necessarily resulted in increased distances of movement for the non-elderly. Movers aged 5–9, 35–39 and 50–54 actually travelled slightly shorter distances on average in 1985–86 than they did in 1983–84.

The manner in which the propensity to migrate over distance changes by age is indicative of the various motivations which influence individuals at various stages in their life cycles. Models of aggregate migration suffer from the need to make assumptions about motivation that are inevitably limited since survey data have shown that longer-distance population redistribution involves a larger proportion of labour migrants changing their jobs as well as moving house, whereas shorter-distance migrants have a higher proportion of individuals who are moving purely for housing and environmental reasons and who will remain in the same workplace. The paucity of data in Britain on migration classified by reason for move necessitates the derivation of methods to separate aggregate flows into the major motivation-specific streams. Gordon suggests such a methodology in Chapter 5 of this volume. An alternative and much simpler approach is to partition the spatial units and to model flows between contiguous areas separately from flows between areas that are not contiguous. The importance of area contiguity

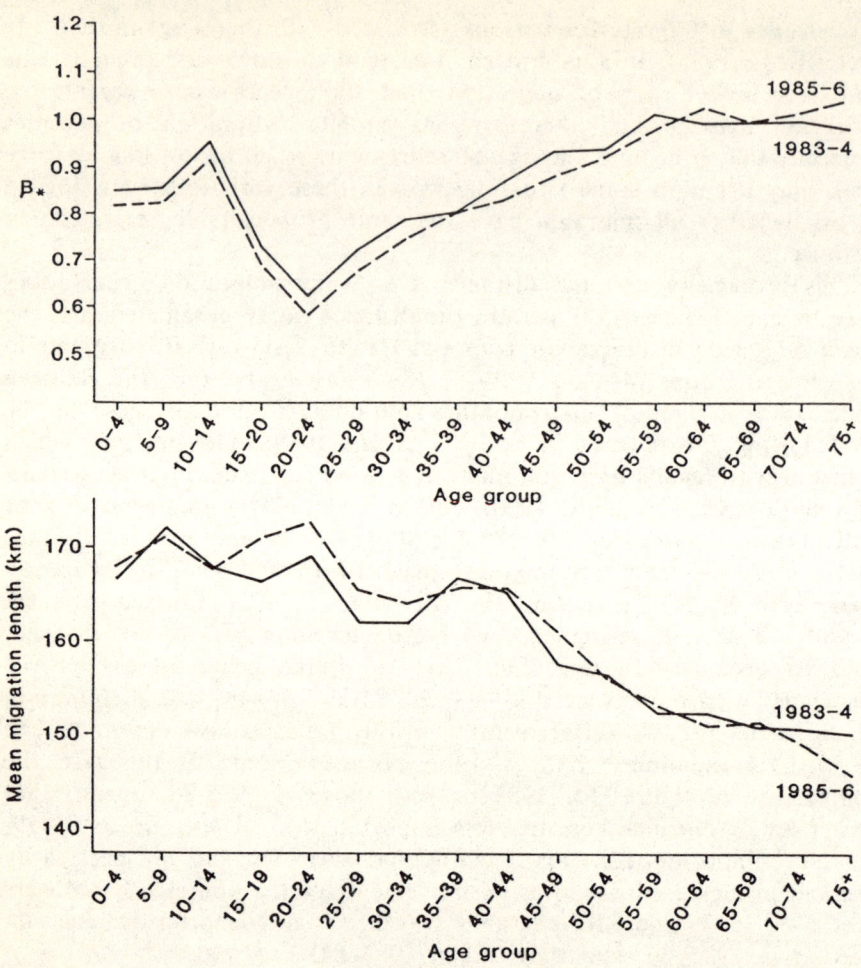

Figure 3.3   Distance decay parameters and mean migration distances by age
group, metropolitan and nonmetropolitan regions, 1983–84 and
1985–86

in modelling migration between British standard regions was investigated
by Weeden (1973), who maintained that a contiguity dummy introduced
into a regression model picked up the effect of short-distance moves that
happened to cross the boundaries of administratively defined (rather than
functionally defined) regions, but which did not necessarily entail a
change of job. The separate modelling of migration between contiguous
areas and between non-contiguous areas has been shown to improve
overall model fits considerably. The application of this approach to the
example of interregional migration for 1980–81 used in Section 3.2
results in reductions in the MAD to 8.7 and the IOD to 4.3, and an
increase in R to 0.9913. A further approach to migration stream

modelling in the intraurban scale is considered in Section 3.4.

Whilst generalized distance decay parameters give an indication of the overall propensity to migrate over distance, they conceal spatial variations that may occur between different origins or destinations. The extent of this geographical variation can be identified by the calibration of models which incorporate zone-specific decay parameters. The optimum generalized parameter is used as the initial beta value for each zone in the calibration procedure, and the Newton Raphson routine is then employed iteratively until convergence between the observed and predicted mean migration distance for each zone has been achieved. In the final stage, the balancing factors and model equation are recalculated with the complete set of optimum zone-specific parameters until convergence between the observed and predicted mean migration distances overall has been achieved and the overall outmigration and inmigration constraint equations are satisfied. Exactly the same procedure is used to calibrate both origin- and destination-specific parameters, but in the case of the latter the original migration matrix has to be transposed and the row and column totals (or attractiveness factors in singly constrained models) for origins and destinations exchanged.

Two examples serve to illustrate the spatial and temporal variation in origin-specific (β_i) and destination-specific (β_j) parameters respectively. The first example is based on migration data from the NHSCR for the system of metropolitan and nonmetropolitan regions used in the previous analysis. The influence of distance on outmovement is shown to vary appreciably in Figure 3.4, even between areas in the same broad regional division. Of the four regions defined as constituting Britain's periphery, outmigrants from Scotland appear to be relatively unaffected by distance, whereas migrants from Tyne and Wear and the remainder of the North have higher values than outmigrants from Wales. Regions in the industrial heartland appear more clustered in terms of the propensities to move over distance and the general trend of decline in the frictional effect of distance is reflected in the schedules for all the metropolitan regions. In the south of the country, there is again considerable variation. Greater London and the rest of the South East have relatively low beta values whereas distance has a much greater effect on migrants from East Anglia and the South West. Over time, an upward trend is observed in the parameter for the East Midlands.

The second example illustrates the spatial variation in the influence of distance on the propensity to move into Family Practitioner Committee (FPC) areas in England and Wales. The negative parameter values range from over 2.0 in the case of inmovement to Powys and Gwynedd to less than 0.5 for Scotland, and less than 1.0 for several of the areas in London (Figure 3.5). Statistical comparison of the decay parameters against mean inmigration distances indicates the lack of a significant relationship. There are areas (e.g. Suffolk and Rotherham) whose inmigrants show a similar propensity to migrate over different mean

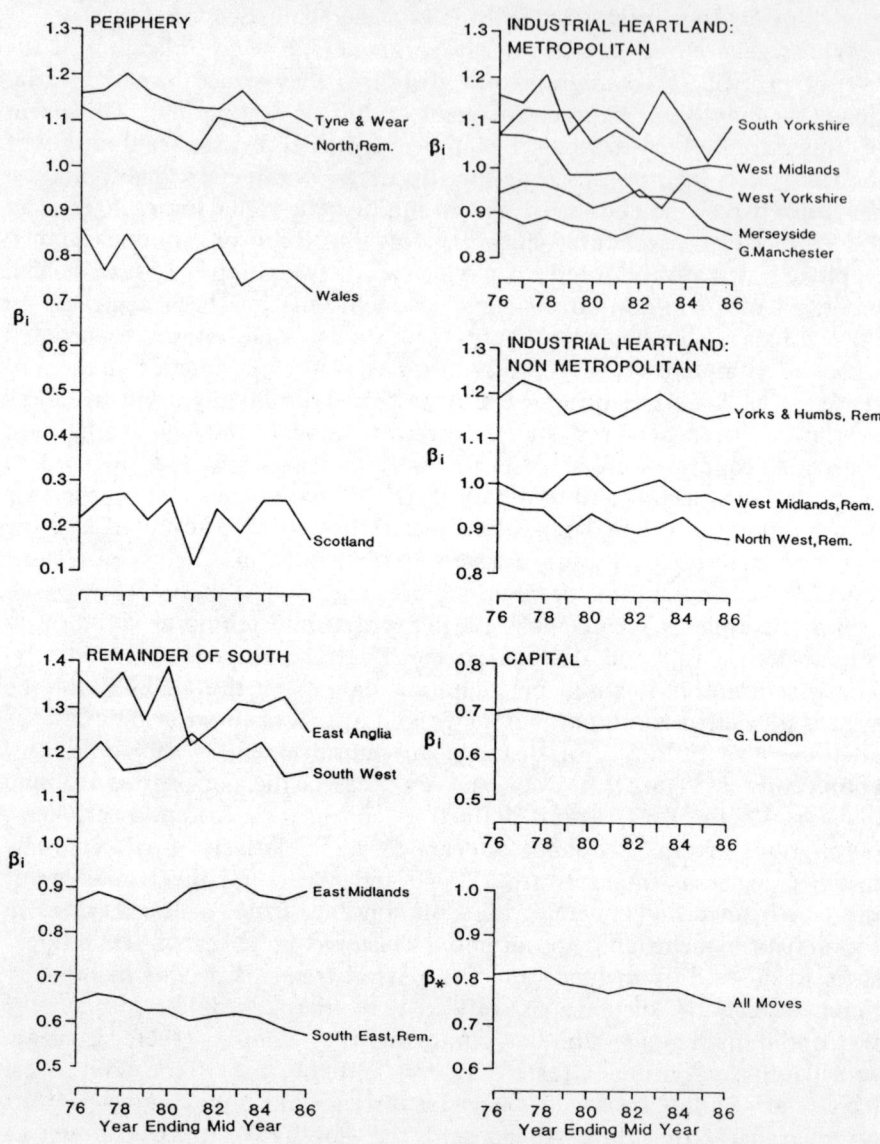

Figure 3.4 Origin–specific distance decay parameters, metropolitan and nonmetropolitan regions, 1975–86

distances. Likewise, there are other areas (e.g. Berkshire and Mid-Glamorgan) with similar mean migration lengths but with very different decay parameters.

The mean inmigration distance is not itself a measure of accessibility but it is likely to be a function of the accessibility of the zone to the rest of the system, as measured by an index of population potential. In this

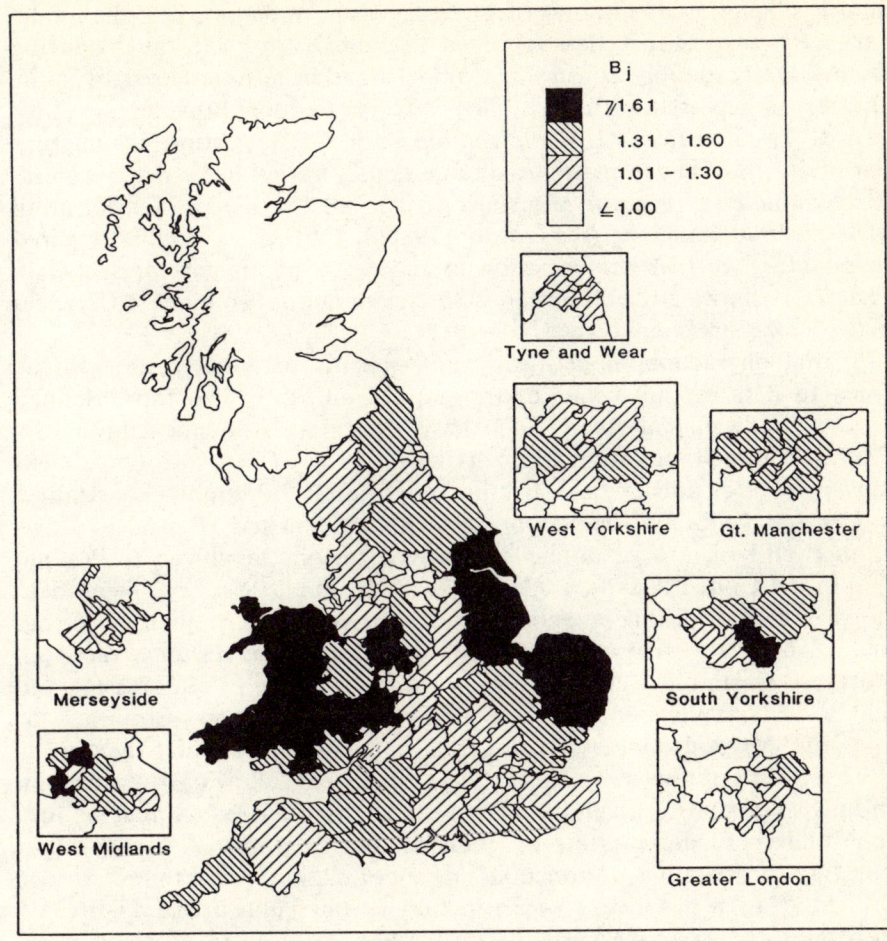

Figure 3.5 Destination–specific distance decay parameters, FPC areas, 1985–86

context, Cliff *et al.* (1974), Johnston (1975) and, more recently, Fotheringham (1986) have drawn attention to the role of accessibility in terms of what has been called the 'map pattern' or 'spatial structure' effect. This refers to the trend for central zones to have less negative decay parameter estimates and peripheral zones to have more negative estimates. However, results reported in the studies mentioned previously have all been associated with unconstrained models which lack internal consistency. In Chapter 4 of this volume, Fotheringham suggests that a more coherent theoretical alternative is required which involves incorporating a factor into unconstrained models which represents the competitive relationships between destinations. However, Gordon (1985b) has argued that explanations of variation in distance decay parameters in terms of 'map pattern' alone are inadequate when a doubly constrained model is being used, since no theoretical reason to assume that the model has been misspecified has yet been presented. In fact, the balancing factors in the doubly constrained model have been interpreted by some authors as representing accessibility effects. Gordon provides an alternative set of substantive explanations for the variation in migrant sensitivity to distance in terms of the spatial variation in real incomes, the economies of scale in transport costs, and the spatial concentration of specialized functions (see Gordon 1985b). Further research is required to establish whether the variation in the decay parameters presented in Figure 3.5 shows any correlation with functional or economic differences between the areas concerned.

Spatial interaction models with zone-specific parameters can also be fitted to data on subgroups of the population other than those defined by age. Stillwell and Rees (1985) have used data from the Universities Central Council on Admissions (UCCA 1978–84) to analyse student movements to universities. In this application, a doubly constrained model was calibrated based on an asymmetric matrix of student flows from twelve regions of domicile to eleven regions of university destination in the United Kingdom. Centroids of the domicile regions were identified and road distances were measured between each region's centroid and each of the fifty-two university locations. The distances between Northern Ireland and elsewhere included the distance of sea crossing and length of ferry routes between Belfast and Heysham, Stranraer or Glasgow. Mean distances between each domicile centroid and the universities within the university cluster were calculated, allowing for variation in university size by weighting each distance by the total number of full-time undergraduate entrants of home fee-paying status. A model incorporating a negative exponential decay function was found to be preferable to a negative power function in this context and Figure 3.6 illustrates the regional variation in destination-specific parameters set against the national trend of decline between 1977 and 1983 for males and females. An increase in the beta parameter over the period is only calibrated for female students moving to universities in the South West.

The pattern of residuals which is generated when the spatial interaction model is calibrated with student migration is dominated by the over-prediction of flows to Northern Ireland. This particular region has its own unique set of religious, political and socioeconomic circumstances which acts as a major disincentive to potential undergraduate students from the rest of the United Kingdom. The 'troubles' in Northern Ireland can be regarded as an additional barrier to student migration, over and above that which is measured by road and ferry-crossing distances. A barrier effect can be introduced into the model explicitly by the addition of a constant to each of the distances between Northern Ireland and elsewhere. The constant is determined through successive spatial interaction model calibrations with a distance matrix adjusted on each iteration, such that the optimum value is achieved where a selected

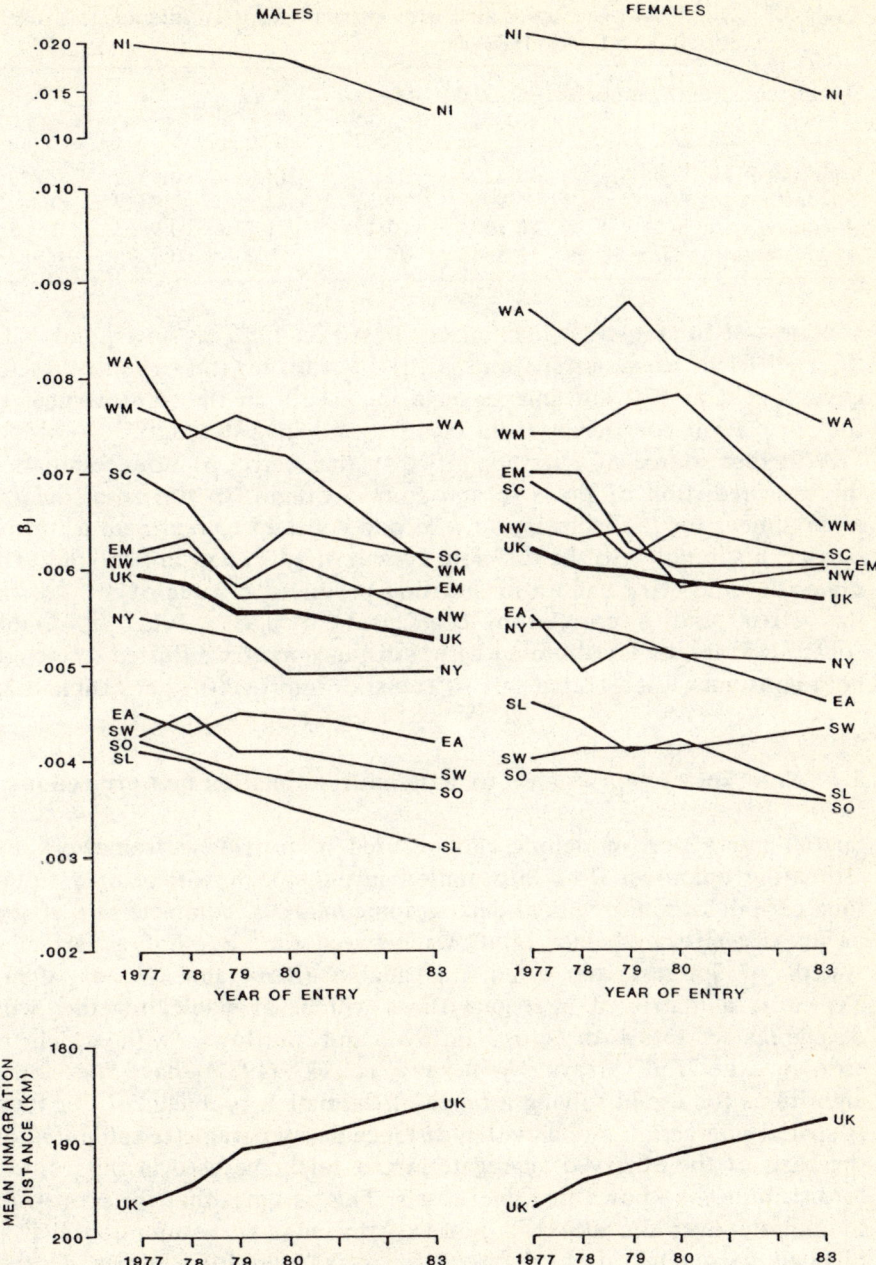

Figure 3.6 Destination-specific distance decay parameters and mean inmigration distances, male and female students, 1977–83

Table 3.2   Goodness-of-fit associated with alternative spatial interaction models for student flows, 1982–83

Doubly constrained model	SSD ('000)	MAD	IOD	R	R^2
Equation 3.13	10 420	25.5	14.8	0.9132	0.8339
+ constant for NI	6 994	22.6	11.3	0.9422	0.8877
+ constant for SC	6 102	22.1	11.1	0.9505	0.9035
+ constants for NI + SC	2 384	16.4	8.2	0.9772	0.9548

goodness-of-fit statistic is maximized. Based on 1982–83 flows, and using the coefficient of determination as the fit statistic, the 'troubles' factor is computed as 890 km and its inclusion results in the improvement of the correlation coefficient from 0.913 to 0.942 (Table 3.2).

A further source of error identified in the matrix of flow residuals is the overprediction of flows to and from Scotland. In this case, there is an argument for the inclusion of a second constant to represent a further barrier, attributable to the different system of education in Scotland. The same trial and error calibration method produced a value of 355 km for this effect and a correlation coefficient of 0.951. When a doubly constrained model is calibrated with a distance matrix adjusted to include both constants, the goodness-of-fit statistics improve further (Table 3.2).

3.4 Spatial interaction models for migration estimation and projection

Spatial interaction modelling can be used to provide a framework for estimating unknown flow information in either a historical or a future time period. In multiregional demographic analysis, complete sets of sex- or age-disaggregated data on flows between the zones of a particular system of interest are often unavailable (Rees and Woods 1986). Typically, a matrix of aggregate flows will be available, together with disaggregated totals of gross inflows and outflows, with which to estimate the full arrays. Willekens *et al.* (1981) have developed algorithms for use in solving a range of estimation problems of this type. A spatial interaction model with a distance decay parameter calibrated on the basis of the observed aggregate matrix might be used in this context to distribute the known marginal totals. This assumes that the propensity to migrate over distance will not vary by age, an assumption that is difficult to defend in the light of the results reported earlier. Consequently it would be appropriate to distribute the age-specific totals using a spatial interaction model with decay parameters adjusted for age variation.

Problems also arise frequently in population analysis because of changes in the boundaries of spatial units over time with local government reorganization or enumeration area reform. Such circumstances may necessitate the adoption of spatial interaction models to distribute known outflow and/or inflow totals for a new, post-revision set of regions, given a base period matrix of flows between a set of old, pre-revision regions. The parameter calibrated on the base period matrix would be used in the model to distribute the 'new' outmigration and/or inmigration totals.

The application of spatial interaction models for the estimation and projection of migration can be effectively illustrated by reference to SWIS, an information and projection system for ward populations and housing developed for Swansea City (Rees *et al.* 1990). Singly constrained spatial interaction models are used in the system to project inter-ward migration flows in three separate streams: (i) a turnover migration stream, comprising those individuals moving from one unit of existing housing to another in Swansea; (ii) a stream of migrants from existing housing into new houses; and (iii) a stream of migrants resulting from housing demolition. Models for each of these streams are required to generate estimates of aggregate internal migration in Swansea for a benchmark period, 1981–86, and for projection periods thereafter. The estimates produced, together with demographic rates of birth, death and external migration, are input to a multiregional cohort component model to generate ward populations by age and gender. The population model relies on the movement concept rather than the migrant transition concept.

The starting point in the migration projection procedure is with the calibration of an origin-constrained model and a destination constrained interaction model for aggregate migration between the twenty Swansea wards during 1980–81, the most recent period for which data (from the 1981 Census) is available at this scale. Observed inmigration and outmigration totals are used as the attractiveness factors in the two models respectively, and two decay parameters $\beta(oc)$ and $\beta(dc)$ are computed.

The next step is to estimate movement out of and into each ward during the benchmark period by transforming the total within Swansea, out of Swansea and into Swansea migration rates for 1980–81 from a 1981 ward basis (twenty wards) to a 1983 ward basis (twenty-three wards). The three rate vectors are multiplied by a transformation matrix, based on detailed enumeration district populations, which distributes 1981 ward values to the new 1983 wards. These transformed rates are then adjusted to account for the difference between Census transition rates and movement rates required by the model, for the different period length, and for changes in the level of migration occurring between 1980--81 and 1981–86. The number of moves to new housing also has to be separated from the turnover migration at this stage.

The origin constrained model used to estimate turnover migration between wards in the benchmark period can be written as:

$$TM_{ij} = A_i \ O_i \ W_j \ d_{ij}^{-\beta(oc)} \tag{3.21}$$

where TM_{ij} = turnover migration between ward i and ward j;
$\quad\quad A_i$ = the balancing factor for origin ward i;
$\quad\quad O_i$ = total estimated migrations originating in ward i;
$\quad\quad W_j$ = the attractiveness of ward j to inmigrants; and;
$\quad\quad d_{ij}$ = the distance between wards i and j.

The attractiveness factors, W_j, turned out to be crucial elements in the model. After some experimentation with alternatives such as total housing stock and vacancies created by the turnover process, a methodology was devised in which the attractiveness factors for each ward were estimated iteratively. The whole projection model is run with a set of attractiveness factors to produce projected 1986 populations. A comparison of these projected populations with independently estimated figures for 1986 leads to adjustment of attractiveness factors to improve the fit between projected and estimated figures on the next iteration. Full details of the iterative methodology for defining the attractiveness factors, which reflect migration choices in 1980–81 and 1981–86 and which correlate quite closely with socioeconomic indicators, are described in Rees *et al.* (1990).

A destination-constrained model is employed to estimate the second stream of migration to new housing in Swansea. It takes the form:

$$HM_{ij} = B_j \ W_i \ D_j \ d_{ij}^{-\beta(dc)} \tag{3.22}$$

where HM_{ij} = new housing migration between ward i and ward j;
$\quad\quad B_j$ = the balancing factor for destination ward j;
$\quad\quad W_i$ = the propensity to migrate from origin ward i; and
$\quad\quad D_j$ = the total migration flow into destination ward j,
$\quad\quad\quad\quad$ defined as:

$$D_j = NH_j \ pph_j \tag{3.23}$$

where NH_j = the number of new housing units in ward j; and
$\quad\quad pph_j$ = the persons per household in ward j.

D_j has to be reduced to allow for migrants from the rest of the United Kingdom moving in to occupy new housing units. The origin term, W_i, is set to the projected total migration within Swansea.

Another origin-constrained spatial interaction model is used to estimate the third component of migration in Swansea — that occurring due to housing demolition. In this case, origin outmigration, O_i, is estimated by multiplying the number of demolished houses in each ward by a suitable person per household figure, and the attractiveness factors, W_j, are defined in connection with turnover migration.

Total migration between each pair of wards in the benchmark period is computed as the summation of the three streams, rates are computed and the aggregate rates are finally disaggregated by age and sex before being used in the population projection program. Clearly the migration models built into this system make demands on data supply, not least in terms of the numbers of dwelling units constructed and demolished. However, the structure of the system and the models within it provide a facility with which a local authority can evaluate what might happen to population under different scenarios of future migration behaviour and housing development.

3.5 Testing projections

When used in a projection context, constrained spatial interaction models require independent projections of total zonal outmigration and/or inmigration. These can be produced using a variety of different methods, some of which have been discussed in the previous section. In the very simplest case, a historical inmigration rate defined as:

$$d_j(t) = D_j(t) / P_j(t_o) \tag{3.24}$$

can be applied to a population associated with the beginning of the projection period, θ:

$$D_j(\theta) = d_j(t) \, p_j(\theta_o) \tag{3.25}$$

Alternatively, more sophisticated projection models can be developed. One example of an approach to inmigration projection, based on the results of previous research at the standard region scale (Stillwell 1980), adjusts the rate of inmigration in the previous historical period by a factor measuring the assumed change in the overall propensity to migrate, g, and the changing distribution of employment between the regions, ES_j. These three features can be combined into an inmigration rate model written as:

$$d_j(\theta) = d_j(t) \, g(\theta) \, ES_j(\theta) \tag{3.26}$$

where ES_j is an employment shift multiplier. The formulation of a migration rate model based on a multiplicative relationship with a selected set of variables contrasts with the additive structure of log linear models where parameters associated with different independent variables and having different degrees of significance are estimated using regression techniques.

Whilst there are very few studies which actually report on tests of the accuracy of alternative migration projection methods, Stillwell (1986) warns that spatial interaction modelling does not generate particularly accurate short-term projections of origin–destination flows. An approach which distributes gross flows on the basis of the historical pattern of migration and excludes an explicit functional relationship between migration and distance is found to generate more accurate projections and this method was preferred by Martin, Voorhees and Bates (1981) as the model for assigning the origin outmigrants by broad age group to destination areas in the assignment stage of the model for generating the migration assumptions for subnational areas in England.

An attempt to assess the relative accuracy of different model projections for 1985–86 can be made using observed NHSCR data on movements between the metropolitan and nonmetropolitan regions of Britain in 1980–81 and 1984–85. For the sake of exemplification, three spatial interaction models are utilized: a production-constrained model which assumes that total outmigration flows for the regions in the system have been projected; an attraction-constrained model which adopts observed total inmigrations as the totals projected exogenously; and a doubly constrained model in which observed outmigration and inmigration totals are assumed as the projection period constraints. The doubly constrained model is calibrated initially with a generalized parameter and subsequently with an origin-specific parameter set.

Three other distribution models are selected for comparison. The first is a rates model which simply applies historical interregional rates to initial populations of the projection period. The second follows the conceptual deconsolidation of the origin–destination flow into a level, generation and distribution component (Willekens and Baydar 1986). The (observed) level of movement in the system is assumed to be known and each flow from origin i to destination j is estimated by applying (i) the historical probability of migration occurring from origin i, and (ii) the historical probability of migration to destination j, given that the move originated from origin i. A final model is included in which a growth factor is used to distribute the observed out- and inmigration totals on the basis of the migration pattern for the historical period. The growth factor for each interregion flow is the product of the ratio of projection to historical period gross outmigration from each origin and the ratio of the projection to historical period inmigration total to each destination.

Summary goodness-of-fit statistics (derived from comparing predicted against observed flows) associated with each of the models selected are presented in Table 3.3, with the results of the rates model providing a benchmark against which to compare the other projections. The mean deviation between projected and observed flows for 1985–86 is 10.1 per cent when 1980–81 rates are applied and this reduces to 7.7 per cent when the more recent rates for 1985–85 are used. There is marginal improvement when a historical probability model is used to disaggregate the observed total level of movement and the best set of projections are generated by the doubly constrained growth factor model, which contains

Table 3.3 Goodness-of-fit statistics for selected migration projection models

Information available for projection period (1985–86)	Type of model	Fit statistic MAD	Fit statistic R^2
	Movement rates model		
Initial populations	based on (a) 1980–81	10.11	0.9922
	(b) 1984–85	7.66	0.9938
	Conditional probability model		
Total moves	based on (a) 1980–81	8.59	0.9935
	(b) 1984–85	7.44	0.9939
	Constrained growth factor model		
Total outmigration and inmigration	based on (a) 1980–81	5,14	0.9982
	(b) 1984–85	2.65	0.9996
	Production constrained SIM		
Total outmigration	based on (a) 1980–81	34.23	0.8423
	(b) 1984–85	34.23	0.8422
	Attraction constrained SIM		
Total inmigration	based on (a) 1980–81	29.58	0.9251
	(b) 1984–85	29.63	0.9247
	Doubly constrained SIM (with β_*)		
Total outmigration and inmigration	based on (a) 1980–81	28.06	0.9303
	(b) 1984–85	27.93	0.9310
	Doubly constrained SIM (with β_i)		
Total outmigration and inmigration	based on (a) 1980–81	20.28	0.9598
	(b) 1984–85	20.33	0.9614

no explicit distance function and where the historical migration is simply adjusted to comply with new row and column totals using balancing factors.

The results generated by the spatial interaction models reflect the magnitude of deviation which arises when information carried forward from the historical period is reduced to one parameter, or a set of parameters in the case of the origin-specific model, describing the relationship between migration and distance. An attraction-constrained model appears to generate more accurate projections than a production constrained model, but accuracy is only improved appreciably when a doubly constrained model with zone-specific parameters is used. The mean deviation is around 20 per cent for the doubly constrained model with origin-specific parameters calibrated on either of the base year matrices.

3.6 Conclusions

Spatial interaction models have the distinctive capability of generating internally consistent migration flow predictions. Their calibration provides the migration analyst with distance decay parameters appropriate for behavioural interpretation. Considerable variation is observed in the frictional effect of distance on migration propensity, that is, between age groups and according to the area of origin or destination. In the case of the latter, the spatial variation appears not to be correlated with the relative location of zones in the system.

Although the results of comparing alternative sets of projections of migration in the short run suggest that spatial interaction models should be treated with some caution, models of this type have been in use in various public planning contexts (especially transportation) for many years, and are now being incorporated into decision support systems for private companies in the retailing and service-based sectors. The importance of the migration component in local and regional population change is resulting in the demand by planners for more advanced modelling and projection tools. An example of one application has been described in this chapter and what is now required is new and imaginative ideas about how to link migration with important behavioural or policy-related variables for which data may be available. This can be achieved in the context which the spatial interaction modelling framework provides.

Chapter 4

Migration and spatial structure: the development of the competing destinations model

Stewart Fotheringham

4.1 Introduction

Understanding the determinants of migration patterns and forecasting such patterns accurately are recognised as important objectives of spatial demographic analysis: in most developed countries, spatial variations in population growth rates can be ascribed mainly to variations in net migration rather than to variations in natural growth rates. As well as being of intrinsic interest to spatial demography, migration forecasting is also an important aspect of government and business planning. Matching the provision of housing, employment opportunities and services to demand necessitates an accurate forecast of individuals' long-term movements over space. Consequently, the modelling of spatial mobility and of migrants' destination choices has a long history — perhaps one of the longest in social sciences, dating at least from Ravenstein in the nineteenth century (Ravenstein 1885).

Despite its relatively long history, however, several problems have persisted in the mathematical modelling of migration that have reduced the reliability of modelling results and have hindered the widespread acceptance of a model-based approach to the analysis of migration patterns. One of these problems, a solution to which is the topic of this chapter, is that of the spatial variation of parameter estimates referred to as 'the spatial structure effect' or 'context dependency'. Following a description of this problem, a simple solution will be outlined that involves the addition of a single variable to a classic migration destination choice model to produce what has become known as 'the competing destinations model'. The psychological basis for this model formulation is discussed and the implications of ignoring the competing destinations effect are described in terms of both parameter estimation and the prediction of migration flows. The competing destinations model is shown to provide a potentially useful breakthrough in understanding the so-called spatial structure effect in spatial interaction modelling and may be a key to unravelling the persistent geographic mystery of why estimated distance decay parameters appear to exhibit unexpected spatial variation.

4.2 The problem: spatial structure and migration models

One of the basic questions in migration research is 'why do people migrate to a particular place?' Faced with a typical migration matrix, the elements of which represent numbers of migrants from various origins to various destinations, it is of interest to discover why certain destinations attract larger numbers of migrants than others. What attributes of a place make it attractive to a migrant and how sensitive are migrants to changes in these attributes? If accurate answers to these questions can be found, then the information could be used in forecasting migration patterns or in attempting to influence migration patterns by altering the attributes of locations.

Unfortunately, it has not yet been demonstrated that it is possible to obtain accurate information on the sensitivity of migrants' destination choices to various destination attributes. The general methodology for obtaining such information is to calibrate a spatial interaction model of the following form:

$$M_{ij} = \frac{O_i W_{1j}^{\alpha_1} W_{2j}^{\alpha_2} \ldots W_{kj}^{\alpha_k} d_{ij}^{\beta}}{\sum_j W_{1j}^{\alpha_1} W_{2j}^{\alpha_2} \ldots W_{kj}^{\alpha_k} d_{ij}^{\beta}} \qquad (4.1)$$

where M_{ij} represents the number of migrants between origin i and destination j, O_i represents the total number of migrants leaving origin i, W_{1j} represents attribute 1 of destination j which affects its overall attraction to migrants and there are k such attributes, the α parameters reflect the sensitivity of a migrants' destination decision to changes in the respective attribute, d_{ij} represents the spatial separation between i and j and is usually measured by distance, and the parameter β represents the sensitivity of a migrant's destination choice to distance and is commonly referred to as a distance decay parameter. Applications of this modelling approach in migration studies are legionary and include Stillwell (1978), Kau and Sirmans (1979), Greenwood and Sweetland (1972), Flowerdew and Salt (1979), Clark and Ballard (1980), Lovett *et al.* (1985), Ishikawa (1989), Fotheringham (1987), Opt'Veld *et al.* (1984) and Boots and Kanaroglou (1987).

The usual type of destination choice model that has been calibrated in migration studies (equation 4.1) will yield information about behaviour that can only be some sort of average across the individual origins. Certain variables, for example, may appear to be insignificant when calibrated for all origins because they have opposite effects for different origins. The effect of house prices on interregional migration is a case in point: migrants from high-priced housing markets might prefer to move to similarly high-priced markets to maintain their housing equity and to avoid capital gains taxes, hence yielding a positive parameter estimate; conversely, migrants from low-priced housing markets might exhibit an aversion for high-priced areas due to their lack of equity in the housing market, hence yielding a negative parameter estimate. The calibration of a single model for all origins would miss this difference and might lead to the conclusion that the house price variable is unimportant. Further examples of the misleading results caused by calibrating an aggregate model are provided by Fotheringham and O'Kelly (1989).

It is clear, therefore, that the calibration of equation (4.1) with a matrix of migration flows could obscure some potentially interesting information on the variation of attribute sensitivity by origin. For example, it might be useful to know whether different values are attached to destination attributes by migrants from peripheral compared with central origins or by migrants from high-unemployment areas in contrast to low-unemployment areas. A clear difference that might be expected would be in terms of a variable representing house prices at each destination, a factor which is likely to be more important to migrants from an area of low house prices than to those from an area of high house prices. To alleviate the problem of obtaining 'average' parameter estimates for a system, it is strongly suggested that equation (4.1) be calibrated separately for each origin in the system. This origin-specific form of the model is written as:

$$M_{ij} = \frac{O_i W_{1j}^{\alpha_{1i}} W_{2j}^{\alpha_{2i}} \ldots W_{kj}^{\alpha_{ki}} d_{ij}^{\beta_i}}{\sum_j W_{1j}^{\alpha_{1i}} W_{2j}^{\alpha_{2i}} \ldots W_{kj}^{\alpha_{ki}} d_{ij}^{\beta_i}} \qquad (4.2)$$

where the parameters all now have a subscript i denoting the origin for which the model is calibrated. Estimates of the parameters in equation (4.2) will thus provide information on the sensitivity of the destination choices of migrants from origin i to the various destination attributes in the model. Disaggregation in this manner is always possible since in a migration matrix the data are available by origin. Clearly, if further data are available, the model could be disaggregated by both origin and person-type. Such models are relatively easily calibrated by various regression-based techniques or by maximum-likelihood estimation. An extended example of the calibration of an origin-specific migration model using UK migration data and eleven destination attributes is provided by Fotheringham and O'Kelly (1989, pp. 98–106).

Spatial variations in origin-specific parameter estimates can thus yield valuable information on migration patterns, but only if it can be assumed that the estimates are reasonably accurate. A controversy has arisen surrounding this point in terms of the spatial variation of estimated distance decay parameters in spatial interaction models of the type represented in equation (4.2). This controversy has been referred to as 'the spatial structure problem'. The problem is essentially this: suppose equation (4.2) is calibrated for each origin in a migration system so that amongst other things a set of estimated, origin-specific, distance decay parameters is obtained. If this set of estimates is mapped or graphed against a measure of origin centrality, a very clear, but

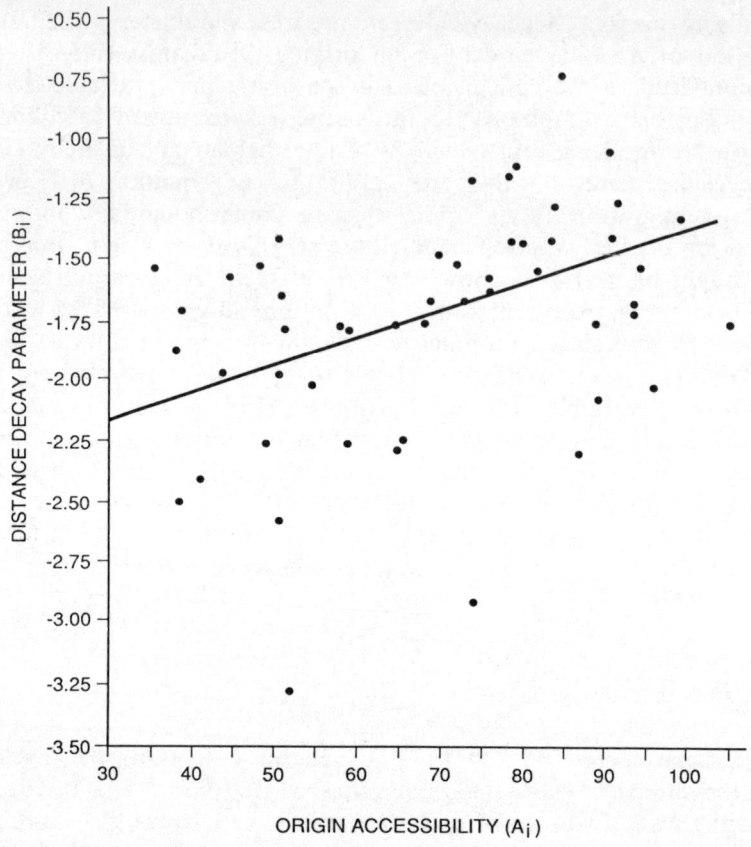

Figure 4.1   Relationship between estimated distance decay parameters from equation (4.2) and origin centrality

behaviourally suspicious, spatial trend is generally apparent with central origins having less negative distance decay parameter estimates and peripheral origins having more negative estimates. This trend is apparent in almost every study of origin-specific distance decay parameter estimates (*inter alia* Greenwood and Sweetland 1972; Chisholm and O'Sullivan 1973; Leinbach 1973; Gould 1975; Stillwell 1978; Fotheringham 1986, 1987; Fotheringham and O'Kelly 1989; Ishikawa 1989). The graph of estimated distance decay parameters against origin centrality from the Fotheringham (1987) study of migration between the fifty-one Dutch housing market areas is presented in Figure 4.1. In this case, origin centrality is measured by a potential accessibility function which is essentially an inverted weighted average of the distance from each origin to all other origins, that is:

$$A_i = \sum_{j \neq i} W_j / d_{ij} \qquad (4.3)$$

where A_i represents the accessibility or centrality of place i, W_j is usually, but not necessarily, measured by destination population size, and d_{ij} represents the distance between i and j in kilometres.

There are several reasons for thinking that the trend exhibited by the parameter estimates in Figure 4.1 is very unreliable as an indication of reality. It is extremely difficult, if not impossible, to explain why migrants from peripheral origins would be deterred to a much greater extent by distance than would migrants from more central origins. In fact, in many systems it would seem more plausible to suggest that migrants from peripheral origins are more willing to make the long-distance moves to the central part of the country rather than the reverse. It is also difficult to believe that the range of behaviour suggested by these parameter estimates can actually exist within a single country. It is not all that uncommon, for example, for positive distance decay parameter estimates to be reported in the calibration of equation (4.2) (*inter alia*, Fotheringham 1981, 1983, 1986), although none is present in the Dutch results. The presence of these positive estimates is perhaps the most damning evidence concerning the validity of equation (4.2) as a basis for migration modelling as they suggest a positive relationship between migration rates and distance *ceteris paribus*. Positive distance decay parameter estimates, where they exist, are always reported for peripheral origins and are clearly an extreme result of the generally observed relationship between an origin's location and its estimated distance decay parameter. A final piece of evidence suggesting a problem with the distance decay parameter estimates is the highly counter-intuitive values of certain estimates. For example, in another context, that of airline passenger interaction in the United States, Fotheringham (1983) points to urban areas such as Syracuse and Rochester having far fewer negative parameter estimates than cities such as Los Angeles and San Francisco. The interpretation that passengers from Syracuse and Rochester undertake greater proportions of long-distance flights than their counterparts in Los Angeles is very unconvincing.

It should be noted that the trends described above are merely evidence that the estimated distance decay parameters for origin-specific migration models are unreliable as indicators of the underlying behaviour they are supposed to represent. However, they do strongly suggest that there may be a problem with the modelling framework represented by equation (4.2) and this problem has become known as the spatial structure effect: its presence causes estimated origin-specific distance decay parameters to reflect not only behaviour but also some attribute connected with origin location. The identification of this latter attribute and the mechanism by which it becomes incorporated into a distance decay parameter has been the topic of much investigation and fairly intense debate (Curry 1972; Johnston 1973, 1975; Curry *et al.* 1975; Cliff *et al.* 1974, 1975, 1976; and Fotheringham and Webber 1980) which is reviewed by Fotheringham (1981). It is also the impetus that led to what has become known as the competing destinations model which will now be described.

4.3 The competing destinations model

Without going into the mathematical details, which are beyond the scope of this chapter (and which are presented elsewhere (Fotheringham 1988; Fotheringham and O'Kelly 1989)), the model formulation of equations (4.1) and (4.2) is predicted on the assumption that individuals consider and evaluate every destination possibility prior to making a decision about where to move. This seems most unlikely: aside from the fact that migrants probably do not possess the information necessary to conduct such a search procedure, there is a fairly substantial volume of evidence suggesting that individuals have a very limited capacity for processing information (*inter alia* Simon 1969; Lindsay and Norman 1972; Newell and Simon 1972; and Norman and Bubrow 1975). That most of us would be incapable of making an evaluation of the large numbers of potential alternatives a migrant generally faces is self-evident. Indeed, in the brand-choice literature, it has been suggested that our limit of information-processing capabilities may be as low as six alternatives (Bettman 1979). Consequently, the assumption underlying classic migration destination choice models, that individuals evaluate and compare all alternatives, is highly implausible and implies that the models are therefore misspecifications of reality.

A more acceptable assumption regarding the method by which migrants process spatial information in order to reach a destination choice is that they do so hierarchically. That is, rather than evaluate all alternatives, they first evaluate clusters or groups of alternatives and then evaluate only alternatives from within a selected cluster. This simple case with only two levels serves as an example, but clearly more complicated hierarchies can exist; the more alternatives that are available, the greater the number of levels there will be in the hierarchical choice process. The rationale for assuming a hierarchical decision process is presented in Figure 4.2, which describes the number of evaluations that are necessary to reach a decision when faced with a certain number of alternatives. When the number of alternatives is small, less than X_1, individuals are able to evaluate every alternative. As the number of alternatives increases beyond X_1, however, the individual cannot process all the required information to evaluate every alternative and some other procedure must be employed to simplify the process. One method is to divide the choice set into clusters, select a cluster and evaluate only the alternatives in that cluster. As the number of alternatives continues to increase, the number of clusters will need to increase until a point is reached where there are too many clusters to evaluate and a new tier in the hierarchy has to be established. For instance, a migrant in the United States cannot be expected to process information on all potential destinations; rather he/she might first exhibit a regional preference (such as wanting to live in the North East), then a preference for a particular state in the North East (such as New York) in which it is possible to evaluate every

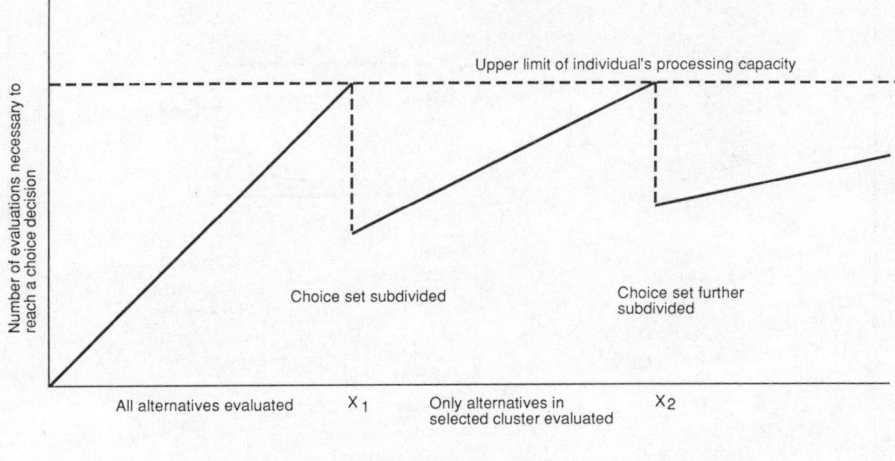

Figure 4.2 A demonstration of hierarchical information processing

alternative (say, metropolitan areas with a population over 500 000). In the UK context, it is not uncommon to hear people express opinions such as 'I would like to live in the South West' or 'I wouldn't want to live in the Midlands or the North', which suggests that many of us initially make evaluations regionally even if we are not fully aware of the decision-making process being employed. Essentially, a large number of potential destinations are never evaluated by migrants, not because of their individual characteristics but because of their general location.

Given that hierarchical choice is an efficient, and sometimes the only way, of processing large amounts of information, how does this affect the form of a migration destination choice model? It seems highly likely that the traditional model forms represented by equations (4.1) and (4.2) are misspecified. How can this misspecification be removed? To answer this question, consider equation (4.2) being represented as:

$$M_{ij} = \frac{O_i V_{ij}}{\sum\limits_{j} V_{ij}} \qquad (4.4)$$

where V_{ij} is an overall measure of the attractiveness of a destination to migrants from origin i and is defined as:

$$V_{ij} = W_{1j}^{\alpha_{1i}} W_{2j}^{\alpha_{2i}} \ldots W_{kj}^{\alpha_{ki}} d_{ij}^{\beta_i} \qquad (4.5)$$

That is, V_{ij} is a summation of all the site attributes of place j that affect the number of migrants it attracts from place i: attributes such as unemployment rate, house prices, distance, and so forth. Solely for the sake of demonstrating the type of misspecification present in equations

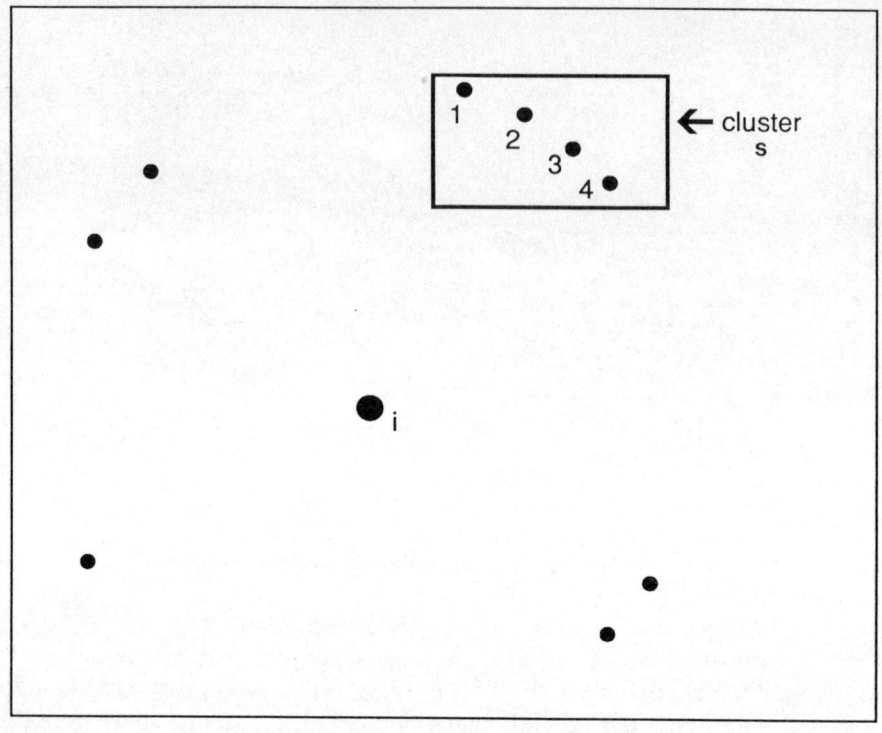

Figure 4.3   A set of alternative destinations with constant V_{ij}

(4.1) and (4.2) and how it can be relieved, consider V_{ij} being constant for any origin; that is, all the potential destinations are equally attractive to the migrants from a particular origin. This situation is represented in Figure 4.3 where it is assumed that the attributes defined in equation (4.2) are equal for all destinations. Mathematically:

$$V_{ij} = V_i \text{ for all } j \tag{4.6}$$

Suppose, again for the purposes of demonstrating the misspecification of equations (4.1) and (4.2), that we are interested in forecasting the combined volume of migration from i to destinations 1,2,3 and 4 which, collectively, we can call cluster s. If migrants evaluate all alternatives without regard to their spatial clustering, the attractiveness of the cluster s is simply the sum of the attractions of the individual destinations within the cluster which is $4V_i$. In general:

$$V_{is} = n_s V_i \tag{4.7}$$

where V_{is} is the attractiveness of cluster s to migrants from the origin i, and n_s is the number of alternatives in cluster s. Clearly, if the

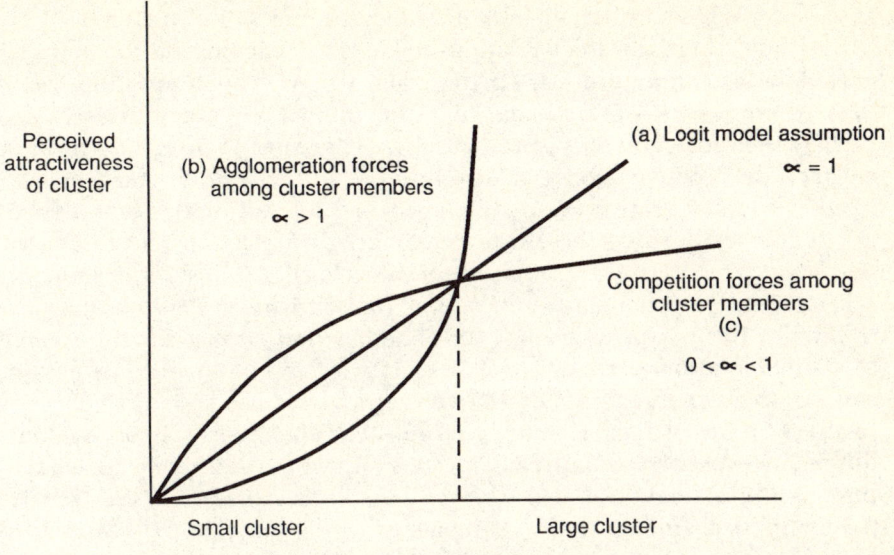

Figure 4.4 Relationships between the perceived attractiveness of a cluster and the size of a cluster

number of alternatives in the cluster increases, the attractiveness of that cluster will increase by a constant amount, V_i, for every added alternative. That is:

$$\partial V_{is}/\partial n_s = V_i \qquad (4.8)$$

which is the situation represented by the slope (a) in Figure 4.4.

The above scenario seems reasonable in choice contexts where there are relatively few alternatives. Suppose, however, that migrants are faced with a large number of destination possibilities where their selection process is necessarily hierarchical. In the above example, a hierarchical choice process implies that a migrant would evaluate the cluster s as a cluster so that equation (4.7) should be replaced with:

$$V_{is} = (n_s V_i)^\alpha \qquad (4.9)$$

where the parameter α reflects the relationship between the perceived attractiveness of a cluster and its magnitude and is assumed to be positive. The rate of increase in the perceived attractiveness of a cluster as its size increases now depends critically on α since:

$$\partial V_{is}/\partial n_s = \alpha n_s^{\alpha-1} V_i^\alpha \qquad (4.10)$$

as is shown in more detail in Fotheringham and O'Kelly (1989).

Basically, three different relationships exist depending on the value of α as described in Figure 4.4. If α is equal to one, equation (4.9) is identical to equation (4.7) and the migration model in equations (4.1) and (4.2) is therefore correctly specified. If α is greater than one, then large clusters are perceived to be relatively more attractive and small clusters relatively less attractive than is assumed in equation (4.2). Such a situation might exist when there are economic advantages to selecting alternatives in large clusters, such as a consumer's choice of a large shopping centre where greater opportunities exist for comparison and multipurpose shopping: there is little ground for thinking that such a situation could exist in migration destination choice. If α is less than one, then large clusters are perceived to be relatively less attractive and small clusters relatively more attractive than is assumed in equation (4.2). If migrants do evaluate clusters of alternatives, then it would be highly unusual if this situation did not exist given the prevalence of the general psychophysical finding that individuals generally perceive large entities to be smaller than they actually are (Stevens 1957). In a migration context, relationship (c) in Figure 4.4 would arise if migrants underestimated the number of potential destinations in large clusters. There is evidence in other, related areas to support this hypothesis (for example, Provin 1977).

Under the assumption that α is less than one and that migrants do perceive large clusters of alternatives to contain fewer potential destinations than actually exist, what implications does this have for modelling the destination choices of migrants? In Figure 4.4, the relationship depicted by the line (a) represents that assumed in equation (4.2) whereas the relationship depicted by the line (c) represents what is likely to happen in reality. Consequently, the use of equation (4.2) will lead to migration to destinations in large clusters of alternatives being over-predicted and migration to destinations in small clusters being under-predicted. Ideally, in order to correct this problem, it would be necessary to incorporate into the model structure a term that represents the size of the cluster in which the destination lies. Unfortunately, in a migration context it will generally be impossible to define the nature of the clusters perceived by an individual (although we may guess), and even if it were possible, it would be necessary to have knowledge of this clustering for all individuals since an individual's partitioning of space will vary by location (Gould and White 1974). However, we can make an assumption to get around this problem: in terms of migrants' perceptions of space, destinations in close proximity to other destinations are more likely to be included in large clusters than are more peripheral destinations. This proximity variable should then be added to the model formulations in equations (4.1) and (4.2) where it would be expected to have a negative parameter estimate: the closer is a destination is to all others, the lower will be the migration to that destination, *ceteris paribus*. It only remains to operationalise the variable measuring the proximity of a destination to all others and many formulations could be used. The one used most frequently is a potential accessibility formulation equivalent to that given in equation (4.3) written in terms of each destination:

$$A_j = \sum_{m \neq j} W_m/d_{jm} \qquad (4.11)$$

where A_j is the potential accessibility of destination j to all other potential destinations m, W_m is a weight generally measured by population, and d_{jm} is the distance between j and m. Other plausible formulas for measuring a destination's centrality are given in Fotheringham (1988). Regardless of which particular formulation is employed, the incorporation of this variable into equation (4.2) yields the competing destinations model:

$$M_{ij} = \frac{O_i W_{1j}^{\alpha_{1i}} W_{2j}^{\alpha_{2i}} \ldots W_{kj}^{\alpha_{ki}} d_{ij}^{\beta_i} A^{\gamma_i}}{\sum_j W_{1j}^{\alpha_{1i}} W_{2j}^{\alpha_{2i}} \ldots W_{kj}^{\alpha_{ki}} d_{ij}^{\beta_i} A^{\gamma_i}} \qquad (4.12)$$

where the parameter γ_i reflects the relationship between migration and a destination's centrality and it will be negative if migrants select destinations hierarchically and if they underestimate the number of opportunities in large clusters. While the logic for expecting the parameter γ_i to be significantly negative seems fairly strong, ultimately the determination of γ_i must be a matter left to empirical investigation.

While the addition of a single variable to equation (4.2) may seem a rather trivial matter, it should be emphasised that the addition of the variable in equation (4.11) is quite different from adding a site variable such as unemployment rate or median house price to the migration model. The addition of site variables does not alter the fundamental structure of the model, whereas the addition of the competing destinations variable in equation (4.11) does. The traditional model in equation (4.2) contains two generally undesirable properties that are not present in the model described by equation (4.12). The first of these is what has become known as the Independence from Irrelevant Alternatives (IIA) property which is that the ratio of the probabilities of selecting any two destinations is independent of any other destination. Consider the ratio of probabilities of a migrant choosing two destinations, 1 and 2, from equation (4.2):

$$\frac{M_{i1}}{M_{i2}} = \frac{W_{1j}^{\alpha_{1i}} W_{2j}^{\alpha_{2i}} \ldots W_{kj}^{\alpha_{ki}} d_{i1}}{W_{12}^{\alpha_{1i}} W_{22}^{\alpha_{2i}} \ldots W_{k2}^{\alpha_{ki}} d_{i2}} \qquad (4.13)$$

It does not make any difference to this ratio if destination 1 is surrounded by other alternatives or is completely isolated; this seems counterintuitive. The equivalent ratio from the competing destinations model is:

$$\frac{M_{i1}}{M_{i2}} = \frac{W_{1j}^{\alpha_{1i}}W_{21}^{\alpha_{2i}} \ldots W_{k1}^{\alpha_{ki}} d_{i1}^{\beta_i} A_1^{\gamma_i}}{W_{12}^{\alpha_{1i}}W_{22}^{\alpha_{2i}} \ldots W_{k2}^{\alpha_{ki}} d_{i2}^{\beta_i} A_2^{\gamma_i}} \tag{4.14}$$

which now depends on other destinations through their differential effects on the A_1 and A_2 variables. For instance, assuming γ_i to be negative, the ratio in equation (4.14) will be lower when destination 1 is more centrally located than when it is located on the periphery of the system.

The other undesirable property of equation (4.2) which is removed by the addition of the competing destinations variable is that it is impossible for the probability of a migrant selecting an existing alternative to increase when a new alternative is added to the system. This can occur with the use of the competing destinations model through the differential effects a new alternative would have on the relative location variable A_j.

It would thus seem that the competing destinations model has a reasonably logical foundation and that it represents a potentially significant improvement in the structure of migration destination choice models. It remains to be demonstrated whether it represents a significant increase in our ability to forecast migration patterns and whether it removes any of the undesired spatial structure effect from estimated origin-specific distance decay parameters. Both of these topics are now addressed.

4.4 The removal of spatial structure effects

To this point, the spatial structure effect in migration destination choice modelling has been outlined and a new model of migration destination choice has been developed after a discussion detailing the potential misspecification of the original model in equation (4.2) caused by disregarding hierarchical choice. It remains to be shown how the spatial structure effect in estimated distance decay parameters can be removed by calibration of the competing destinations model. For reasons of exposition, assume that the accessibility variable in the latter, A_j, is uncorrelated with any of the site attributes, the W_j's, but may be correlated with the distance variable. Indeed, as will become clearer, by definition these two variables must be correlated for certain origins. Under these conditions, Fotheringham (1984) has shown that the expected value of $\hat{\beta}_i$ in equation (4.2) is:

$$E(\hat{\beta}_i) = \beta_i + \delta_i \gamma_i \tag{4.15}$$

where γ_i is the destination accessibility parameter from equation (4.14) and δ_i is the slope parameter obtained in regressing destination accessibility on distance from each origin. The bias $\delta_i \gamma_i$, which is caused

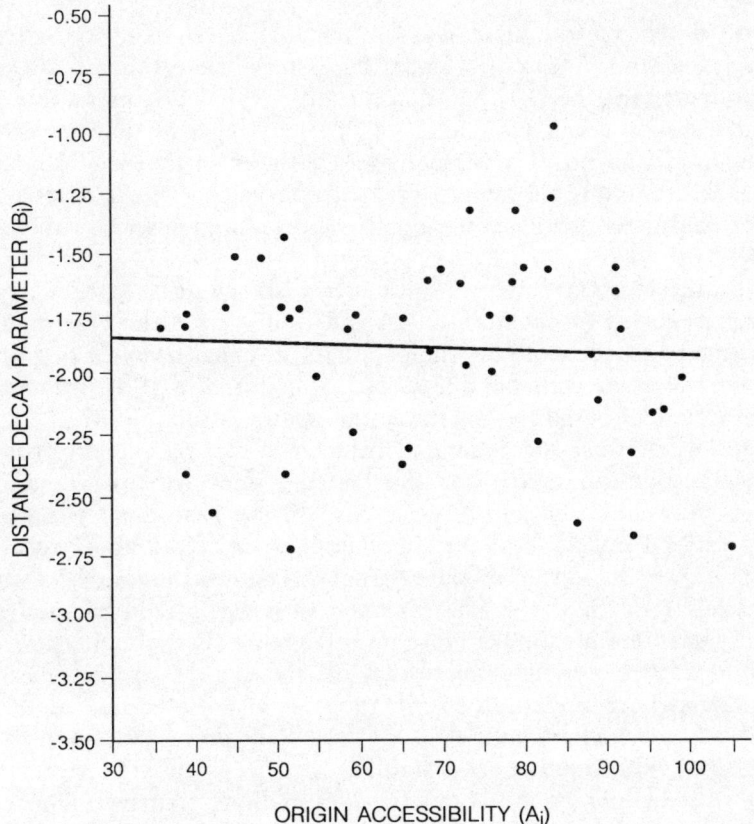

Figure 4.5 Relationship between estimated distance decay parameters from equation (4.14) and origin centrality

by the misspecification of equation (4.2), can thus be interpreted as the indirect relationship between migration and distance: γ_i represents the relationship between migration and destination accessibility; and δ_i represents the relationship between destination accessibility and distance. Clearly, if either of these relationships does not exist, the bias is eliminated. If the former does not exist, then the implication is that destination choice is not hierarchical; if the latter does not exist, then there is no relationship between destination accessibility and distance for that origin.

From equation (4.15) it is possible to speculate on the direction of the bias for different origins since γ_i is likely to be negative for all origins. The parameter δ_i, reflecting the relationship between destination centrality and distance from origin i, will be negative for centrally located origins (as the distance between the origin and a destination increases, the destination must become less centrally located) and positive for peripheral origins (as the distance between a peripherally located origin and a destination increases, the destination is likely to become increasingly centrally located). Hence, the bias in the estimated distance decay parameter will be positive for centrally located origins so that the estimated distance decay parameter will be less negative than its actual value and it will be positive for peripheral origins so that the estimated parameter will be more negative than its actual value. This is exactly the pattern of parameter estimates frequently reported and described above in Figure 4.1.

If the spatial structure effect in estimated distance decay parameters is indeed that reported in equation (4.15) and results from the type of mis-specification of the destination choice model in equation (4.2) described above, then the parameters obtained from the calibration of the competing destinations model should not exhibit the spatial structure effect. As a demonstration of this, the estimated distance decay parameters from a competing destination model for the Dutch migration study described above are shown in Figure 4.5. It is easy to see that these parameter estimates suffer from none of the characteristics described above that led to suspicion over the nature of the original estimates in Figure 4.1. There is no spatial trend in the estimates, their variance is reduced, and the individual interpretations make more intuitive sense (Fotheringham 1987).

Similar evidence of the superiority of the competing destinations framework has been presented elsewhere (*inter alia*, Fotheringham 1983, 1986, 1987; Fotheringham and O'Kelly 1989; Boots and Kanaroglou 1987; and Ishikawa 1989). In all of these studies, there is evidence to suggest that not only will the use of the competing destinations framework provide more accurate parameter estimates in destination choice models but it will also produce more accurate predictive models. The empirical research reported by Fotheringham and O'Kelly (1989), for example, demonstrates the significant improvement in goodness-of-fit when the competing destinations variable is added to five different models of UK migration. It also demonstrates that the origin-specific competing destinations parameter, γ_i in equation (4.14), is significantly negative for all thirty origins in the study. Similar findings are reported by Fotheringham (1983, 1986, 1987).

In a slightly more detailed examination of goodness-of-fit, Fotheringham (1984) demonstrates that there is a spatial pattern to the improvements in model performance when a competing destinations variable is added to the traditional destination choice framework. In a study of origin-specific improvements in goodness-of-fit, it is shown, not unexpectedly perhaps, that improvements in model accuracy are relatively small for origins where the relationship between destination centrality and distance is strong. Conversely, the improvement is greatest for origins where the relationship is weakest. Where destination centrality and distance are strongly related, as in the case of very central origins and very peripheral origins, the addition of the competing destinations variable will add little to the explanatory power of the model but it will be important in removing the bias in the estimated distance decay parameters since in equation (4.15) the parameter δ_i will be large in absolute magnitude. Where destination centrality and distance are weakly related, as in the case of origins which are neither extremely centrally located nor extremely peripherally located, the addition of the competing destinations model will add significantly to the explanatory power of the model but will have relatively little effect on the estimated distance decay parameter because in equation (4.15) the parameter δ_i will be small in absolute magnitude.

4.5 Summary and discussion

The theme of this chapter is that conventional migration destination choice models are likely to be misspecified because they assume that migrants select a destination after evaluating and comparing all potential alternatives. This misspecification leads to a bias in estimated distance decay parameters which is often referred to as the spatial structure effect. The misspecification can be corrected very easily, and the spatial structure effect removed, by the addition of a variable measuring the centrality of a destination with respect to other destinations. This new model is referred to as a competing destinations model because it is based on the much more plausible behavioural assumption that migrants make destination choices hierarchically which leads to a 'competition' effect between destinations in large clusters. In effect, migrants underestimate the opportunities in large clusters of destinations. The competing destinations model appears to be superior in terms of both parameter estimation and forecasting ability.

The concept of hierarchical choice is certainly not new and there are other choice models based on such assumptions — perhaps the best known is the nested logit model (for discussion see Wrigley 1985 and Ben-Akiva and Lerman 1985). However, the competing destinations model is an explicitly spatial choice model based on the psychological premises that not only do individuals make choices hierarchically but also they underestimate the size of large clusters of alternatives. A big advantage of the model formulation is that it is not necessary to specify the form of each individual's hierarchical mental representation of space. Models such as the nested logit do not have this capability and the user needs to specify a priori the underlying structure of each individual's choice hierarchy. While this is possible in contexts where the choice hierarchy is clear, such as in the selection of a class of product and then a particular brand, or in the selection of a shopping centre and then a particular shop, in most spatial choice contexts it is impossible to know how individuals define clusters of alternatives, and, by implication, space in general, in their choice hierarchies. However, for the reasons described above, it seems highly reasonable to expect that the more central is a destination with respect to other destinations, the more likely it is to be included in a large cluster of alternatives and hence the less likely it is to be chosen, *ceteris paribus*.

The competing destinations framework suggests several avenues for future research. One major area is to investigate empirical regularities in the spatial distribution of the competing destinations parameter. Given that this parameter indicates the extent to which individuals make choices hierarchically, it would be interesting to discover any empirical relationships between spatial location and the degree to which individuals make selections hierarchically. It would be equally interesting to disaggregate migration data by attributes such as age, sex and income and discover if there are differences in the degree of hierarchical choice related to differences in these variables.

Another area of research concerns the spatial aggregation of alternatives and the traditional finding that estimated distance decay parameters vary as interaction data are aggregated (Putnam and Chung 1989). The evidence presented here suggests that estimated distance decay parameters will contain a misspecification bias when obtained from traditional destination choice models at low levels of aggregation where the number of alternatives is large. When the data are aggregated to levels where there are relatively few destinations, such as major regions of the country for example, traditional models will no longer be misspecified since it is then reasonable to assume that every alternative can be evaluated by an individual. It would be interesting to discover if and where such changes occur.

Overall, the competing destinations model provides us with a new perspective on several perennial problems in destination choice modelling. Issues such as the spatial structure effect and the aggregation problem may now be viewed in a different manner and possibly removed or reduced. It is interesting to speculate on what volume of existing empirical research on migration is brought into question by the doubts on the validity of traditional models that are raised in this chapter.

Chapter 5

Multi-stream migration modelling

Ian Gordon

5.1 Introduction

People move house for many different reasons or combinations of reasons. Diverse situations impose varying degrees of constraint on movement. Migrants have quite different perceptions as to the available opportunities, and move either singly or in company with others from their own or previously separate households. In many respects this considerable heterogeneity need present no fundamental problem for the would-be migration modeller. Most models admit a random or stochastic element which is understood to cover the multitude of causal factors which are not explicitly or adequately represented by independent variables. Typically, however, some restrictive statistical assumptions are made about this stochastic element, which require it either to reflect the summation of a large number of independent influences, or random behaviour by independent members of a homogeneous population.

In reality, there seems to be a fairly small number of quite distinct types of migration (or migration stream), each characterised by distinct combinations of motive, constraint and perceived opportunity. For example, people who are seeking to change both their employment and their residence can be distinguished from those seeking a new residence within reach of an existing job. If this is the case, then the statistical assumptions of any single-stream migration model are likely to be invalidated, because the migration population is far from homogeneous.

More pertinently perhaps for most users of these single-stream models, they will prove inefficient as explanatory or forecasting tools, because flows between certain origins and destinations will be dependent on influences different from those affecting flows between other origins and destinations. It is much less likely, for example, that flows between neighbouring zones will be influenced by labour market factors than would be the case for moves between areas more remote from each other. In this case there is an interaction between the effect of distance and of some area-related variables, which cannot be appropriately represented or unscrambled within any conventional migration model. The reason for this is that the observed migration flow between any pair of areas is a mixture (i.e. a linear, additive function) of migration streams, each of which depends on a multiplicative combination of distance-related and area-related factors.

A conventional gravity type model, of the form:

$$M_{ij} = A_i B_j \, f(d_{ij}) \, e_{ij} \qquad (5.1)$$

where M_{ij} = the volume of migration from area i to area j;

     A_i = a generalised 'push' factor for area i;

     B_j = a generalised 'pull' factor for area j;

     $f(d_{ij})$ = a monotonic function of the distance from i to j; and

     e_{ij} = a stochastic disturbance,

would require influences such as differential wages, or rates of house-building (both imbedded in the A and B factors), to exert the same proportionate effect (absolutely and in relation to each other) over any distance range, and irrespective of whether the move was from suburb to inner city, or vice versa. The implications of an alternative simple model, the linear counterpart to equation (5.1):

$$M_{ij} = A_i + B_j + f(d_{ij}) \qquad (5.2)$$

are no better in that the relative influences of variables such as wages and house-building are still independent of distance, and there is now nothing to forbid the prediction of negative volumes of movement between pairs of areas.

In order to avoid such evident unrealism, it is necessary either to restrict the domain of application of the model to a subset of flows which involve a more homogeneous sample of moves (e.g. only inter-regional moves, or only those moves reported as involving a change of workplace as well as a change of residence), or to find a means of working with a multi-stream interaction model, of the form:

$$M_{ij} = \sum_s A_i^s \, B_j^s \, f^s(d_{ij}) \, e_{ij}^s \qquad (5.3)$$

where s denotes a specific migration stream. Though simpler, in many contexts the former alternative is not available, since the most substantial sources of migration data notably (in Britain) the Census of Population and NHS Central Register, include no supplementary information about moves (as distinct from those making them). Furthermore, observed flows between many origin–destination combinations will involve a mixture of migration streams. Hence, the work reported here has concentrated on the latter approach, specifying and estimating a multi-stream model — although in doing so some use has been made of the tactic of looking initially for reasonably homogeneous subsets of flows.

The multi-stream model is an aggregate model in the gravity model tradition in that it seeks to account for the volume of migration between pairs of places, during a specific time period, rather than using disaggregate data to predict individuals' chances of making a move. Each approach has specific strengths, relating to the different sources of variability which can be identified from aggregate and from disaggregate data sources. The particular advantage of aggregate data sources, such as the Census of Population, lies in the sheer volume of flows which they record (far larger than any more intensive survey), and consequently in the large number of distinct origin and destination areas across which reliable comparative data are available to identify area-specific and distance-specific influences on movement. Conversely, disaggregate data can allow more direct investigation of motives, decision processes, perceived alternatives and the influence of personal or household factors, as well as the estimation of discrete choice models deduced from personal and situational variables specific to an individual. The two approaches are, or should be, clearly complementary. Thus the development of the multi-stream 'motivation-specific' model has been informed by analyses of data on individual decision-making, while the specific functional forms adopted in its latest version derive directly from an investigation of discrete choice models. But the exchange is not all one way; aggregate models can provide the basis for much more precise specifications of areal variables in disaggregate analysis, and have already highlighted the central importance of the stock or flow of opportunities in destination areas, a factor largely ignored in disaggregate analyses (Gordon and Vickerman 1982).

The remainder of this chapter is organised in five sections which in turn discuss the theoretical basis of a multi-stream model, outline its formal specification, clarify methods of estimation, report some results from empirical applications, and consider extensions and broader implications of the multi-stream approach.

5.2 Theoretical basis of multi-stream modelling

Observed migration movements are the outcome of a multi-stage decision process in which typically an individual has to engage in some form of search before uncovering opportunities for movement, which must be accepted or rejected in turn as they arise. This search process may be long or short, and may be abandoned at any time if it proves too costly and/or frustrating. In any case the two key decisions are, first, to look (or stop looking) for opportunities, and then to accept or reject specific opportunities — rather than committing oneself to move somewhere, and then deciding where, as has sometimes been suggested (e.g. Brown and Moore 1970). How the process works out may vary a lot between individuals, notably between those planning on 'speculative' moves, for whom only a coarse search for sets of possible opportunities would actually precede the move, followed up by more specific search on the spot; and those requiring 'contracted' moves, with the assurance of a specific house and/or job being a precondition for any commitment to move (Molho 1986). Occasionally the whole process may be collapsed into a single moment, when a person not actively contemplating a move is confronted with an 'offer that they could not refuse'. More commonly, however, potential migrants have some control over the way in which search proceeds — if not over what it reveals — and people with different motives (and constraints) will choose to search in different ways. These different modes of search may vary in intensity, cost, tightness of focus and in the primary channels of information which are used. The latter may be formal or informal; spatially organised locally, regionally, nationally or internationally; and internal or external to some more extended organisation such as a firm or profession. In each case, however, where people look for opportunities inevitably conditions where (if anywhere) they eventually move to — and this includes the issue of how far afield they look, and then move.

As the gravity model framework (presented in equation (5.1)) makes clear, how far individuals actually move must depend partly on the relative attractiveness of (and the flow of opportunities within) near as compared with more distant destinations — and this obviously also impinges on where they start looking. But when the attraction factor is controlled for, there remain some more specifically distance-related factors. How these affect individuals' search behaviour will depend partly on how great the costs of eventual movement would be for them, but also, for example, on whether there is a need for household members to retain an existing job or other local connections requiring regular trips back towards the area of origin. In addition, behaviour should depend on the expected costs of acquiring information about closer and more distant opportunities, since the more 'cosmopolitan' groups in the population (for example, professional, managerial and technical workers, especially in large organisations) have readier access to national and international networks of information than do their 'localist' counterparts. A further consideration is the degree of specialisation in the opportunities sought by particular groups of migrants, since the less common they are, the less also is the likelihood that one will appear during a given time period in a more local field of search; hence, prospective migrants in such a group who are not prepared to wait for long may have to look further afield to satisfy their requirements.

The chances of somebody moving from a given area to a specific destination during some time period can then be seen as the outcome of three conditional probabilities:

(i) $p(S_s|i,c)$, the probability during that period for an individual in area i with characteristics c of seeking movement opportunities using search mode s;

(ii) $p(O_j|i,s)$, the probability, given the current area of residence and that mode of search, of receiving information about a relevant opportunity in area j; and

(iii) $p(A_j|O_j)$, the probability, given such an opportunity, of choosing to accept it.

For any short period the probability of a move from i to j for a person with characteristics c is then given by:

$$p(M_j|i,c) = \sum_s p(S_s|i,c) \cdot p(O_j|i,s) \cdot p(A_j|O_j) \tag{5.4}$$

while the actual volume of moves would be given by:

$$M_{ij} = \sum_c p(M_j|i,c) \cdot P_{ic} \tag{5.5}$$

where P_{ic} = the population in area i with characteristic c.

This simple representation of the process underlying migration behaviour has two significant features. First, it emphasises the role of different modes of search, of which there could clearly be many, but which can in practice be grouped into a few sets. Theoretically these sets of search modes are identified with specific migration streams — hence the use of the same index (s) to denote the various search modes, in equation (5.4), and the resulting migration streams, in equation (5.2). Secondly, it indicates how the choices of individuals — embodied in probabilities $p(S)$ and $p(A)$ — interact with exogenous factors — embodied in probability $p(O)$, and the distribution of populations at risk P_{ic}, as well as the characteristics of areas to which they are responding.

In relation to the different modes of search, our primary concern is with those which involve significantly different spatial patterns of information. An important consideration here is the way in which the main media of communication are organised. Thus Saunders and Flowerdew (1987), investigating the effects of employers' advertising strategies on labour migration, found themselves able to work with a simple distinction between 'locally' and 'nationally' advertised agencies, although in some situations 'regional' media might also be expected to play a distinct role. A second key factor which also leads to a spatial clustering of modes of search is the centrality of paid employment in most people's lives, making the issue of whether or not an existing workplace is to be retained after the change of residence (and thus constraining its location) a strategic issue in decisions about appropriate fields of search. Indeed, the early work with multi-stream models focused exclusively on a binary division between 'housing' and 'employment' moves based on the primacy of this question of whether the workplace as well as the residence was to be changed. However, while some such division could be found in different studies, it did not always appear to be the same one (cf. Hyman and Gleave 1976 with Gordon 1975). In fact, earlier survey results (Harris and Clausen 1967) had suggested that different sets of motives for moving were associated with (at least) *three* distinct distance profiles of actual movement. Average distances moved were longest for those moving for job reasons, and shortest for those moving for housing reasons (or marriage), while environmental and familial moves formed a third intermediate group. More detailed analysis of survey data on the fields of search which prospective migrants were prepared to consider also pointed to *two* divisions associated with distinctive combinations of motive and constraint (Gordon *et al.* 1983). Specifically, a discriminant analysis found that those only searching locally were characterised by purely housing motives (notably for a larger house) as well as particular attachments to the area and to friends; regional searchers, who tended to be younger and seeking owner-occupation, displayed a wider range of motives, of which the most characteristic was the desire for a 'better area'; national searchers, on the other hand, tended to be motivated by employment considerations and were biased towards the young and single. On this basis we hypothesise that there should be *three* distinct streams of internal migrants within the country, in turn national, regional and local in range, and primarily (if not exclusively) associated with the dominance of employment, environment and housing motives, respectively.

In relation to the role of migrants' choices in the determination of actual patterns of movement, the representation in equations (5.4) and (5.5) indicates that the latter can be partially — but only partially — explained in terms of the (presumably rational) choices which individuals make. Thus, while distance deterrence can partly be understood in terms of the trade-offs which prospective migrants make between the expected benefits of life in alternative locations and the associated costs of transferring home there, it must also reflect the impact of distance on information flows about relevant opportunities, given a specific mode of search. Similarly, while the pattern of 'pushes' and 'pulls' must partly reflect the perceived costs and benefits of living in each area, for a specific type of movers, it also clearly depends on the distribution of populations 'at risk' of these sorts of move, and of current opportunities for each kind of move. Hence, while there is much which can be learned about appropriate specifications of aggregate migration relationships from disaggregate models of migrants' choices between discrete alternatives, the latter can only represent one element of an overall model of migration outcomes.

The most familiar version of such a disaggregate model is based on the so-called 'random utility' hypothesis (McFadden 1973; Maier and Weiss in Chapter 2 of this volume). This postulates that individuals will always choose an alternative offering the highest level of 'utility' to them, but that this utility may depend not only on characteristics identified and observed by the analyst but on other more or less idiosyncratic features representable in terms of a stochastic (i.e. random) distribution.

Straightforward applications of this approach require identification of a relatively homogeneous set of alternatives, with more or less equal degrees of substitutability among them as far as the typical migrant is concerned, the so-called 'independence of irrelevant alternatives' (IIA) assumption. If the likelihoods of being in search at any point of time and choosing any single opportunity are both low, the resulting multinomial logit model can be further simplified to yield for the product of the two choice probabilities:

$$p(S_s|i,c) \cdot p(A_j|O_j) = \exp(\sum_k -\alpha_k X_i^k) \exp(\sum_k \alpha_k X_j^k) \exp(-\gamma C_{ij}) \qquad (5.6)$$

where X_i^k = is a measure of valued characteristic k of area i;
$\quad \alpha_k$ = the marginal utility afforded by k to a representative individual;
$\quad C_{ij}$ = the total 'cost' of moving from i to j; and
$\quad \gamma$ = the marginal utility of movement costs.

There are two points to make about this model. The first is that, where the costs of movement simply depend on distance, it is consistent with the general gravity model formulation (equation (5.1)), with probabilities being proportional to a cluster of variables specific to an origin, a second cluster specific to a destination, and thirdly to a function of the distance separating them. And this remains the case when it is extended into a full model of migration by incorporating populations-at-risk, the flow of opportunities and a distance deterrence effect on information transmission. But the second point is that the IIA assumption means that separate submodels are required to deal with any sets of migration opportunities which are not equally substitutable for each other, i.e. those relevant to differently motivated (or constrained) groups in specific migration streams. Hence the random utility approach leads, at the aggregate level, to specification of a multi-stream model, of the form of equation (5.3). The exogenous (non-choice) factors also require such a disaggregation because of the likely differences between streams in the type and distribution of populations-at-risk and of opportunities, as well as the quite distinctive distance decay profiles of information in the local, regional and national search media.

Two further theoretical propositions have a particular relevance to the multi-stream model. The first is that even successful search does not necessarily lead to migration. Individuals who are prepared to move both their residence and their workplace, and who are searching for job opportunities in a national field, from which migration in the national stream is the expected outcome, may end up choosing a relatively nearby opportunity and decide not move their residence at all because the costs of doing so outweigh those of additional commuting. Hence there is one additional conditional probability which should be added to equation (5.4), whose effect is to introduce the possibility that the national stream (alone) may not have a monotonic distance function, but rather one which first rises and then falls with increasing distance.

The second proposition is that recent in-movers to an area are more likely than longer-term residents to move on again, whether because of a particular disposition to mobility, or because duration of residence affects the opportunity costs of movement. Hence high rates of inflow tend to generate high rates of outflow. In the multi-stream case this may not only apply within a particular stream, for example in the national stream which contains many repeating labour migrants. There may also be particular links across streams. For example, informational constraints may encourage long-distance movers to pursue a strategy of successive approximation, with an exploratory national stream move being followed by regional or local adjustments, as they learn more about their new environment.

5.3 Model specification

The theoretical discussion in the previous section suggests that an aggregate migration model can appropriately be represented at a formal level in terms of the multi-stream gravity model of equation (5.3), with an expectation that internal movement within the country comprises *three* fairly homogeneous migration streams. These streams would differ both in their distance profiles, and in terms of the characteristic motives and constraints of the movers concerned, especially in relation to the role of employment, environmental and housing factors. Much of the substance of a migration model is, however, buried within the generalised 'push' and 'pull' factors (A_i and B_j), which now need to be represented in terms of identifiable variables.

For the 'push' and 'pull' factors, our theoretical argument implies the following general specifications:

$$A_i^s = P_j(\sum_c \mu_{cs} H_{ci}) \cdot \exp(\sum_k -\alpha_k X_i^k) \ e_{si}' \tag{5.7}$$

$$B_j^s = P_j(\sum_l \lambda_{ls} G_{lj}) \cdot \exp(\sum_k \alpha_k X_j^k) \ e_{sj}'' \tag{5.8}$$

where P_j = population of area j;
H_{ci} = characteristics of the population of i;
μ_{cs} = a weighting factor for stream s;
G_{lj} = rates of flow, growth or turnover in sets of opportunities such as house/job vacancies in area j;
X_{ls} = weighting factor for stream s; and
e_{si}', e_{sj}'' = stochastic disturbances.

The terms involving an exponential function in these two equations both derive from equation (5.6), which represented determinants of the two choice probabilities contributing to the overall likelihood of movement. (The third element in that equation is now subsumed within the distance function, discussed below.) The earlier terms in equations (5.7) and (5.8) derive from the deterministic factors which also impinge on the level of movement. Those in equation (5.7) represent the determination of the population 'at risk' of movement, weighted by those characteristics of the population (such as youth, education and unemployment) with a general effect on the disposition to consider moving. The comparable terms in equation (5.8) represent the numbers of relevant opportunities becoming available in potential destination areas, weighted by the salience of particular types of opportunity for a specific migration stream. The specific variables to be included in the equations would clearly differ between the migration streams, reflecting the distinctive motives and constraints of those involved. Thus the national stream equations should incorporate measures reflecting the number and quality of employment opportunities, and the local stream equations comparable indicators of housing opportunities, while in the regional stream equations environmental factors might figure more centrally. In each case, however, the A (push) equation should incorporate predictors of individuals' propensity to move (including some indicator of recent inmigration as well as, for example, age, occupation and housing tenure), together with characteristics of living and working conditions in the area (such as earnings, unemployment, house prices and environmental quality); the B (pull) equations should include the environmental characteristics entering potential migrants' comparisons of opportunities, but also indicators of the flow of relevant opportunities in the area (for example, house-building or employment growth rates, and/or predictors of the turnover in these markets).

The distance deterrence function in the 'formal' interaction model has a dual role, combining (multiplicatively) the effects of the distance decay of information (within a given stream or mode of search) and the movement cost component of potential migrants' utility function. Theory tells us that, in the standard case considered in Section 5.2, the latter factor should be an exponential function of the movement costs, which presumably vary more or less linearly with distance. Informational flows might well also decay exponentially with distance, although there is little or no evidence on which to ground such expectations. The overall distance deterrence function would then also be negative exponential:

$$f(d_{ij}) = \exp(\beta d_{ij}) \qquad (5.9)$$

where β is a parameter <0, but other forms cannot be ruled out a priori. Historically at least, most empirical studies have suggested that flows conform to a power function:

$$f(d_{ij}) = d_{ij}^{\beta} \qquad (5.10)$$

but while this may appear a better representation when all flows are lumped together, that would not necessarily be the case for any or all of the separate migration streams now being distinguished.

There are also some a priori arguments for more complex forms of distance function. For example, some research on commuting patterns (Molho 1990) suggests that over short distances behavioural or perceptual distances may vary less than proportionately with measured, Euclidean distance, and some allowance for this non-linearity could be incorporated in the distance deterrence function for the (local) stream (Gordon 1988a). On a rather more fundamental level it can be argued that the simplifying assumption introduced in Section 5.2, to the effect that the chances of acceptance of any independent alternative are small to negligible, probably does not apply in the *regional* stream, where many migrants effectively make their choice in relation to broad areas before considering specific housing opportunities (Gordon 1988a). In this case a better approximation to the distance relationship would be the logistic function:

$$f(d_{ij}) = \frac{\exp(\beta d_{ij})}{\exp(\beta d_{ij}) + \theta} \tag{5.11}$$

where θ is a parameter >0.

Finally, if (as we suggested earlier) prospective migrants in the *national* stream could at the end of the day choose to commute to the new job which they had chosen, rather than to move house, if it was less costly to do so, it may give rise to a non-monotonic distance function of the form:

$$f(d_{ij}) = \exp(\beta d_{ij}) (1 - \exp (\phi \, d_{ij})) \tag{5.12}$$

where ϕ is a parameter <0. As with equation (5.11) this is evidently a generalisation of the exponential function (5.9), collapsing to the latter when $-\phi$ approaches infinity, as (5.11) does when θ becomes very large.

5.4 Model fitting

The next step clearly is to confront the model with empirical data on the origins and destinations of migrants during some period, and see how adequately it can represent these.

For the fitting of the 'formal' model represented by equation (5.2), the basic data requirements are for a matrix containing flows between a set of origins and destinations in some specific period, and a corresponding matrix of inter-area distances. The completeness of the matrix is not critical, but if all three streams are to be identifiable with any precision this matrix must include a wide range of distances. At the short end of the range, the point is only that if there is a lack of flows in the 0–5-mile band for any area, parameters relating to the local stream will be poorly estimated. But at the long end of the distance range, a lack of flows of 150 miles or more for any area is liable (with the estimation technique outlined in this section) to produce unreliable estimates for *all* of the migrant streams. If measured distances between centroids are to be representative of those facing prospective migrants, the areas involved (especially in the shorter-distance flows) should also not be too extensive. Thus the best results so far have been obtained with a national matrix of district–district flows, derived from the 1981 Census (Gordon 1988a). But where coarser areal units (such as regions) have to be used, corrected average distances appropriate to specific migration streams can be calculated by first predicting flows for a finer set of areal units, using a simplified interaction model, then aggregating and computing the matrix of distances which would have exactly predicted the aggregated matrix of flows, given the same model (Gordon 1975; Gordon and Molho 1987). For the district–district analysis, however, the distance matrix was based simply on straight-line distances between centroids, diverted where necessary around estuaries and other inlets.

To fit a 'substantive' model, accounting for the push and pull (A and B) factors, requires additional data for each area on the set of relevant population, quality-of-life, and opportunity variables. In the most successful substantive analysis to date, relating to areas in the London metropolitan region, these additional variables included measures of occupational and age structure, housing tenure, construction and demolition rates, earnings and house prices, employment growth and unemployment, housing conditions and perceived environmental quality (Gordon and Lamont 1982).

This model fitting stage is intended to do three things: (i) to identify the most appropriate of some alternative specifications, particularly of the distance decay functions; (ii) to provide a disaggregation of the observed pattern of flows into estimates of the constituent migration streams; and (iii) to test the significance and practical importance of the various substantive factors which have been hypothesised to influence rates of inflow to and outflow from areas in each of the specific migrant streams.

This is not a particularly simple exercise with the multi-stream model, and a number of methodological questions need to be addressed about the fitting process, some of which are common to all aggregate migration models, and others of which arise from the particular form of the multi-stream model.

We should start by considering the general issues as they emerge when a conventional, single-stream spatial interaction model (of the form represented in equations (5.1), (5.7), and (5.8)) has to be fitted. Two broad approaches have been developed for this task. The first involves the use of some form of regression analysis, using each cell (or each off-diagonal cell) of the migration matrix as an observation, and seeking to generate a set of predictions of the flow volume in each, from the set of independent variables, such as to minimise some function of the prediction error in each cell. The simplest version of this regression approach makes use of logarithmic transformation in order to linearise the model (thus converting it from a multiplicative to an additive form), and then uses the familiar Ordinary Least Squares (OLS) criterion to fit the linear model. One objection to this approach involves its assumptions about the statistical distribution of the stochastic component (or error term) in the model. It has been shown quite clearly that the use of OLS in this context produces biased estimates of parameters in the model, and that maximum likelihood estimation requires the use of a Poisson regression model (Flowerdew and Aitkin 1982; Flowerdew in Chapter 6 of this volume).

But a second objection may be made to any form of regression analysis that is applied directly to a reduced form of the interaction model. The reduced form is that obtained when equations (5.7) and (5.8) are substituted into equation (5.1), in order to produce an equation relating migration flows directly to area characteristics, as well as to distance variables. The problem with a direct (one-stage) regression approach to this reduced-form relationship is that it combines three sets of error (or stochastic) components — one (from equation (5.5)) relating to a whole row of the migration matrix, one (from equation (5.8)) relating to a whole column, and one (from equation (5.1)) specific to particular cells — and treats their combination as varying independently across the cells of the matrix. That assumption of independence will be seriously in error if the first two sets of errors substantially outweigh the second, and this will generally be the case. The reason is that, while it is not difficult (particularly with the multi-stream model) to specify 'formal' gravity models, such as are represented in equations (5.1) and (5.3), which fit observed flows pretty well, it is much more difficult to specify adequate 'substantive' explanations of the variation in 'push' and 'pull' factors across areas, as Section 5.5 will illustrate. This is particularly the case where the small number of areas involved restricts the number of degrees of freedom and allows few significant independent variables to be identified.

A false assumption of independence in the stochastic terms can lead both to inefficient estimates of all or any of the parameters, and to exaggerated estimates of the significance of independent variables relating to the areas. Thus, if a regression approach is to be used, it needs to be carried out in two stages. First, a version of the 'formal' interaction model (equation (5.1)) should be estimated, by including as independent variables only a suitable distance function and two sets of dummy variables for the relevant origin and destinations: coefficients on the latter then provide estimates of the 'push' and 'pull' factors (A and B). These then have to be inserted as dependent variables in a set of substantive regressions using versions of equations (5.7) and (5.8).

The alternative standard approach, the iterative method developed in parallel with the popular regression approach, necessarily involves such a two-stage division, since it is essentially a methodology for calibrating the 'formal' interaction model. As proposed by Hyman (1969), it focuses not on minimising error across the set of origin–destination cells, but rather on achieving an exact fit to a set of crucial characteristics of the observed matrix (cf. Stillwell in Chapter 3 of this volume). These characteristics (or constraints) are equal in number to the number of parameters in the model, and their selection follows from a specification of the underlying stochastic process. In this respect, Hyman's method is a maximum likelihood approach, like the Poisson regression, and similarly avoids the biases of OLS regressions. When, as commonly assumed in this tradition, the distance function is specified in its exponential form, the appropriate characteristics of the actual flow matrix which have to be matched by the predictions are: (i) the total flow from each origin; (ii) the total flow to each destination; and (iii) the average distance moved by the set of migrants. (If the distance relationship were a negative power function, the last condition would involve the average logged distance.) Computationally, an exact fit to all of them is achieved by iterating through three steps: (a) fixing a value for the distance parameter and computing the predicted flows (initially with the push and pull factors both set to unity); (b) adjusting the push and pull factors iteratively (via so-called RAS or balancing-factor methods) so as to bring the row and column totals in line with actual values; and (c) calculating the mean distance in flow miles, and adjusting the distance parameter in an appropriate direction to correct the discrepancy from the actual mean distance (e.g. raising its absolute value, thus increasing distance deterrence, if the predicted mean distance is too long). When convergence is achieved (quite rapidly with suitable algorithms), the set of push and pull factors then have to be used as dependent variables in 'substantive' regressions, corresponding to equations (5.7) and (5.8), as with the first approach. This iterative method yields identical results to the Poisson regression method when the latter is applied to the 'formal' interaction model of equation (5.1) (Baxter 1982).

The multi-stream version of the migration model presents some additional estimation problems since equation (5.3) cannot be linearised — it already includes linear relationships between the streams — nor can Hyman's method be directly applied to it. Non-linear regression methods could be used, but with so many interrelated parameters there are extreme difficulties in practice in achieving optimisation of the fit. Hence a more *ad hoc* procedure has had to be developed in order to fit the multi-stream model.

The basis of this procedure is a series of attempts to generate flow estimates relating only to a single stream, to be modelled on its own, using Hyman's method for the first stage 'formal' analysis. (It should be noted that the second, 'substantive' stage of analysis remains quite separate, and that since this follows the disaggregation of overall flows into separate streams, the multi-stream formulation presents no distinctive problems for this stage of the work, although proportionately more regression equations are involved, i.e. two for each stream.)

The point of departure is the postulation of a distance cut-off beyond which all but the longest-distance migration stream (i.e. the national stream) should have negligible flows. In the inter-district analysis, after some experimentation this was set at 100 miles. A subset of cells — all those involving distances exceeding this cutoff — is then distinguished to which a submodel for this first stream can be fitted. Next a further subset of cells is distinguished on the basis of a second distance cut-off postulated to exclude any significant flows in the third (local) stream. In the inter-district analysis this was eventually set at 25 miles. The first-stream submodel is used to predict national stream flows for these cells, on the basis of the estimated A and B factors and distance function. These represent a sort of extrapolation, or 'back-projection' of the flow pattern observed beyond the first cut-off distance. The differences between observed flows and these first-stream predictions are then used as estimates of the second (regional) stream, for the fitting of a second submodel. Finally, these two streams are then back-projected in the same way for the remaining cells, and the residuals used as a basis for fitting the third submodel.

When the commuting option is included in the model (as in equation (5.12)) — and/or the logistic distance function for the regional stream — appropriate values for the additional parameters (θ and ϕ) have been chosen on the basis of experimentation, guided by a chi-square test on the distribution of actual and predicted flows by distance bands. Choice of appropriate distance cut-offs has also been a matter of experimentation. A balance has to be struck between larger values for a cut-off, which would more clearly separate the streams (avoiding bias in the distance parameter estimates), and shorter values which allow a larger sample of cells to be used in fitting the first- and second-stream submodels (reducing variance in the parameter estimates). The principal criterion used in striking this balance has been an overall R^2 statistic for the migration matrix. For the full district–district matrix the selected cut-offs were at 100 and 25 miles, but with matrices offering fewer long-distance observations lower values have to be used for the first cut-off (cf. Gordon 1982).

This method of back-projection and residuals is not very robust in the face of misspecification of the distance functions, particularly for the first/national stream, and this is clearly a weakness if it is to be used mechanically. However, in the context of an ongoing research process the reverse has been the case, with 'nonsense' results in the experimental phase (including the prediction of negative flows within some streams) leading to a closer examination of the model specification — including, in particular, the implications of the migration/commuting choice. This process emphasises the importance of looking at more than one or two indicators of the 'shape' of distance distribution of migration in order to assess the adequacy of any migration model. And that is especially the case if model-building is to serve as a means of developing an understanding of migration behaviour, rather than as an end in itself, or the basis for mechanical forecasts.

5.5 Model results

Several different versions of this multi-stream model, of varying degrees of sophistication, have been applied to a number of different data sets, mostly relating to internal movement within Great Britain, but with differing spatial units, degrees of aggregation of population groups and observation periods. The most developed version of the 'formal' model, distinguishing three streams and the commuting option, has been implemented for district-to-district flows across Great Britain in 1980–81, but 'substantive' results reported here for the effects of factors other than distance come from a series of applications with earlier versions of the model. These include both cross-sectional analyses focused on the London region (Gordon and Lamont 1982; Gordon and Molho 1985) and mixed cross-section/time series studies of interregional flows (Gordon and Molho 1987; Molho 1984b).

All of these studies support the hypothesis that a number of quite distinctive migration streams can be identified, each with characteristic patterns of origin and destination as well as differing degrees of sensitivity to distance. In terms of the shape of distance decay functions, the studies suggest that the classic inverse power function which has been used to represent the aggregate pattern of movement is a rather coarse approximation to the sum of a number of negative exponential functions (or the variants on these outlined in Section 5.3) (Gordon and Pitfield 1982). Where the studies provide a reasonable coverage of shorter-distance flows, they are consistent with each other in identifying *three* broad streams of internal migrants. If all residence moves are considered, the local stream is clearly the largest of these, accounting for about 70 per cent of the total, against 13 per cent in the national stream, and 17 per cent in the regional stream (Gordon 1988a). For inter-district moves alone all three streams appear of similar importance. At the interregional level, the local stream is clearly not very important, but the regional and local streams together still account for some 13 per cent of flows (Gordon and Molho 1987). Typical distance parameter estimates for the negative exponential function (with distances in miles) are around 0.005, 0.1 and 0.5 for the three streams. The modal distances moved are around 100, 10 and 1 or 2 miles respectively, although substantial overlaps are evident in the range of distances associated with the three streams (see Figure 5.1).

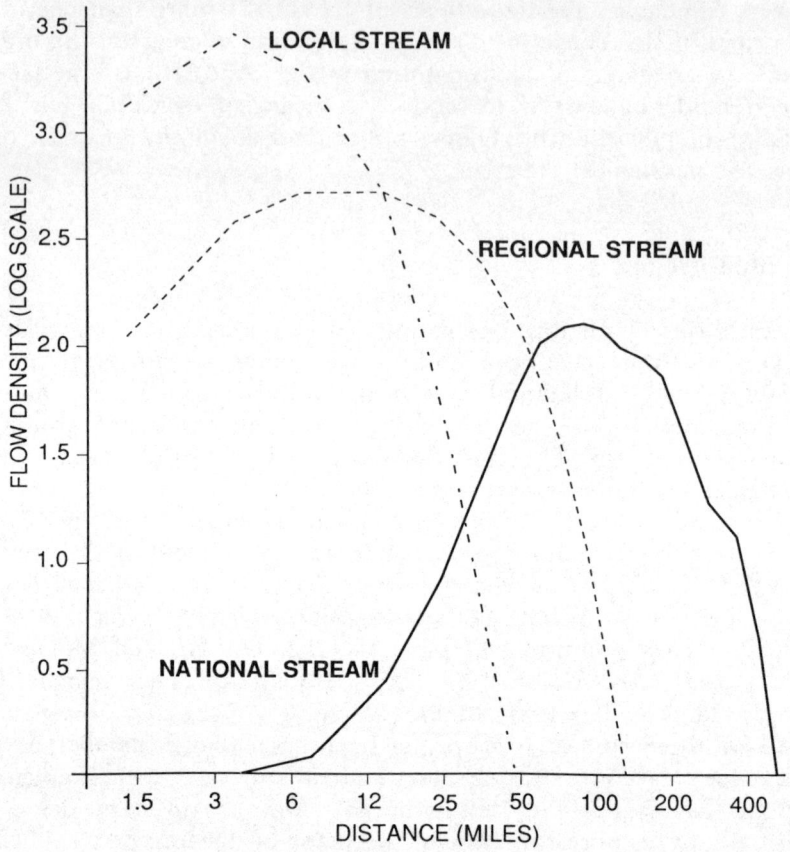

Figure 5.1 Density of migration flows by stream and distance

The power of single- and multi-stream models can be compared through parallel analyses of the Census data on flows between the 459 districts in Great Britain (Table 5.1). At this level of disaggregation close fits are much harder to achieve than with regional data, as can be seen by comparing the results, in terms of R-squared, for the single-stream power function model here with those for the equivalent doubly constrained model in Table 3.1 of Stillwell's chapter. In fact R-squared is not a very sensitive measure of performance for these models since the iterative fitting procedure does not necessarily maximise this statistic for any specific model. Nevertheless, it can be seen that either the two or three stream models are evidently preferable to a single-stream model, although this criterion does not discriminate clearly between the multi-stream models. As in other studies, the power function for distance seems clearly preferable if only a single stream is specified, but this is not the case for multi-stream specifications (cf. Gordon 1982). Consideration of a second important statistic, the chi-square value for the distance

Table 5.1 Parameters and goodness-of-fit statistics for spatial interaction models fitted to inter-district flows, Great Britain, 1980–81

Model	Distance function	β_1	β_2	β_3	R^2	Chi-square
1-stream	Exponential	—	—	—	0.225	49 987
1-stream	Power	1.550	—	—	0.729	5 648
2-stream	Exponential	-0.0071	-0.236	—	0.828	1 322
3-stream	Exponential	-0.0044	-0.058	-0.33	0.802	298
3-stream	Modified Exponential	-0.0044	-0.067	-0.33	0.823	56

Notes:
(i)   All results relate to the off-diagonal elements of a 459 square matrix of inter-district flows by economically active males, and to distances measured in miles.
(ii) The distance cut-offs selected were: 100 and 15 miles for the 3-stream models; and 30 miles for the 2-stream model.
(iii) The modified exponential model employed equations (5.11) and (5.12) to represent the first- and second-stream distance functions.
(iv) The chi-square statistic is based on a comparison of actual and expected moves over 17 distance ranges.

profile of flows, however, demonstrates much more clearly the superiority of a three-stream model, and particularly of the modified form allowing for a commuting option and the grouping of options in the regional stream.

Further evidence that there are real differences between the streams, going beyond the niceties of distance decay functions, can be found by comparing the distribution of net flows in each stream, across the set of areas. With the last of the models reported in Table 5.1, this comparison revealed a complete absence of correlation between the national stream and either the regional stream (r = 0.099) or the local stream (r = 0.034), while the latter pair were negatively correlated (r = −0.458). Substantive analyses of the pattern of 'pushes' and 'pulls' in the respective streams (fitting versions of equations (5.7) and (5.8)) corroborate this evidence of the distinctness of the three sets of flows. For example, an analysis in the London region showed that the national stream (alone) was strongly responsive to the rate of employment growth in destination areas; regional stream moves reflected tenure patterns in origin areas, relative house prices, the environment of destination areas, and rates of private construction there; while the local stream was primarily determined by relative rates of construction (Gordon and Lamont 1982). Such results bear out many of the hypotheses developed in Section 5.2 of this chapter. In general, however, the fit achieved with the push–pull factor regressions has been less impressive than that with the 'formal' interaction model. In the study just cited, for example, 77 per cent of the variance in the original flow matrix was accounted for, while the average

R^2 for the six push-pull equations was only 58 per cent. Comparable analyses for the full district–district model have yet to be completed. However, results from the earlier studies offer considerable support for the view that the multi-stream model cannot only provide better fits to observed sets of flows, but also substantive explanations of these flows which are more readily intelligible in relation to the situations of specific migrants.

5.6 Applications and extensions

One pragmatic reason for making a distinction between the principal migrant streams is that each is sensitive to quite different influences which need to be recognised if intelligent forecasts are to be made of future migration trends in particular areas. In part this follows from the evidence (discussed in the previous section) that cross-sectional variations in migration rates have to be explained with quite different sets of variables for each of the three streams, although it must be conceded that few of these independent variables are easy to forecast themselves at a local level. But there are also time-specific influences on general mobility which only apply to particular migration streams, and which may be rather easier to track. In the case of the employment-related national stream there is a strong expectation that liquidity and informational constraints, together with uncertainty avoidance will severely inhibit mobility from all areas when the national economy is in recession. And evidence from a time-series analysis of Scottish migration, which should be effectively confined to national stream movements, appears to show that, for a given incentive to move, flows are much reduced when general unemployment is high (Gordon 1985a). In the case of the regional and local streams, where much movement is associated with demands for an improved quantity or quality of housing, often requiring extended commuting as well as additional housing expenditure, key influences on mobility should be the strength of effective demand for housing services (influenced by interest rates, etc.) and the relative costs of transportation. Their effects could be particularly strong in the regional stream where more moves appear to be discretionary in character, rather than being necessitated by changes in household composition. And again there is evidence from a time-series study to support these hypotheses, this time relating to net flows from Greater London which are dominated by the regional stream (Gordon 1988b). Given these mobility effects on different streams, migration trends can well vary between areas in the short and medium term for reasons which have nothing much to do with local factors, but simply with the way in which the external environment impinges on different mixes of migration streams.

The strengths of the multi-stream approach are twofold. First, it connects more directly than do other aggregate models with theoretical analyses of the migration process and situational factors affecting individuals' movement decisions. Secondly, it can now match the actual pattern of observed flows a good deal more closely than can single-stream models. The possible problems are threefold. First, it has lacked a simple and reliable method of calibration — the iterative MSTREAM program outlined in Section 5.3 now fills that gap, although more efficient simultaneous procedures are still sought. Secondly it multiplies the number of separate regression analyses required, with six push–pull factors to be modelled rather than two. Thirdly, it opens up more possible choices about the form of distance deterrence functions and so on. If formal modelling is to contribute to (rather than assume) an understanding of migration behaviour, however, not all of these may actually be negative characteristics. But in any case it is hard now to justify the use of single-stream models which ignore the compound character of migrational flows, except in the case of very long- or very short-distance flows.

Key issues for future research on multi-stream modelling relate, firstly, to the dynamics of the interaction between migration streams, which have considerable implications for housing markets and the transmission of house price fluctuations. Longer-distance, economically motivated moves into areas (such as London) with an inelastic supply of housing must sooner or later stimulate outmigration in the shorter-distance streams. If this reaction is delayed, a ripple of house price increases and subsequent decreases will accompany the secondary migration. Secondly, there is a need for considerably more disaggregate work, modelling flows among specific groups of migrants, distinguished by occupation, gender, age, marital status and housing tenure. Another important area for further work is on the trade-off between migration and commuting. In order to preserve symmetry in the distance functions, the present model represents this choice solely in terms of the two sets of movement costs. Allowances should also be made for the role of housing cost differences — since migration will be the more attractive option when the new workplace is in an area of cheaper housing — but this will require a significant modification to the form of model.

Chapter 6

Poisson regression modelling of migration*

Robin Flowerdew

6.1 Introduction

By the late 1970s, a large volume of literature already existed which described, analysed and attempted to account for the pattern of migration movements taking place within countries. Characteristically, a data set was available, usually derived from a national census or perhaps a population register, consisting of a square matrix, whose rows and columns represented a set of places within a country, filled up with entries representing the number of people living in the row place (i) at one time and the column place (j) at a subsequent time. The places might be a set of regions which together made up the whole country, or a set of towns or cities. Diagonal matrix entries might or might not be included; if they were, they could represent either people who had moved within the place concerned, or people who had stayed in the same place. Usually the matrix would have a few large values for moves between large places or between neighbouring places and a large number of much lower values for the other entries. If the analysis was based on counties or other relatively small units, many of these low values could be zero. The larger the number of places considered, the greater the proportion of zero and very small values.

Inspection of such a migration matrix would usually reveal that the larger places tended to have both more inmigrants and more out-migrants. If size was controlled for, it was fairly obvious that the larger flows tended to be between places near to each other. Other effects, such as economic factors, might or might not be detectable as well. Analysis of migration matrices could be directed either at assessing the strength and nature of the size and distance effects, or at going beyond these to investigate more subtle influences. In either case, some method was necessary to systematise the analysis.

* I am indebted to the Social Science Research Council (now ESRC) for supporting my research on Poisson regression in 1983–84. Murray Aitkin of the Centre for Applied Statistics at Lancaster University first told me about the method, and he and others at the Centre have been consistently helpful and supportive. Many people have helped me develop my work on this subject (but of course are not responsible for its shortcomings), especially Andrew Lovett, Richard Davies and Joe Whittaker. The data used to exemplify the methods were kindly supplied to me by David Owen and Tony Champion.

Two main approaches to the analysis of migration matrices had developed by the later 1970s and are still in use today. One, developing from the gravity model of Stewart (1948), uses multiple regression analysis to relate migration flows to origin size, destination size, distance and a range of other variables. This approach was particularly common in economics and sociology, and is reviewed, for example, by Olsson (1965) and Greenwood (1975). The second approach, developed in parallel with studies of other interaction matrices (for example, traffic flows or journey-to-work flows), uses mathematical rather than statistical methods to work out estimates of what the flows should be on the basis of the attributes of the origin and destination and the distance between them. The approach, which involves the calibration of a model which can then be used as a basis for prediction, is sometimes termed spatial interaction modelling to contrast with gravity modelling. Wilson (1967, 1970) justified the methods used by showing that the estimated flows were entropy-maximising (i.e. they constituted the most probable configuration of flows, given a set of constraints defining the system). Stillwell explains the approach more fully in Chapter 3 of this book.

The next section of this chapter will be devoted to comparing the strengths and weaknesses of these two approaches. After this, Poisson regression analysis, which, it will be argued, combines the strengths and avoids most of the weaknesses of the two approaches, will be introduced. There will be a general discussion of Poisson regression: what it is, how it works and how it can be put into practice. The following section will cover the application of Poisson regression analysis to the analysis of a migration matrix, and the interpretation of the results. This will be followed by an examination of the relationship of Poisson regression and spatial interaction models and the incorporation of origin and destination constraints in the Poisson regression approach. Poisson migration models are not always appropriate as they stand for migration analysis, for reasons to be explained later, and a section of the chapter examines developments of the Poisson model which take these reasons into account. Before concluding, a series of problems relating to the use of the Poisson regression models will be covered.

6.2 A comparison of statistical and entropy-maximising approaches

The statistical approach usually incorporates population figures to represent size, and usually assumes that the relationship between migration and distance is a negative power function. In contrast, the entropy-maximising approach uses the number of flows originating and ending at each place as measures of size, and usually models distance as having a negative exponential relationship with migration. The statistical approach is likely to exclude the migration occurring within a place while the entropy-maximising approach usually includes it. The statistical approach usually excludes small places, whereas the entropy-maximising approach aims to include the whole system of regions in which migration can occur. The most important differences, however, concern five factors: flexibility, constraints, consistency, stability and evaluation.

The statistical approach is highly flexible in that it is a simple matter to incorporate new variables; for example, migration models of this type have frequently included economic variables such as wage rates or unemployment rates, and a wide range of other variables including welfare benefit levels, housing variables, and even climatic variables. The inclusion of a new variable in the model is as simple as specifying a new independent variable in a multiple regression. Incorporating an additional variable into an entropy-maximising model is usually possible but somewhat more complicated. This must be done by modifying one of the three components of the model — in Stillwell's terms, the origin attractiveness factor, the destination attractiveness factor or the distance impedance function. Usually an assumption must be made about how the new variable will change the relevant factor, either a priori or based on an exogenous estimation procedure. Alternatively, an iterative process may be developed which optimises model fit with respect to both the new variable and the standard spatial interaction parameters, perhaps by fitting the spatial interaction model several times for different values for the new variable's coefficient and choosing the best fit.

A second important consideration is the treatment of constraints. In entropy-maximising approaches, it is common to fit a model so that it meets origin and/or destination constraints: in other words, that the number of outmigrants predicted from each place is equal to the number observed (origin-constrained or production-constrained model) or that the number of inmigrants predicted to each place is equal to the number observed (destination-constrained or attraction-constrained model). Statistical approaches do not usually incorporate these constraints. Entropy-maximising models are often based on an explicit distinction between the generation of migrants and their distribution between destinations. Such a distinction fits in well with the use of an origin constraint; the number of outmigrants from a place is assumed to be generated by a different process from the one influencing where they go, and is treated as exogenous to the spatial interaction model. It is arguable whether this approach is appropriate for modelling migration or not. Some behavioural work on migration has suggested that people decide whether or not to migrate and only then choose a destination. Others see migration decisions in terms of a choice between accepting a specific job or housing opportunity at place j and not accepting it (and remaining at i). This dichotomy is related to Silvers's distinction (1979) between 'speculative' and 'contracted' migration (see also Molho 1986). In the context of contracted migration, the generation and distribution of migrants cannot sensibly be separated.

It is also possible to argue for destination-constrained models of migration; if the number of inmigrants to a place is regarded as fixed because of a fixed number of job opportunities or housing opportunities, it may be reasonable to employ destination constraints. The existence of unfilled job or housing vacancies and unemployed or homeless migrants in most labour markets, however, suggest that destination constraints are seldom appropriate (except perhaps in societies where all migration is centrally planned). Doubly constrained models may be appropriate where the arguments for both origin and destination constraints are accepted.

An advantage of entropy-maximising approaches over traditional statistical approaches is that the latter are inconsistent, in that the total number of migrants estimated by a model is not necessarily equal to the total observed, and can often be a great deal less. This systematic underestimation of migration results from bias involved in Ordinary Least Squares regression conducted on a logarithmic scale (Haworth and Vincent 1979). Even the unconstrained spatial interaction model is free of this problem.

Statistical approaches have the further disadvantage of instability when they are used with migration matrices containing zero or very small flows. Such flows tend to have an importance in fitting the model disproportionate to their intuitive significance. Further, because it is impossible to take the logarithm of zero, some adjustment to zero flows must be made; this is usually done by adding a small constant but, as Flowerdew and Aitkin (1982) show, the arbitrary choice of this small constant can have a major impact on the model fitted. The problem is not encountered in spatial interaction models.

Evaluation of model fit is generally straightforward in statistical approaches to migration modelling, where the goodness-of-fit statistic is derived directly from the statistical model adopted. In spatial interaction models, goodness-of-fit has not always been considered important — the model produces the most likely set of flows, and just how likely they are compared to other sets is not the central issue (e.g. the discussion in Wilson and Kirkby 1980). On other occasions, a range of goodness-of-fit measures have been reported and compared, often with little theoretical argument for preferring one to another (Black and Salter 1975; Pitfield 1978). Baxter (1983), however, has done a great deal to clarify statistical issues in spatial interaction modelling.

In summary, the statistical approach has a number of advantages, especially the flexibility of introducing new explanatory variables and the availability of goodness-of-fit measures. In contrast, it has (in its traditional form, Ordinary Least Squares regression) some severe drawbacks, including the difficulty of introducing origin and destination constraints, its inconsistency in the sense discussed above, and its instability when confronted with zero and very small flows. These drawbacks are sufficiently major for Senior (1979) and others to warn potential users away from them. However, other statistical methods are available which do not suffer from these problems and which are in any case theoretically more appropriate for analysis of count data. Such a method, Poisson regression analysis, is outlined in the next section.

6.3 Generalised linear models and Poisson regression

Poisson regression analysis is part of a wider set of regression models that are grouped together as generalised linear models, a concept introduced by Nelder and Wedderburn (1972). Textbooks on generalised linear models include Aitkin *et al*. (1989) and McCullagh and Nelder (1989). It is a framework which links together a number of different models and techniques, all of which involve relating a response variable to a linear predictor (a linear function of one or more explanatory variables). These include Ordinary Least Squares regression, logit regression, and log-linear models for contingency table analysis. Generalised linear modelling is applicable to response variables distributed according to any probability distribution within the exponential family. The statistical packages GLIM and GENSTAT have been developed to fit models within the generalised linear modelling approach.

A generalised linear model has the following structure:

$$Y_i = f(\sum_i \beta_i X_i) + \epsilon_i \tag{6.1}$$

in which a response variable Y_i is equal to the sum of the systematic component and a random component. The systematic component is derived from a linear combination of explanatory variables and associated coefficients ($\sum \beta_i X_i$) which is linked to the response variable by a link function f. The random component is determined by the probability distribution of the response variable (the error distribution). A generalised linear model is defined by the error distribution and the link function.

Many commonly used statistical models are special cases of the generalised linear model. In Ordinary Least Squares regression, the error distribution is Normal and the link is the identity function; in other words, the estimated mean is equal to the linear predictor:

$$Y_i = \sum_i \beta_i X_i + \epsilon_i \tag{6.2}$$

where ϵ_i is a normally distributed error term. In logit models, the error distribution is Binomial and the link is the logit function.

In log-linear modelling, the error distribution is Poisson and the link is logarithmic. The most common application of log-linear modelling is in contingency table analysis, where a set of cases is cross-classified according to observed values on two or more categorical variables. The response variable is the number of cases in each cell of the contingency table, and the explanatory variables are the categorical variables which define the rows and column of the table. Because the response variable is a count, the error distribution must be a discrete probability distribution rather than a continuous distribution like the Normal. The Poisson is the appropriate discrete distribution to use if each case is assumed to be independent of the others, but all cases are assumed to be influenced in the same way by the explanatory variables. In the contingency table case, the linear predictor is constructed entirely from the categorical variables defining the table.

Sometimes, however, a count variable may be related to interval- or ratio-scale explanatory variables. In the case of migration, the number of migrants from one place to another is a count, and the gravity model variables are ratio-scale. In this situation, a discrete error distribution is still appropriate although the data cannot be expressed in contingency table form. Poisson regression is a generalised form of log-linear modelling for use when some or all of the explanatory variables are not categorical.

A Poisson regression equation can be written:

$$Y_i = \exp(\sum_i \beta_i X_i) + \epsilon_i \tag{6.3}$$

where Y_i has a Poisson distribution whose expected value is equal to $\exp(\sum_i \beta_i X_i)$; equivalently, the natural logarithm of Y_i is equal to the linear predictor. In the gravity model case, the response variable is M_{ij}, the number of migrants from i to j, and the appropriate explanatory variables are the natural logarithms of origin size (P_i), destination size (P_j) and distance (d_{ij}), and the Poisson regression equation becomes:

$$M_{ij} = \exp(\beta_0 + \beta_1 \ln P_i + \beta_2 \ln P_j + \beta_3 \ln d_{ij}) + \epsilon_i \tag{6.4}$$

If additional explanatory variables are to be introduced, they and their associated parameters become part of the linear predictor.

In generalised linear modelling, a likelihood ratio statistic is used to assess how well the model fits the data. This statistic is known as the deviance. In the Poisson case, the formula for the deviance is:

$$D = 2 (\sum_i \sum_j M_{ij} \ln (M_{ij} / \hat{M}_{ij})) \tag{6.5}$$

where M_{ij} is the observed number of migrants from i to j and $\hat{M}_{ij}$ is the number estimated by the model. The distribution of the deviance is asymptotically chi-squared; in other words, as the number of flows and the size of the flows increases, it converges to the chi-squared distribution. This means that the size of the deviance can be used to assess the goodness-of-fit of the model. If the deviance is greater than the critical chi-squared value at an appropriate significance level with $n - k$ degrees of freedom (for n flows and k coefficients in the linear predictor), the model can be rejected as not providing an acceptable fit to the data. In addition, alternative models can be compared according to their deviance values, assessing, for example, whether introducing an additional explanatory variable into the linear predictor produces a significant reduction in deviance; the new variable reduces the overall degrees of freedom by 1, so the reduction in deviance is compared to the critical chi-squared value with 1 degree of freedom.

In terms of the discussion in Section 6.2 above, Poisson regression retains the advantages of flexibility in the introduction of new explanatory variables and of a theoretically appropriate measure of goodness-of-fit. Unlike Ordinary Least Squares, it is consistent in that predicted and observed flows have the same overall total. It is also stable with respect to the problem of zero flows, which do not have to be recoded to a small positive value as is necessary in log-linear Ordinary Least Squares regression. Further, the Poisson model has the property that the variance for each case is equal to its mean, in contrast to the Ordinary Least Squares assumption that each case has the same variance as all the others. This means that cases with larger estimated flows (and hence larger variances) are weighted more heavily in the fitting process, and that the Poisson model, unlike ordinary least squares, will not suffer major distortions as a result of numerically small but proportionately large differences between observed and estimated flows. The issue of constraints will be discussed in a later section.

6.3.1 Fitting Poisson regression models to migration data

A data set on migration between the thirty largest places in Great Britain in 1980–81 will be used to illustrate the method. The areal units are Functional Regions (FRs), devised to approximate local labour market areas by staff at the Centre for Urban and Regional Development Studies at the University of Newcastle upon Tyne (Champion *et al.* 1987; Coombes *et al.* 1982). There are 280 FRs in Great Britain, but for reasons of convenience we have restricted our analysis to migration among the thirty largest (Poisson regression of the full migration matrix is perfectly possible, except that a larger than standard version of GLIM is needed, and fitting constrained models would be very time-consuming). These thirty FRs all exceed 300 000 in population.

The data set contains 870 cases (30 × 29) as migration within FRs is not considered. The total number of migrants is 149 335, with a mean of 171.6, with a minimum of 3 and a maximum of 3 619. In this particular data set, therefore, there are no zero and few very small values.

Before fitting a Poisson regression model, an Ordinary Least Squares model was fitted for comparative purposes. This produced the regression equation:

$$\ln \hat{M}_{ij} = -14.88 + 0.913 \ln P_i + 0.823 \ln P_j - 0.731 \ln d_{ij} \qquad (6.6)$$
$$\quad\; (0.71)\,(0.035) \qquad\quad (0.035) \qquad\quad (0.036)$$

Note that no error term appears in this and subsequent equations because they are phased in terms of estimated migrant flows rather than observed values. The standard errors of the parameters are in parentheses under the terms to which they refer.

The R^2 value for this model is 0.66. Because the R^2 measure is not comparable to the deviance measure used in Poisson regression, Pearson's χ^2 was also calculated. This has the value 120 398 with 866 degrees of freedom (870 cases minus 4 parameters fitted). It may also be noted that the estimated total number of migrants in this model is 109 283.

In fitting a Poisson model, it is usual to start by fitting a null model (or Grand Mean model) in which case migration from i to j is estimated simply as the mean flow $\overline{M}$ (171.6 in this case). This then serves as a baseline with which we can compare estimates based on the explanatory variables. The deviance of the null model is 313 445 (with 869 degrees of freedom).

The Poisson regression model produces the following equation:

$$\hat{M}_{ij} = \exp(-16.06 + 0.974 \ln P_i + 0.917 \ln P_j - 0.867 \ln d_{ij}) \qquad (6.7)$$
$$\quad\;\; (0.054)\,(0.002) \qquad\quad (0.002) \qquad\quad (0.003)$$

This model, unlike the previous one, has the property that the total of the predicted flows is equal to the total of the observed flows. The totals predicted to leave each origin and to arrive at each destination are not the same as the observed totals, however, as this is an unconstrained model.

The deviance value is 58 405 with 866 degrees of freedom. Comparing this with the deviance of the null model, we can say that this model accounts for 0.81 of the overall deviance. The χ^2 value for this model is 77 914, which is clearly better than the Ordinary Least Squares model.

For the model to be regarded as providing an adequate fit, however, the deviance value should be the same order of magnitude as the degrees of freedom; in fact, it is 67 time greater. If, as here, a model fails to fit, there are two main alternative explanations. It may be that a Poisson model is inappropriate; more will be said about this later in the chapter. Or it may be that other explanatory variables are needed to improve the model. Often there will be theoretical reasons to suggest other variables which can be tried; sometimes examination of the residuals may suggest other hypotheses. Some variables may be difficult to measure or otherwise be unobtainable, but many variables relevant to migration, including wage rates, unemployment, housing conditions and cultural factors, should be relatively easy to obtain and to incorporate into the model.

New variables can be incorporated into a Poisson regression model as

Table 6.1 Variables used in the analysis

Variable	Definition
P_i	Population of i, 1981
P_j	Population of j, 1981
O_i	Number of outmigrants from i to other places in the data set, 1981
D_j	Number of inmigrants to j from other places in the data set, 1981
d_{ij}	Straight-line distance between centroids of i and j
A_j	Accessibility measure ($A_j = \sum_k P_k/d_{jk}$)
I	Origin factor with one category for each i
J	Destination factor with one category for each j
C_{ij}	Contiguity (1 if Functional Regions i and j are contiguous; 0 if not)
OLD_i	Percentage at i of pensionable age, 1981
OLD_j	Percentage at j of pensionable age, 1981
$ECINACT_i$	Economically inactive per 100 economically active at i, 1981
$ECINACT_j$	Economically inactive per 100 economically active at j, 1981
$EMPCH_i$	Employment change (%) at i, 1978–81
$EMPCH_j$	Employment change (%) at j, 1978–81
U_i	Unemployment rate change (% point) at i, 1971–81
U_j	Unemployment rate change (% point) at j, 1971–81
U_{ij}	$U_i - U_j$
$MGRPRF_i$	% economically active in managerial and professional SEGs (1–4, 13) at i, 1981
$MGRPRF_j$	% economically active in managerial and professional SEGs (1–4, 13) at j, 1981
$CARS2_i$	% households with 2 or more cars at i, 1981
$CARS2_j$	% households with 2 or more cars at j, 1981
$HOUSE_i$	Average house price at i, 1980
$HOUSE_j$	Average house price at j, 1980

Note: Several of the variables are used in logged form in some models, as indicated in Table 6.2. Origin-specific terms are written $I \cdot X_j$ and destination-specific terms are written $J \cdot X_i$ where X_i and X_j can refer to any of the available variables.

easily as into an Ordinary Least Squares model. They can be origin-specific or destination-specific; they can also refer to both origin and destination in combination. A migration model could thus include the origin unemployment rate, the destination rate, or the difference in rates between origin and destination; or it could include all three. It could include other ways of specifying separation between i and j, such as a contiguity dummy variable (origin-specific and destination-specific dummy variables can also be used); it can also include an intervening opportunities variable (Stouffer 1940) or a competing destinations variable (Fotheringham 1983). In their introduction to Poisson regression, Lovett and Flowerdew (1989) suggest a strategy for the systematic examination of a set of explanatory variables.

Within a few minutes, a set of models were fitted to the Functional

Table 6.2 Summary list of models fitted to the data

Model	Variables included	Degrees of freedom	Deviance
1	$\ln P_i$, $\ln P_j$, $\ln d_{ij}$ (Ordinary Least Squares: $R^2 = 0.66$)		
2	null model	869	313 445
3	$\ln P_i$, $\ln P_j$, $\ln d_{ij}$	866	58 405
4	$\ln P_i$, $\ln P_j$, $\ln d_{ij}$, C_{ij}	865	52 903
5	$\ln P_i$, $\ln P_j$, $\ln d_{ij}$, $\ln A_j$	865	41 752
6	$\ln P_i$, $\ln P_j$, $\ln d_{ij}$, U_i	865	52 443
7	$\ln P_i$, $\ln P_j$, $\ln d_{ij}$, U_j	865	37 374
8	$\ln P_i$, $\ln P_j$, $\ln d_{ij}$, U_{ij}	865	55 704
9	$\ln P_i$, $\ln P_j$, $\ln d_{ij}$, U_i, U_j	864	34 925
10	$\ln P_i$, $\ln P_j$, $\ln d_{ij}$, C_{ij}, U_i, U_j	863	27 755
11	$\ln P_i$, $\ln P_j$, $\ln d_{ij}$, $\ln A_j$, U_i, U_j	863	29 504
12	$\ln P_i$, $\ln P_j$, $\ln d_{ij}$, C_{ij}, $\ln A_j$, U_i, U_j	862	23 881
13	$\ln P_i$, $\ln P_j$, $\ln d_{ij}$, C_{ij}, $\ln A_j$, U_i, U_j, OLD_i, OLD_j, $ECINACT_i$, $ECINACT_j$, $EMPCH_i$, $EMPCH_j$, $MGRPRF_i$, $MGRPRF_j$, $CARS2_i$, $CARS2_j$	852	20 552
14	I, $\ln P_j$, $\ln d_{ij}$	838	43 812
15	J, $\ln P_i$, $\ln d_{ij}$	838	26 633
16	I, J, $\ln d_{ij}$	809	18 060
17	I, $\ln P_j$, $\ln d_{ij}$, $\ln A_j$	837	30 324
18	I, $\ln P_j$, $\ln d_{ij}$, C_{ij}, OLD_j, $ECINACT_j$, $EMPCH_j$, $\ln U_j$, $MGRPRF_j$, $CARS2_j$, $\ln HOUSE_j$	830	17 706
19	I, $\ln P_j$, $\ln d_{ij}$, C_{ij}, $\ln A_j$, OLD_j, $ECINACT_j$, $EMPCH_j$, $\ln U_j$, $MGRPRF_j$, $CARS2_j$, $\ln HOUSE_j$	829	15 682
20	J, $\ln P_i$, $\ln d_{ij}$, $\ln A_j$	837	26 424
21	J, $\ln P_i$, $\ln d_{ij}$, C_{ij}, $\ln A_j$, OLD_i, $ECINACT_i$, $EMPCH_i$, $\ln U_i$, $MGRPRF_i$, $CARS2_i$, $\ln HOUSE_i$	830	17 190
22	I, J, $\ln D_{ij}$, C_{ij}	808	11 787
23	I, $I \cdot \ln P_j$, $I \cdot \ln d_{ij}$	780	29 989
24	I, $I \cdot \ln P_j$, $I \cdot \ln d_{ij}$, $I \cdot \ln A_j$	750	17 898
25	I, $I \cdot \ln P_j$, $I \cdot \ln d_{ij}$, C_{ij}, OLD_j, $ECINACT_j$, $EMPCH_j$, $\ln U_j$, $MGRPRF_j$, $CARS2_j$, $\ln HOUSE_j$	772	12 917
26	I, $I \cdot \ln P_j$, $I \cdot \ln d_{ij}$, C_{ij}, $I \cdot \ln A_j$, OLD_j, $ECINACT_j$, $EMPCH_j$, $\ln U_j$, $MGRPRF_j$, $CARS2_j$, $\ln HOUSE_j$	743	9 109
27	I, $I \cdot \ln P_j$, $I \cdot \ln d_{ij}$, $I \cdot C_{ij}$, $I \cdot OLD_j$, $I \cdot ECINACT_j$, $I \cdot EMPCH_j$, $I \cdot \ln U_j$, $I \cdot MGRPRF_j$, $I \cdot CARS2_j$, $I \cdot \ln HOUSE_j$	554	7 705
28	I, $I \cdot \ln P_j$, $I \cdot \ln d_{ij}$, $I \cdot C_{ij}$, $I \cdot \ln A_j$, $I \cdot OLD_j$, $I \cdot ECINACT_j$, $I \cdot EMPCH_j$, $I \cdot \ln U_j$, $I \cdot MGRPRF_j$, $I \cdot CARS2_j$, $I \cdot \ln HOUSE_j$	524	5 326
29	J, $J \cdot \ln P_i$, $J \cdot \ln d_{ij}$, $J \cdot C_{ij}$, $J \cdot OLD_i$, $J \cdot ECINACT_i$, $J \cdot EMPCH_i$, $J \cdot \ln U_i$, $J \cdot MGRPRF_i$, $J \cdot CARS2_i$, $J \cdot \ln HOUSE_i$	554	6 277
30	I, J, $I \cdot \ln d_{ij}$, $J \cdot \ln d_{ij}$, C_{ij}	749	7 052
31	$\ln d_{ij}$ (offset $\ln O_i + \ln D_j$)	868	38 783
32	d_{ij} (offset $\ln O_i + \ln D_j$)	868	56 844
33	$\ln O_i$, $\ln D_j$, $\ln d_{ij}$	866	35 983
34	$\ln O_i$, $\ln D_j$, d_{ij}	866	54 834
35	— (offset $\ln O_i + \ln D_j - 0.6862 \ln d_{ij}$; satisfies mean distance constraint)	869	39 528

Region data set, using explanatory variables from Champion *et al.* (1987), together with house price data from the Nationwide Building Society and contiguity and competing migrants variables calculated from the data (Table 6.1). The most successful single variable was the destination unemployment change (U_j); when this was added to the gravity model variables, deviance was reduced from 58 409 to 37 374. As expected, this variables had a negative coefficient though, contrary to classical economic theory, origin unemployment change (U_i) also had a negative coefficient (i.e. areas of increasing unemployment had lower outmigration). Both contiguity and the competing destinations variable significantly improved the model fit; when the linear predictor included these, in addition to the gravity model and the unemployment variables, deviance was reduced to 23 881. Incorporating some of the other variables in Appendix 2 of Champion *et al.* (1987) reduced deviance further to 20 552. Details of the models fitted and their results are given in Table 6.2.

The decision as to whether particular explanatory variables should be included or left out can be based on three grounds. First, deviance can be calculated for a model including a new explanatory variable and compared to the deviance without that variable; the change in deviance is assessed by a chi-square test, comparing reduction in deviance with the chi-squared value with degrees of freedom equal to those lost when the new variable is used — normally 1 unless the variable is categorical. If the reduction in deviance is significant, the variable is worth including in the model. Second, a standard error and an associated t value can be calculated for each explanatory variable. If the t value is insignificant, the variable can be excluded from the model. Care is necessary when using either of these criteria: a variable may seem significant at first, but may lose its significance when another variable enters the model; alternatively, a variable may seem insignificant until another variable is introduced. These events occur when there is multicollinearity among the explanatory variables; examples are found in the analysis in Lovett and Flowerdew (1989). The third basis for inclusion or exclusion of explanatory variables (arguably the most important) is whether they make theoretical sense; practitioners differ in the importance they give to this criterion.

A further advantage of Poisson regression is that there is less ambiguity about the goodness-of-fit of a model. Whatever value of the R^2 statistic in Ordinary Least Squares regression, it can never be unequivocally stated that a model does or does not fit because an apparent poor fit may be attributable to a high variance for the normally distributed error term. In Poisson regression, the variable for each observation is known (and is equal to the mean), and so cannot be used to explain away a poor model fit.

It is easy, therefore, to say whether a Poisson model does or does not fit a particular data set. As with any regression analysis, a model which fits the data successfully cannot be regarded as proof for any causal explanation: the model might no longer fit for a larger data set, a different set of variables might give just as good a fit, or the explanatory variables may be correlated with other variables which have more to do with generating the observed response. Nevertheless, if a model has an appropriate theoretical basis, a successful fit can be viewed as a testable hypothesis surviving a test.

6.3.2 Introducing constraints

The Poisson regression migration models discussed so far are unconstrained. It is a property of the method, unlike Ordinary Least Squares regression, that the total number of migrants estimated by the model is equal to the observed total. It is not the case, however, that the totals estimated as leaving or arriving at each place will be equal to the observed totals. If an origin constraint is desired in the model, it can be imposed in a Poisson model by introducing a categorical variable ('factor' in GLIM terminology) which has a different value for each origin. If I is such an origin factor, for example, it could take the value 1 for all flows from place 1, 2 for all flows from place 2, and so on for all n places. Fitting I as an explanatory variable in a Poisson model is equivalent to fitting a dummy variable for each origin. The coefficient of dummy variable I(i) automatically takes a value which scales all estimated flows from i such that the origin constraint is satisfied for i; the resulting model is origin-constrained, in the sense that observed and estimated outmigration will be equal for each place.

Similarly, a factor J can be set up with different values for each destination. Thus, for an observation of migration from i to j, I would have a value of i and J would have a value of j. Introducing J into a Poisson model gives a destination-constrained model, and introducing both I and J gives a doubly constrained model. Note that if I is used in a model, it will subsume all origin variables, and origin population or origin unemployment cannot be introduced into the regression. This is also the case for J and variables referring to destination conditions. This method was suggested by Baxter (1984) and operationalised by Flowerdew and Lovett (1988). It should be noted that fitting origin and destination constraints may be quite demanding of computer time if there is a large number of places in the system under study.

When an origin-constrained form of the standard gravity model is fitted to the Functional Region migration data, therefore, the explanatory variables comprise the origin factor, the logarithm of destination population and the logarithm of distance. This model has a deviance of 43 812, a considerable advance on the comparable unconstrained model (58 405). However, the origin-constrained model has only 838 degrees of freedom instead of 866 (there is no parameter for origin population, but there are separate parameters fitted for each of the thirty origins, one of which is subsumed in the constant term). It could also be argued that the origin-constrained model has only to account for the distribution of migrants among the available destinations, while the unconstrained model is also accounting for the generation of migrants.

The analogous destination-constrained model has a deviance of 26 633 with 838 degrees of freedom, dramatically less than the origin-constrained version. This seems to suggest that there is a weaker relationship between population and inmigration among the thirty FRs than there is between population and outmigration. The doubly constrained model reduces deviance to only 18 060 with 809 degrees of freedom.

As with the unconstrained model, it is easy to introduce further explanatory variables which may improve the model, and the results of some of these models are reported in Table 6.2. These variables can be used to reduce the deviance of the origin-constrained model to 15 682. Introducing additional variables to the destination-constrained model reduces the deviance to 17 190, and adding contiguity to the doubly constrained model reduces deviance to 11 797. As stated above, origin variables cannot be used in an origin-constrained model and destination variables cannot be used in a destination-constrained model. The only additional variables which can be introduced into a doubly constrained model are those which relate to both origin and destination (such as distance, contiguity, and the difference between i and j in economic and other conditions).

It is also possible to assume that the effect of the explanatory variables may differ between origins or between destinations. This is frequently done with the distance parameter in spatial interaction models; for example, Stillwell's chapter in this book includes a discussion of zone–specific distance decay parameters. Origin-specific distance parameters may be appropriate if it is thought that outmigrants from certain places may be deterred by distance less than outmigrants from other places. Similarly, the use of destination-specific distance parameters may reflect the idea that certain places attract inmigrants from a long distance while the appeal of others is more local.

In Poisson regression, zone-specific parameters may be fitted as interaction terms between the origin or destination factor and other variables. Lovett and Flowerdew (1989) provide an example in which the effect of distance on migration was hypothesised to vary regionally. Moreover, not only distance but other variables can be treated as zone-specific; the only drawbacks are the degrees of freedom lost (29 for each zone-specific parameter when there are 30 places in the data set) and the time taken by GLIM to fit models containing large numbers of zone-specific parameters. Fitting zone-specific parameters to the Functional Regions data set reduced deviance to 5 326 for 524 degrees of freedom in an origin-constrained model. More details are given in Table 6.2.

A further question concerns when it is appropriate to use constrained models. Many uses of spatial interaction models refer to journey-to-work flows where it is fairly clear that constraints are desirable — no model should predict more flows leaving zone i than there are workers resident in zone i. In the case of migration, the case for constraints seems less clear-cut. The view is taken here that employing an origin constraint is appropriate if migration is seen as a two-stage decision, in which people first decide whether to leave place i or to stay put, and then select a destination. If a migrant is seen as receiving information about a job opportunity in zone j and then deciding (in one stage) whether to move or to stay, an unconstrained model may be more appropriate.

6.4 Relationship to spatial interaction models

Despite the distinction drawn at the start of the chapter between statistical and spatial interaction approaches to fitting gravity models, there are equivalences between the two approaches in certain cases, as shown by Baxter (1982). In particular, a Poisson regression model can be constructed which is equivalent to a spatial interaction model with or without origin and destination constraints. An unconstrained spatial interaction model might be written:

$$M_{ij} = k \ O_i \ D_j \ exp \ (\beta \ d_{ij}) \tag{6.8}$$

where O_i is the total number of outmigrants from i, D_j is the total number of inmigrants to j, and k is a constant of proportionality.

To fit this model in Poisson regression, $\ln O_i$ and $\ln D_j$ must be used instead of $\ln P_i$ and $\ln P_j$, and unlike an ordinary log-linear regression model, they are constrained to have coefficients of exactly 1. This can be accomplished in GLIM using the OFFSET command. If a quantity equal to $\ln O_i + \ln D_j$ is declared as an offset and M_{ij} then regressed on d_{ij}, the resulting model is the same as the unconstrained spatial interaction model. The intercept term in the GLIM model is equal to the natural logarithm of the constant of proportionality k.

As might be expected, the model performs better when $\ln O_i$ and $\ln D_j$ are used instead of $\ln P_i$ and $\ln P_j$, because it no longer has to account for the differences in the generation and attraction of migrants. With this particular data set, however, the negative exponential form of the distance decay is far worse than the power function form. In the first case, deviance is 56 844; in the second, 38 733. In order to investigate the effect of constraining the coefficients of $\ln O_i$ and $\ln D_j$ to be 1, the power function version of the model was run without the offset. The best-fit coefficients for $\ln O_i$ and $\ln D_j$ were 1.082 and 1.115 respectively, and the deviance was reduced to 35 983. This suggests that constraining the coefficients to be 1 does reduce model performance in the unconstrained case, but that the effect is not very great.

If the spatial interaction model is used with a negative exponential distance decay term, as in equation (6.8), the entropy-maximising solution has the property that the total distance moved in the fitted model is equal to the total observed distance. This is equivalent to saying that the mean migration distance in the model is equal to the mean observed migration distance. This property is sometimes (rather questionably) regarded as an important feature of an adequate model, and is used as a constraint in deriving equation (6.8). Often spatial interaction models are stated in terms of cost rather than distance as the measure of separation between places, and so this property is called the total cost constraint. This cost constraint may be used in calibrating a spatial interaction model, as is the case, for example, with the IMP program Stillwell describes in Chapter 3 of this book.

If distance is regarded as having a negative exponential distribution in Poisson regression (i.e. the term d_{ij} is fitted as an explanatory variable), the resulting model will also satisfy the cost constraint. If it is fitted as a power function (involving the term ln d_{ij}), this constraint is not satisfied, although in a good model observed and fitted mean migration distances should not be very different. The observed mean migration distance is 141.9 kilometres; the unconstrained standard gravity model (model 3 in Table 6.2) has a mean migration distance of 139.0 kilometres. When additional explanatory variables are added to improve model fit (model 13 in Table 6.2), the mean migration distance becomes 140.6 kilometres.

The power function version of the Poisson model, however, has a slightly different property: the sum of the logged distances of the moves estimated by the model is equal to the sum of the logged distances of the observed moves:

$$\sum_i \sum_j M_{ij} \ln d_{ij} = \sum_i \sum_j \hat{M}_{ij} \ln d_{ij} \tag{6.9}$$

This property may seem less intuitively plausible than the total cost property which applies with a negative exponential characterisation of the effect of distance. However, the contrast in deviance between models 33 and 34 in Table 6.2 suggests that, for this data set at least, the power function gives a better fit.

In his discussion of goodness-of-fit, Wilson (1974, Chapter 12) derives this result and generalises it for any arbitrary function of distance. If the function is written in the form $\exp(-\beta \ln (d_{ij}))$, then a maximum likelihood model (such as Poisson regression) will have the property that the predicted sum of ln (d_{ij}) in the model will be equal to the sum in the observed data set. Correspondingly, a spatial interaction program should satisfy the constraint that the observed and fitted sums of ln (d_{ij}) should be equal. The total cost constraint is only appropriate for a negative exponential distance function.

In a constrained model, origin and/or destination factors must be declared as described in the previous section. Offsets are used in singly constrained models, equal to ln D_j in an origin-constrained model and ln O_i in a destination-constrained model. No offset is needed in a doubly constrained model. In all cases, regressing M_{ij} on d_{ij} produces a result equivalent to the corresponding spatial interaction model. In constrained models, the spatial interaction model is usually written:

$$\hat{M}_{ij} = A_i \, B_j \, O_i \, D_j \, \exp(\beta \, d_{ij}) \qquad (6.10)$$

where the A_i and B_j terms are place-specific constants, often called balancing factors, which ensure that the constraints are met.

In a constrained Poisson regression model, a set of coefficients is produced for each origin (and/or destination). In a single constrained model, these coefficients are equal to the natural logarithms of the equivalent balancing factors plus the natural logarithms of their respective origin (or destination) totals. In an origin-constrained model, therefore:

$$\beta_o + \beta_i = \ln A_i + \ln O_i \qquad (6.11)$$

where $\beta_o + \beta_i$ is the coefficient of the origin factor for place i (GLIM output presents these coefficients as contrasts with the coefficient for place 1). In a destination-constrained model:

$$\beta_o + \beta_j = \ln B_j + \ln D_j \qquad (6.12)$$

where $\beta_o + \beta_j$ is the coefficient of the destination factor for place j. In a doubly constrained model, the sum of the coefficients output by GLIM is equal to the sum of the logarithms of both balancing factors and both attractiveness terms:

$$\beta_o + \beta_i + \beta_j = \ln A_i + \ln B_j + \ln O_i + \ln D_j \qquad (6.13)$$

Although spatial interaction models can be fitted in more sophisticated ways which allow more general measures of attractiveness or different distance decay functions, they are less flexible than Poisson regression models, first because the latter allow all the terms to have parameters fixed within the model, whereas spatial interaction models only allow the distance decay parameter to vary. Second, in a spatial interaction model, origin and destination attractiveness terms must be determined separately from the model, while in Poisson regression they can be estimated simultaneously.

6.5 Dispersion

6.5.1 Overdispersion

Usually the deviance of a Poisson regression model is bigger than the critical chi-squared value, at least if the data set is large. As stated earlier, this may be because there are other important explanatory variables not in the model, or because the Poisson assumption (that all migrants from i to j move independently and with the same probability) does not hold. In the case of migration, there may well be reasons why the Poisson assumption does not hold. This in itself should not be taken as an argument against using a Poisson regression methodology, because spatial interaction models also, implicitly, make the Poisson assumption.

The most obvious reason why migration may not be a Poisson process is because individual migrants do not always make independent decisions. In the words of Odland and Ellis (1988), 'migration behaviour has generally been analyzed . . . as if all migrants were autonomous individuals who do not cooperate with other members of a household.' In practice, if one member of a household moves from i to j, it is highly likely that the rest of the household will make the same move. Apart from the household effect, there may be other reasons why one person's move from i to j will not be independent of other people. For example, if a company relocates from i to j, many of its employees may make the same move; another company at j may concentrate recruitment efforts at i, leading to several non-independent movers from i to j. Individual migrants from i to j may be influenced by each other's moves; perhaps friends or relatives may be encouraged or helped by each other's support, or several people in i may be influenced by information reaching them from j through previous migrants or other information channels. All these processes may invalidate the Poisson assumption, usually in a manner which will lead to a pattern more clustered than the Poisson. Whereas the Poisson distribution has the property that its variance is equal to its mean, these processes have the property that the variance is greater than the mean.

It may be possible to model such processes using a probability distribution akin to the Poisson, such as compound or generalised Poisson. The negative binomial is one such distribution, which is compatible with several such processes. For a large class of models, the parameters estimated in a Poisson model will still be unbiased in such a model, as will expected migration flows (Davies and Guy 1987). The deviance statistic for the Poisson will not apply however; nor will the Poisson standard errors.

Davies and Guy (1987) review methods for fitting models of this type, including quasi-likelihood and pseudo-likelihood approaches, discussed in the context of migration by Congdon in Chapter 7 of this volume. Aufhauser and Fischer (1985) have applied quasi-likelihood methods to the study of migration in Vienna.

6.5.2 Household-size models

In the case where the Poisson assumption is violated because of the tendency for households to move together, it is possible to model the process explicitly. Flowerdew and Lovett (1989) assumed that the migration of a household was a Poisson process, and that this process was generalised by an empirically observed household-size distribution to give a distribution for the total number of migrants. Such a model is considerably more realistic than a Poisson, although their work still makes the questionable assumption that the probability of a household migrating is independent of household size. In this model, flows of 1 migrant become less likely, and flows of 0 and 3 to 6 migrants (i.e. 1 household) become more likely.

The parameters and fitted values are the same for this model as for the Poisson. The calculation of deviance is more complicated, however, and must be done using a recursive formula. It is possible to calculate the log-likelihood of there being no migrants from i to j. It is also possible to calculate the log-likelihood of there being p migrants for any number p, given the log-likelihood of there being any smaller number of migrants. The log-likelihood of a large flow must therefore be calculated by first calculating the log-likelihood of all smaller flows. Details are given in Flowerdew and Lovett (1989).

The results of fitting this model are that the deviance is greatly reduced, although not necessarily to the point where it is less than the relevant critical value of chi-squared. In contrast, quasi-likelihood methods reduce the deviance to be equal to the degrees of freedom, so that the model must fit. Modelling the source of extra-Poisson variation explicitly, as in the household-size model, does not necessarily result in a bad model displaying a perfect fit, and is more helpful in that it gives scope for comparing models employing different sets of explanatory variables.

6.5.3 Underdispersion

As stated above, it is common for Poisson models to be overdispersed. However, in some cases, especially where the data matrix is sparse, with many zero or very small entries, the deviance value may actually be less than the critical chi-squared value. This has been observed, for example, in attempting to model inter-ward migration, using the Special Migration Statistics from the 1981 Census. This would suggest that the migration process is more regular than the Poisson, something which is hard to explain theoretically.

This phenomenon appears to be an artefact of the data set, resulting from the failure of deviance to follow the chi-squared distribution when there are many very small flows. This invalidates its use as a measure of goodness-of-fit. One approach to this problem is to use simulation methods to work out the probability of a given deviance measure being observed. First, the Poisson model is fitted in the normal way, resulting in a set of estimates for each pair of places. These estimates are then used to generate simulated flows, drawing random numbers and assigning an 'observed' flow to each observation using the estimate as the Poisson parameter. The model can then be refitted using the simulated data, and the deviance recorded. If many sets of simulations are done, the range of deviances for the simulated flows can be used to assess the deviance for the real set of flows. The deviances for the simulated data sets are likely to be substantially lower than the critical chi-square value if the data set contains many zero and very small flows and the model can only be regarded as fitting satisfactorily if the real deviance is within the range of simulated deviances.

A simulation approach to assessing goodness-of-fit is particularly useful for models where the Poisson variance is greater than the mean, such as the household-size model discussed above.

6.6 Problems in fitting Poisson regression models

Few statistical analyses are free of problems and, although Poisson regression is a relatively flexible method, it is no exception. Some of the problems discussed in this section are applicable to many methods while others are more specific to Poisson models.

As in any linear regression, multicollinearity between independent variables can make the interpretation of the results problematic. In migration modelling, the explanatory variables will refer either to the origin or to the destination or to both in combination. It is highly likely that interesting explanatory variables will be correlated with each other; for example, housing, wage rates, unemployment and wealth indicators are all likely to be correlated. This means that using one of these variables may appear to improve model fit when it is really another closely correlated variable that is important. The best approach to this problem is to explore the effects of such variables on the model individually and in combination, to consider theoretical arguments about their likely influence on migration carefully, and to avoid jumping to causal conclusions on the basis of a good model fit.

As suggested earlier, assessing goodness-of-fit can be a problem for sparse migration matrices. Again, it must be remembered that a model which fits a particular data set may be only one of a large set of adequate models. Often a model will appear to fit satisfactorily not because it is a good model but because there is insufficient data on which to base rejecting it. Similarly, the failure to establish that a hypothesised influence on migration improves goodness-of-fit may mean not that the influence does not exist but merely that it is too weak to emerge clearly from the data set used. A Poisson model, however, does allow us to say more about goodness-of-fit than is possible with Ordinary Least Squares.

Using GLIM, it is possible to fit Poisson regression models on quite large data sets in a few seconds. For example, models can be fitted to the 30×30 inter-FR migration data set mentioned above in a few seconds on Lancaster University's Sequent Symmetry. An exception to this occurs when constrained models are fitted, when the fitting procedure expands to a minute or two for a data set of this size. The household-size model is also relatively time-consuming to fit. In both cases, however, it is hoped that improvements to the algorithm could speed up the process greatly.

The existence of spatial autocorrelation in a data set has been argued to cast doubt on the results of applying conventional statistical methods (Griffith 1987). There is good reason to suppose that this is a problem for spatial interaction modelling, and no reason to suppose that Poisson models are not liable to be affected by it. To the author's knowledge, no work has yet been done on methods of estimating and controlling for spatial autocorrelation effects in Poisson regression.

A further problem is that of areal unit definition. The number of migrants between i and j is clearly dependent on the boundaries of the two places. If distance is to be used as an explanatory variable, problems result from the fact that the distance actually moved by a migrant may be far less than the distance between the geometric centres of i and j; this is a particular problem where i and j are contiguous. One way of looking at the impact of zone definition is to compare models calibrated for small units with models calibrated after these units have been aggregated into larger zones. This type of analysis is an application of Openshaw's approach to the modifiable areal unit problem (1984). Openshaw reports that the results of fitting spatial interaction models are highly sensitive to aggregation. Work by Amrhein and Flowerdew (1989) on migration between Canadian census divisions, however, detects only a minor effect. The discrepancy may be related to data peculiarities, or to the volatility of the R^2 goodness-of-fit measure employed by Openshaw.

6.7 Conclusions

Poisson regression is a relatively new approach to migration modelling, but it is now fairly well established and easy to put into practice. At the beginning of the chapter, approaches to migration modelling based on a statistical approach and based on the spatial interaction modelling approach were contrasted. Poisson regression, which is actually closely related to spatial interaction modelling in substance if not in style, combines the advantages of both approaches. It does not suffer from the disadvantages which led many migration analysts to reject the statistical approach, and benefits from the flexibility that is the statistical approach's main advantage.

This is not to say that Poisson regression models are the complete answer to the migration analyst's prayer. The later sections of the chapter have discussed some problems which have been encountered in using Poisson models and some extensions to the general method which show promise of overcoming them. There are other areas where the general approach is capable of further development.

Overall, however, Poisson regression is an approach to migration modelling which is theoretically sound and is capable of dealing with large and sparse data sets. Almost as important, it is relatively easy to put into practice if GLIM or GENSTAT is available, and the basic principles should be within the grasp of anybody with experience of multiple regression.

Chapter 7

An application of general linear modelling to migration in London and South East England

Peter Congdon

7.1 Introduction

In classical economic models of migration between regions, migration is regarded as an adjustment mechanism which equilibrates spatial differences in income and unemployment, and which regulates the supply of and demand for labour in competitive regional labour markets. The more recent human capital mode (Molho 1986) also expects — when aggregating over individual decisions — that migration will tend to be away from areas of lesser opportunity towards those of greater opportunity.

Recent migration research has, however, cast doubt on the nature of migration's equilibrating role in spatial labour markets. Thus several studies have found migration flows to be largest between regions of economic strength, with a high correlation between grows inflows and outflows, and little evidence of equilibrating net outflows from less prosperous regions (Gleave and Cordey-Hayes 1977).

If such 'parallelism' or turnover effects are operative, then the direction of the effects of economic variables on migration flows will not be as expected under a model of equilibration. Thus if migration were equilibrating one would expect that migration from a region would increase as its unemployment rate increased, but decrease as its income increased. Many studies do find 'incorrect' signs when evaluated against classical push–pull predictions: the effects of income or unemployment, especially on outmigration (i.e. at the origin), are not signed as expected or are not statistically significant. It may be that such findings are a real reflection of migration processes: of turnover rather than push–pull. However, it is argued below that the signs and significance of regression coefficients can often depend to a marked extent on the choice of regression method, and that some methods have drawbacks in their treatment of the migration dependent variable.

This chapter considers regression methods adapted to the discrete nature of migration flows between areas, focusing on migration in London and the South East region. This context is interesting in that the region contains a local diversity of growth rates and prosperity: with growth zones such as the 'M4 corridor' counties; prosperous though less fast growing suburban areas in outer London and the counties immediately adjacent to London; and some deprived inner city areas. Does migration in the South East act to reduce these intraregional inequalities, and how does the statistical methodology chosen condition the conclusions reached?

The subsequent sections of the chapter consider the nature of migration's role in job and housing markets, as evidenced by the flows in the South East. The next section considers in more detail the questions of (a) migration equilibration and (b) migration's role in a complex and extensive metropolitan region. Succeeding sections contrast the often used log-linear model with generalised Poisson models; these both reflect the true nature of migration and allow for 'extravariation' beyond that expected under a simple random (Poisson) assumption. Finally some implications of disaggregation by age and social group are considered.

7.2 Migration in labour and housing markets

Findings contrary to migration equilibration may be attributable to real forces in labour and housing markets. In labour markets, it has been argued that high vacancy rates and low unemployment in growth areas encourage migrant turnover and increase outmigration as well as attracting inmigrants (Gleave and Cordey-Hayes 1977, Chapter 6); while in housing markets certain types of tenure may have a similar effect in raising migrant turnover.

Another reason why the push–pull relationships may not be observed (at first sight) is the compositional effect due to chronic or repeat migrants which induces a positive correlation between inmigration and outmigration (Mueser and White 1989; Miller 1973). This compositional effect is recognised by proponents of the turnover hypothesis: areas of high inflow and outflow attract the residentially footloose with both occupational skills and few family ties. However, it may act to conceal the 'true' push–pull nature of factors such as earnings or job growth, or at least suggest that push-pull and turnover streams operate simultaneously (providing an alternative basis for multi-stream models to the usual 'distance bands' approach).

A major reason why classical predictions may not be met in practice is the operation of constraints on migration ('market imperfections') — again such constraints would act to conceal the basically push–pull nature of migration. Constraints on migration operate not only in the labour market itself but also in the housing market. Thus labour migration — motivated by prospects of gain in the labour market and undertaken by economically active persons over long distances — necessarily involves a change of housing as well as of job (Johnson *et al.* 1975). Many shorter-distance moves are predominantly related to housing factors. Access to housing is thus a major factor in facilitating or limiting geographic mobility within and between geographical labour markets.

For example, restrictive conditions for inmigrants in terms of entry to municipal housing (Hughes and McCormick 1987) and marked regional house price differentials hinder labour migration, especially by lower- and middle-income groups. Simple imbalances between housing demand and supply, often associated with planning constraints, reduce affordable housing opportunities, especially in more prosperous regions such as South East England. Housing market constraints may operate with considerable force for intermediate occupational groups with fixed group skills but restricted opportunities in the private housing market.

Labour market barriers to migration are of course also operative. Poor information flows and the geographically restricted labour markets of low-skill workers may reduce any tendency to equilibration by migration within these occupational groups. The geographical mobility of such workers, already often hindered by dependence on municipal housing, is further reduced by occupational barriers in terms of training and admission requirements (Johnson *et al.* 1975). So migration may tend to match labour demand and supply better in occupational categories with high training investments and inelasticity of supply within the local labour market. There are also ties associated with family and social factors which inhibit mobility: such residential inertia is likely to be greater for older workers and tends to produce differences between individuals in the relation between the movement decision and the length of residence.

It is evident from this argument that classical labour market equilibration in terms of the supply of jobs and spatial differences in earnings needs to be supplemented by information on housing market structure, on the supply of (new) houses and on house prices. Thus, in the quantitative analysis undertaken below, both labour and housing market factors are included as 'predictors' of the amount of migration between areas. It is also clear that a disaggregate analysis by age group and occupational group is preferable because of heterogeneity in migratory response and in the impact of economic variables.

7.2.1 Migration within metropolitan regions

The necessity to account simultaneously for both job and housing market factors is also apparent when shorter-distance moves are taken into account. Many of the moves between London boroughs and between South East counties which are considered here would be expected to be short-distance moves where the influence of housing type and house prices is of major importance. Thus, the traditional model of residential relocation within urban areas is formulated in terms of changing demands for housing space associated with household and family transitions (for example, marriage, family formation, and retirement). Much of the decentralisation in London and the South East will be associated with moves — by households undergoing such transitions — away from areas of high house prices and towards areas where new housing is still being built and house prices are lower.

However, the influence of labour market factors on intrametropolitan and intraregional migration also needs to be taken account of. This is related to labour market differentiation within London and the South East and to the increasingly polycentric nature of metropolitan regions (Gordon *et al.* 1986). These changes cast doubt on monocentric models whereby most decentralising workers retain central workplaces via extended commuting (Buck *et al.* 1985). Several studies have pointed to the close grouping and overlapping nature of labour markets in London and the South East, and to the difficulties of delimiting local labour markets on a comparable basis throughout the United Kingdom. The high degree of commuting overlap between neighbouring labour markets in the London region means that application of uniform national criteria reduces London to a single labour market, as in the CURDS scheme (Coombes *et al.* 1982), or alternatively two labour markets, as in the scheme of the Department of Employment (Smart 1981). Lower commuting thresholds (as in Smart 1974, Chapter 5) show a more fragmented pattern. It is likely that an overlapping rather than disjointed approach to delimiting local labour markets would be more appropriate to the London region and would give a better impression of the degree of labour markets segmentation (Isserman *et al.* 1986).

The part that migration plays in the multiple overlapping labour markets of London and the South East is apparent from labour market accounting — a procedure matching changes in employment (labour demand) with changes in labour supply due to net migration, changes in unemployment and economic participation, and (possibly) changes in commuting balances (Congdon and Champion 1989a, 1989b). Such accounts show that migration and commuting (a) act to some degree as alternative labour market responses in London and the South East and (b) act in an equilibrating fashion within the labour market. The latter finding may be challenged as spurious (for example, as really due to house price differentials) and hence the necessity to control for housing market factors in assessing the influence that job supply has on migration between areas in the South East. However, at least initially this evidence suggests that the London region is not a homogeneous labour market in which differentials in labour demand are eliminated by commuting, but that residential relocations also occur in response to differentials in labour demand. It also suggests that equilibration rather than turnover is predominant in the London region and that migration may contribute to reducing unemployment differentials as in the classical model.

One implication is that decentralisation of population to the outer London suburbs and beyond is at least partly linked to the faster growth of jobs and earnings there and to higher unemployment in inner London. Census data on the workplaces of recent migrants from inner to outer London and from London to the rest of the South East confirm a high rate of workplace relocation within a year of residential relocation (Congdon 1989a).

However, job migration takes place within the context of a differentiated housing market. Excess labour demand in the 'Sunbelt' counties to the west and south of London generally coincides with the highest house prices — and planning constraints on new housing. By contrast, the eastern parts of the region, such as the 'Lower Thames corridor', have considerably lower prices (SERPLAN 1988). House price differentials have been seen as a cause of segmented migration, with middle- and lower-income groups moving from London in search of cheaper housing (Barlow 1989). Over time the influence of house prices in relation to family incomes has been found important in predicting net migration (Congdon and Champion 1989b; Muellbauer and Murphy 1988).

A further trend indicating the breakdown of traditional models of residential location is the selective inmigration by higher-income workers ('gentrification') to formerly working class districts of the inner city. This has been linked (Hamnett 1984) to changes in the pattern of labour demand, especially the growth of financial services and quaternary employment in central metropolitan areas.

7.3 Migration models and specification

The results of quantitative analysis of migration are conditioned by the methods chosen. Questions of the significance or direction (i.e. positive or negative sign) of independent variables may depend strongly on the form of the dependent variable, the type of regression method chosen, assumptions as to error structure and so on. Some studies make an implicit assumption of a two-stage decision process (often for reasons of methodological as well as theoretical convenience): namely that the choice of destination is conditional on a prior choice to migrate and therefore that total rates of outmigration ('generation') and destination probabilities ('allocation') are separate objects of explanation.

However, several studies question the assumption that the decision to move is independent of the choice of alternative destinations and their characteristics (Ginsberg 1978; Congdon 1989b). Indeed such an assumption is at variance with migration models (such as the human capital approach) which stress the comparison of origin and destination in the evaluation of the discounted returns to moving or staying. There is evidence that 'incorrect' or insignificant coefficients may occur in models either of generation or of allocation (Cushing 1989). For example, origin characteristics are likely to be misrepresented in models of the total outflow rate (Congdon 1989b, p. 98) because of the lack of a comparison between origin and destination. Hence the analysis below is conducted with dependent variables which are migration flows between origins and destinations.

Incorrect specification of the regression equations used to predict rates or flows of migration between origins and destinations may, however, lead to incorrect or insignificant coefficients on independent economic variables. The commonly used log-normal approach involves ordinary least squares except for a logarithmic transformation applied to the migration flow (and possibly also the independent variates). This method, used by Gleave and Cordey-Hayes (1977, p. 18) and found by them to give wrongly signed or insignificant coefficients, has a number of problems when calibrated using migration count data. The assumption of log-normality (normality in the log scale of a variable), intended to be applicable to numbers on a continuous scale — and often appropriate, for example, for incomes data — is often not appropriate for count data such as migration flows. Problems arise in the choice of the constant to be added to zero flows so that logarithms can be taken (Flowerdew and Aitkin 1982).

A further issue of specification may affect the direction and size of coefficients, but is more often particularly associated with the random error assumption underlying tests of their statistical significance. For example, statistical distributions adapted to count data, such as the Poisson distribution, may have an error specification which is not appropriate to ('does not fit') the data. The Poisson distribution basically assumes a uniform migration rate for individuals and randomness in migration behaviour. A number of studies have found the Poisson to be incorrectly specified in terms of the available degrees of freedom (the number of observed flows less the number of constraints placed on the data by the regression procedure). Measures of error specification such as the deviance and generalised chi-square (readily available in the GLIM package) should be approximately equal to the degrees of freedom if a Poisson distribution is appropriate.

However, typically these measures exceed the degrees of freedom — this is known as excess or 'extra-Poisson' dispersion, and substantively implies non-randomness in migration patterns and variability in the migration rates of individuals. There are a number of possible sources for this (analysed further below), including spatial clustering effects and unobserved heterogeneity in migration behaviour which may arise from aggregating migration counts over one or more important explanatory factors. Excess dispersion may be remedied by adopting a different distribution which allows for excess variation (such as the negative binomial) or by some form of scaling.

The main import of incorrect error specification to the assessment of migration models is that the standard errors will be understated if there is variation in excess of that expected under the Poisson model. This is relevant to assessing the statistical significance of independent variables (e.g. job and housing growth) used to predict migration because if standard errors are understated then significance (assessed by comparing regression coefficients and standard errors) will be overstated, e.g. job growth at destination will be seen as significant when it is not in fact so.

A general linear modelling approach is adopted in this chapter to estimating Poisson models and discrete probability models which allow for excess variation. This approach can be implemented by iterative least squares, necessitating only that one specify the relation between variance and mean (e.g. in the Poisson they are assumed equal) rather than the full distribution.

7.3.1 The gravity model and testing migration theories

These generalisations of the Poisson model are applied to the so-called gravity model of migration. This model is directly derived from the Newtonian model for gravitational attraction between two bodies. This attraction is proportional to the mass of each and inversely related to the square of the distance between them. Allowing for the influence of economic variables and for other factors (e.g. 'contiguity') is a major motivation for applying gravity models.

The analysis here is based on aggregate migration flows between areas and on predicting these using information on the characteristics of areas and their populations. Nevertheless, the gravity model may be related to the processes underlying individual migration choices and to models (e.g. human capital or random utility models) which attempt to represent the factors governing these individual choices. To quote Molho (1986, p. 416), the gravity model 'provides a general empirical discipline which encompasses different micro-based theories of migration, and may be used to provide empirical evidence for or against competing hypotheses'.

Indeed, apart from their computional difficulties, micro-level studies do not provide a complete view of migration, especially the effect of regional and local labour and housing market processes on the mover–stayer decision. Micro-level models will generally aggregate to generate some form of gravity formulation, especially if such aggregation is performed over relatively homogeneous populations in terms of micro theory (e.g. over age groups at similar stages in their life and career cycles, or over persons with similar occupational skills).

Of course, there remain problems with the gravity model as a test of the human capital and other migration theories. The labour and housing market determinants of migration are typically represented by average earnings or house prices or by average growth rates (in jobs and houses). The implicit assumption is that individual opportunities are related to these averages. However, many migrants will move in the 'wrong' direction whether equilibration or turnover is predominant (e.g. some migrants will move to high unemployment areas or to high house price areas). This is one reason why it is important to allow for unobserved heterogeneity in migration regressions. A second major problem is simultaneity: endogeneity between migration and the factors used to predict it. For example, a positive relation between inmigration and employment growth could be because areas of high growth have more job vacancies and attract more migrants. But it could also be because inmigration raises demand for certain goods and services (housing, welfare services) which in turn leads to job creation (Vanderkamp 1986). A third problem is selectivity: if the dependent variable is a count of movers, then the decision process of stayers is unobserved. This set of persons may have been unable to overcome barriers to migration and their experience is of obvious relevance to assessing migration theories.

7.3.2 *Variable measurement and data availability*

The choice of economic variables in the present study is nevertheless guided by recent migration theories. Thus — as far as the labour market is concerned — the search model of migration reviewed by Molho (1986) predicts that migration patterns will be affected by the spatial distribution of job generation as well as by spatial relativities in average earnings or unemployment rates. Similarly, the turnover models of Gleave and Cordey-Hayes (1977, pp. 33), emphasize the relation between migrant turnover, occupational mobility and job vacancy rates. The necessity for some measure of the probability of gaining employment or housing (e.g. vacancy rates or employment/housing growth) in alternative potential destinations, in addition to knowledge of wage averages, is apparent in view of imperfections in labour and housing markets.

The absence of full employment and wage flexibility in real labour markets invalidates the neoclassical assumption that wages are sufficiently flexible to induce migration until any wage differentials are eliminated. In housing markets house price differentials within and between regions impede migration but flexibility in the supply of new housing is limited by planning constraints and again migration may tend to be disequilibrating (to increase pressure on house prices in more prosperous regions) rather than equilibrating.

Proxies for vacancy creation in the employment and housing stock are available for the London boroughs and South East counties. Notified vacancy rates for jobs are not reliable and change in workplace employment is used instead: for the 1971–81 analysis, the comparison is based on data from the two population censuses, while for the 1980–81 and 1984–87 analyses, comparisons are based respectively on the 1978 and 1981 employment censuses and on the 1984 and 1987 employment censuses. The 1978–81 employment growth rate is converted to an annual rate to match the one-year migration data for 1980–81.

Income relativities or differences in rates of earnings increase will also be expected to reflect labour demand differences and to influence the migration decision especially where job-related factors are of partial or major importance. This is true both for the neoclassical model of equilibration (where migration is stimulated by and acts to reduce spatial differences in earnings) and for more recent models such as that based on human capital — where migration is based on a comparison of present values of lifetime earnings between origin and destination. Incomes data for both boroughs and counties can be extracted from the annual New Earnings Survey which gives workplace-based average earnings.

Dwelling stock change — either in total or in the private and public sectors separately — is provided by Department of Environment returns on housing completions. In the South East outside London, especially in the 1980s, most new housing has been built by the private sector (131 000 out of 155 000 housing units in the calendar years 1985–87), and it seems reasonable to take total stock change as a proxy for housing opportunities. Even much of the new public housing outside London has been intended for migrants, as in the remaining New Town developments in Milton Keynes and Crawley.

Within London, new public housing has been built primarily to meet local demand, though it may stimulate migration via the creation of vacancies in private renting as new public housing is occupied. It has been argued (Gordon and Lamont 1982) that, in contrast to new public housing to meet local housing need, new private housing is likely to be particularly oriented to migrants, especially longer-distance movers with little information about the existing stock. For this reason (i.e. to test the proposition that migration is led by new private housing) new private completion rates alone are used as a predictor of London interborough migration.

In fact the evidence indicates that the great majority of new private housing in London and the South East is taken by short-distance intrazonal movers (it may be that a higher proportion of longer-distance movers than short-distance movers enter new houses rather than the existing stock but the longer-distance stream is much smaller than the short-distance stream). Building society surveys show the high proportion of new private houses in London taken by intrazonal movers — 60 per cent from within 5 miles according to the surveys quoted in SERPLAN (1986, p. 52).

Another major qualification to the role of new private housing in influencing migration flows, especially within London but also within the South East generally, is that the volume of new private housing in London is low in relation to inmigrant flows. Thus new private housing in the capital has averaged 6.5 thousand a year in the 1980s (45.3 thousand units totalled over the calendar years 1981–87), mostly in outer London. The annual volume of migrants to outer London according to the 1981 Census stands at 143 000 (from inner London, the rest of

Britain and overseas) and this total excludes intrazonal movers between the outer London boroughs. Thus any 'statistically significant' coefficient relating inmigration to new private housing must be seen in the light of the actual numbers of migrants and new houses involved.

The limited extent to which new housing can or does meet the housing demands of migrants enhances the importance in migrant decisions of house price relativities relating to the existing as well as new stock (as is apparent from above, most movers even over longer distances are moving into the existing stock). Data on house prices for South East counties are available from surveys by the Nationwide Building Society (SERPLAN 1987, p. 41). For London boroughs, house price averages for 1971–81 are based on the 20 per cent Inland Revenue survey of house prices, undertaken between 1974 and 1980, while for 1980–81 the Nationwide data relating to 1981 is used (SERPLAN 1988).

7.4 Regression specification of the gravity model: the log-normal and Poisson representations

In the baseline gravity model for migration, the flow between areas i and j, M_{ij}, is directly proportional to the population masses of the two areas, P_i and P_j, and inversely proportional to the distance d_{ij} between the area centroids. Assuming multiplicative errors ϵ_{ij} and applying a logarithmic transformation gives:

$$\log(M_{ij}) = \beta_0 + \beta_1\log(P_i) + \beta_2\log(P_j) + \beta_3\log(d_{ij}) + \epsilon_{ij} \tag{7.1}$$

where β denotes the regression coefficient associated with the relevant population or with distance. Typically β_1 and β_2 are near one in value and β_3 is negative (less migrants as distance increases).

This framework may be extended to include predictions of the human capital model: that individuals will migrate to that area which offers highest discounted returns in relation to the resources of potential migrants, where such returns are evaluated over a future, possibly lifetime, horizon (Molho 1984a; Hart 1973). A move from i to j is predicted to occur if the discounted net gain G_{ij} from migration is positive, i.e.:

$$G_{ij} = (V_{ij} - V_{ii}) - C_{ij} > 0 \tag{7.2}$$

where V_{ij} is the present value of the expected real income stream if an individual moves to area j, V_{ii} is the present value of expected real income in the current area of residence, and C_{ij} are the costs of search and moving (which increase with distance). V_{ii} and V_{ij} may be regarded as the deterministic or strict components of area utility and written as functions of known characteristics of housing and labour markets, and of the characteristics of potential migrants.

The extension of model equation (7.1) to include such characteristics assumes that the comparison of V_{ij} and V_{ii} is in terms of known independent variates X_{ik} and X_{jk} (where $k = 1, \ldots p$ denotes the range of covariates). There are separate regression effects for origin and destination values of each covariate, i.e. it is not assumed that a single coefficient multiplies the destination–origin difference $(X_{jk} - X_{ik})$. However, the coefficients are not usually origin specific, though there is nothing preventing separate analysis for clusters of origins or even single origins (cf. Fotheringham, Chapter 4 of this volume). Hence — in the absence of origin specificity — V_{ij} may be conceived as $\beta_1^d X_{j1} + \beta_2^d X_{j2} + \ldots + \beta_p^d X_{jp}$ and V_{ii} as $\beta_1^o X_{i1} + \beta_2^o; x_{i2} + \ldots + \beta_p^o X_{ip}$ (where the superscript d denotes destination and the superscript o denotes origin).

Under this model, errors ϵ_{ij} and hence dependent variables M_{ij} are assumed to be log-normally distributed continuous variates, and the variance of the errors is constant regardless of the size of the migration flow. Difficulties with estimation include biased estimation of the M_{ij}, a tendency to underpredict large flows, and the treatment of zero flows (Haworth and Vincent 1979; Flowerdew and Aitkin 1982; Congdon 1989b). A small positive constant must be added to flows so that logarithms are defined, but parameter estimates may differ considerably according to the size of constant, especially if there are many zero or small flows.

Nevertheless comparison of the log-normal with other regression techniques, based on the Poisson distribution and its generalisations, should be considered in terms of the accuracy of the regression prediction of the migration flows. As discussed further below, goodness-of-fit measures oriented to assessing error specification may exaggerate the impression of 'lack of fit' of the log-normal.

Unlike the log-normal, the Poisson model recognises that each flow variable from a particular origin to a particular destination is a number or count of persons with only integer values, and follows a discrete probability distribution. Under this model, the probability of M_{ij} persons moving from origin i to destination j is given by:

$$\Pr(M_{ij}) = \frac{\exp(-\mu_{ij})\mu_{ij}^{M_{ij}}}{M_{ij}!} \tag{7.3}$$

where $-\mu_{ij}$ is the mean of the Poisson distribution. Unlike the log-normal, the variance of the migration flows is not constant but equals μ_{ij}. The mean of the Poisson may be linked logarithmically to a linear combination of logged independent variables (the latter being logged to ensure compatibility with the original gravity form).

If there are I origins and J destinations, then the regression will be over $I(J-1)$ cases since the migration within an area is not usually included in the model (e.g. for 32 London boroughs, there will be

(32)(31) = 992 origin–destination flows constituting the cases). This is the usual form of analysis, though as noted above a smaller number of flows would be involved in a regression analysis specific for (clusters) of origins.

The Poisson model can be expressed as a general linear model within the exponential family. A general linear model allows for analysis of counts in a similar way as the standard linear model for continuous variates, and permits estimation by iterative least squares. A general linear model for M_{ij} has three major features (McCullagh and Nelder 1983): an expected value of M_{ij} (such as the Poisson μ_{ij}) under a distribution specifying the random or error (unexplained) component of the data; a regression or systematic term used to explain the observed M_{ij}, which is usually a linear combination of the independent variable $\eta_{ij} = \beta X_{ij}$; and a link function relating the regression term to the mean, e.g. a logarithm in the case of Poisson regression since $\beta X_{ij} = \log(\mu_{ij})$. Estimation of the Poisson can be implemented within the GLIM package (Payne 1987) using the commands $ERROR POISSON and $LINK LOG.

The fit of the overall model (and of individual explanatory variates) and its performance against, say, the log-normal can be assessed in several ways. A distinction may be drawn between measures of fit primarily oriented to error specification and those primarily oriented to the adequacy of the regression in predicting the data. General linear models are generally assessed (as in GLIM) in terms of the deviance and the generalised chi-squared. The deviance is the log likelihood-ratio statistic comparing the model fitted to a saturated model which predicts the data exactly because there is a parameter for every case. Unlike the ordinary chi-squared (the sum of the squared residuals divided by expected values), the generalised chi-squared divides each squared residual by the variance of the expected value μ_{ij}.

When fitting count data, both these statistics reflect the appropriateness of the Poisson model for the error term, i.e. the assumption that the variance of a flow equals its expectation. For a model which correctly specifies the random error structure, the generalised chi-square and deviance should be similar in size to the number of available degrees of freedom — the number of cases minus the number of independent variables (Baxter 1985; Davies and Guy 1987). For example, the available degrees of freedom for London borough migration predicted using ten covariates including the constant is $992 - 10 = 982$. In terms of GLIM output these two measures of fit are given by %X2 and %DV respectively (though the latter is strictly the scaled deviance S, where $S = D/\theta$, where θ is the GLIM scale parameter %SCALE).

If a Poisson model if fitted and there is a considerable excess of these statistics over the available degrees of freedom, then the data are described as overdispersed relative to the Poisson. One solution is to scale up the standard errors by the ratio of the generalised chi-square to the available degrees of freedom (i.e. in GLIM a second Poisson fit is performed but with the scale parameter set as $SCALE %S, calculated from the first Poisson fit, where %S = %DV/%DF or %S = %X2/%DF).

Such a scaling dramatically improves the deviance and generalised chi-squared statistics and the standard errors of the coefficients are much closer to those values implied by the random component in the data. However, the regression predictions $\hat{\mu}_{ij}$ of the migration flows are unchanged. Hence measures of simple fit to the data (i.e. adequacy of the regression specification), such as the error sum of squares or ordinary chi-squared will be unchanged. So also will be other measures of data fit for interaction matrices such as information gain, distance statistics, and so on, reviewed by Knudsen and Fotheringham (1986).

7.4.1 Empirical comparison of the log-normal and Poisson

Empirical comparison is based on migration flows between the 32 London boroughs and between the 13 counties of the South East. Three sources of migration data are used. First, the Census of 1981 provides information on moves in the pre-censal year, 1980–81. Second, the National Health Service Central Register provides migration counts (over yearly intervals) on a continuous basis since 1976 using patient re-registrations. The analysis here using NHSCR data focuses on the period 1984–87 with counts aggregated over the three relevant years. Third, the Longitudinal Study, a 1 per cent sample of census respondents linking equivalent records between the 1971 and 1981 Censuses (and extending to the forthcoming 1991 Census), provides information on migration over the ten-year interval 1971–81. Both the Longitudinal Study and the NHSCR data provide a longer time frame than the Census but the latter suffers from sampling and registration bias.

Tables 7.1 and 7.2 show the estimates of the log-normal and Poisson models for these three migration data sets using the fundamental measures of job and housing opportunities and house price relativities outlined in the previous section. This set of covariates was found to produce 'sensible' results (in accordance with expectations for migration relations in job/housing markets) across the three sets of data. In addition a contiguity dummy was included for South East counties as this has been shown to improve fit in other studies (Flowerdew and Lovett 1988, p. 301; Molho 1984a). A constant of unity has been added to all flows to ensure that zero flows are non-negative under the log-normal model.

Comparison of the fit statistics in Tables 7.1 and 7.2 show that the Poisson is not uniformly superior to the log-normal in terms of simple data fit (adequacy of the regression formulation). For example, the phi statistic recommended by Knudsen and Fotheringham (1986) is lower under the Poisson for the census and NHSCR data but higher for the

Table 7.1   Migration in London and South East England, log-normal model parameters and their standard errors

	London Boroughs 1981 Census 1980–81		London Boroughs Longitudinal Study 1971–81		South East Counties NHSCR 1984–87	
	β	SE(β)	β	SE(β)	β	SE(β)
Constant	−447.2	73.96	−33.64	8.975	14.87	3.759
Distance	−1.828	0.03614	−1.411	0.04564	−0.8369	0.1152
Population, origin	1.432	0.07909	0.7005	0.1174	0.8781	0.06149
Population, destn	1.299	0.07514	1.019	0.1039	0.5720	0.04829
House prices, origin	0.5397	0.07280	0.1890	0.1001	−0.02403	0.2169
House prices, destn	−0.2293	0.07026	−0.8751	0.1193	−1.168	0.1779
New housing, origin	−84.33	14.60	−5.745	1.758	−4.295	4.451
New housing, destn	182.8	13.13	11.17	1.504	−3.794	3.135
Growth in employment, origin	−1.322	0.8631	−0.8712	0.3617	1.886	0.5775
Growth in employment, destination	−0.2754	0.8668	2.124	0.3566	2.051	0.3749
Contiguity					0.5338	0.06898
Phi statistic*	0.138		0.203		0.051	
Error sum squares	23.41E46		5578		845E + 6	
Degrees of freedom	982		982		145	

*The phi statistic increases as goodness-of-fit declines. It has the form:

$$\phi = \sum_i \sum_j p_{ij} \ln (p_{ij}/q_{ij})$$

where:

$$p_{ij} = M_{ij}/\sum_i \sum_j M_{ij}$$

and:

$$q_{ij} = \hat{\mu}_{ij}/\sum_i \sum_j \hat{\mu}_{ij}$$

OPCS Longitudinal Study. The error sum of squares is generally lower for the log-normal, despite the tendency noted by Flowerdew and Aitkin (1982) for underprediction of large flows by the log-normal. Drawing attention to such results is not to advocate the use of the log-normal for migration counts, but to clarify its performance in terms of commonly used measures of data fit (including measures of regression specification) for spatial interaction models.

What is also apparent, and significant in terms of the theme of migration models and method dependence, is the possibility of sign reversal and changes in statistical significance under different types of model. Thus the log-normal model for London borough census data (the first two columns of Table 7.1) shows a move away from boroughs with low growth in jobs, whereas the Poisson model for the same data in Table

Table 7.2 Migration in London and South East England, Poisson model parameters and their standard errors

	London Boroughs 1981 Census 1980–81		London Boroughs Longitudinal Study 1971–81		South East Counties NHSCR 1984–87	
	β	SE(β)	β	SE(β)	β	SE(β)
Constant	− 456.2	12.42	− 48.10	10.67	14.25	0.1612
Distance	− 2.063	0.004301	− 2.101	0.04807	− 1.012	0.004426
Population, origin	1.352	0.01107	1.071	0.1345	0.8516	0.002016
Population, destn	1.404	0.01090	1.393	0.1183	0.6609	0.001884
House prices, origin	0.4219	0.009790	0.4266	0.1076	− 0.1027	0.009565
House pries, destn	− 0.1235	0.009903	− 1.320	0.1287	− 1.024	0.009102
New housing, origin	− 49.55	2.088	− 6.822	2.029	− 4.628	0.1415
New housing, destn	144.7	1.936	14.69	1.738	2.048	0.1249
Growth jobs, origin	0.8694	0.1327	− 1.710	0.4107	1.406	0.02660
Growth jobs, destn	1.907	0.1317	3.123	0.4030	1.511	0.02466
Contiguity					0.5533	0.003345
Ordinary chi square	54413		1936		103483	
Phi statistic	0.126		0.527		0.045	
Error sum squares	27.63E + 6		5788		1015E + 6	
Degrees of freedom	982		982		145	

7.2 shows a tendency to turnover between boroughs with high rates of job growth. Both models agree on showing equilibration in the period 1971–81 based on Longitudinal Study migration. By contrast, the NHSCR data shows migration turnover in labour markets to be predominant in the mid-1980s under both types of model.

Statistical significance means the extent to which a positive or negative sign actually affects migration in the quantitative sense: a positive sign on, say, new housing at destination may not be statistically significant, in which case it may be regarded as simply positive by chance. It is still possible that a statistically 'significant' coefficient is not significant in terms of real world processes — if there is a marked discrepancy between numbers of new houses and numbers of inmigrants, as noted above in the case of London. Statistical significance in migration models should be regarded as a necessary but not sufficient condition for significance in terms of real-world migration processes. In simple terms a coefficient which is twice the size of its standard error in absolute terms is statistically significant (at the 5 per cent level), though if only 'one tail' of a coefficient in the expected direction is considered, the ratio necessary for significance is reduced to around 1.7 (at the 5 per cent level) and 1.3 (at the 10 per cent level).

If we consider the effect of house price relativities at origin and destination, these have the expected sign and are statistically significant for London boroughs in the pre-censal year and in the 1971–81 decade. Both models show a move away from high-cost boroughs to lower-cost boroughs for these periods. For South East counties in 1984–87, however, only the destination effect is correctly signed. The origin effect is negative under both models, contrary to expectation. Substantively, this may be interpreted as representing the predominantly short-range nature of decentralisation at the county scale: more moves than expected to the counties of the outer South East (where house prices are lowest) are from the adjacent relatively low housing cost counties than from more distant counties. It is apparent that this origin effect is only statistically significant under the Poisson model. A separate estimation for single origins or for clusters of origins may obviate this problem (see Fotheringham, Chapter 4 of this volume).

Similar considerations apply to the effects of housing growth on migration. As was argued above, any statistical effects of this variable need to be seen in conjunction with real-world levels of house-building in relation to migration. Both models show a move away from boroughs with low rates of new private house construction towards those with higher rates (even if these rates of new construction are low in relation to migration numbers). This is so whether the period 1971–81 or the pre-censal year are considered. However, for South East counties in the mid-1980s, while the Poisson model does reproduce this expected relation, the log-normal shows an unexpectedly negative sign at destination. The impression of method dependence in theory assessment receives further backing.

While the effects of population mass and contiguity are similar as between the two models, a final contrast is apparent in the size of the distance deterrence parameter: generally greater under the Poisson specification. Indeed, it may be shown that choice of a different constant to add to flows under the log-normal affects the size of the deterrence coefficient and the direction/significance of economic variates (Flowerdew and Aitkin 1982, p. 195, Congdon 1989b, p. 90). This is, however, only likely to be a major problem when there are a large number of zero or small flows, the correction of which exerts an undue influence on the estimation.

7.5 Error specification in general linear migration models

The above section has compared the Poisson and log-normal models as applied to migration counts with particular reference to implementation using a generalised linear modelling approach. It has shown that their relative performance is best assessed using measures of regression specification and depends also on features of the data such as the general size of flows and the number of zero flows. When, however, we consider that part of a general linear model specifying the error distribution of the random component, then different criteria apply.

The Poisson assumption implies that the variance of a flow equals its expected value. So for a correctly specified model (in terms of its error structure) the measures of fit adapted to assessing error specification, such as the generalised chi-square, should be close to the available degrees of freedom. If they considerably exceed the latter then we need to model the extra-variation. If the extra-variation is not allowed for then the standard errors of the regression coefficient will be understated and their significance (e.g. as assessed via t-ratios) will therefore be overstated.

It is evident from Table 7.2 that all three data sets exhibit substantial overdispersion, albeit greater for the NHSCR data for counties of the South East than for the London borough LS data. Thus for the LS data we have a generalised chi-square of 1936 compared to degrees of freedom 982, suggesting that the standard errors are about half what they should be and the t-ratios about double what they should be. We obviously may reach incorrect conclusions about the statistical significance of an economic variate in influencing migration if its t ratio is incorrectly two rather than one as it should be.

There are several reasons why such extra-variation may occur and why it needs to be incorporated in a general linear model with both a correct regression and error specification. The use of migration counts as the response variable, with aggregation of the binary migration choice (Y = 1 for movers, Y = 0 for stayers) over individuals, may mean that important explanatory variables have been aggregated (Aitkin *et al.* 1989, p. 106). A similar potential problem from aggregation lies in the independent variables: these are typically averages (e.g. of earnings, unemployment and job growth), and taken to represent area utility. In practice there is considerable variance in opportunities and many individuals will undertake moves in response to opportunities which are in the 'wrong' direction in terms of overall averages (Molho 1986; Vanderkamp 1986).

Unobserved heterogeneity may to some extent be represented via disaggregation by age or skill group (these being important variables in the calculation of discounted lifetime returns to migration for individuals), but variation in migration behaviour will remain. This may reflect (in terms of search theories of migration) variable search strategies between individuals or households.

In technical terms, the error component is known as random utility and contrasted with strict utility to be maximized according to, say, human capital criteria. Different assumptions about the error term and form of dependent variable lead to different specifications for the distribution of the random component of the general linear model.

The Poisson model assumes that migration events are independent over time, over space and between individual movers. Over time, the Poisson model is equivalent to the assumption that the individual decision to move (hazard rate) is independent of the time already spent in an area.

There are reasons why this may not be so — the propensity to move among certain groups may decrease with duration of stay ('cumulative inertia'). Such compositional effects have been proposed as one source of parallelism — the high correlation between in and out-migration (Mueser and White 1989). Areas which attract higher numbers of migration-prone individuals — individuals who have already migrated and are likely to move again soon — will have both high inmigration and high outmigration. The behaviour of chronic movers contrasts with that of long-term residents characterized by cumulative inertia. Accordingly at the individual level a model for migration counts which allows for extra-variation corresponds to the assumption that the migration hazard rate is related to duration of stay.

In spatial terms, the Poisson assumption implies an absence of interaction or clustering, whereas in practice there is strong evidence of migration clustering. The Poisson will be invalidated by such spatial correlation.

Another departure from randomness may occur in the act of migration itself. If most migrations are taken by household units collectively rather than by individuals acting independently, then the number of persons migrating would follow a compound Poisson determined by the rate of migration and the distribution of household size. The evidence from Table 7.3 is that overdispersion exists even when household heads are the unit of analysis, suggesting that there are likely to be additional sources of residual variation even when the tendency to move as household units is taken account of.

To represent extra-variation analytically, we let an error term e_{ij} be introduced for every origin–destination pair:

$$\mu_{ij} = \exp{(X_{ij}\gamma + e_{ij})} = \nu_{ij} \exp{(X_{ij}\gamma)} \tag{7.4}$$

This implies a tractable form for the probability of different numbers of moves M_{ij} only under certain assumptions. Assume ν_{ij} follows a gamma distribution with index $1/\sigma^2$, then the probability of different numbers of migrations M_{ij} follows a negative binomial distribution. The expected value of the migration random variable remains as μ_{ij}, predicted by $\hat{\mu}_{ij}$ = $\exp{(X_{ij}\hat{\gamma})}$, but its variance becomes $\mu_{ij} + \mu_{ij}^2\sigma^2$, where σ^2 is known as 'extraneous variation' (variation beyond that expected under the Poisson randomness model). Note also that the negative binomial regression coefficient, γ, is different from that of the Poisson, β.

This distribution may be fitted by a procedure known as quasi-likelihood (denoted QLNB and equivalent to full maximum likelihood) which ensures that the generalised chi-square statistic equals the available degrees of freedom. Hence the standard errors are correctly stated and the true statistical significance of the effects of economic variates on migration can be assessed.

Table 7.3 compares the baseline Poisson with models allowing for

Table 7.3　Migration by economically active household heads, Longitudinal
Study, 1971–81, a comparison of models

	Poisson		Proportional scaling		Quasi-likelihood negative binomial	
	β	SE(β)	β	SE(β)	β	SE(β)
Constant	−48.10	10.67	−48.10	14.95	−52.95	18.67
Distance	−2.101	0.04807	−2.101	0.06736	−2.272	0.08784
Population, origin	1.071	0.1345	1.071	0.1884	1.054	0.2218
Population, destn	1.393	0.1183	1.393	0.1658	1.180	0.2008
House prices, origin	0.4266	0.1076	0.4266	0.1508	0.5752	0.1743
House prices, destn	−1.320	0.1287	−1.320	0.1803	−1.177	0.2043
New housing, origin	−6.822	2.029	−6.822	2.843	−4.632	3.368
New housing, destn	14.69	1.738	14.69	2.435	13.84	3.016
Growth in jobs, origin	−1.710	0.4107	−1.710	0.5755	−2.057	0.6932
Growth in jobs, destn	3.123	0.4030	3.123	0.5647	3.355	0.6847
Orinary chi square	1936		1936		1992	
Phi statistic	0.527		0.527		0.540	
Generalised chi square	1936		982		982	
Degrees of freedom	982		982		982	

extra-variation in the error specification (the simple scaling-up procedure
and the negative binomial procedure). It uses migration by economically
active household heads from the Longitudinal Study. It is apparent that
the standard errors are increased in the proportional scaling approach.
Nevertheless all covariates remain significant. In the quasi-likelihood
negative binomial method not only the standard errors but the coefficients are subject to change as compared to the Poisson.

The QLNB version does show a reduction to near non-significance of
one independent variate, new housing at origin, though under a one-
tailed 10 per cent test for a coefficient in the 'expected' direction
significance is retained. That is, there is no longer a (markedly) significant tendency for higher outmigration from boroughs with lower rates of
new private housing development. The sizes (elasticities) of coefficients
also change under the QLNB model, though not their direction (cf. the
comparison of Tables 7.1 and 7.2 above). Such results point to the
importance of the extra-variation specification in assessing the role of job
and housing markets in migration.

It is finally noticeable that equilibration in both housing and employment markets is apparent for migration in London over 1971–81, with significant effects at origin as well as destination. Moves from inner to outer London seem to be generated not only by a search for lower house prices but by a comparison of job opportunities between inner and outer London, with higher rates of job growth and hence opportunity in the suburbs. This finding is in conformity with high rates of relocation apparent in the workplaces of recent migrants from inner to outer London. Thus over 30 per cent of economically active migrants from inner to outer London in the pre-censal year 1970–71 had an outer London workplace (15 560 out of 49 730 migrants), whereas only 10 per cent of continuing inner London residents had an outer London workplace (132 210 out of 1 238 420).

7.6 Disaggregation and migration theories

It was argued above that excess variation over the Poisson independence assumption may be due in part to aggregation of migration counts over independent variables at the micro level which are relevant to the migration decision. Such aggregation camouflages the effects of personal characteristics and also possibly distorts the effects of labour and housing market area characteristics. One way to test for this without resorting to modelling micro migration data is disaggregation by relevant variables. While area characteristics (ideally including both average and variances in opportunities) govern the comparison of returns in different potential destinations, individual or household characteristics govern the response to differences in area utility.

These individual characteristics, including age and accumulated skills, determine (a) the probability of gaining employment (or upward occupational mobility) in the area of destination, (b) the length of time under which returns to migration accrue (e.g. the length of time remaining in an individual's working career), and (c) the social and pecuniary costs of migration. Thus older individuals with greater ties to the existing area of residence, including familial commitments and/or partners also economically active, are less likely to move than young unmarried adults. Moreover, the gains to migration will accrue over a shorter period of the working life.

Skill type may be expected to influence both the size of the 'migration field' (the distance over which migration will be considered) and the influence of job and housing covariates. More educated workers may be less attached to particular locations, better informed about jobs advertised nationally, and have jobs which often require a relatively long-distance move, whether within the promotion ladder of the same firm or by changing employers. Housing costs are less likely to be a deterrent for such workers. A national labour market reflects both the relative scarcity and inelastic supply of highly skilled occupational groups. By contrast, unskilled manual workers are generally recruited within a local labour market and these types of jobs are widely available, reducing the incentive to long-distance migration (though wide labour demand differentials between areas affect the local availability of even low-skill jobs). The financial costs of moving tend to be more prohibitive (especially in areas of high house prices such as South East England), and often such workers may be inhibited by reliance on council rented housing, the allocation rules of which discourage longer-distance migration between districts and regions.

Intermediate occupational groups — including lower-paid professionals, clerical and technical workers, and skilled manual workers — may have relatively fixed occupational skills and relatively spatially extensive labour markets for these skills. This would, by itself, imply relatively high geographic mobility. On the other hand, their relatively lower incomes might place constraints on housing mobility and they would be more dependent on housing availability at reasonably low cost. Middle-income worker mobility would, for example, be constrained to potential destination areas with high labour demand but also high housing costs — a pattern characteristic of more prosperous growth zones of the South East, generally counties to the south and west of London.

Table 7.4 applies the negative binomial model to one-year census migration between South East counties in 1980–81 with a breakdown by four socioeconomic groups. Table 7.5 performs a similar disaggregation by age group of the working population. It is apparent from Table 7.4 that the responsiveness of middle-income groups to housing availability and price is greater than for professional and managerial workers. The greatest responsiveness to house price differences and to new housing is exhibited by skilled manual workers. House price effects are statistically more significant than new housing supply — perhaps a reflection of the relatively low absolute size of new housing in relation to the size of migrant flows, and the high proportion of new houses taken by local households rather than longer-distance migrants. House price differentials are significant even for low skill manual workers.

It may be noted that the 'unexpected' direction of the origin effect for house prices reflects the short-distance radial nature of decentralising moves, so that moves to low-cost counties on the periphery of the region are disproportionately from adjacent relatively low-cost counties rather than more distant high-cost counties. It is likely that a smaller spatial scale (such as the borough scale of Table 7.3) would show the expected positive effect of house prices at origin. The negative effect at origin is statistically significant only for low-skill manual workers and might be taken as evidence for spatial segmentation of the owner-occupied market by occupational group — this phenomenon has been discussed by Barlow (1989) and involves moves by lower-income workers from and to areas of lower housing cost, albeit within a generally high-cost region.

Table 7.4 Migration by socioeconomic group, South East counties, 1980–81, results from the quasi-likelihood negative binomial model

	Professional/managerial		Other non-manual		Skilled manual		Semi/unskilled manual	
	β	SE(β)	β	SE(β)	β	SE(β)	β	SE(β)
Constant	10.88	9.018	20.38	9.067	37.99	14.16	28.97	10.65
Distance	−1.767	0.1231	−2.034	0.1236	−2.489	0.1945	−1.960	0.1474
Population, origin	0.9479	0.07444	0.9849	0.07394	0.9153	0.1170	0.9180	0.08861
Population, destn	0.8400	0.07283	0.9597	0.07317	0.8126	0.1140	0.9165	0.08813
House prices, origin	−0.1679	0.5687	−0.6936	0.5731	−0.7990	0.8915	−1.460	0.6712
House prices, destn	−1.084	0.5741	−1.529	0.5777	−2.883	0.9184	−1.612	0.6817
New housing, origin	0.2540	5.761	−1.362	5.798	−6.324	9.127	−8.768	6.886
New housing, destn	5.765	5.735	7.886	5.783	12.86	9.172	8.002	6.840
Growth in jobs, origin	2.763	2.148	3.107	2.158	2.941	3.399	7.653	2.559
Growth in jobs, destn	5.720	2.153	4.859	2.160	3.734	3.385	5.585	2.558
Income growth, origin	−2.565	2.169	1.365	2.176	2.237	3.455	1.150	2.622
Income growth, destn	1.823	2.169	4.522	2.178	0.04591	3.443	3.072	2.614
Generalised chi square (= D.F.)	144		144		144		144	
Ordinary chi square	642		1169		756		521	
Phi statistics	0.069		0.077		0.166		0.119	

Table 7.5 Migration by age, South East counties, 1980–81, results from the quasi-likelihood negative binomial model

	15–29		30–44		45–retirement	
	β	SE(β)	β	SE(β)	β	SE(β)
Constant	37.66	7.641	26.20	6.768	33.83	8.285
Distance	−1.793	0.1024	−1.821	0.09068	−1.714	0.1113
Population, origin	0.8629	0.05660	0.9526	0.05024	0.9370	0.06321
Population, destn	1.022	0.05688	0.8260	0.05002	0.5692	0.06144
House prices, origin	−1.408	0.4838	−0.8880	0.4281	−0.1135	0.5222
House prices, destn	−2.268	0.4839	−1.554	0.4290	−3.009	0.5276
New housing, origin	−8.618	4.794	−0.4671	4.239	−1.468	5.192
New housing destn	2.813	4.785	3.230	4.238	−10.70	5.227
Growth in jobs, origin	5.848	1.791	2.618	1.584	2.165	1.942
Growth in jobs, destn	7.456	1.790	7.249	1.586	12.21	1.952
Income growth, origin	1.434	1.767	0.8163	1.562	2.279	1.921
Income growth, destn	4.048	1.765	1.714	1.563	0.6051	1.931
Generalised chi sq	144		144		144	
Ordinary chi sq	10844		11249		5012	
Phi statistic	0.072		0.052		0.085	

There is, however, less evidence that responsiveness to job opportunities is differentiated by skill. As in the analysis of NHSCR data for South East counties (Table 7.2), turnover rather than equilibration in the labour market is predominant at this spatial scale. Job growth effects at destination are significant for all but skilled manual workers, the lack of significance for this group possibly reflecting the location of manufacturing job change as distinct from change in total jobs. Differentials in labour demand seem to be pronounced enough to overcome the spatial search effect for low-skill workers. Also somewhat contrary to a priori expectations, the greatest distance deterrence is observed for middle-income rather than low-income manual workers. These results suggest that once low-skill workers overcome the barriers to labour mobility they exhibit similar patterns of response to job and housing opportunity as other income groups (except the highest-income professional and managerial workers). In this connection it must be remembered that the results of Table 7.4 are subject to a 'selectivity bias' in considering only those who undertake migration and not the more extensive set of stayers unable to overcome constraints to moving.

Among age groups mobile young adults show the greatest responsiveness to both job and income growth, and so exhibit the most consistent response to indicators of excess labour demand. For this group also, turnover in growth labour markets appears most pronounced (as can be seen from the high positive coefficient on employment growth at origin, pointing to higher outmigration from growth counties). These age groups seem most likely to contain repeat migrants making short-term moves between areas of greater economic opportunity. However, high housing costs are a greater disincentive to move for this age group than for the younger middle age groups at later stages in their careers. By the time retirement is approaching house price differentials may again assume greater importance (the destination house price effect nearly doubles as between the over 45 and 30–44 age groups).

7.7 Conclusions

This chapter has considered the specification of general linear models for migration. These models can be framed to take account of the discrete nature of the migration dependent variable, a factor important in specifying the form of the regression when there are many small flows. They can also be generalised from the Poisson baseline model to take account of extra-variation in the error component arising from non-randomness in migration over time, space and between individuals.

These issues of specification are important not only for technical reasons but for assessing the predictions of different migration models: for example, the turnover as against the push–pull hypothesis of job migration. In general, the chapter has found support for equilibration in labour and housing markets with significant effects at both origin and destination. Equilibration does, however, seem to be less evident in the 1980s, especially at the county scale.

The chapter has also shown how spatial scale (county versus district level analysis) can affect the direction and significance of the correlates of migration, and how important disaggregation by skill and age may be in capturing some of the micro-level influences which may be aggregated out in analysis of migration counts between areas.

General linear models are not the 'last word' for migration analysis. For example, the regression specification might be improved by, say, adopting an additive rather than multiplicative error in equation (7.1) which implies iterative estimation outside the general linear framework (Haworth and Vincent 1979). However, the general linear model approach, especially when the Poisson model is generalised to procedures for extra-variation in the error component, provides a simplified as well as a rigorous approach to the modelling of migration flows.

Chapter 8

The human capital model and its econometric estimation

William Milne

8.1 Introduction

The human capital model has had a long history in economics. Indeed, as far back as the writings of Adam Smith, it was recognized that education could be treated as a form of 'investment in human resources'. The human capital model has its basis in the theory of investment (in structures or machines) where a firm's decision to invest depends on the present discounted flow of revenues from the project less the project's cost. The question facing the firm becomes: is the project to be undertaken economically worthwhile? To make this concept clear, consider the decision by a firm to purchase a machine. If the machine is purchased, then it will generate increased revenues over the life of the machine through the increased output the machine can produce. In order to convert this flow of future revenue into a concept that is meaningful today, it must be discounted. That is, because of inflation and the opportunity cost associated with purchasing the machine, the revenue flow generated over the lifetime of the machine must be expressed in present value terms. If the difference between this present value flow and the cost of the machine is positive, then the firm would choose to purchase the machine.

This decision by the firm can also be applied to an individual or household decision to undertake a particular activity. Thus, the human capital model has been used to explain the decision to obtain more education or training through a comparison of the private and social benefits and costs (see, for example, Becker 1964 or Mincer 1974), to undertake job search by both employers and potential employees, and has even been applied to decisions regarding child-bearing. The focus of this chapter is the use of the human capital model to provide empirically testable propositions about labour migration.

The outline of this chapter is as follows: in the next section, the human capital model as applied to labour migration is set out. This includes a statement of the decision based on human capital considerations and the model as derived from individual (or household) utility maximization. In addition, the empirical hypotheses arising from the human capital framework are presented. In Section 8.3, the econometric modelling of migration flows based on the human capital model is discussed. Special emphasis is placed on the definition of the dependent variable, on the determinants of migration and their measurement, on the different econometric problems associated with cross-section versus time series modelling of migration, and an overview of empirical results that apply the human capital model to migration. In Section 8.4, possible future applications are considered which focus on techniques used in other areas that can be effectively used in the econometric modelling of migration.

8.2 An overview of the human capital model as applied to migration

To begin, it is important to note that the human capital model provides a way that, on an individual (or household) level, a decision is made to invest in human resources, whether in additional education and training or, as in this case, the decision to migrate. Therefore, the human capital framework suggests determinants of the decision that can be used in empirical analyses. In this section, a consideration of the determinants in the instance of labour migration is undertaken.

One of the first uses of the human capital model can be attributed to Sjaastad (1962). In this model, migration is viewed as an investment through which income can be augmented. The basic concept weighs the benefits of moving against the cost of moving. If the benefits outweigh the costs, then the individual (or household) should move. In the simplest model, the benefits of migrating are represented by the present discounted value of the differences in lifetime earnings at the destination and the origin. The present discounted value, as indicated in the introduction, ensures that the decision is made in today's value terms. That is, it returns the future income stream in today's prices in order that the effect of inflation, for example, can be removed. The costs are typically borne immediately and include the actual cost of moving as well as psychological costs (for example, leaving other family members and friends). The individual decision to migrate from region i to region j is based on a calculation of the following:

$$NB_{ij} = \int_{t_0}^{T} e^{-r(t-t_0)} (W_{jt} - W_{it})\, dt - C_{ij} \tag{8.1}$$

where

NB_{ij} = net benefit of moving from region i to region j;
W_{it} = earnings in the origin region i;
W_{jt} = earnings in the destination region j;

r   = discount rate, which returns the future earnings to present day prices;

C_{ij} = costs (both actual and psychological) of moving from i to j;

t_0 = current time period;

T   = end of individual's working life;

t   = the movement of time from the current time period (t_0) to the end of the individual's working life (T); and

e   = an exponential function.

The discounting in equation (8.1) is done in continuous time terms which results in the use of the exponential function. Discounting can also be done in discrete time terms. In this case the integral would be replaced by a summation (with index of summation t and initial and terminal points t_0 and T respectively) and the difference in earnings between the regions would be divided by $(1+r)$ raised to the power of $(t-t_0)$. The individual (or household) computes equation (8.1) for each possible destination and migrates to the destination where NB_{ij} is maximized, provided it is positive.

The human capital model implies that individuals will move to regions with the highest incomes. This increases the supply of labour in these regions and decreases the supply in low-income regions. As a result of the increased supply in high-income regions, there is downward pressure on wages and upward pressure on wages in the low-income regions due to the decreased supply. Therefore, this model implies that income differentials will be eliminated. This is the same result as in neoclassical growth models where factors of production (labour, capital) move to seek their highest returns and therefore these returns are equalized across regions over time.

The human capital model can be derived from an individual utility-maximization problem. The potential migrant evaluates the utility, or satisfaction, that can be obtained by living in a particular region. This utility depends on the goods and services consumed in the region as well as the amenities available in the region. Of course, the total satisfaction an individual can attain from the goods and services consumed is constrained by the income he/she receives, termed the budget constraint. Given that the individual maximizes utility subject to the budget constraint in each region, then the differences between the maximum utility associated with moving to a new region is greater than staying in the origin region, the individual should move.

In terms of the migration decision, it is more convenient to represent this utility in terms of the indirect utility function which expresses utility in terms of prices and income. This indirect utility function is obtained by maximizing the direct utility function subject to the budget constraint to obtain the optimal bundle of goods and services consumed as functions of prices and income. These optimal quantities are then substituted into the utility function to obtain the indirect utility function which has prices and income as arguments. This provides a specification similar to the migration function which is typically based on prices and income. The individual decision to choose to live in a particular region j can be written in terms of the indirect utility function (v) as:

$$v(P_j, W_j, OY_j, A_{ij}) > v(P_i, W_i, OY_i, A_{ji}) \quad \text{for all } i \neq j \tag{8.2}$$

where

P_i = vector of price of goods in region i;
W_i = individual's wage in region i;
OY_i = individual's other (non-wage) income in region i; and
A_{ij} = vector of other variables (for example, climate, availability of public goods, employment opportunities, etc.) that represent characteristics of region j from the point of view of an individual living in region i.

Adding a time dimension to the maximization problem that leads to equation (8.2) results in an equation similar to (8.1), that is, it is the difference between the wages, prices and other variables between the regions that determines if an individual migrates. Both of these equations, however, provide a theory underlying the decision to migrate and, in an effort to undertake econometric estimation, it is necessary to arrive at a specification that can be estimated. Consequently, the general formulation of the human capital model used in empirical studies posits that the flow of migrants from origin i to destination j can be written as:

$$M_{ij} = f_{ij}(X_i, X_j, c_{ij}) \tag{8.3}$$

where

X_i = a vector of variables in the origin region i which influence the decision to migrate;
X_j = a vector of variables in the destination region j which influence the decision to migrate;
c_{ij} = the cost of migrating from i to j; and
f_{ij} = a particular functional form (for example, linear or log-linear).

Equation (8.3) allows for the possibility that many variables can influence the flow of migrants between two regions. This moves away from the early uses of the human capital model where only discounted income was included. Here, the vectors X_i and X_j include all benefits associated with living in region i or region j. Because of the importance of the variables that can be used to proxy benefits, these are discussed in more detail next.

The income variable is often measured by the average wage in the region (although, as noted in the next section, this depends on the data used). While the human capital model, as given in equation (8.1), requires discounting of future income streams, this is usually not done for two reasons: first, future income is unknown and is typically proxied by current income, and, second, the discount rate is the same across regions and is therefore, in empirical work, eliminated from the specification.

Early uses of the human capital model to model migration flows ignored uncertainty, that is, they ignored the possibility that an individual may face the possibility of being unemployed if he/she moves. There are a number of ways to incorporate employment opportunities. In a theoretical way, using the utility-maximization approach, the problem can be solved by using an expected utility approach where the weights forming the expected utility would be the probability of being employed and the probability of being unemployed in the destination region versus the expected utility based on these probabilities in the origin region.

Alternatively, as followed in the model developed by Todaro (1969) for developing countries, equation (8.1) can be modified by adjusting the destination wage by the probability of employment in that region (as given by 1 minus the proportion of the labour force in the destination region that is unemployed). However, this specification forces a particular relationship between income and employment prospects and is therefore, too restrictive. To avoid this restriction, it is common to include the wage and the unemployment rate (or the employment rate) as separate explanatory variables.

However, as Isserman *et al.* (1986) indicate, measuring the probability of obtaining employment is very difficult. Using the aggregate unemployment rate ignores those workers who have left the labour force because they are discouraged. Further, it does not adequately measure the dynamics of the labour market through measurement of job vacancies on the demand side of the labour market and supply factors such as new entrants and retirements. Fields (1976) demonstrates how vacancy and job turnover rates may be better measures of labour market conditions.

Extending the model to include benefits beyond those related to earnings and employment prospects allows for many different variables to be incorporated in the specification. One interesting, and potentially important, set of variables is the effect of regional government tax and expenditure policies on interregional migration. Boadway and Flatters (1982) have shown that if migration is affected by regional fiscal policies, the equilibrium allocation of labour across regions may be inefficient in the absence of some scheme to equalize the regional governments' incomes. If, due to resource base or some other economic advantage, governments in some regions can offer more services or offer lower taxes, there may be more inmigration than would be desirable from the point of view of maximizing national output. Consequently, an empirical examination that verifies that these local government expenditures and taxes affect migration among the regions can provide a justification for a national equalization scheme. This is a continuing important issue in internal migration research since, as outlined in the next section, there is no conclusive result to date.

Another set of variables that can be viewed as benefits and, therefore, influence the migration decision are quality of life variables. Such variables include climate, as measured by temperature or average precipitation in the region, population density as a proxy for crowding and crime problems, pollution, etc. Even such qualitative variables as the desire to live near mountains or near the coast can be included.

It is also important to measure the costs of migrating (the c_{ij} in equation (8.3)). As indicated above, the most obvious of these are the direct costs of moving but they also include the cost of information-seeking and the psychological cost of leaving the neighbourhood in the origin region. Often these costs are proxied by distance between the origin and destination regions since distance is directly related to the actual cost of the move and also reflects the notion that information is more costly to obtain as distance increases. However, it may be possible to incorporate some data on the nominal cost of moving in addition to just the distance (for example, through rail freight or air costs).

In an n region system, often researchers have modelled inmigration and outmigration or net migration for each region i, where inmigration is defined as:

$$D_i = \sum_j M_{ji} \tag{8.4}$$

where outmigration is defined as:

$$O_i = \sum_j M_{ij} \tag{8.5}$$

and where net migration is defined as:

$$NM_i = D_i - O_i \tag{8.6}$$

It is noteworthy that the bi-regional flow in equation (8.3) is only determined by conditions in the origin region and the destination region. This is the traditional way that empirical research has been undertaken. However, even with this simple specification for M_{ij}, D_i, O_i and NM_i depend on the X vectors for *all* regions. That is, in modelling in, out or net migration, variables from all regions must enter the specification. In this way the migration model becomes multiregional in nature.

There is one further extension worth noting before leaving this discussion of the general specification of the human capital model. The concept of intervening or alternative opportunities was introduced by Stouffer (1940). In this case, the potential migrant may not know a priori the destination, and therefore the probability of selecting a particular destination depends on the number of possibilities that exist along the way. In particular, the chances of choosing a particular destination depends, in part, on conditions in alternative destinations. In this case equation (8.3) would have to include conditions in all possible destinations as given by:

$$M_{ij} = f_{ij}(X_1, X_2, \ldots, X_n, c_{ij}) \tag{8.7}$$

where there are n regions in the system. This specification allows the bi-regional flow to be influenced by conditions in all regions and, therefore, allows for the multiregional modelling of migration flows. However, as described in the next section, this can lead to serious degrees of freedom problems.

Before leaving this discussion it is useful to summarize some of the testable hypotheses based on the human capital model. *Ceteris paribus*:

(i)   if the wage in the destination region rises, inmigration to the destination will increase;
(ii)   if the wage in the origin region rises, outmigration from the origin will decrease;
(iii) if employment prospects in the destination region improve, inmigration to the destination will increase;
(iv)   if employment prospects in the origin region improve, outmigration from the origin will decrease;
(v)   if the bundle of amenities in the destination improves in quantity or quality, inmigration to the destination will increase;
(vi)   if the bundle of amenities in the origin improves in quantity or quality, outmigration from the origin will decrease;
(vii) if the cost of migrating to the destination increases; inmigration to the destination will decrease;
(viii) the young will migrate more than the old since the young can obtain the higher income needed to offset the cost of moving in the destination region over a longer period of time.

In the next section, the specification of models to test these hypotheses and the results will be discussed.

8.3 Econometric estimation based on the human capital model

In this section an examination of the econometric modelling of the human capital approach is undertaken. Studies based on two types of data are examined: cross-section modelling, which involves the estimation of migration of individuals or households in a particular way, and time-series modelling, which considers the modelling of migration flows over time. Both of these data types are important in testing the hypotheses outlined above and in predicting future migration flows.

8.3.1 Cross-section migration modelling

There are numerous studies of the cross-section econometric modelling of migration. This is typically because these data are more readily available from a census of the population or from a survey of individuals than are time-series data.

Usually questions about migration in a census ask either about whether you migrated in a particular period (for example, within the last year, which would allow the calculation of the one-year migration rate) or about where you were born (which allows for the calculation of the lifetime migration rate). It is quite common in developing countries for only the lifetime migration question to be asked because of respondent difficulty in interpreting the one-year question. However, for the social scientist the one-year question is preferable for several reasons. First, the lifetime migration flow, as enumerated in the census, may have taken place many years before the census or have involved many intervening moves. Planners and policy-makers may, therefore, find the determinants of these lifetime flows of only limited use since they are more concerned with recent moves. In addition, the determinant variables are usually taken from a census (or a survey) and therefore are only appropriate for a decision to migrate in a period before the census.

Whether the data are based on the period rate or the lifetime rate, the responses are either 1, indicating that the respondent moved, or 0, indicating that the respondent did not move. There are two ways to arrive at data for analysis in this case. The first method would involve aggregating the data to find how many people moved in a particular region. For example, suppose you were interested in modelling the migration between ten regions in a country. From the census data, an aggregation would be made to obtain the flow of migrants from each origin i to each destination j. This would result in a data matrix containing ninety observations of the migration flows between the regions to be used as the dependent variable. The second method is to deal with the individual data as provided from the census or survey. In this case, the data take the form of 1 if the respondent migrated and 0 otherwise. This result is what is termed a discrete dependent variable and the number of observations is equal to the number of respondents in the census or survey. In this case there are considerably more observations than would be available by aggregating the flows.

Following the first approach, the dependent variable used in a multivariate regression is usually defined in terms of the flow from i to j divided by the population in the origin i or the flow from i to j divided by the number of stayers (that is, the population less the number of out migrants in i) in the origin i. Either of these represents the migration rate between i and j, m_{ij}. This rate can either be between the regions of a country, between the subregions of a region or between cities of a country (for example, between Standard Metropolitan Statistical Areas (SMSAs) in the United States or Census Metropolitan Areas (CMAs) in Canada).

There have been many studies that estimate the determinants implied by the human capital model using aggregate cross-section census data (for convenient reviews, see Greenwood 1975 or Isard 1975).

The explanatory variables, as suggested by the derivation of the human capital model, involve measuring the benefits and costs of moving. As indicated in Section 8.2, it is common to use the average industrial wage in a particular region as a measure of income. It is preferable to use a wage rate rather than a broader concept like personal income since the latter includes income that is not dependent on a particular location (for example, savings or investment interest income). Measuring employment opportunities is more difficult. Data on both vacancies and job-seekers would be ideal. However, this is not usually available and, as a result, other proxies must be used. The most common of these is the aggregate unemployment rate in the region, but other researchers have used the growth in employment (Greenwood and Hunt 1984b), the employment to population ratio or the rate of new hirings (Fields 1976, 1982). Some variables to measure quality of life are often included. These can range from population density (as a measure of crowding or crime problems), climate conditions (Graves 1980), or cultural differences across the regions (for example, differences in languages across regions). Government fiscal variables have been used successfully in cross-section studies by Cebula (1979) in the United States and Shaw (1986) in Canada. Care must be taken in choosing these variables in order to highlight the regional fiscal variation. In this regard, national income taxes (which have the same rates across regions) are not important, but regional variations in income and sales taxes may influence the migration decision. On the expenditure side, regional government spending on goods and services are important as a measure of the public goods provided in the region while, if there is regional variation in transfer payments due to unemployment, for example, this should also be included.

The timing of these explanatory variables is also important. If the migration data comes from a census and the migration question provides a one-year migration rate, then the explanatory variables should be those of the year before the census. If the explanatory variables are in the same year as the census there can be a problem of simultaneity. That is, some of the explanatory variables may depend on the migration rate. For example, the wage rate in the destination region is likely to depend on the rate of inmigration to that region (due to increased supply of labour). The estimated parameters in this case will be biased. In order to obtain unbiased (or, at least, consistent) parameter estimates, a more sophisticated estimation technique must be used. Typically this involves estimation by two- or three-stage least squares which purges the explanatory variables of their simultaneity with the error term. Vanderkamp (1986) indicates that this system estimation approach makes a substantial improvement in the estimated parameters both in terms of meeting sign expectations and significance.

As indicated above, most often the distance between the origin and destination regions is used to proxy the costs of migrating (see Greenwood 1975).

Having outlined some of the important explanatory variables, it is useful to consider the results of some of the empirical studies. Most important, do the determinants implied by the human capital model actually explain the flows of migrants between regions? Overwhelmingly, the answer to this question is yes. In the studies surveyed in Greenwood (1975, 1985), economic variables such as wage rates, unemployment rates, etc. are important and statistically significant determinants of the flow of migrants. Second, through interpretation of the estimated parameters, most studies find that the significant variables are more important, both in magnitude and statistical significance, than the origin variables (see Shaw 1986; Fields 1982). This is somewhat at odds with the human capital theory which would predict that both origin and destination variables should have similar effects. This is one reason, as noted below, why more recent research has been undertaken with individual data.

Distance continues to play a strong role in these cross-section studies, and, as Isserman *et al.* (1986) indicate, the elasticity of migration with respect to distance (as measured by the road distance between the centres of the regions) is in the range of -0.5 to -1.5.

Quality of life variables have had mixed results in the empirical results although climatic variables tend to perform the best. Local fiscal variables have been shown to be important in influencing migration in the United States (Cebula 1979) and in Canada (Shaw 1986). In the Canadian case, Shaw concludes that these fiscal variables tend to 'crowd out' more traditional market variables. He suggests that variables like wage rates and employment prospects have less influence in determining migration among the CMAs in Canada in the decade of the 1970s than in the period before 1971. Consequently, to date, the results of whether net fiscal benefits affect migration are mixed.

Finally, Levy and Wadycki (1974), Wadycki (1979) and Feder (1979, 1980) have demonstrated that incorporating intervening opportunities plays an important role in determining migration flows.

A second approach to the econometric modelling of migration involves individual data for a given time period. These data generally come from a survey. The advantage of this approach is that there are many more observations on the individual data and, therefore, degrees of freedom problems disappear. However, with a discrete variable, estimation by

Ordinary Least Squares (OLS) is not appropriate since the unknown disturbance terms are not normally distributed. Further, estimation by OLS may result in predictions of the probability of moving that are less than zero or greater than one. Consequently, it is common to estimate this model by using either a logit (based on the logistic distribution) or a probit (based on the cumulative normal distribution) model. The use of either of these models solves the problem of bias and ensures that the fitted values lie in the range of 0–1 inclusive.

One of the advantages of using individual data is that it is closer to modelling the decision to migrate, rather than modelling the migration flow. However, there are other special problems introduced through the use of individual data. In particular, there are only observations on the benefits in the destination region for those that migrated. Both Nakosteen and Zimmer (1980) and Robinson and Tomes (1982) have shown how important the adoption of appropriate estimation schemes can be in the case of individual data. Consider the following problem. An individual chooses to migrate if the wage in the destination region is greater than the wage in the origin region. But with individual data, the wage in the destination region for those that choose to stay in the origin region is not observed. Consequently, if an equation is specified for the wage in the destination region which depends on individual characteristics (age, education, etc.) and location-specific variables, the parameter estimates will be inconsistent since the sample does not include stayers and is therefore truncated. This problem can be viewed as one of an omitted variable. In such a case, Heckman (1976) has suggested the following two-stage procedure. First, estimate the reduced form equation for whether the individual chooses to migrate for the complete sample. Since the dependent variable is discrete, this estimation is undertaken with a probit model which includes all the exogenous variables in the system. These exogenous variables again will include both individual characteristics and location-specific variables. In estimating the determinants for those who moved to the destination region, a variable constructed from the parameter estimates in the reduced form is included to account for the selection of only those individuals who moved. In order to obtain a model for individual migration which includes the wage directly (known as a structure model), it is necessary to have wages for all individuals — including the stayers. These wages are obtained by using the parameter estimates in the estimated wage equation to infer what wages the stayers would have obtained if they had migrated to the destination region. Based on this constructed wage data for the complete sample, a structural equation for potential migrants can be estimated that will show the effect of the benefits (in this case only wages, although this approach could be used for other variables) in the destination versus the origin regions. Robinson and Tomes (1982) find that a failure to account for selectivity overstates the returns to migration. Consequently, this is a very important technique which should be used more often in the future as more micro data sets become available and computers and their software can more readily handle large amounts of data (see Section 8.4).

Besides allowing for a closer examination of the human capital model through the use of individual data, it is also possible to test the hypothesis that young people have higher rates of migration than older people. As indicated above, this follows since young people have a longer period of time to offset the costs associated with migrating. There is strong support for this hypothesis (for example, Morgan and Robb 1981; Schlottmann and Herzog 1984).

Finally, the use of micro (or individual) data, also has the advantage of assisting in solving some of the unexpected empirical findings using aggregate data. For example, DaVanzo (1978) showed that unemployment rates in metropolitan areas in the United States are very important in determining individual level migration, although in aggregate data the effect is often obscured.

8.3.2 Time-series migration modelling

In time-series modelling of migration flows the data are typically aggregate. That is, it is uncommon to find data by individual (or household) over time. Even time-series data on aggregate flows are difficult to obtain and must often be estimated from published data. For example, to obtain interstate time series on net migration in the United States, a residual method must be used. Net migration is computed as:

$$\text{net migration} = \text{population change} - \text{births} + \text{deaths} \qquad (8.8)$$

Consequently, most studies in the United States rely on net migration flows. In Canada, time-series data exist for the origin–destination flows for all ten provinces and the two territories by quarter from 1961 based on data from family allowance statistics and, in recent years, supplemented by information from Revenue Canada. This is a unique data set that has been used effectively for analysis of both net and gross migration (see, for example, Foot and Milne 1989; Ledent 1986b; Winer and Gauthier 1982).

In time-series modelling of internal migration, there is an important system-wide constraint allowing for the multiregional nature of the decision process that must be imposed. A person exiting one region must enter some other region or the total number of inmigrants must sum to the number of outmigrants:

$$\sum_i D_i = \sum_i O_i \qquad (8.9)$$

in each time period. This non-stochastic adding-up constraint imposes consistency on the system and must be incorporated into the estimation scheme through cross-equation restrictions on the parameters. Placing the required restrictions on the parameters often produces more reliable estimates since, in effect, it adds more information. This adding-up constraint is relatively new in the econometric literature and has been used for net migration flows in the United States by Milne (1981) and Greenwood and Hunt (1984b) and, for Canada, by Foot and Milne (1984). Gross flows incorporating the adding-up constraint have been estimated by Foot and Milne (1989) for Canada.

The adding-up constraint highlights an important difference between time-series modelling and cross-section modelling. In the previous section, the dependent variable was either a migration rate or a discrete variable. In time-series modelling, the adding-up constraint is imposed on the flows, not the rates. This, of course, creates problems since the size of the population in the origin region determines the number of potential migrants. Therefore, in this case it is important to include, as explanatory variables, the population in the origin and destination regions. (See Vanderkamp 1976 for a further discussion of the use of population as an explanatory variable in migration models.) The other alternative is to ensure that the adding-up constraint holds even with the dependent variables expressed in rate terms. However, the parameter restrictions which must be imposed, based on the rates, are intractable.

The explanatory variables are, in general, the same as discussed for the cross-section studies. The difference, of course, is that it is necessary to have a time series of the explanatory variables.

When dealing with time-series data, care must be taken in the valuation of income. In particular, while in a cross-section model the wage rates and other income variables are in nominal (or current price) terms, it is important in time series estimation to take into account the movement of prices. This explains why both prices and wages appear in the indirect utility function of equation (8.2). It is likely that migration decisions are based on real incomes rather than nominal incomes. Consequently, most time-series migration studies put income variables in real or constant price terms. This could be made a testable hypothesis by including both current price and income variables separately. The estimated parameters could then be tested to see if they conform to homogeneity of degree zero in income and prices. That is, a testable hypothesis would be: if prices and incomes increase by the same proportion in all regions, there is no effect on net migration between the regions.

As indicated in Section 8.2 in modelling in, out or net migration, variables from all regions must enter each equation. Depending on the number of explanatory variables included, this can result in severe degrees of freedom problems (an econometric expression meaning that the number of parameters to be estimated is approaching the total number of observations). With ten regions, if the explanatory variables consist of real wage rates, unemployment rates, a government fiscal variable and population, there would be forty-one parameters (including the intercept) to estimate each equation. Given that the data used are typically annual, there are not usually more than thirty observations available. Therefore some method of conserving degrees of freedom must be found. Greenwood and Hunt (1984a) accomplish this by aggregating regions to a very small number. Alternatively, the variables for the regions other than the origin can be aggregated following a procedure suggested by Feder (1979, 1980). This method weights variables in all other regions inversely to their distance from the origin region. This is the method used in the Foot and Milne (1984, 1989) multiregional migration models.

As in most time-series models, serial correlation is likely to be a problem which occurs when the error terms are related to each other over time. Often, of course, the presence of serial correlation implies that a respecification of the migration equation to include an omitted variable is included. However, given the paucity of regional economic data on a time-series basis, the other approach is to include the autocorrelation coefficient directly into the estimation. In a multiregional framework, where the adding-up constraint is required, Foot and Milne (1990) have shown that the only tractable solution which is consistent with adding-up is for the autocorrelation coefficient to be the same in all regions. This is a very strong restriction and further research needs to be undertaken to generalize this result and also to allow for the possibility of spatial autocorrelation (which would allow the error terms across regions to be correlated).

Of course, one of the major advantages of time-series models is the ability to take into account the dynamics of the migration decision. That is, it is likely that because information takes time to acquire, migration responds with a lag to the explanatory variables. Once again, however, there can be serious degrees of freedom problems if many lags on several variables are included.

In sum, again the determinants of the human capital model have been shown to be important determinants of the migration flow in a time-series context.

8.4 Future applications of the human capital model

Perhaps the most important development in the econometric modelling of internal migration is the development and use of individual, or micro, data. By using these data, individual characteristics of the potential migrant, as well as location-specific characteristics, can be included. In this research, a better measure of the benefits versus the costs can therefore be made. There are also difficult econometric problems involved since there are sample selection and censoring biases introduced. The use of these data sets can also permit more of the migrant history of the individual to be considered. In this sense, some measure of return migration can be incorporated.

Perhaps the next most important area for further work is in the definition of the explanatory variables. While in the basic human capital model only lifetime income and costs enter, this chapter has noted that there are many other variables that are important. These include many location-specific variables and the introduction of uncertainty. In cross-sectional data sets, the level of educational attainment can influence the migration decision. Different measures of the net fiscal benefit in a region must be developed and tested empirically.

With the emergence of more time-series data a number of important developments can be expected. First, the system estimation of aggregate internal migration should become more common. The adding-up constraint that is placed on the system should not be overlooked in time series modelling. Further, this system estimation allows for two important testable hypotheses borrowed from the study of demand systems. First, the system can be tested for homogeneity. That is, if, for example, wage rates in all regions rise by 10 per cent, *ceteris paribus*, there should be no effect on migration. This hypothesis can be tested in this system-wide approach region by region. Second, the hypothesis of symmetry can be tested. In this case the hypothesis states that the effect of the wage rate in region i increasing on the flow of migrants to region j is the same as the effect of the wage rate in region i increasing and the effect on the flow of migrants to region j. These, and other, testable restrictions should form part of the econometric modelling and testing for time-series models of internal migration.

In addition, as a longer time series of migration flows becomes available, it will soon become possible to look for changes in the parameter estimates over time. Shaw (1986) has done this using census data for Canada, but the empirical analysis would be much richer using a time-series approach. In this way it would be possible to determine whether the traditional variables (for example, wage rates and unemployment rates) used in migration modelling have decreased or increased in significance over time.

There is also an important need to understand the dynamics of the migration decision in more detail. That is, not a great deal of literature has been undertaken into the lag structure associated with the explanatory variables in influencing current period migration. Associated with this is the need to explore the relationship between in- and outmigration and therefore return migration. Once again, an extended time series will help research in this regard.

Finally, particular note should be made of recently available data sets. These are panel data sets from administrative records which trace individuals over time. With these data sets the detail provided by individual level data together with the time series (and the adding-up constraint) can provide new insight into the determinants of migration implied by the human capital model.

Chapter 9

Migration and regional labour market adjustment in West Germany*

Ursula Bilger, Joachim Genosko and Georg Hirte

9.1 Introduction

Since the Second World War, many attempts have been made to give a quantitative representation of regional labour markets (Rouwendal and Nijkamp 1987). Such work is only a part of the extensive literature on regional labour markets in general (see, for example, the different articles published in Fischer and Nijkamp 1987). Research is focusing again on how regional labour markets work, since a number of recent studies have found only a weak statistical connection between the cyclical sensitivity of regional employment and unemployment (see, for example, Gordon 1985; Genosko 1988a). This weak connection reflects the complexity of regional labour market adjustment, with several possible consequences of a rise in regional employment demand — including increased labour participation as well as net migration (Chalmers and Greenwood 1985).

This 'missing link' between unemployment and employment suggests that it would be worthwhile investigating how labour supply adjusts to labour demand in regional labour markets, using an econometric model which is macro-economic in nature.

One should first consider the response of interregional net migration and of regional labour force participation rates (see Chalmers and Greenwood 1985, as well as Blattner 1981, Schubert *et al.* 1987).

However, in order to describe as completely as possible the adjustment *mechanism* it is necessary to include in our considerations changes in employment, unemployment rates, and changes in regional earnings as well as the already mentioned migration and labour force participation rates. Commuting is eliminated since the regions in our study are delimited in the way that they internalise commuting 'by definition' (Schubert *et al.* 1987).

The second section of this chapter deals with the derivation of the theoretical connection between the different components of the adjustment mechanism. Although there are many studies which employ single equation models (see the overview of Chalmers and Greenwood 1985),

*We would like to thank E. Dieterich for his helpful support in collecting data.

Table 9.1 Anticipated signs of the model of the regional labour market adjustment processes

Endogenous variable		Independent variable				
		nm	ẏ	b	ė	u
Unemployment rate	u	−	−	+/−		
Net migration rate	nm		+	+/−	+	−
Labour participation rate	b	+/−	+/−		+	−
Change in employment sector	ė	+	+/−			
Change in earnings	ẏ	+		+/−	+	−

the appropriate approach to use is a simultaneous equations model, because there are simultaneous interdependencies between the five variables identified. If simultaneity is not allowed for, the coefficients of the variables will be estimated with bias.

In Section 9.3, we present the data set and the research sample which we use for our econometric study investigating the regional labour market adjustment processes. Then we give the empirical findings for territorial units, which coincide largely with the German states (*Bundesländer*). The chapter closes with some conclusions on regional and labour market policies derived from the empirical results obtained.

9.2 The theoretical background

As already noted, there is a close mutual link between net migration, unemployment rate, labour force participation rate, and regional growth in earnings and employment. In the following sections we will explore the nature of the relations and determine which signs can be expected from the regression estimates for the different coefficients in the empirical part of the chapter, considering each endogenous variable in turn (Table 9.1).

9.2.1 Regional unemployment

First of all we will consider regional unemployment rates. They can be influenced by positive migration in a twofold way. First, net inmigration brings both employed and unemployed people into a region. So the relationship between regional unemployment rates and net migration is dependent on the proportions of both groups (Mincer 1966). If one refers to the current results of migration studies, according to which interregional migration is primarily stimulated by employment opportunities (see Gordon 1985b, and the literature quoted there), a negative sign for the coefficient relating unemployment to net migration is expected. This sign is additionally upheld by the fact that a positive balance of migration increases regional consumption and investment demands, by which token, other things being equal, regional unemployment and hence the regional unemployment rate is reduced too. The opposite is true in the case of a negative net migration.

A negative relationship also seems probable between regional unemployment rates and the changes in regional earnings. This has to do with the fact that earnings include overtime pay and the like: if an economic recession arises, firms will initially respond by shortening overtime. If the unfavourable economic trend continues, enterprises will make layoffs as the next step. A further effect argues in favour of a negative sign on the 'income' coefficient — a decreasing income per employee will have an adverse effect on the demand for products and services with disadvantageous consequences to investment and employment (demand for labour).

It is interesting to consider what kind of relationship will exist between regional unemployment and labour force participation rates (with unemployment both as effect and cause). In order to judge this relationship we should acknowledge that 'the decision to participate is more precisely a decision to undertake a job search and the costs of search and the probability of successful search may itself affect the participation decision . . . The most commonly used measure of this probability is the unemployment rate, although it is recognised that this may not adequately represent labour market conditions' (from Schubert *et al.* 1987; see also Genosko 1979).

Following this quotation, one might believe that the 'discouraged worker' or the 'additional worker' hypotheses determine the sign of the 'labour force participation' coefficient. The 'discouraged worker' hypothesis contends that labour market slackness as manifested by a rise in unemployment rate discourages people from entering the labour market and from job search, whereas the 'additional worker' hypothesis claims 'that unemployment of one family member may lead other family members to seek employment in an effort to maintain household income' (from Schubert *et al.* 1987; see also Jüttner 1972).

If both hypotheses are truly valid, the sign of the 'labour force participation' coefficient would be an open question. Since most evidence, however, indicates a dominance of the 'discouraged worker' hypothesis, we could expect a negative correlation between labour force participation and unemployment rates (Wachter 1972). In a macro context, an interpretation in terms of the 'discouraged worker' hypothesis versus the 'additional worker' hypothesis does not seem to be permitted as Mincer (1966) explains. Mincer emphasizes that a negative relationship in a regional analysis may reflect some selectivity of migration, i.e. a tendency for more job-determined individuals to move to areas with better economic opportunities.

It cannot be necessarily excluded, however, that there is a positive correlation between regional unemployment rates and regional labour force participation rates.

In particular areas of expanding job opportunity . . . and high net inmigration of labour force, individuals may have high labour force participation rates and high unemployment rates. The latter may reflect a large amount of frictional unemployment as a relatively large proportion of individuals are temporarily between jobs because of recent movement to the area and/or because the rapidly expanding job market encourages increased quits and search for improved jobs by the resident population (Schubert *et al.* 1987).

9.2.2 Net migration

With regard to migration rates, we can infer positive signs on the regional changes in earnings and employment variables, since increases in regional income and employment will promote inmigration and slow down outmigration. Higher regional unemployment rates tend to have the opposite effect (Chalmers and Greenwood 1985). With respect to the connection between regional labour force participation rates and net migration, we should expect a negative correlation because, strictly speaking, an increased labour force participation of the indigenous population would restrain and displace inmigrants. But we cannot rule out the possibility that people outside a region interpret increased labour force participation as signalling favourable regional economic development. Moreover, increased labour force participation will presumably provide additional jobs. Both facts could stimulate inmigration and at the same time render superfluous outmigration. To sum up, we can state that the sign of the regional labour force participation rate included in the regression estimate of regional net migration need not be so un-equivocally negative as might appear at first glance.

9.2.3 Labour force participation

Regional net migration rates for their part affect regional labour force participation rates because they influence labour supply. Other things being equal, an increased labour supply will lengthen the period necessary for job-searching — an effect which could extend the situation described by the 'discouraged worker' hypothesis (Jüttner 1972) and lead to a diminution of the labour force participation rate. However, before actually moving, an individual will usually be sure of getting a job in the region of destination (Rouwendal and Nijkamp 1987). Moreover, the balance of migration can alter the structure of the regional population (e.g. sex, age) by virtue of which the regional labour force participation rate may either be enhanced or may decline. For example, inmigration of large families increases the population more than the labour force and therefore labour force participation rates decrease.

Therefore we cannot, on balance, specify a priori what impact net migration will have on regional labour force participation rates, even though we tend to expect a positive correlation.

Basically we can expect increases in employment positively to influence regional labour force participation rates, since an increased labour demand should encourage people who are not currently in the labour force to become employees. (We equate labour demand and employment, although employment is a measure of already manifested labour demand. Vacancies would doubtlessly be a better demand variable, but the (official) figures on job openings are hardly reliable.) Conversely, a high unemployment rate will possibly deter (potential) employees from searching for a job and hence will lower labour force participation rates. In this case, displaced workers will leave the labour market and persons from the 'hidden reserves' will desist from searching for a job. It is assumed implicitly that individuals perceive unemployment rates as indicators for labour market conditions. As already indicated above, however, the unemployment rate is subject 'to so many shortcomings that its value as labour market indicator is more than questionable' (Genosko 1979). Regional labour force participation rates also respond to changes in regional earnings.

The simplest connection would be that labour force participation rates are higher the greater the rate of increase of regional earnings. But the relation between labour force participation rates and change in earnings may be more complex. Following (micro) economic theory we have to distinguish between the income effect and the substitution effect in the case of labour supply (labour force participation rate is a proxy for labour supply). Since both effects have opposing signs, we cannot, a priori, determine which sign the overall effect has, though usually the income effect dominates the substitution effect.

9.2.4 Employment

Another regression equation deals with regional changes in employment. Net migration rates have an impact not only on the region's labour supply, but also on its labour demand. This influence is based on the fact that in- and outmigration occur selectively, especially with regard to age and personal endowment with human capital. Furthermore, migrants will generally differ from the indigenous population and from non-migrants respectively (Genosko 1980). What the 'balance' of selection looks like depends on the type of region considered. In any case, selection influences local labour productivity.

In addition, migrants take assets with them and perhaps have income at their disposal which does not stem from labour services. Moreover, as already mentioned, migrants will induce investment (for example, investment in infrastructure facilities and in housing). Finally, migrants influence the prices of goods and services via the changes in demand they cause; in addition, they contribute to the growth of markets. Consequences of growing markets include larger production units which can realize economies of scale as well as localization and urbanization advantages (advantages of agglomerations), i.e. positive externalities for already settled production and consumption units (Chalmers and Greenwood 1985). All in all, we can draw the conclusion that there is a positive correlation between the dependent variable, changes in regional employment, and the independent variable, regional net migration rates.

As regards the development of earnings, we have to distinguish two effects. On the one hand, an increase in median earnings will promote employment via possible demand effects. On the other hand, from a neoclassical point of view, increasing earnings can affect employment via their cost effect. In view of these different effects, the expected sign of the relation between changes in regional employment and in regional earnings cannot be unequivocally fixed theoretically.

Additionally we would expect there to be a negative connection between changes in regional employment and regional unemployment rates. But such a relation between these two variables may lack statistical significance. Although Congdon (1983) as well as Congdon and Champion (1989a) arrive at different findings for metropolitan areas, Gordon (1985a) and Genosko (1988a) show in their studies that this finding is universal for greater areas, especially for rural ones. Since in our study we use regions which are very heterogeneous in nature, we see our findings as universal. In terms of labour market theory, the weak statistical connection in question follows from differences between job requirements and manpower qualifications. In metropolitan areas these differences are not so distinct since the labour market is more homogeneous.

According to economic theory, earnings should be handled in real terms. But we support in this case Friedman's (1968) argument that money illusion in labour supply has to be allowed for. In particular, workers contract in money wages, so perceived money wages invariably equal actual money wages. This is not always the case for real wages, since workers may implicitly evaluate money wages by a price level which is not the actual current one (Schubert *et al.* 1987). According to economic theory, we should also take into account non-labour income. But since no regionalized data are available for this issue we cannot include a relevant variable in our regression estimates.

9.2.5 Earnings

Finally, we will deal with changes in regional median earnings, since we also consider earnings per employee as an endogenous variable. A rise of regional unemployment rates should lead to a decrease of median regional earnings because we can assume that increasing unemployment symbolizes an economic slackening and will lead to a reduction of over-time. Reduced overtime pay, however, will reduce earnings, of which overtime pay is part. In addition, more unemployed persons (and hence an increasing excess labour supply) will slow down the monetary wage increase. The opposite with apply in the case of an economic upswing.

Analogous to the previous arguments, more employees should positively influence changes in regional earnings per employee. This argument, however, holds only if the increase in earnings exceeds the increase in employees. This, in turn, is only true if predominantly higher-wage employees are hired in the region concerned.

On the other hand, there will be a negative relation expected between increases in labour force participation rates and regional median earnings. This assertion can be deduced from the fact that low labour force participation rates mean a low regional labour supply (or a positive excess labour demand) and hence an increase in earnings according to the usual supply–demand frame. Since, however, labour force participation rates also include unemployed people according to official statistics, a positive sign on the labour force participation variable cannot be completely excluded. Something like the 'additional worker' hypothesis could appear and (unemployed) migrants could be attracted by such a region respectively. Both facts would increase labour force participation. Presumably a positive relationship exists between the change of average earnings and net migration because 'the presence of higher wages in other regions may be an important cause of the desire to migrate' (Rouwendal and Nijkamp 1987, p. 101).

9.3 Empirical evidence

9.3.1 The data set

In this section we briefly describe the data employed for estimating the equations which we will formulate below following our explanations in Section 9.2.

First, we should emphasize that the estimated period of our time series analyses extends from 1963 and 1964 respectively to 1986. The Federal Republic of Germany (excluding West Berlin) forms the research sample. In principle the research sample consists of the German states except that the cities of Hamburg and Bremen are annexed to the states of Schleswig-Holstein and Lower Saxony. We follow this procedure so as to take into account the fact that migration in Hamburg and Bremen, if taken as independent units, would be relatively strongly characterized by non-labour-market-conditioned motives (see on this latter issue Rouwendal and Nijkamp 1987 and the literature quoted there). The exclusion of West Berlin is determined by the special geographical and political situation of the city which would also bias the net migration

Table 9.2 Average values of the defined variables, 1963–86

Region	$\dot{e}_i$	nm_i	$\dot{y}_i$	u_i	b_i
Schleswig-Holstein/Hamburg	1.0083	0.00247	1.0696	4.13	0.4335
Lower Saxony/Bremen	1.0084	0.00194	1.0703	4.77	0.4168
Nordrhein-Westfalen	0.9970	0.00166	1.0696	4.21	0.4088
Hessen	1.0127	0.00515	1.0706	3.03	0.4378
Rheinland-Pfalz/Saarland	1.0104	0.00140	1.0687	3.92	0.4124
Baden-Württemberg	1.0152	0.00402	1.0713	2.17	0.4603
Bavaria	1.0186	0.00461	1.0721	3.69	0.4638
Unweighted average over all regions	1.0101	0.00304	1.0703	3.70	0.4333

rate within our survey. Rheinland-Pfalz/Saarland is treated as a unit conditioned by data availability. Accordingly, the research sample contains seven 'regions'. All (raw) data are taken from the official statistics as they are published in the Statistical Yearbook of the Federal Republic of Germany, in the Official News of the Federal Labour Office, and in the Social Statistics of the Secretary of Labour.

Definitions of the variables used are as follows: $\dot{e}_i$ the rate of change of employment in region i, is a quotient consisting of the employment in year t as numerator and the employment in year $t - 1$ as denominator, where the respective figures are taken from the annual micro-census; nm_i, the regional net migration rate, is calculated using the regional migration balance (inmigrants minus outmigrants) of the economically active population (people dependently employed plus unemployed) in year t and the accompanying regional population in year $t - 1$; $\dot{y}_i$, the rate of change of median (gross) earnings, where the earnings are determined by the weekly wages of industrial workers and by the monthly salaries of employees in manufacturing industry and commerce; u_i, the unemployment rate of region i, where the figures are taken from the Statistical Yearbook; and b_i, the labour force participation rate of region i, is expressed as the proportion between region's i employees and population. The average values of the variables are presented in Table 9.2.

The variables just defined are elements in the following estimate equations:

$$u_i(t) = \alpha_0 + \alpha_1 nm_i(t) + \alpha_2 b_i(t) + \alpha_3 \dot{y}_i(t-1) + \alpha_4 \dot{e}_i(t-1) + e_1 \qquad (9.1)$$

$$nm_i(t) = \beta_0 + \beta_1 u_i(t-1) + \beta_2 \dot{y}_i(t) + \beta_3 \dot{e}_i(t) + \beta_4 b_i(t-1) + e_2 \qquad (9.2)$$

$$b_i(t) = \delta_0 + \delta_1 u_i(t-1) + \delta_2 \dot{y}_i(t) + \delta_3 \dot{e}_i(t) + \delta_4 nm_i(t-1) + e_3 \qquad (9.3)$$

$$\dot{e}_i(t) = \epsilon_0 + \epsilon_1 nm_i(t-1) + \epsilon_2 \dot{y}_i(t) + \epsilon_3 u_i(t-1) + e_4 \qquad (9.4)$$

$$\dot{y}_i(t) = \mu_0 + \mu_1\hat{u}_i(t) + \mu_2\hat{e}_i^2(t) + \mu_3\hat{b}_i(t) + \mu_4\hat{n}m_i(t) + e_5 \tag{9.5}$$

In order to estimate the equations (9.1)–(9.4) we can use the common ordinary least square procedure (OLS), though we assume mutual links among the variables employed. This is possible, since the employed lag structures fix unambiguously the directions of relations among the variables. In other words, we need not fear simultaneous equations bias for these four equations. But our statements are not correct with regard to equation (9.5). If we consider $\dot{y}_i(t)$ as an endogenous variable, we have to use the two-stage, least square methods (2SLS) on equation (9.5).

We have not described the chosen lag structures in detail since they can be taken from Genosko (1989). We would just like to point out that we have chosen the special lag structure because of data availability and not by chance. Some other aspects, such as identification, underline this choice. As mentioned above, we have described the adjustment mechanism of the five correlated labour market determinants and not micro-behavioural equations. We are conscious of possible biases, but they influence only the size and not the direction of the coefficients (e.g. autocorrelation of the residuals).

With regard to the resulting temporal autocorrelation of the residuals, it is worth noting that an additional time-dependent variable, such as a business-cycle indicator, would diminish these problems but it would create multicollinearities. Since we are interested only in the correlation between the above-presented variables and in the signs and approximate magnitudes of the coefficients we will accept the resulting distortions.

The last point we would like to mention is our preference for the use of a two-tail test on account of the theoretically equivocal sign of most coefficients (a one-tail test is used when we can be sure a coefficient can only be expected to have one sign).

9.4 The findings

The results of our estimates based on the equations in Section 9.3 are presented in Tables 9.3–9.7 (although the tables do not contain estimated values of the intercepts).

9.4.1 Regional unemployment

Starting with the results in Table 9.3, we can see that regional net migration rates (nm_i) show the predicted negative effects on unemployment. However, the coefficients are only statistically significant for the regions Schleswig-Holstein/Hamburg, Nordrhein-Westfalen, Baden-Wüttemberg, and Bavaria (for the other areas the sign is only significant at a 10% level). With regard to the size of the coefficients, considerable differences

Table 9.3   OLS estimates of regional unemployment rates

	$nm_i(t)$	$b_i(t)$	$\dot{y}_i(t-1)$	$\dot{e}_i(t-1)$	$\bar{R}^2$	DW
Schleswig-Holstein/	69.08 [†]	6.05	− 5.44 [†]	− 4.07	0.567	0.497
Hamburg	(2.289)	(1.116)	(2.530)	(0.188)		
Lower Saxony/	− 38.022	1.243	− 6.271[†]	− 1.430	0.496	0.510
Bremen	(1.394)	(0.244)	(2.615)	(0.901)		
Nordrhein-	− 40.865*	− 15.340*	− 3.077[‡]	3.466	0.660	0.818
Westfalen	(2.871)	(3.054)	(2.140)	(0.994)		
Hessen	− 3.671	− 0.752	− 4.030[†]	− 1.456	0.462	0.683
	(1.465)	(0.254)	(2.684)	(1.459)		
Rheinland-Pfalz/	− 48.696	3.837	− 2.799	− 1.135	0.323	0.464
Saarland	(1.629)	(1.012)	(1.465)	(0.995)		
Baden-Württemberg	− 19.825*	0.782	− 3.404*	− 0.123	0.655	0.580
	(4.200)	(0.501)	(3.853)	(0.232)		
Bavaria	− 36.773*	2.479	− 3.233*	− 0.634	0.711	0.916
	(4.562)	(1.706)	(3.126)	(1.295)		

Notes:
(i) Critical t-values in brackets.
(ii) $\bar{R}^2$ is the adjusted R^2 (R^2 divided by the number of observations. $\bar{R}^2$ is used in order to compare different estimations).
(iii) * Significant at the 1% level.
  [†] Significant at the 2% level.
  [‡] Significant at the 5% level.
(iv) DW = Durbin–Watson statistic.

exist. Since the negative correlation between these variables depends on the net migration structure, it is not surprising that high unemployment areas tend to be characterized by high values of these coefficients. It is absolutely plausible that in such areas the proportions of inmigrants among the employed and the proportions of outmigrants among the unemployed are especially high. However, as Egle and Apfelthaler (1979) show, a high unemployment rate does not necessarily mean difficult labour market conditions. This depends rather upon what brought about the high unemployment rate.

All coefficients of the labour force participation rates in Table 9.3 are insignificantly positive with the exception of Nordrhein-Westfalen and Hessen areas. In both areas the sign is negative, but it is only significant in the case of Nordrhein-Westfalen. According to our exposition in Section 9.2, three different kinds of explanations are basically possible. But we believe that the positive signs can be best explained by expanding job opportunities in the regions concerned. On the other hand, the negative signs point at a selectivity in migration, i.e. more job-determined individuals move to these areas. In our opinion this is especially true in the case of Nordrhein-Westfalen.

As expected, the relations between regional median earnings and regional unemployment rates are negative in all cases and statistically significant, too. Only the Rheinland-Pfalz/Saarland region shows no statistical significance in its negative sign.

Confirming the studies quoted in Section 9.1, we can make no remarks

Table 9.4 OLS estimates of regional net migration rates

	$u_i(t-1)$	$\dot{y}_i(t)$	$\dot{e}_i(t)$	$b_i(t-1)$	$\bar{R}^2$	DW
Schleswig-Holstein/Hamburg	−0.000002	0.049*	0.008	0.012	0.553	0.977
	(0.015)	(3.257)	(0.686)	(0.410)		
Lower Saxony/Bremen	0.00009	0.072*	0.008	0.004	0.589	1.259
Nordrhein-Westfalen	−0.00022	0.058*	0.104*	−0.009	0.764	1.665
	(1.122)	(3.689)	(3.688)	(0.186)		
Hessen	−0.001	0.139	0.083	0.114	0.185	2.105
	(0.577)	(0.888)	(0.785)	(0.450)		
Rheinland-Pfalz/Saarland	−0.00003	0.033‡	0.009	0.001	0.318	0.920
	(0.210)	(2.202)	(0.894)	(0.047)		
Baden-Württemberg	−0.00017	0.100‡	0.051‡	0.080	0.475	0.969
	(0.244)	(2.438)	(2.161)	(1.377)		
Bavaria	−0.00008	0.081*	0.01	0.028	0.495	0.563
	(0.228)	(3.034)	(0.704)	(0.867)		

Notes: See Table 9.3

on the connection between changes in regional employment and the regional unemployment rates. The hypothesis of an absence of relation between the two variables cannot be rejected. Therefore it is not worthwhile to speculate about the signs of these coefficients for different German areas.

To conclude, we can state that regional unemployment rates depend in principle on net migration and regional median earnings. The first determinant imparts the impression that the regional labour supply is primarily determined by (net) migration.

9.4.2 Net migration

In Table 9.4 all coefficients of $\dot{y}_i(t)$ and $\dot{e}_i(t)$ have positive signs according to our discussion in Section 9.2. With the exception of Hessen, all regions have significantly positive signs of $\dot{y}_i(t)$, whereas in the case of $\dot{e}_i(t)$ only Nordrhein-Westfalen and Baden-Württemberg show a significant relation between $\dot{e}_i(t)$ and $nm_i(t)$. Since net migration is in general shaped more by regional earnings than by regional employment (Nordrhein-Westfalen excluded), we can draw the tentative conclusion that migration *per se* is not stimulated primarily by vacancies, but depends above all on expected earnings. This corresponds with the fact that the states of Hessen, Baden-Württemberg and Bavaria, which show the highest net migration rates (Table 9.2) also have the highest 'income' coefficients.

As was derived theoretically in Section 9.2, the signs of the lagged unemployment rates are negative. But they are not significant and do not entirely come up to our expectations. With the exception of Nordrhein-Westfalen, all signs on the labour force participation variable are

Table 9.5 OLS estimates of regional labour force participation rates

	$u_i(t-1)$	$\dot{y}_i(t)$	$\dot{e}_i(t)$	$nm_i(t-1)$	$\bar{R}^2$	DW
Schleswig-Holstein/	0.00008	−0.008	0.018[‡]	0.084	0.292	1.032
Hamburg	(0.793)	(0.589)	(2.280)	(0.505)		
Lower Saxony/	−0.0007	−0.099	−0.130[‡]	1.797	0.314	0.445
Bremen	(0.763)	(0.935)	(2.138)	(1.604)		
Nordrhein-Westfalen	−0.002*	−0.073	0.266[‡]	−0.064	0.501	0.530
	(2.860)	(1.115)	(2.184)	(0.084)		
Hessen	−0.00051	−0.136	0.114	0.208	0.167	0.914
	(0.277)	(0.885)	(1.531)	(0.925)		
Rheinland-Pfalz/	0.002	0.058	0.101	1.367	0.191	0.969
Saarland	(1.436)	(0.466)	(1.648)	(0.705)		
Baden-Württemberg	0.002	−0.129	0.136[‡]	1.641[‡]	0.344	1.088
	(0.758)	(0.874)	(2.122)	(2.081)		
Bavaria	0.005	0.00048	0.082	1.991	0.169	0.968
	(1.732)	(0.002)	(1.119)	(1.105)		

Notes: See Table 9.3

positive, but the coefficient sizes are in the most cases relatively small. Therefore we can infer that increasing labour force participation rates promote inmigration and retard outmigration because of their signalling effect and because of the resulting multiplier effect. Only in the case of Nordrhein-Westfalen does an increase in labour force participation seem to displace inmigration. This is not amazing because Nordrhein-Westfalen has the lowest labour force participation rate among all states considered and hence it has to make up 'indigenous employment' to a certain, even though small extent. Finally, the results of this table show that regional net migration rates are mainly determined by regional labour demand. In other words, migration is for the most part labour market-oriented (Genosko 1980; Schubert *et al.* 1987).

9.4.3 Labour force participation

If we have a look at Table 9.5, we gain the impression that regional labour force participation rates are quite differently influenced by the various explanatory variables in the different states. As we argued in Section 9.2, the signs on the lagged net migration rates are predominantly positive (but only significant in the case of Baden-Württemberg). This suggests indeed that migrants tend to have already a new job when they move to another region and that persons attached to the labour force are most likely to migrate. Only in the case of Nordrhein-Westfalen do we seem to have a situation quite similar to that described by the 'discouraged worker' hypothesis or a situation in which people who are not attached to the labour force are more likely to move into this state. All in all, this means that in fact net migration tends to increase labour supply.

Almost all changes in regional employment show the expected positive signs which are significant in the cases of Schleswig-Holstein/Hamburg, Nordrhein-Westfalen and Baden-Wüttemberg. A very striking result, however, is the significantly negative correlation between the changes in employment and the labour force participation rate for Lower Saxony/ Bremen. Does this sign hide an economically explicable connection or not? In our opinion it does, since the 'additional worker' hypothesis — which works especially in areas of high unemployment — could provide an explanation of the 'special case' of Lower Saxony/Bremen, since Lower Saxony/Bremen has the highest unemployment rate (Table 9.2). This means a great part of the new hired employees are 'additional workers'. Another explanation may be our regional delimitation. Since Hamburg is located at the border between Schleswig-Holstein and Lower Saxony, some people may work in Hamburg and live in Lower Saxony. In this case they are counted as employees in Schleswig-Holstein/ Hamburg and as resident in Lower Saxony. In this context commuting is not completely internalized.

The signs on $\dot{y}_i(t)$ are mainly negative in Table 9.5. This corresponds largely with our discussion in Section 9.2. Perhaps the 'special cases' of Rheinland-Pfalz/Saarland and Bavaria can be explained by the relatively low income levels in these states measured on West Germany's average.

The predicted negative correlation between regional unemployment rates and regional labour force participation rates appears only in the cases of Lower Saxony/Bremen, Nordrhein-Westfalen and Hessen, where only in the case of Nordrhein-Westfalen is the sign statistically significant. To verify our statements in Section 9.2, we think the unexpected positive signs can be explained by the 'additional worker' hypothesis. As we can see from Table 9.2, Nordrhein-Westfalen and Lower Saxony/ Bremen are characterized by above-average unemployment rates. Therefore it would seem obvious to use the 'additional worker' hypothesis for explanation. In the case of Hessen, further investigations are necessary since it may be possible that non-economic factors are responsible for this finding (for example, the attitude to the labour force participation of women).

9.4.4 Regional employment

With regard to Table 9.6, we need not go into detail, since there are no significant relations at all and the sizes of the coefficients are for the most part negligible. It is therefore pointless to reason about the sign of these coefficients. Furthermore the R^2 values of the estimate equations are extremely low. We merely would like to emphasize that in all areas apart from Hessen the absolute values of the coefficients of $nm_i(t-1)$ are considerably higher than those of $\dot{y}_i(t)$ and they are again clearly different from those of variable $u_i(t-1)$.

Table 9.6 OLS estimates of changes in regional employment

	$nm_i(t-1)$	$\dot{y}_i(t)$	$u_i(t-1)$	$\bar{R}^2$	DW
Schleswig-Holstein/Hamburg	1.549	0.271	0.002	0.059	1.935
	(0.364)	(0.852)	(0.694)		
Lower Saxony/Bremen	−1.566	0.158	−0.003	0.070	2.272
	(0.381)	(0.406)	(0.760)		
Nordrhein-Westfalen	2.063	−0.045	0.00063	0.133	1.884
	(1.576)	(0.379)	(0.441)		
Hessen	−0.013	−0.176	−0.005	0.055	1.819
	(0.019)	(0.382)	(1.036)		
Rheinland-Pfalz/Saarland	3.848	−0.314	−0.004	0.070	2.167
	(0.594)	(0.809)	(0.809)		
Baden-Württemberg	1.007	−0.115	−0.004	0.040	2.134
	(0.366)	(0.222)	(0.481)		
Bavaria	−4.779	0.376	−0.007	0.069	2.063
	(0.885)	(0.587)	(0.789)		

Notes: See Table 9.3

9.4.5 Median earnings

Though the R^2 values in Table 9.7 are very high, we would like to stress here that in our opinion the success of our study does not depend on the R^2 values, because we are not so interested in prognosis, but rather in the diagnosis of the labour market adjustment mechanism and hence in the testing of hypotheses.

As expected, the signs of the unemployment rate coefficients are all negative, but they are only significant in the cases of Lower Saxony/Bremen, Baden-Württemberg and Bavaria. This suggests that a reduction in overtime and hence in wages plays an important role, especially in these regions. This is plausible for Baden-Württemberg and Bavaria with their low unemployment rates and high labour force participation rates (Table 9.2). For these regions a decreasing unemployment rate leads to increasing overtime and thus to increasing wages, since their labour force potential seems to be exhausted, at least in the short run. We cannot explain, however, the case of Lower Saxony/Bremen at this stage of our study.

On the other hand, the $\dot{e}_i(t)$ coefficients are positive with the exceptions of Hessen, Rheinland-Pfalz/Saarland and Baden-Württemberg. In relation to our statements in Section 9.2, this means that in these atypical regions relatively more low-paid employees than high-paid employees are additionally hired. This might have something to do with the economic structure of these regions. In order to verify this, we would need to make further investigations.

With the exception of Bavaria, all labour force participation rates correspond to our theoretical analysis with their negative signs. The signs

Table 9.7   2SLS estimates of changes in median earnings

	$u_i(t)$	$\dot{e}_i(t)$	$b_i(t)$	$nm_i(t)$	R^2
Schleswig-Holstein/Hamburg	−0.000097	0.049‡	−0.074*	1.530*	0.981
	(1.376)	(2.268)	(3.801)	(12.136)	
Lower Saxony/Bremen	−0.0002*	0.037‡	−0.028	1.077*	0.975
	(3.268)	(2.443)	(1.619)	(12.589)	
Nordrhein-Westfalen	0.00018	0.017	−0.236*	1.113*	0.805
	(0.579)	(0.227)	(2.953)	(6.057)	
Hessen	−0.000085	−0.096*	−0.175*	0.440*	0.906
	(0.420)	(3.527)	(4.874)	(9.235)	
Rheinland-Pfalz/Saarland	−0.0001	−0.004	−0.115*	2.260*	0.882
	(0.693)	(0.317)	(2.954)	(8.094)	
Baden-Württemberg	−0.001*	−0.053	−0.099*	0.457*	0.928
	(4.588)	(1.979)	(4.800)	(5.570)	
Bavaria	−0.00034‡	0.039*	0.046‡	0.813*	0.974
	(2.094)	(3.1)	(2.180)	(8.694)	

Notes:
(i) R^2 is not adjusted.
(ii) See Table 9.3 for other notes.

are statistically significant in almost all cases. The unexpected sign of Bavaria's coefficient may be explained as follows. A rising labour force participation compensates for income losses caused by past unemployment. Therefore a development similar to the 'additional worker' hypothesis can possibly explain the positive $b_i(t)$ coefficient. This means that more high-paid workers hired than low-paid workers or unemployed individuals increase the labour force participation. Conversely, in all other regions reduced labour supply tends to increase overtime and/or wage rates and vice versa.

Finally, as elucidated above, the regional net migration rates positively influence the changes in regional median earnings, and all signs are significantly different from zero. Moreover, the last-mentioned variable exerts the strongest impact on changes in regional average earnings, considerably stronger than the $b_i(t)$ variable.

9.5 Summary and conclusions

In view of labour market adjustment processes the central outcome of our research is: bringing labour supply into line with labour demand occurs first of all via the balances of migration. Nevertheless, we must not leave out the regional labour force participation rate as a measure of the indigenous employment potential of a region, because its importance is not insignificant for the regional labour market adjustment mechanism, at least in some regions.

The last observation suggests that labour market adjustment processes are not regionally uniform. As the results in Table 9.3 and Table 9.4 indicate, (net) migration tends to play a somewhat more important role for the labour markets in Baden-Württemberg and Bavaria than for the labour markets in many other areas of West Germany. Among other things this is surely based on the high labour force participation rates of these states (Table 9.2). These rates seem to be caused not only by economic factors, but also by sociological ones, for example, the attitude to the labour force participation of women.

The conclusions with regard to regional policy are somewhat more difficult to draw, not least because the areas which have been used for investigation are relatively highly aggregated. If it actually holds true that labour market balance works above all via (net) migration, then apart from the labour market attraction of an area — by this is meant the regional employment and income conditions — its locational attraction additionally comes into play in a broader sense. Attractive areas cannot only attract migrants, but are also better able to hold their own population. If we assume that currently existing and potentially available (qualified) regional manpower is still important for the location decisions of firms and for the localization of business activities (Genosko 1987; 1988b), then the implications with respect to regional economics and regional policy are easily discernible: differences in attraction contribute to regional disparities, and are therefore to be reduced by regional policies, in so far as they are politically manipulative. In other words, regional structural policy should be more oriented to quality. This holds particularly if we take into account that readiness to migrate has decreased and simultaneously migration has become more selective (Mieth and Genosko 1982).

The activation of the indigenous employment potential should first of all challenge (regional) education and labour market policy, especially in the form of qualifying measures. These should make it possible for the human capital of the indigenous potential to enter into competition with migrants. This is of less concern to 'classic' regional structural policy. And as mentioned previously, non-economic obstacles can prevent the indigenous employment potential of a region from being exhausted.

Despite the material presented here, regional labour market adjustment processes still need further research. Apart from a more meaningful spatial structure, which should simultaneously be connected with a distinction of regions in accordance with their industrial structure — developing versus lagging geographical areas — it should be of special interest to process data disaggregated by sex. Furthermore, more polished econometric methods should be of interest. In this chapter we have only been able to deliver the first approach to research in this field for West Germany.

Chapter 10

Youth migration in the United States: analysis of a deindustrializing region

Donald Haurin and Jean Haurin

10.1 Introduction

This chapter focuses on migration to and from a region changing its primary employment base from manufacturing to services. Previous research on aggregate data has shown that during such a period of transformation, unemployment rates attain unusually high levels relative to the national average and the region experiences net outmigration, especially of youths or young adults aged 14–21. Our micro-level model analyses the determinants of migration from, and return migration back to, such a deindustrializing region.

One reason for our focus upon youth movement is that the economic rewards of migration are realized over a long period of time. We therefore expect the youth age group to be relatively more mobile than other age groups. Also, because of rapid changes in life-course events (marriage, births, divorce) for young adults, their costs of migration vary more than those of middle-aged households. At the regional level, a focus on youth movement is justified because of the interest in migration as an equilibrating force within a national economy.

In previous work on aggregate data, we found that during a regional recession, the net outmigration of youths can be large (Haurin and Haurin 1988). Although this result is predicted by regional equilibrium models, it is difficult to say which individuals in the region are most likely to react; aggregate models do not identify the factors that lead to the migration of particular individuals or families. One goal of our research is to determine if individuals migrate in response to changes in regional macro-level economic factors. We also investigate whether regional macro-economic signals are read differently by youths with different levels of educational attainment.

Another goal of this study is to determine the influence of micro-level factors on the benefits and costs of migration. Included among our benefit measures are an individual's unemployment experience and the wage differentials between the current home region and the alternative location. A variety of factors that may affect the cost of migration are also tested for their importance.

Our methodology involves applying a discrete time duration technique to a nine-year longitudinal data set. This approach allows us to avoid two problems that have plagued studies using cross-sectional data. First, potential wages in other regions are estimated based on current outcomes rather than on post-migration realizations. This approach should better model the decision process of individuals who must choose a location before they know the wage outcome in alternative areas. Second, we use contemporaneous (i.e. time-varying) values of exogenous variables to explain migration. Other cross-sectional studies analysing migration over some time period (say, five years) are forced to use either beginning of period values or an average value for the period. Because the characteristics of youth migration and regional macro-level indicators change rapidly, use of current period values for explanatory variables is necessary to predict the occurrence and timing of migration.

A measurement problem encountered in many studies of migration occurs because of the nature of the sample from which regional wage data are derived; specifically, non-workers are excluded from the sample. This limitation may result in biased estimates of the alternative wage that could be earned (Maddala 1986, p. 222). In consequence, measurement of the locational response of youth to the calculated regional wage differential is not reliable. Our methodology allows us to include data on workers and non-workers; thus the entire population of youths is in the pool of potential migrants.

To estimate regional wage differentials, we must derive potential wages that could be earned in both the home and alternative regions. For those youths residing in the home region, wages in the alternative region are not observed and must be estimated based on the wages of individuals who already live in that region. However, the residents of the alternative region may not be representative of those in the home region, as their wages would not reflect the earnings that could be attained upon relocation. This econometric problem is referred to as 'selection bias' and we use a methodology that corrects for this problem.

We also clarify the relative contributions of studies that use aggregate (macro) data and those that use individual level (micro) data sets. Formal studies of regional economies can be classified as representing static equilibrium models or dynamic growth models. In the static equilibrium framework, migration is the response to disturbances that occur somewhere in the spatial distribution of population. However, the predicted response is in terms of net migration, not gross population flows. Although theoretical equilibrium models identify the factors that will affect net migration (Haurin 1980), they do not predict which individuals in a region will migrate. Growth models differ in that they may predict continuous population movements even if no shocks occur to the system; however, they are similarly non-informative in terms of indicating which individuals will relocate.

The theoretical model of individual economic behaviour used here fills this gap because it indicates who is most likely to migrate. Based on the standard economic paradigm of lifetime welfare maximization, this model predicts that in a frictionless world, individuals and families will move through a series of localities that yields the highest level of lifetime benefits (discounted to reflect the usual preference for current benefits compared to future benefits). However, in a world with costly relocation, only those who perceive the benefits of migrating to be greater than the costs will undertake a move. The empirical implementation of this framework allows us statistically to test a variety of factors hypothesized to influence either the benefits or costs of relocating.

Which factors affect migration at the micro-level cannot be inferred from aggregate studies. It would be fallacious to assume that because macro-level unemployment rates have been found to influence net migration flows, individual level migration will be influenced by personal unemployment experiences. Rather, personal unemployment must be tested for its explanatory power. Analysts using aggregate data may be subject to the ecological fallacy; they attribute to individuals results found at the aggregate level (Simon 1978, p. 327). The detail of micro-level research is required to make the proper attribution of causes and constraints on migration.

One hypothesis we introduce is that individuals will view changes in regional unemployment rates (relative to the national average) as a signal of a structural change in the local economy. Faced with a rising rate, an individual may decide that both future employment prospects and the growth rate of wages have declined. The resulting decrease in the level of lifetime benefits occurs even if the youth is currently employed. We further test whether the response to this regional unemployment signal is different among youths with varying levels of education. Our results show that highly educated youths are the group most likely to move if a downturn occurs in their home region's economy.

In the next section of the chapter we provide descriptive tables comparing aggregate net migration of a cohort of youths in our study region with that in regions in the United States that were not deindustrializing. We then summarize the micro-level econometric model of (a) duration until first outmigration from the Midwest region and (b) duration until first return migration. The estimation of wage differentials is then described and the results of our longitudinal analysis are presented.

10.2 Characteristics of the Midwest and comparative regions

The Midwest region of the United States includes Ohio, Michigan, Indiana and Illinois, an area that contained 16.3 per cent of the US population in 1980. Manufacturing employment in the Midwest declined substantially during the study period. From 1977 to 1982, the number of

Table 10.1 Net youth migration and unemployment rate deviations (%)

Years	Midwest net migration	$U_r - U_n$	South Atlantic net migration	$U_r - U_n$	Texas net migration	$U_r - U_n$
1979–80	− 1.19	1.8	1.07	− 0.6	0.73	− 1.6
1980–81	− 0.92	2.4	− 0.38	− 0.8	5.05	− 2.1
1981–82	− 2.68	2.7	− 0.39	− 0.9	4.21	− 2.5
1982–83	− 1.99	2.9	2.09	− 1.3	0.92	− 2.2
1983–84	− 1.20	2.4	0.05	− 1.4	2.59	− 0.6
1984–85	− 0.05	1.9	− 0.03	− 1.3	1.82	− 0.8
1985–86	− 0.91	1.4	2.22	− 1.4	1.66	0.9
1986–87	0.41	1.1	1.71	− 1.5	− 4.55	2.3

Notes:
(i) The youth cohort is aged 14–21.
(ii) Location is recorded on the survey date which is generally in February or March.
(iii) Unemployment rates are average values of the two single-year rates.

employees in manufacturing industries fell by 13.5 per cent, and from 1977 to 1985 the percentage reduction was 17.3 per cent. The corresponding falls for the United States as a whole were 2.5 per cent and 4.1 per cent. By contrast, for the South Atlantic region (similar in size to the Midwest and including Delaware, Maryland, the District of Columbia, Virginia, North and South Carolina and Georgia), there were increases in manufacturing employment of 0.4 per cent and 1.7 per cent for the two time periods.

One result of the change in employment base in the Midwest was a high unemployment rate relative to the rest of the country. Table 10.1 lists the difference between Midwest's adult unemployment rate (U_r) and the national rate (U_n) in percentage points. It also lists net youth migration expressed as a percentage of the youth population for each pair of years from 1979 to 1987. Comparative statistics are presented for the South Atlantic region and for Texas, a large state which benefited from the oil boom but which experienced a severe recession when oil prices declined.

A strong negative correlation between net youth migration to a region and the local unemployment rate deviation from the national average is evident (the correlation coefficient equals − 0.77). In aggregate terms, youths respond quickly to this signal of a decline in their potential earnings and outmigration occurs. Additional evidence that youths respond quickly to changes in regional unemployment is found in the data for Texas. The turnaround in the Texas economy in 1985–86 resulted in a reversal of the continuous net inmigration (1979–86) and a large net outmigration occurred in the year following the 1986 survey.

Summary measures of the duration of stay in a region by the

Table 10.2 Percentage of the youth population remaining continuously in a region after 1979 (%)

Year	Midwest	South Atlantic	Texas
1979	100.0	100.0	100.0
1980	91.3	90.4	94.4
1981	86.1	83.6	89.1
1982	81.0	79.6	85.1
1983	75.8	77.2	80.8
1984	70.5	73.5	77.4
1985	66.5	71.1	73.5
1986	61.8	67.9	70.4
1987	58.2	64.3	67.4

Table 10.3 Return migration to the Midwest (%)

	Year return						
Year leave	1981	1982	1983	1984	1985	1986	1987
1980	22.7	28.8	40.2	37.7	35.3	36.7	40.5
1981	—	27.6	26.8	24.8	31.0	35.1	37.5
1982		—	31.3	31.5	38.4	30.9	41.6
1983			—	17.9	28.3	38.2	42.2
1984				—	15.0	23.3	31.0
1985					—	15.8	27.0
1986						—	26.4

Note: Percentages may not rise monotonically because some return migrants leave the region after having returned.

respondents in our sample are presented in Table 10.2. In the Midwest, 58.2 per cent of the 1979 resident youths remained in-state for the entire 1979–87 period. This value is lower than the percentages observed in both Texas and the South Atlantic region.

Return migration to the Midwest is reported in Table 10.3. The first row records the cumulative percentage of the youth population that returned to and remained in the region after having left in 1980. Over one-fifth of those who left between survey dates in 1979 and 1980 returned by 1981. The percentage stabilizes three years after the time of outmigration, yielding a 40 per cent return rate. In the second row of Table 10.3, outmigration occurs in 1981 and the percentage returning to the region is measured for 1982–87. A return migration rate of about 40 per cent is consistently observed for youths who outmigrated between 1980 and 1983. Return migration rates were slightly higher in Texas and slightly lower in the South Atlantic region compared to the rates observed for the Midwest.

10.3 An econometric model of time until first outmigration

A household (either a married couple or a single youth) is assumed to compare the benefits attained in the home region (the Midwest) with those attained in an alternative location. In this econometric study, the alternative region is defined as the remainder of the United States, although the model can be generalized to any interregional comparison (Falaris 1987). Benefits may include the regional differences in wages (adjusted for differences in the cost of living), differences in employment probabilities, and, perhaps, differences in amenities. Movement may be constrained by a variety of costs including hauling of household goods, loss of job tenure, costs of selling an owned home, loss of contact with family members or current friends, and search costs for a new residence and job.

The standard econometric model of this decision is a regression model with endogenous switching. In the existing literature on migration, this approach is referred to as the 'mover–stayer' model (Nakosteen and Zimmer 1980; Robinson and Tomes 1982). A switching regression model contains multiple equations; in the current application they are benefit equations. Each equation represents an estimate of the benefits attained in a particular region. A youth can migrate between regions and thus switch between benefit equations. The maximization implies that this switching depends upon which benefit outcome is best for the individual, so that the selection of the appropriate equation is determined within the model (it is endogenous).

We assume locational choice is based upon a comparison of benefits in the Midwest (B_M) to those in the alternative region (B_A):

$$B_M = \beta_M' X + \epsilon_M \tag{10.1}$$

$$B_A = \beta_A' X + \epsilon_A \tag{10.2}$$

The vector of variables, X, are the determinants of benefit levels. The cost of relocation is C, a function of a different vector of explanatory variables, Z:

$$C = \delta' Z + \epsilon_C \tag{10.3}$$

The three stochastic error terms in equations (10.1–10.3) are assumed to have a trivariate normal distribution.

The comparison of the differences in benefits between the Midwest and the alternative region to the costs of relocating yields the observable locational choice (if the youth remains in the Midwest, $I = 0$; if the alternative region is selected, $I = 1$). Thus:

$$I = 0 \text{ if } (B_A - B_M) < C \Rightarrow I^* < \epsilon$$

$$I = 1 \text{ if } (B_A - B_M) \geq C \Rightarrow I^* \geq \epsilon \tag{10.4}$$

where: $\epsilon = \epsilon_M + \epsilon_C - \epsilon_A$ (10.5) and $I^* = \beta_A' X - \beta_M' X - \delta' Z$ (10.6). Equation (10.4) is referred to as the structural locational choice model.

Once unbiased estimates of the coefficients in the benefit equations are computed, the structural locational choice equation can be estimated using a technique appropriate for dichotomous dependent variables such as the probit method. A probit model transforms the (0,1) dependent variable to a continuous variable. We thus avoid some econometric problems that occur if the ordinary least squares method is used to model the migration decision (Maddala 1986, p. 16).

10.3.1 Wage equations

Frequently, benefits are equated with wages, and wages are only observed for those youths that have selected to live in a particular region. A number of econometric studies have shown that estimates derived from a partial sample may be biased if the subsample respondents are not randomly drawn from the population (Heckman 1979). Self-selection into a region is one example that may lead to bias. Our correction methodology involves a two-step procedure. In the first step, we estimate a reduced form regional selection equation for each year using probit maximum likelihood. The sample is all civilian youths aged 18 or older in the National Longitudinal Survey of Youth (NLSY) data set which contains information on 11 406 civilian youths. Siblings are over-estimated in the NLSY and therefore we select only one youth per family to avoid clustering bias (Center for Human Resources Research 1988, pp. 41–2). From these results we compute two selection correction variables, λ_M and λ_A.

We assign the value 0 to the alternative region and 1 to residence in the Midwest (a reversal of the definitions used in the structural probit equation (10.4)). We define:

$$\lambda_{M_i} = \phi(I_i^*)/\Phi(I_i^*) \tag{10.7}$$

and:

$$\lambda_{A_i} = \phi(I_i^*)/(1 - \Phi(I_i^*)) \tag{10.8}$$

where ϕ is the density function and Φ is the cumulative distribution function of the standard normal distribution. Both ϕ and Φ are evaluated at I_i^* (the inverse normal distribution function of the predicted probability of locating in the Midwest).

In the second step, consistent estimates of the coefficients of the benefit equation are obtained if λ_M is included in the Midwest region's equation and λ_A in the alternative region's equation (Maddala 1986, pp. 257–8). If the sample is randomly distributed across regions, the correction will not matter. We follow other researchers in measuring benefits by wage rates with some exceptions noted below.

A problem not addressed by others is the limitation of observations of wage data to workers only. Migration occurs among both workers and those unemployed or out of the labour force. Estimation using only the sample of youths who select to work and application of the results to the locational choice decision of all youths is incorrect, just as ignoring potential selectivity in locational choice may bias coefficients in the wage equations. We estimate our wage equations using a tobit analysis and include all youths in a region. The tobit methodology allows the dependent variable to be partially observed (wages for working youth), while for non-working youths wages are not observed (Maddala 1986, p. 151). The potential wage a youth could earn is defined to be the predicted value from this estimation. Wage equations are estimated for single males, single females, married respondents, and respondents' spouses in each year from 1979 to 1987 and for two regions (a total of seventy-two equations).

Our wage equations are based on the standard human capital model. To allow for possible differences in the wage determinants for young men and young women, the equations for single males and females are estimated separately. Information about a spouse is limited, thus among married couples the wage rates of respondents and spouses are estimated separately. Sample size limitations prevent estimation of separate equations for married male and female respondents; we simply include a dummy variable for gender in respondent and spouse equations. Wage rates are spatially deflated using the US Bureau of Labor Statistics cost of living index as extended to states by McMahon and Melton (1978). This measure is updated over time using the regional consumer price index series.

Youths are assumed to make their migration decision in a multiperiod planning context. They account not only for current differences of wages among regions, but also for the growth in future wages. We calculate the present value of the potential wage using a five-year horizon. Estimated wage growth changes as the respondent ages; this effect is captured in the age and age-squared variables. The final conversion of this stream of wages is to an annuity, $(\bar{w})$, whose present value equals the present value of the time-varying wage, (w_t), over the planning period:

$$\bar{w} = [\sum_t (w_t/(1+r)^t)]/[\sum_t (1/(1+r)^t)] \tag{10.9}$$

The summations are from $t = 1$ to 5 and the real discount rate, r, is assumed to equal 0.035.

The variable that is entered in the migration equation is the difference in (annuitized) wage that a Midwestern youth could earn comparing the home region to the alternative regions.

We assume that residents of the Midwest compare the potential wage that could be earned in the Midwest to the wage they could earn in the alternative region. The expected wage in the Midwest by youths located in the Midwest is:

$$W_{M,M} \equiv E(W_M | \text{reside in } M) = \beta_M' X - \sigma_{M\epsilon} \lambda_M \tag{10.10}$$

where $\sigma_{M\epsilon}$ is the covariance of ϵ_M and ϵ. The probability of migration is based on the differences between $W_{M,M}$ and the expected earnings of Midwestern residents if they were located in the alternative region ($W_{A,M}$). To derive this expression note that the expected earnings of the non-truncated sample in the alternative regions $E(W_A)$ is:

$$E(W_A) = \text{Prob(reside in } A) \, E(W_A | \text{reside in } A)$$
$$+ \text{Prob(reside in } M) \, E(W_A | \text{reside in } M) \tag{10.11}$$

The expected wage of the current residents of the alternative region is:

$$E(W_A | \text{reside in } A) = \beta_A' X + \sigma_{A\epsilon} \lambda_A \tag{10.12}$$

The probability of residing in M is Φ and in A is $1 - \Phi$. Substitute these expressions and that for λ_A into (10.11) and recognize that the unconditional mean earnings are $\beta_A' X$, then solve for $E(W_A | \text{reside in } M) \equiv W_{A,M}$:

$$W_{A,M} = \beta_A' X - \frac{\phi}{\Phi} \sigma_{A\epsilon} = \beta_A' X - \sigma_{A\epsilon} \lambda_M \tag{10.13}$$

The difference in potential wages for Midwestern youths between home and alternative region is:

$$\text{WAGEDIFF} = W_{M,M} - W_{A,M} = (\hat{\beta}_M - \hat{\beta}_A) X + \lambda_M (\hat{\sigma}_{A\epsilon} - \hat{\sigma}_{M\epsilon}) \tag{10.14}$$

If the estimated coefficients of the lambdas ($\hat{\sigma}_{M\epsilon}$ and $\hat{\sigma}_{A\epsilon}$) are not significantly different from zero in the year t, then the wage differential in year t equals $(\hat{\beta}_{M_t} - \hat{\beta}_A) X_t$ which is the standard measure used in the migration literature. Estimation of the reduced form probit equation yields the values of λ_M and λ_A and the estimation of the wage equations yields values for $\hat{\beta}_M$, $\hat{\sigma}_{M\epsilon}$, $\hat{\beta}_A$, and $\hat{\sigma}_{A\epsilon}$. With this information the predicted wage differences can be calculated.

Regional cost of living indices may not fully reflect differences in living costs, one reason being the existence of unpriced goods (e.g. highway congestion). Differences in amenity levels affect locational choices but their value is difficult to measure directly. The study by Haurin (1980) indicates that compensatory wage differences among regions persist if amenity levels vary among regions. Thus, migrants may not respond to differences in the level of potential wages; rather they may respond to intertemporal changes in these differences. For example, assume the difference in potential wages between home ($6.00) and alternative region ($5.50) is $0.50 per hour for a particular youth. If, because of a structural change in the home region, the potential wage for this person falls to $5.75, the difference is now $0.25 and the extended model predicts outmigration from the home region even though a wage advantage persists. We tested for the effect on migration of this more complex measure of the change in the differential; however, the results were inferior to those derived with the simple wage measure.

An example of a tobit wage estimation for married respondents living in the Midwest in 1986 is presented in Table 10.4. Among the seventy-two regressions, variables frequently achieving statistical significance at the 5 per cent level include TENURE in job (+), being MALE (+), employment in the MANUFACTURING sector (+), and occupation as a PROFESSIONAL (+), or OPERATIVE (+). Generally, a concave relation is observed for AGE, EDUCATION and an achievement test score (AFQT). Significant less frequently were a dummy variable for race (WHITE), poor HEALTH (−), and the measure of population DENSITY (+).

Urban theory suggests that metropolitan wage rates will be positively correlated with the population size and the density of the urban area. Our measure of population DENSITY is for the respondent's county of residence. Job TENURE is measured in weeks. MANUFACTURING is a dummy variable for the respondent's industry classification. The omitted category for the respondent's occupation (PROFESSIONAL, CLERICAL, OPERATIVE) consists of service and unskilled jobs. The Armed Forces Qualification Test (AFQT) is a general measure of trainability for the armed forces and is used by the military as a test of enlistment eligibility. Rarely significant are measures of job TRAINING or the regional selection variables (λ_M and λ_A). We define a dummy variable to be 1 if the respondent received job training in at least one month during the past year. TRAINING is the sum of the dummy variables for the prior two years.

The lack of significance of the regional selection correction variables suggests that the simple present value wage differential measures are adequate; further adjustment of the wage differential for prior regional selection by youth is unnecessary. Of the seventy-two λ_M and λ_A that appear in the wage equations, only seven differ from zero at the 5 per cent significance level. This result is plausible in our particular sample. The respondents mostly live in the region where they were born, or if they have migrated, it was as children. In an analysis of migration by older adults, this correlation procedure could be most important.

Table 10.4   Sample tobit wage regression for married Midwestern respondents, 1986

Variable	Coefficient	t-value
Constant	−61.70	0.9
AGE	3.04	0.6
AGE^2	−0.06	0.6
EDUCATION	2.23	1.7
EDUCATION^2	−0.07	1.4
AFQT	0.02	0.2
AFQT^2	−0.00	0.1
TENURE	0.01	4.4[†]
MANUFACTURING	1.96	1.8
PROFESSIONAL	7.88	6.0[†]
CLERICAL	6.43	5.9[†]
OPERATIVE	5.21	3.9[†]
MALE	3.99	4.5[†]
HEALTH	−3.27	1.3
DENSITY(10^{-4})	−0.25	0.1
TRAINING	−0.39	0.0
WHITE	−0.64	0.4
HISPANIC	0.73	0.3
λ_M	−0.78	1.3
N	342	
Log-likelihood	−858.48	

* For the respondent, the wage variable is constructed as calendar year earnings divided by annual hours supplied; for the spouse, wages are annual earnings divided by the product of weeks worked annually and the typical number of hours per week; outliers (wage greater than $30 per hour) are deleted from the sample.
[†] Statistically significant at p = 0.01.

10.3.2 Migration estimation

Limitations of the data set require location to be measured as of the annual survey date. Other variables are also converted to annual values or are measured as of the survey date. Because our dependent variable is discrete rather than continuous, we select an estimation methodology consistent with this limitation.

Duration models are the appropriate estimation technique if the data set is a time series of observations of outcomes of an individual's choice process. A frequent problem with this type of data is censoring: the lack of observation of the completed series of choices. For example, in our study of migration, some youths never move. Duration models have been developed to account for this problem. We follow Allison's (1982, p. 72) approach to duration analysis with discrete data and define the hazard rate (h_{it}) as:

$$h_{it} = \Pr[T_i = t | T_i \geqslant t, X_{it}] \tag{10.15}$$

The hazard rate is the probability that migration will occur for individual i at some moment in time given that the person has not migrated before that time. T is the time of migration and X_{it} is a vector of exogenous explanatory variables (time-varying). As explained by Lee (1980, p. 12), the hazard rate is related to the more familiar survival rate. The survival rate at time t equals the probability that a person with characteristics X_{it} will not have migrated by time t. As shown by Brown (1975), the log-likelihood for this model is the same as that for the regression analysis of dichotomous dependent variables. Designating first migration with a 1 and remaining in the Midwest with a 0, the sample consists of all observations with runs of 0's (i.e. all the years over which an individual stays in the Midwest), up to and including the first 1. Thereafter, the observation drops from the sample. Time-varying explanatory variables are easily included in the analysis. We assume a constant underlying hazard rate, but test whether the rate varies with the age of the respondent. One limitation of this approach is that we assume there are no persistent unobserved variables that affect the probability of migration; that is, there is no autocorrelated error in the hazard function.

Our benefit measures include wage differentials and both macro-level and micro-level variables that are related to unemployment. The macro-level measure is the difference in unemployment rates between the Midwest and the rest of the nation ($U_M - U_A$). Variations in this measure are assumed to reflect structural changes in the region's economy relative to the rest of the country. We assume these variations act as a signal of changing future earning capacity. This variable is then interacted with variables that indicate the level of education of the respondent and spouse. HIGH-ED equals one if either adult family member has attained more than fourteen years of education; LOW-ED equals one if both adult family members have fewer than twelve years of education; the control group is the rest of the sample. Previous research (Sandefur and Scott 1981; Sandell 1977) suggests that highly educated youth are more mobile; however, we test a slightly different hypothesis. We expect changes in $U_M - U_A$ to be interpreted as a signal of changes in the regional economy. By including the series of interaction variables and $U_M - U_A$ in the migration equation, we test whether highly educated youths react to this signal differently than do youths of lower educational attainment. (The coefficient of $U_M - U_A$ reveals whether the control group reacts to the unemployment rate differential.) We also test two micro-level unemployment measures; one is a measure of the number of weeks of unemployment in a year experienced by the individuals, and the other is the number of weeks of unemployment in which unemployment compensation was not received. Schlottman and Herzog (1982) used a dummy variable (1 if unemployed at any time) and found it to be important in explaining migration in a reduced form probit analysis of migration. They also found their variable to be quite important in explaining repeat migration.

Included in the cost of relocation variables (Z from equation (10.3)) are whether the youth owns a home (HOME OWNER), reflecting the substantial transaction cost of selling a house, and a variable measuring the loss of job TENURE if the youth relocates. Increases in the levels of these variables are expected to reduce the probability of migration and to have a negative coefficient. A measure of whether the respondent has a work-limiting health problem (POOR HEALTH) is expected to lower the probability of migration (negative coefficient). Finally, we test whether single youths have lower relocation costs associated with migration than married youths and whether households with children have higher costs due to household disruption.

The sample includes male and female respondents and their spouses (if married). We identify wage and unemployment variables separately for men and women, but all other measures are for households. Included among the explanatory variables is a dummy variable for gender; it tests whether males migrate more frequently when other factors are held constant. We also test for differences in migration rates by race, self-employment and enrolment in college, factors found to influence migration in previous studies (Sandefur and Scott 1981; Spitze 1984). Finally, DaVanzo and Morrison (1981) and Sandefur and Scott (1981) have found that the probability of migration is higher for households with a history of migration. The longer an individual resides in an area, the more extensive become their personal and family ties to the location. We enter a series of three dummy variables to test for this possibility, RESIDE 4–6 YRS, RESIDE 7–9 YRS, and RESIDE 10+ YRS. They measure the length of time the respondent has lived in the Midwest prior to the survey year.

All explanatory variables are measured prior to the period in which migration could occur. As an example, for the 1980–81 migration decision, health status is measured on the survey date in 1980 and the regional difference in wages (WAGEDIFF) is measured for calendar year 1979. Migration decisions are measured from 1980–81 to 1986–87. The measure of wage difference is set to 0 for the spouse WAGEDIFF variable if the respondent is married. WAGEDIFF is defined as WAGE(HOME)–WAGE(AWAY). An increase in this variable is expected to reduce the probability of migration, thus a negative coefficient is expected.

Variable means are presented in Table 10.5 for migrants from the Midwest and for those who remained. Significant differences in means are found for job tenure, poor health, $U_M - U_A$, children, percent home ownership, percent white, residence in the Midwest for at least ten years, being enrolled in college, the female wage difference and the interaction variable of high education and $U_M - U_A$. These differences are all in the direction predicted by theory or found in previous research. The wage difference variable is negative for female migrants, indicating that a higher wage could be earned in the alternative region. The value of this

Table 10.5 Means of variables for migrants from the Midwest and non-migrants

Characteristic	Migrant from Midwest	Non-migrant	t-ratio*
TENURE	56.06	74.18	2.96[‡]
POOR HEALTH	0.03	0.07	3.06[‡]
$U_M - U_A$	2.39	2.24	3.38[‡]
CHILDREN	0.31	0.44	2.33[‡]
HOME OWNER	0.10	0.18	2.94[‡]
WHITE	0.83	0.74	2.66[‡]
SELF-EMPLOYED	0.02	0.04	1.38
SINGLE	0.74	0.67	1.80
AGE	22.80	23.20	1.84
RESIDE 4–6 yrs	0.14	0.85	1.75
RESIDE 7–9 yrs	0.11	0.10	0.49
RESIDE 10+ yrs	0.59	0.76	4.22[‡]
LOW-ED[†] $(U_M - U_A)$	0.36	0.37	0.18
HIGH-ED[†] $(U_M - U_A)$	0.54	0.29	2.99[‡]
ENROLLED	0.28	0.20	2.14[†]
M-WAGEDIFF	0.51	0.37	0.22
F-WAGEDIFF	−0.61	0.27	2.06[†]
M-UNEMPLOYMENT	6.46	5.29	1.27
F-UNEMPLOYMENT	2.36	2.68	0.46

* The t-ratio is for a difference of means test.
[†] Statistically significant at p = 0.05.
[‡] Statistically significant at p = 0.01.

variable is positive for female stayers, again consistent with our expectations. However, the wage difference variable is unexpectedly positive for male migrants, contrary to our hypothesis. It is also unexpectedly larger than the value for male stayers.

10.4 Results of analysing the time until first migration from the Midwest

Our estimates of time until first outmigration indicate that highly educated youths respond more to regional unemployment rate differentials and that the cost of migration is influenced by lost job tenure, poor health, and the cost of selling a home. We also find that women migrate from the Midwest if wage opportunities are better elsewhere. Other variables important in explaining migration are race and prior duration of residence in the Midwest. Dummy variables indicating whether the respondent was a male or was self-employed were entered in the regression, but they were not significant. We followed Henretta (1987) in treating the repeated observations of a youth over time as a clustered sample. The design effect is found to be 0.888 and our reported t-ratios are adjusted for this small effect. See Kish (1965) for further explanation

Table 10.6   Probit estimates of time until first migration, Midwest, 1980–87

Characteristic	Coefficient	t-value
Constant	−0.98	6.2
M-WAGEDIFF(10^{-1})	0.03	0.6
F-WAGEDIFF(10^{-1})	−0.15	1.9*
POOR HEALTH	−0.45	2.1*
HOME OWNER	−0.36	2.8[†]
TENURE(10^{-2})	−0.11	2.0*
SINGLE*CHILDREN	−0.15	1.2
WHITE	0.22	2.1*
ENROLLED	0.10	1.0
LOW-ED*($U_M - U_A$)	−0.02	0.4
HIGH-ED*($U_M - U_A$)	0.14	3.0[†]
RESIDE 4–6 yrs	−0.34	2.0*
RESIDE 7–9 yrs	−0.48	2.7[†]
RESIDE 10+ yrs	−0.71	5.4[†]
N	2100	
Log-likelihood	−500.09	
Mean dep. vbl.	.070	

* Statistically significant at p = 0.05.
[†] Statistically significant at p = 0.01.

of the problems resulting from a clustered sample and suggested correction methods.

The results reported in Table 10.6 reveal that highly educated youths are the group most likely to outmigrate during a regional recession. In another estimation, we included $U_M - U_A$ as a separate variable but it was not significant. So we conclude that mainly highly educated youths respond to the unemployment rate signal of regional decline.

The wage differential variable for females is significant in explaining migration. This finding is consistent with the substantial difference in means for F-WAGEDIFF reported in Table 10.5. We also interacted the F-WAGEDIFF variable with SINGLE to test whether the reaction to wage differentials differs for single as compared to married women. The coefficient of the interacted variable is near zero and insignificant, suggesting that all women's locational choices are influenced by wage opportunities. The wage differential for males is not significant. The mean value of their wage differential suggest that relatively high wages could be earned in the Midwest if they could find work. The regional recession in the early 1980s appears to have primarily resulted in a lower probability of obtaining employment, not a lower wage for jobs typically occupied by male youths. If this hypothesis is correct, male youths would migrate in response to employment prospects, not wage differentials.

Measures of respondent's or spouse's personal unemployment experience are not important factors in the explanation of migration (the estimation results are not reported). The coefficient of males' unemployment experiences was positive as expected, but the t-ratio was only 1.1. Apparently the influence of high regional unemployment manifests itself as a macro-level signal of regional decline and even employed youth who can find a job in the Midwest may leave if the prospects for the region decline.

Factors significant in increasing the cost of migration are the loss of job tenure, home ownership, and having a health limitation that affects the ability to work. Increased job tenure in the year prior to the migration decision reduces the likelihood of leaving the region.

We could have reset the job TENURE variable (measured in weeks) to zero when calculating the wage that could be earned in the alternative region; however, we chose to enter it directly in the migration equation as a measure of the cost of relocation. Also significant are the three variables that measure the prior duration of stay of the respondent up to the year before the migration decision. Their values indicate that the longer a youth resided in the Midwest prior to the survey date, the greater the reduction in the probability of outmigration. A dummy variable for the respondent's race (WHITE = 1) is positive and suggests lower outmigration by blacks during this period of regional recession. Perhaps black youths view employment possibilities outside the Midwest as more limited than white youths. Spitze (1984) also found that blacks were less likely to migrate than whites. In her tests of alternative models, she rejects the complex version that allows regression coefficients to differ by race and concludes that only allowing for a difference in intercept is warranted.

Not significant in the migration equation are a dummy variable measuring whether the youth is enrolled in college or a variable interacting SINGLE and CHILDREN. The college enrolment variable is entered to test whether the positive coefficient for HIGH-ED* $(U_M - U_A)$ reflects only outmigration of college-bound youths. Entering the ENROLLED variable in the estimation does not affect the interaction variable's coefficient, further supporting the hypothesis that highly educated youths are reacting to regional employment prospects. Experimentation with SINGLE, CHILDREN, and their interaction led us to only include the interaction variable. The negative coefficient is plausible; single parents migrate less, but the t-ratio is only 1.2. In a separate estimation, we entered the age of the respondent as an explanatory variable, but its t-ratio was less than one; thus the hazard rate appears to be uniform across the age range in our sample.

10.5 Return migration

Earlier, we presented data that suggested a fairly high return migration rate to the Midwest. We test two theories that explain remigration: one is that return migration is simply a result of a reversal of economic conditions; the other is that return migrants are 'unsuccessful' outmigrants. The first theory appears to be generally consistent with our aggregate data; the Midwest suffered a severe recession in 1981–82 and recovered through 1987. If the reason for leaving the Midwest was eliminated, and later reversed, return migration should occur. Support for this theory would be found in our micro-data analysis if return migration occurs as $U_M - U_A$ declines, or if the WAGEDIFF variables are significant. In the return migration analysis, the wage variables are redefined to measure the difference between the potential wage of a youth located in the alternative region and that youth's wage in the Midwest (WAGE(AWAY)-WAGE(HOME)).

The alternative theory (Yezer and Thurston 1976) is based on a model where outmigrants are selectively optimistic, this optimism affecting their pre-migration calculation of expected wages and employment opportunities. If so, then the post-migration realization of earnings in the alternative region may modify their calculation of the benefits of remaining in that region. Particularly unsuccessful outmigrants — that is, those experiencing relatively long periods of unemployment — would be likely candidates for return migration.

We compare the explanatory power of these two theories by analysing return migration to the Midwest between 1982 and 1987. The duration analysis generally includes the same set of explanatory variables as the outmigration equations, their values updated over time. Costs may again reduce the probability of moving; however, some cost measures are lower in value because of the recent relocation. For example, the average job tenure is about 40 per cent lower and ownership rates are 60 per cent lower among outmigrants compared to those who never migrated from the Midwest. The results are presented in Table 10.7.

The only variable among the benefit or cost measures that is significant (at the 5 per cent level) is the unemployment experience of male youths in the period following outmigration. The aggregate unemployment variable, $U_M - U_A$ interacted with HIGH-ED, has the anticipated sign but it is not significant. Increases in $U_M - U_A$ would discourage return migration; thus a negative sign is expected. When we enter $U_M - U_A$ independently, its coefficient is negative, but near zero and insignificant. These results are consistent with the empirical findings of Herzog and Schlottman (1983) and they support the theory of Yezer and Thurston (1976) that return migrants are unsuccessful optimists.

10.6 Conclusions

Over the time period for this study, the Midwest region lost jobs in manufacturing resulting in an increase in the regional unemployment rate relative to the rest of the nation. The region experienced a net outmigration of youths; however, a significant amount of return migration occurred.

Table 10.7 Probit estimates of return migration to the Midwest, 1982–87

Characteristic	Coefficient	t-value	Mean
Constant	−1.51	5.2	
M-WAGEDIFF(10^{-1})	0.01	0.0	−2.24
F-WAGEDIFF(10^{-1})	0.08	0.6	−1.60
POOR HEALTH	0.51	1.0	0.03
HOME OWNER	0.07	0.2	0.07
TENURE(10^{-2})	0.01	0.0	53.17
SINGLE*KIDS	0.11	0.8	0.23
WHITE	0.39	1.6	0.75
ENROLLED	−0.43	1.4	0.09
LOW-ED*($U_M - U_A$)	−0.17	1.2	0.31
HIGH-ED*($U_M - U_A$)	−0.16	1.4	0.54
M-UNEMPLOYMENT	0.02	2.1*	3.59
F-UNEMPLOYMENT	0.02	1.4	3.14
N	261		
Log-likelihood	−97.28		
Mean dep. vbl.	0.134		

* Statistically significant at p = 0.05.

Our study develops a micro-level econometric model of regional choice. The methodology typically used to study migration in cross-sectional data sets (the mover–stayer model) is extended, enabling us to analyse youth migration from 1980 to 1987. We include the potential wages of both husband and wife as determinants of locational choice and use tobit equations to extend the analysis to non-workers.

We find evidence that interregional migration is influenced by the expected benefits of moving and the cost or relocating. An increase in regional unemployment relative to the national average indicates a change in a regions' economic base. Our evidence suggests that highly educated youths interpret this change as a signal of reduced potential earnings in the home region, thus increasing their probability of inter-regional outmigration. At the aggregate level, empirical findings by Haurin and Haurin (1988) supported the hypothesis that aggregate net migration occurs to re-equilibrate utility levels among regions. The current study supports the re-equilibration hypothesis at the micro level, the agents being relatively highly educated youths.

We find support for the hypothesis that women, but not men, migrate in response to personal interregional wage differentials. Our extension of the wage differential measure to include amenities proved unsuccessful.

Costs of relocation affect the tendency to migrate. Important are the loss of job tenure, poor health, and transaction costs associated with sale of an owned home. We also find that long-term residence in the Midwest apparently increases attachment to the region, thus reducing the probability of migration.

Finally, we find the return migration probability to be associated only with a measure of personal unemployment experience. This finding suggests that unsuccessful outmigrants — those experiencing relatively long periods of unemployment in their destination region — are the most likely candidates for return migration.

Chapter 11

Race, local labour markets and migration in the United States, 1975-1983*

Gary Sandefur, Nancy Tuma and George Kephart

11.1 Introduction

There is a growing concern with the problems of poor people living in the central cities of large metropolitan areas in the United States. Some problems seem to have reached epidemic proportions in these areas. Rates of violent crime are very high, and the sale and use of 'crack' and other drugs have created what some commentators view as unmanageable situations for metropolitan police forces (Carpenter *et al*. 1988). In addition, many of these areas have high rates of out-of-wedlock births and single-parent families (Wilson 1987). Further, these areas have disproportionate numbers of adults who are unemployed or completely out of the labour force (neither holding nor looking for a job), and very high rates of utilization of public welfare and food stamps (Ricketts and Sawhill 1986). These problems have racial overtones for both social scientists and the general public because the most depressed areas of large metropolitan areas have very large black populations.

Many observers assert that a lack of adequate employment opportunities is a principal cause of these problems (for example, see Kasarda 1988; Wilson 1987). Further, the higher incidence of social problems among blacks than among whites is attributed to differences in job opportunities for the two racial groups. Wilson, for example, argues that the higher incidence of single-parent families among blacks is due to the lack of employment opportunities for black men, which makes them less able to support a family and therefore less desirable marriage partners.

Not everyone agrees that higher rates of un- and underemployment of blacks result from a lack of jobs. In fact, there has been extensive

* The research was supported by grant HD19473 to Gary Sandefur and grant HD21738 to Nancy Tuma from the National Institute of Child Health and Human Development (NICHD). Sandefur received additional support through a center grant from NICHD to the Center for Demography and Ecology and from the Institute for Research on Poverty. Tuma received additional support from the Hoover Institution on War, Revolution, and Peace and from the Center for Advanced Study in the Behavioral Sciences with funds from the National Science Foundation (BNS87–00864). We thank Jingsheng Huang, Jiwon Jeon, Ray Mirikatani, and Dan Powers for their able research assistance.

debate about the causes of black/white differences in labour force participation, employment rates, and annual hours of work. Some observers (e.g. Kasarda 1985) emphasize the lack of jobs that are open to individuals with few skills and education; others (e.g. Culp and Dunson 1986) emphasize the hiring habits and prejudices of predominantly white employers in central cities; and still others (e.g. Viscusi 1986) emphasize the opportunities in the informal and illegal labour markets of central cities, which are not reported in official labour statistics.

The current focus of social scientists and policy-makers on central cities is understandable given the concentration of poverty, economic disadvantages, and social problems in these areas. Still, understanding the factors that underlie these problems, especially the employment problems of unskilled black men, might be facilitated by expanding our view beyond central cities. There is reason to believe that social and economic changes in central cities are part of a larger phenomenon of economic restructuring of the United States, which involves rural and smaller urban areas as well as large metropolitan areas and central cities.

Some individuals are in a better position to deal with the consequences of social and economic changes than others. Individuals who can relocate to areas with better employment opportunities are more likely to escape the adverse consequences of economic decline and restructuring. As shown by previous research (Long 1988), whites are more likely to migrate than blacks, and the probability of migration increases with education. There are a variety of reasons for these differentials. For one, highly educated individuals have more extensive knowledge of alternative job opportunities. For another, whites and highly educated individuals tend to have higher incomes and can afford to search widely for better employment opportunities. For yet another, whites and more educated individuals are more likely to have professional, technical, and managerial occupations, which operate as national rather than local labour markets. Consequently, in situations of rapid economic change, such as those that occurred in the United States during the 1970s and 1980s, we expect whites and the highly educated to tend to move to areas with more opportunities, leaving blacks and the poorly educated 'trapped' in depressed areas.

If this is the case, then the urban crisis reflects larger economic and social changes, and we should observe the effects of the immobility of the disadvantaged not only in central cities, but throughout the country. In this chapter, we examine whether the evidence on the relationship between race, local unemployment rates, and migration is consistent with this view. More specifically, our first main question is: to what extent were black and less-educated individuals concentrated in areas with high unemployment rates during the 1970s and 1980s?

Second, an implicit assumption among those (e.g. Wilson 1987) who favour the 'mismatch hypothesis' (that jobs have moved to the suburbs and the Sun Belt while blacks have remained in or moved to central cities and the Rust Belt) is that migration provides a way that individuals can improve their opportunities. However, we do not know much about the relationship between migration and the characteristics of the labour markets between which individuals move. What we do know is based mainly on net migration flows between areas rather than on analyses of migration behaviour of individuals. Thus, our second main question is: how is the likelihood of migration related to characteristics of individual decision-makers as well as to employment opportunities in local labour markets? Does migration depend, for example, on income, employment situation, and family situation as well as on race and education?

Our third main question concerns the consequences of migration for the characteristics of the local labour market to which an individual moves. Do migrants indeed tend to move to places with better job opportunities? Does this tendency depend on characteristics of migrants, such as their race and education?

11.2 Local labour markets and migration decisions

Any association between attributes of individuals and characteristics of labour markets in the United States results mainly from individuals voluntarily deciding whether to remain in their present location or to move to a new one. (Children and members of the armed forces are the main groups who can be considered as moving involuntarily.) Our model of the migration decision-making process (cf. De Jong and Fawcett 1981) has three main components: (i) the decision to search for a better location than the present one; (ii) the process of searching for a better location; and (iii) evaluation of the desirability of moving from the present location to one of those considered in the search. Whether individuals are deciding to search or to move, we think that they are basically deciding if the expected gain from the activity is greater than zero, and that they perform the activity if the expected gain exceeds zero. Although gains may involve personal and familial considerations (e.g. opportunities for contact with family members and friends), an individual's employment situation is usually a major factor and is the one we stress below. A formal development of our assumptions is possible but is not needed for present purposes. Instead, we briefly discuss some key implications of these assumptions.

The decision to search is a function of the benefits received from living in the current location, the expected costs of searching for a better location, the expected benefits from living in a new location selected through the search process, and the expected costs of moving to another location. If expected gains from searching exceed zero, individuals search; otherwise, they do not. Once individuals have decided to search and have evaluated the benefits in various locations that they have selected for serious consideration (as well as the benefits in the current location), the

decision to move is based on the expected benefits from living in potential new locations, the benefits of living in the current location, and the
expected costs of moving. If their expected gains from moving exceed
zero, they move; otherwise they do not. We assume that the destination
is the potential new location in which the expected gain is greatest.

Previous findings on racial and educational differentials in migration
in the United States are easily interpreted within this decision-making
context. For example, the high degree of racial segregation in housing
and the relatively small percentage of blacks in the population (roughly
12 per cent in 1980) increase considerably the costs of searching and
decrease the expected gain from moving for blacks as compared to
whites. Partly this is simply because fewer localities are realistic destinations for blacks. That is, when blacks contemplate moving, they must
rule out many communities because they may not be allowed to locate
there due to racial discrimination in the housing market, or because their
white neighbours may make it very costly (socially and/or economically)
for them if they do move there. The model suggests, then, that blacks
are less likely to search than whites, *ceteris paribus*, because the
perceived costs and difficulties of searching are much higher for blacks
than for whites. Because blacks are less likely to search, we expect them
also to be less likely to move.

Similarly, the costs of searching for the highly educated tend to be
lower because they tend to be in professional, technical, or managerial
occupations, which often have national labour markets in which job
opportunities in other areas are widely publicized and relatively easily
monitored through widely dispersed personal networks. Moreover, when
considering potential employees who are highly educated, many
employers are willing to bear part of search costs (e.g. by inviting a job
candidate for an interview) and moving costs. Consequently, we expect
the highly educated to search more readily and also to be more likely to
move.

If we consider these arguments about race and education together, they
clearly imply that less educated blacks are much less likely to move than
highly educated whites. For example, white civil engineers in
deteriorating local labour markets are likely to know about job opportunities for civil engineers elsewhere in the state, region, and perhaps
country. Further, in most areas they are likely to find housing that they
can afford and that is open to them. On the other hand, poorly educated
black janitors in deteriorating local labour markets are likely to have at
best only vague notions about job opportunities elsewhere, and their
choices among possible new locations are constrained by difficulties in
finding affordable housing that is open to them.

Benefits of search depend on individuals' current situations, in
particular on their employment situation, and also on the economic
vigour of the local labour markets in which they reside. Those employed
full-time are unlikely to improve upon their current situation unless wage

rates in a locality do not adequately reflect human capital inputs adjusted for local costs of living. In contrast, those working part-time or not at all can often improve their current economic situation by migrating. Similarly, we expect higher unemployment rates in potential migration destinations to be associated with lower expected benefits of moving to them; therefore, we expect migrants to be less likely to move to places with relatively high unemployment rates.

During the 1970s and early 1980s, migration decisions took place in a context of increasing unemployment and changes in the distribution of job types — a decline in manufacturing jobs and a rise in service jobs (Kasarda 1988). Kasarda (1988, 1989) pointed out that the employment problems of blacks living in central cities resulted not only from a decrease in job opportunities, but also from a change in the nature of the jobs that were available. Similarly, throughout the country, some local economies lost jobs and others gained jobs, and the types of jobs changed. Whites more than blacks, and the highly educated more than the uneducated, were able to adapt more readily to these changes in local economies. Uneducated blacks had the best chances if they lived in areas that experienced an economic resurgence involving the creation of new jobs for those with no education and few skills, but such areas were few in number. Otherwise, they were likely to be 'trapped' in areas with declining opportunities. Uneducated, underemployed blacks were the most likely of all to be 'trapped' in such areas.

The combination of 'normal' racial and educational differentials in migration with changing, and often deteriorating, local labour markets leads to three specific predictions. First, we expect those with weak positions in the labour market (i.e. blacks and those with limited education, low income, and nonprofessional occupations) to be concentrated in areas with relatively poor employment opportunities. Second, after controlling for local labour market characteristics, we expect those with weak positions in the labour market to be less likely to migrate. In other words, we predict that they will be less likely to respond to local labour market conditions through migration. Third, we expect moves to be away from sluggish markets and towards more vigorous labour markets. However, we expect this effect to be greatest for those with strong positions in the labour market (i.e. whites and those with high education, high income, and professional occupations) and smallest for those with weak positions.

11.3 Data

11.3.1 Sample

The 1968–84 waves of the Panel Study of Income Dynamics (PSID) are the source of the data we analyse (Morgan 1986). The PSID is a longitudinal study of members of a sample of approximately 5000 families who were first interviewed in 1968. It collects information on a variety of items pertaining to household structure, income, employment, education, and geographical mobility. The original sample consisted partly of a nationally representative sample and partly of an oversample of low-income families. Re-interviews have been attempted annually since 1968. Although attrition has led to losses of some families and their members, these losses have been offset by the addition of new families due to children setting up their own households and by the addition of new members to many families, primarily because of births, but also because of newly formed marriages.

We focus on black and white male heads of households who were aged 18–64 in 1975–83. We follow men in this age range through time, beginning in 1975 or the first year in which they were a head of household, until they were no longer interviewed, left the labour force, ceased to be head of household, or reached age 65. We excluded men in the military from our analyses of migration and its consequences because their moves may not have been voluntary.

11.3.2 Variables and measures

We use a variety of explanatory and control variables in the analyses reported below.

INTERCOUNTY MIGRATION

We define intercounty migration as having occurred if the county of residence at one interview differs from that at the previous interview. It should be noted that this measure misses some intercounty moves when a person makes two or more intercounty moves between interviews.

UNEMPLOYMENT RATE

We use estimates of the annual unemployment rate in each county each year, which are prepared by the US Bureau of Labor Statistics and distributed by the US Bureau of the Census (1986). Although these estimates are subject to error, they provide a year-to-year view of unemployment trends for small labour market areas — a considerable advantage over information from the decennial censuses or the annual Current Population Surveys.

US UNEMPLOYMENT RATE

Since we are primarily interested in variation across local labour markets, and since county unemployment rates are highly correlated with the national unemployment rate, it is important to control the overall unemployment rate in the United States. The latter is reported annually in the Statistical Abstract of the United States (1986).

RACE

Although the PSID includes a few individuals whose race is other than black or white, there are too few to compare them. Consequently, we excluded individuals other than blacks and whites in the analyses reported below.

EDUCATION

The PSID reports years of completed schooling for each individual in 1968, in the first year that they were interviewed (if they entered the sample by marrying one of the original members of the sample), or at the interview at which they reported discontinuing their schooling. In the analyses reported below we code education into three categories: less than 12 years, 12 years (which usually indicates high school graduation), and more than 12 years (i.e. some college).

AGE

It is generally believed that the probability of migrating declines as age increases. Consequently, we include the individual's age in years as a control variable in our analyses.

LENGTH OF RESIDENCE

Length of residence has long been argued to be an important predictor of the probability of migrating (McGinnis 1968). Persons who have migrated recently are more likely to migrate again. We measured length of residence as the number of years that the person was continuously observed in the same county. The observation period extended back to the 1968 interview, wherever possible. Moreover, sample members were asked in 1968 how long they had lived in their current residence. Their response was added to the years actually observed in the county if they had lived in the same county continuously since 1968.

EMPLOYMENT SITUATION

As one indicator of a person's employment situation, we used a measure of the hours worked in the previous year. We computed this measure by multiplying weeks worked in the previous year by the reported average hours worked per week when employed. We treated 2080 hours (40 hours per week times 52 weeks) as full-time employment. We then categorized annual hours of work as follows: 0–1040 hours (low hours), 1041–1760 hours (medium), 1761–2160 hours (normal), and 2061–5060 hours (high). This admittedly arbitrary scheme was chosen partly on the basis of the empirical distribution of total annual hours of work and partly on the basis of what most people are likely to consider 'low', 'moderate', 'normal', and 'high' hours of work per year. The distribution across these four categories in the sample we analysed is 9.8, 15.7, 43.5, and 31.0 per cent, respectively.

Occupation is another important aspect of a person's employment situation. In accord with our earlier remarks, we created a dummy (0–1) variable to distinguish persons in professional, technical, managerial, official and proprietorial occupations from those in other occupations.

INCOME

Both searching for better employment opportunities in other locations and actually moving there can be expensive, as we noted earlier. Individuals with high levels of income are better able to afford search and moving costs and therefore may be more likely to move. The PSID data include a measure of family income in each year, which we transformed into relative levels of income within the sample for each year. We computed income quartiles for each year on the basis of total family income for the weighted sample of PSID families. In the analyses reported below, we included a dummy (0–1) indicator for a family income in the *lowest* quartile (low income) and another for an income in the *highest* quartile (high income). Family income in the 26–75 percentile range was the omitted category.

FAMILY SITUATION

A few aspects of a person's family situation are important to control, even though they are not central to the hypotheses being tested. We included a dummy (0–1) indicator for being married, and another for having children in the household. We also included a dummy (0–1) indicator for being a homeowner rather than a renter. We expected those who are married, have children, and own their home to be less likely to move.

SAMPLE

As we mentioned earlier, the original sample was drawn from two sources. One, known as the Survey of Economic Opportunity (SEO) sample, oversampled low-income families; it has a high proportion of blacks and is atypical in a variety of other ways. So, we created a dummy (0–1) indicator to denote the SEO sample. As we also noted above, some individuals drop out of the study. We also created a dummy

(0–1) indicator to denote this so-called 'nonresponse' sample, which may also be atypical. Finally, some individuals were in the original sample, and others joined the survey later, usually by marrying one of the original female members of the sample. We created another dummy indicator to distinguish individuals in the original sample from those who joined the survey after 1968.

YEAR

We analyse data on individuals from 1975 through 1983 because data on the county unemployment rate was unavailable prior to 1975. The 1984 interview was the most recent one available when we began our analyses; consequently, it was necessary to end our analyses with 1983. We intend to extend our analyses into the future as subsequent data become available.

11.4 Methods

We raise three main questions and estimate a different model to address each question.

Our first main question is: to what extent are blacks and less educated individuals concentrated in areas with high unemployment rates during the 1970s and 1980s? To address this question, we formulated models of the unemployment rate in individual n's county of origin i at time t, $u_{ni}(t)$, in terms of various characteristics of the individual expressed by the vector of variables $X_n(t)$. Naturally, $u_{ni}(t)$ tends to covary with the overall unemployment rate in the United States at time t, $U(t)$. Since we are interested in the distribution of individuals in terms of relative employment opportunities in different local labour markets, it would make sense to examine either the deviation of the local unemployment rate from the national rate, $u_{ni}(t) - U(t)$, or the relative unemployment rate, $u_{ni}(t)/U(t)$. In preliminary analyses, we examined both. Though overall results were similar, we prefer the latter, which we report below, because it avoids implausible predictions (e.g. $\hat{u}_{ni}(t) < 0$) and because we obtained a better overall fit to the data. Thus, the basic form of the model used to address the first question is:

$$u_{ni}(t)/U(t) = f(X_n(t)) \tag{11.1}$$

where $f(\cdot)$ is some function of the vector of variables $X_n(t)$. For purposes of estimation, we transformed this equation by taking logarithms, adding a random disturbance, and rearranging it as follows:

$$\log u_{ni}(t) - \log U(t) = \beta' X_n(t) + \epsilon_n(t)$$
$$\log u_{ni}(t) = \gamma_1 \log U(t) + \beta' X_n(t) + \epsilon_n(t) \tag{11.2}$$

where β is a vector of parameters indicating the effect of variables $X_n(t)$ on the relative unemployment rate in individual n's county of origin i, and $\epsilon_n(t)$ is a random disturbance with mean zero and variance σ^2. We estimated equation (11.2) by ordinary least squares. If the basic model fits well, we expect estimates of γ_1 to be approximately 1.0, which they were (see below).

Our second main question is: how is the probability of migration related to characteristics of individual decision-makers as well as to local employment opportunities? To address this question, we estimated models of the probability of individual n making an intercounty move between two annual interviews, $p_n(t)$. Such models are sometimes called discrete-time hazard models. We estimated a logistic regression model, which assumes that the log odds of the probability of migrating is linear in $X_n(t)$, log $u_{ni}(t)$, and log $U(t)$:

$$\log \frac{p_n(t)}{1-p_n(t)} = \gamma_0 \log u_{ni}(t) + \gamma_1 \log U(t) + \beta' X_n(t) \tag{11.3}$$

where β is a vector of parameters giving the effects of the variables in $X_n(t)$, and γ_0 and γ_1 are parameters giving the effects of the local and US unemployment rates, respectively. We chose a logistic regression model over a linear probability model because it constrains probabilities to lie within the (0–1) range, and we chose it over a probit model because it is easier to interpret and is known to give qualitatively similar results in most instances. We estimated the logistic regression model by the method of maximum likelihood.

Our third main question concerns the outcome of migration: do migrants indeed tend to move to places with better employment opportunities? Which migrants are most likely to move to better places? To address these questions, we formulated a model similar to that in equation (11.2), except that we examined the unemployment rate in j, the county to which a person n moved, relative to the unemployment rates in the county that was left, $u_{nj}(t)/u_{ni}(t)$. If this relative unemployment rate equals one, it means that individuals' employment opportunities in destination j and origin i are the same on average. If it is less (greater) than one, it means that on average they move to places with better (worse) opportunities. We want to know if the magnitude of this ratio depends on characteristics of the individual, $X_n(t)$. The basic form of our model is:

$$u_{nj}(t)/u_{ni}(t) = f(X_n(t)) \tag{11.4}$$

where $f(\cdot)$ is some function of $X_n(t)$. For purposes of estimation, we also translated this equation by taking logarithms, adding a random disturbance, and rearranging it as follows:

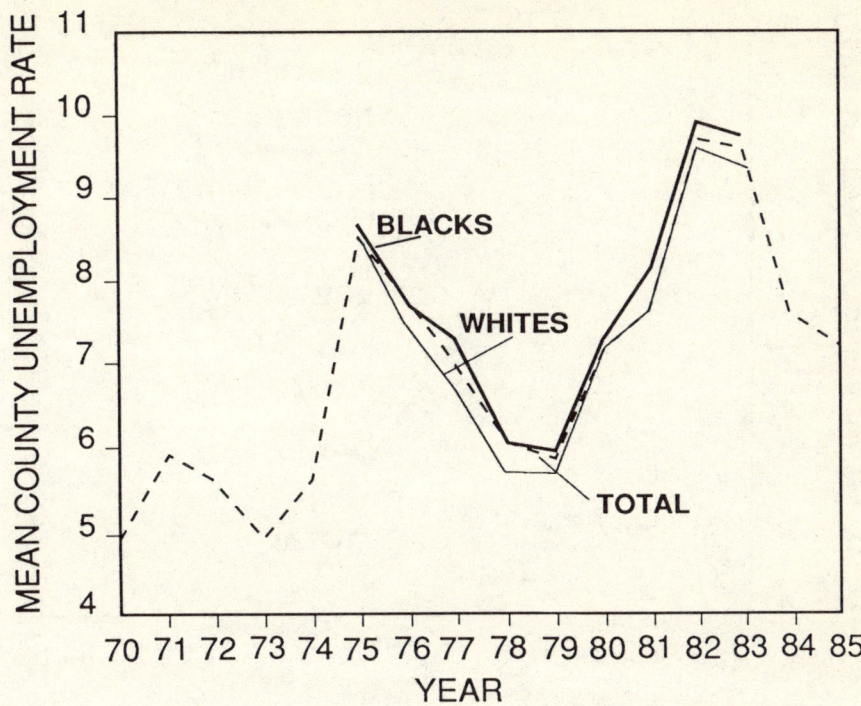

Figure 11.1   Mean county unemployment rates in the US by year for black and white male heads of households aged 18–64

$$\log \, u_{nj}(t) - \log \, U_{ni}(t) \; = \; \beta' X_n(t) + \epsilon_n(t)$$

that is:

$$\log \, u_{nj}(t) \; = \; \gamma_0 \, \log \, U_{ni}(t) + \beta' X_n(t) + \epsilon_n(t) \qquad (11.5)$$

where β is a vector of parameters indicating the effect of variables $X_n(t)$ on the unemployment rate in the county of destination j relative to that in the county of origin i, and $\epsilon_n(t)$ is a random disturbance with mean zero and variance σ^2. We estimated equation (11.5) by ordinary least squares. Naturally, we estimated models addressing the third question only from data on individuals who changed counties of residence.

11.5 Results

11.5.1 Black/white differences in county unemployment rates

Figure 11.1 shows the average county unemployment rate for black and white male household heads aged 18–64 computed from the PSID data

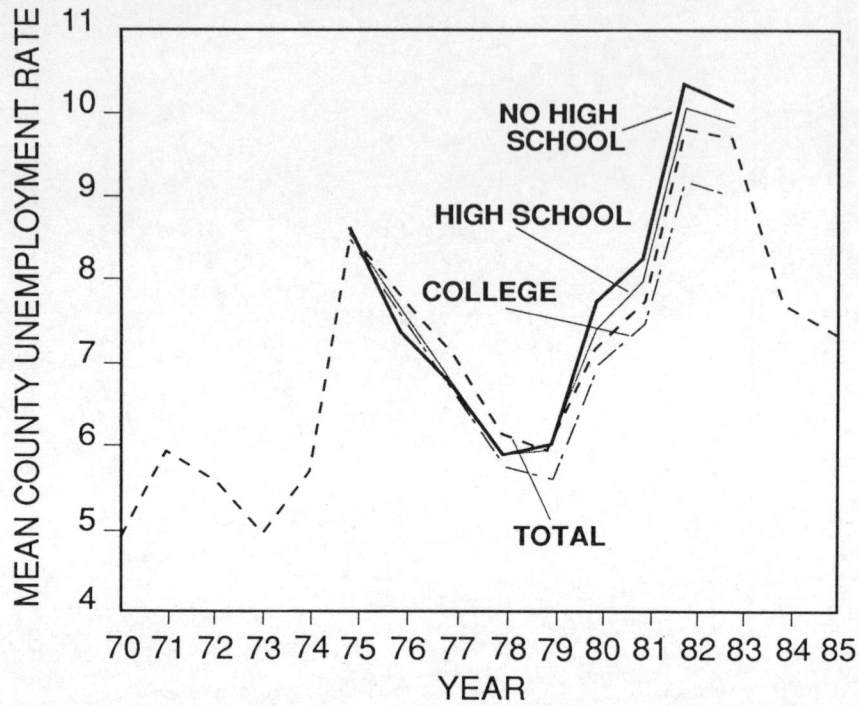

Figure 11.2   Mean county unemployment rates in the US by year for male
heads of households aged 18–64 with different education levels

for the period 1975–83 (solid and dotted lines, respectively). We used the
sample weights provided in the PSID to calculate these averages; consequently, they should reflect the averages for the US population of black
and white male household heads aged 18–64 during this period. The
figure includes the overall US unemployment rate for 1970 through 1985
(dashed line) for comparative purposes.

Examining the curves from left to right, one can see how the US
economy fluctuated between 1970 and 1985. Especially noticeable are the
economic recessions in the mid-1970s (peaking in 1975–76) and in the
early 1980s (peaking in 1982–83), followed by periods of economic
recovery. One can also see that the county unemployment rates have
been higher on average for black men than for white men, indicating that
blacks lived in counties with fewer job opportunities during the 1975–83
period.

Figure 11.2 displays the average county unemployment rates in 1975–
83 for male household heads with different levels of education. The
overall US unemployment rate for 1970–85 is again included for
reference. This figure shows that, during most of the period 1975
through 1983, on average unemployment rates were highest in counties
in which men with less than 12 years of schooling resided and lowest in

counties in which men with more than 12 years of schooling resided. Differences among the three educational groups are especially marked from 1978 to 1983; this pattern may indicate the growing difference in employment opportunities for men with different educational levels due to the economic restructuring under way during this period.

The displays in Figures 11.1 and 11.2 are informative, but they do not indicate whether the observed racial and educational differentials are statistically significant. One would also like to know if black/white differentials are the same at every level of education. Graphical displays are inadequate for these purposes. A multivariate model lets one relate the county unemployment rate to individual characteristics, which helps in assessing whether the racial and educational differentials observed in these two figures are genuine or due to other characteristics associated with race and education.

11.5.1 County unemployment rates and individual characteristics

Table 11.1 reports results of a linear regression model of the logarithm of the unemployment rate in the county of origin in year t (see equation (11.2)) for black and white men combined and separately. In all three models γ_1, the coefficient of the US unemployment rate is close to 1.0, as expected. In the combined sample, the coefficient of the dummy indicator of Black is about 0.01; this indicates that the county unemployment rate is about 1 per cent higher where black men live than where otherwise comparable white men live on average.

As indicated by the F statistics reported at the bottom of the table, all three models improve significantly upon the null model, in which coefficients of all variables are zero. However, the F statistic for the test that race interacts with the other variables is statistically significant at the 0.001 level. This implies that the association between the county unemployment rate and individual characteristics differ for black and white male heads of households. We therefore focus our discussion pertaining to the first question on the separate results for black and white men.

Less-educated black men are significantly more likely to live in counties with relatively high unemployment rates, whereas more educated white men are significantly more likely to live in counties with relatively low unemployment rates. In sum, men with more (less) schooling tend to live in counties with better (worse) employment opportunities.

Not surprisingly, there is also an association between county unemployment rates and employment situation. Those whose own employment situation is favourable tend to live in counties with relatively low unemployment rates. Thus, Table 11.1 indicates that white men with a professional, technical, or managerial occupation are significantly more likely to live in counties with relatively low unemployment rates. For

Table 11.1   Effects of variables on the log of the unemployment rate in the individual's county of residence

Variable	Whole sample		Black sample		White sample	
	Coeff.	p	Coeff.	p	Coeff.	p
Intercept	− 0.1143	0.1509	0.2125	0.0891	− 0.2567	0.0107
Black	0.0110	0.0630	—	—	—	—
Log U(t)	1.0071	0.0000	0.9640	0.0000	1.0254	0.0000
Educ'n < 12 years	0.0087	0.1045	0.0225	0.0033	0.0003	0.9654
Educ'n > 12 years	− 0.0132	0.0136	− 0.0120	0.2395	− 0.0136	0.0341
Occupation P, T or M	− 0.0111	0.0409	− 0.0061	0.6022	− 0.0134	0.0336
Worked 0–1040 hours	0.0692	0.0000	0.0556	0.0000	0.0782	0.0000
Worked 1041–1760 hours	0.0281	0.0000	0.0098	0.2589	0.0389	0.0000
Worked 2161 + hours	− 0.0323	0.0000	− 0.0283	0.0017	− 0.0319	0.0000
Low income	0.0032	0.6501	0.0147	0.0852	− 0.0198	0.0708
High income	0.0024	0.6395	− 0.0020	0.8352	0.0005	0.9301
Age (years–18)	0.0003	0.2640	− 0.0002	0.5043	0.0005	0.1051
Length of residence	0.0013	0.0002	0.0027	0.0000	0.0006	0.1528
Married	− 0.0098	0.1702	− 0.0239	0.0237	0.0002	0.9824
Children	− 0.0040	0.4123	− 0.0047	0.5829	− 0.0025	0.6710
Homeowner	− 0.0163	0.0014	− 0.0386	0.0000	− 0.0049	0.4584
SEO sample	0.0368	0.0000	0.0374	0.0001	0.0369	0.0000
Original sample	− 0.0096	0.0630	− 0.0235	0.0033	− 0.0031	0.6422
Nonresponse sample	− 0.0043	0.4965	− 0.0245	0.0032	0.0110	0.2192
R-squared	0.213		0.250		0.199	
F statistic vs. null model	443.3		179.0		296.5	
(df)	(18,29411)		(17,9140)		(17,20254)	
Sample size	29 430		9 158		20 272	

Source: Computations based on male heads of households aged 18–64 in the 1975–84 Panel Study of Income Dynamics.

both white and black men, there is also a negative association between annual hours worked in the previous year and the county's unemployment rate. That is, those who worked the most hours in the previous year tended to live in counties with relatively low unemployment rates and those who worked the fewest hours tended to live in counties with relatively high unemployment rates.

There is no association between having a family income in the highest quartile and county unemployment rates for either white or black men. However, there is an association between having a family income in the lowest quartile and the county unemployment rates. Low-income black men tend to live in counties where the unemployment rate is relatively high, but, surprisingly, low-income white men tend to live in counties where this rate is relatively low. We think that not much should be made of the findings for white men unless it can be replicated in other studies.

Age is not associated with county unemployment rate for either black or white men. However, length of residence is associated with a relatively high unemployment rate for black men, but not white men. This suggests that black men do, indeed, become 'trapped' in counties with unfavourable labour markets.

Family situation is not associated with county unemployment rate for white men. However, black men who are married or own their home are more likely to live in counties with relatively low unemployment rates. This provides some indirect support for Wilson's (1987) thesis that poor labour market opportunities are at least one reason why so few black men are married.

The three indicators of sample subgroups (SEO, Original, and Non-response samples) have some significant associations with county unemployment rate. However, we will not discuss them because these variables were introduced strictly as controls.

In sum, then, the results in Table 11.1 indicate that male heads of household in the United States are not randomly distributed across local labour markets. Black men with less education, less favourable employment situations, and lower income tend to live in counties with relatively high unemployment rates. In contrast, white men with more education, professional or managerial occupation, and high annual hours of work tend to live in counties with relatively low unemployment rates.

11.5.2 The probability of an intercounty move

Table 11.2 reports results of our logistic regression model of the probability of moving to another county. We report results for the combined sample because race interactions were not statistically significant for this model. The likelihood ratio χ^2 statistic for the test of the model reported in Table 11.2 versus the null hypothesis in which there is a constant probability of migrating is 1379.5 with 19 degrees of freedom, which is statistically significant at the 0.001 level.

The economic literature suggests that a high unemployment rate helps to spur people to move in order to find better employment opportunities. The coefficient of the US unemployment rate is positive (0.748), which supports this view. On the other hand, the coefficient of the county unemployment rate is negative (-0.181), which indicates that individuals have a lower probability of moving away from a county with a relatively high unemployment rate than from a county with a relatively low unemployment rate. These findings are consistent with those of Kephart (1989) but not with those of DaVanzo (1978). Whatever the causal explanation of this finding, it indicates that there is some process leading men to become 'trapped' in places with relatively unfavourable labour markets.

Table 11.2   Effects of variables on the log odds of migrating to a different county

Variable	Coeff.	p
Intercept	− 5.3970	0.0000
Black	− 0.8637	0.0000
Log u(t − 1)	− 0.1807	0.0166
Log U(t − 1)	0.7482	0.0000
Educ'n < 12 years	− 0.0025	0.9746
Educ'n > 12 years	0.1175	0.0936
Occupation P, T, or M	0.3750	0.0000
Worked 0–1040 hours	− 0.1998	0.0729
Worked 1041–1760 hours	0.1890	0.0199
Worked 2161 + hours	0.2557	0.0001
Low income	0.3394	0.0000
High income	0.1983	0.0080
Age (years−18)	− 0.0211	0.0000
Length of residence	− 0.1112	0.0000
Married	− 0.1248	0.1436
Children	− 0.0471	0.4884
Homeowner	− 1.0344	0.0000
SEO sample	0.0205	0.7727
Original sample	0.0347	0.6141
Nonresponse sample	− 0.3442	0.0002
Likelihood ratio Chi-sq. (vs. null model)	1379.5	(19 df)
Number of person-years	29320	
Proportion migration	0.0493	

Source: Computations based on male heads of households aged 18–64 in the 1975–84 Panel Study of Income Dynamics.

In agreement with the previous literature, we find that black men are significantly less likely to migrate than otherwise comparable white men. The estimated coefficient for Black, − 0.864, implies that the probability of migrating for black men is 0.42 (= $e^{-0.864}$) times the probability for white men. We included an interaction between race and county unemployment rate in another model (not reported here), but it was not statistically significant. Thus, blacks simply seem to be less likely to migrate than whites, whatever the employment opportunities in the local labour market.

Also in agreement with the previous literature, we find that men with some college education are more likely to migrate. But an even more important indicator is occupation: men with a professional, technical, or managerial occupation have a relative risk of migrating that is 1.45 (= $e^{0.375}$) times as great as that of men in other occupations.

Hours worked in the previous year also have significant effects on the probability of an intercounty move, but the nature of these effects is not what economic theory might lead one to expect. The men with the highest probability of migrating are those who worked an unusually large number of hours — more than 2160 hours in the previous year. This variable may be an indicator of high skills and other unobserved characteristics associated with employability, and these men may choose to move to another location where their skills and abilities are valued but they can work a normal number of hours. In contrast, men who are employed less than half-time (0–1040 hours) in the previous year are significantly *less* likely to migrate than men who are employed essentially full-time (1761–2160 hours). Thus, under-employed men, whom economic arguments predict will be most likely to migrate to find better employment opportunities, are actually *less* likely to move than those fully employed. Those who were employed somewhat less than full-time (1041–1760 hours) are significantly more likely to migrate than those employed full-time. It appears that these men do have valuable work skills but cannot find full employment in their county of origin, and they do tend to move to find better job opportunities. In short, only those who are appreciably under-employed (i.e. employed less than half-time) seem to have migration behaviour that differs from what economic arguments would lead one to expect. Of course, if these men are the core of the 'hard to employ', then it may be rational for them not to move to other ares with more favourable labour markets.

Most of the control variables in the model have significant effects in the expected direction. Thus, the probability of migrating declines significantly with age and with length of residence. It is worth noting that the magnitude of the effect of age is appreciably less than that of length of residence. And, not surprisingly, homeowners are significantly less likely to migrate than renters. The effects of being married and of having children are negative, as expected, but are not statistically significant. Finally, only the indicator of the nonresponse group has a significant (negative) effect. By definition, the nonresponse subgroup eventually drops out of the panel survey; perhaps some of these departures are due to migration to other places where these individuals cannot be located. Thus, the significant negative effect of this variable may indicate under-reporting of migration for this subgroup.

11.5.3 *Consequences of migration*

The third question we wish to address concerns the consequences of migration, in particular, the nature of employment opportunities in the places to which individuals move. To examine this issue, we regressed the logarithm of the unemployment rate in the county of destination on the logarithm of the unemployment rate in the county of origin, plus various individual characteristics, for migrants. Table 11.3 reports the results for black and white migrants separately and combined.

First, all three models improve significantly upon the null model, which contains no variables, only constants. But we again found

Table 11.3   Effects of variables on the log of the unemployment rate in the destination county of migrants

Variable	Whole sample		Black sample		White sample	
	Coeff.	p	Coeff.	p	Coeff.	p
Intercept	3.2984	0.0000	4.5133	0.0000	3.0940	0.0000
Black	0.0115	0.6945	—	—	—	—
Origin log u(t)	0.4861	0.0000	0.3065	0.0000	0.5172	0.0000
Educ'n < 12 years	−0.0351	0.1855	−0.0545	0.3303	−0.0247	0.4223
Educ'n > 12 years	−0.0247	0.2859	−0.0283	0.6606	−0.0233	0.3523
Occupation P, T or M	0.0302	0.1867	0.0341	0.6372	0.0331	0.1693
Worked 0–1040 hours	0.0791	0.0333	0.0067	0.9230	0.1068	0.0179
Worked 1041–1760 hours	−0.0053	0.8460	−0.1030	0.0718	0.0258	0.4139
Worked 2161+ hours	−0.0381	0.0909	−0.0632	0.3461	−0.0316	0.1867
Low income	0.0119	0.6616	0.1467	0.0144	−0.0262	0.4034
High income	0.0103	0.6889	−0.0822	0.3631	0.0182	0.4956
Age (years−18)	0.0012	0.3428	0.0015	0.6357	0.0010	0.5110
Length of residence	−0.0009	0.7116	−0.0065	0.2083	0.0019	0.4974
Married	0.0253	0.3796	0.0779	0.3260	0.0150	0.6319
Children	−0.0255	0.2713	−0.0494	0.4859	−0.0214	0.3831
Homeowner	−0.0190	0.4204	0.0826	0.2870	−0.0325	0.1917
SEO sample	0.0106	0.6477	0.0231	0.7195	0.0023	0.9283
Original sample	0.0276	0.2425	−0.0037	0.9575	0.0265	0.2936
Nonresponse sample	−0.0207	0.5053	−0.1018	0.0995	0.0045	0.9024
R-squared	0.244		0.146		0.280	
F statistic vs. null model	25.42		2.56		26.18	
(df)	(18,1416)		(17,254)		(17,1145)	
Sample size	1435		272		1163	

Source: Computations based on male heads of households aged 18–64 in the Study of Income Dynamics who migrated during the period 1975–84.

significant interactions between race and the other variables in the model ($F = 29.57$ with 18 df). Therefore, we concentrate on the results for the separate black and white samples. We include the results for the combined sample for purposes of comparison.

In contrast to Table 11.1, where the estimate of γ_1 (the coefficient of the US unemployment rate) was close to 1.0, the estimate of γ_0 (the coefficient of the unemployment rate in the origin county) is appreciably less than 1.0 in Table 11.3. The implication of the estimated intercept and estimated coefficient of the log unemployment rate in the origin county is that the log unemployment rate in the destination county tends to be higher for blacks than for whites and also less dependent on the log unemployment rate in the origin county for blacks than for whites.

The other notable finding is that individual characteristics (at least those we measured) have very little impact on employment opportunities in the labour markets to which these male heads of household moved. In particular, neither educational level nor having a professional occupation have significant effects in any of the three samples. There is some tendency for white men who worked less than half-time in the previous year to move to destinations where the county unemployment rate is higher. In contrast, there is tendency for black men who worked 1041–1760 hours in the previous year to move to destinations where the county unemployment rate is lower. Low-income blacks are significantly more likely than middle- and upper-income blacks to move to counties with higher unemployment rates. Thus, there is little evidence that migration is an important mechanism by which black men manage to escape labour markets with few opportunities.

11.6 Summary and conclusions

Our research has demonstrated several important features of the spatial distribution and internal migration of black and white men in the United States. First, black men, especially those with less than a high school degree, resided in counties with relatively high unemployment rates during the 1975–83 period. In contrast, white men, especially those with more than a high school degree, resided in counties with relatively low unemployment rates during this period. Since we do not have data prior to 1975, we cannot tell whether this is a continuation of a fairly consistent historical pattern or a recent phenomenon. Given the concentration of African Americans in rural Southern areas in the early part of this century and their more contemporary concentration in either rural Southern areas or declining central cities in the Midwest or Northeast, it is likely that the 1975–83 pattern reflects a situation that has existed for some time.

Second, we found that during the 1975–83 period black and less-educated men were less likely to move than white and more educated men. This was found to be true, even after controlling the national unemployment rate and the relative county unemployment rate. This finding means that blacks are less likely to migrate in order to improve the quality of the local labour market in which they reside. Coupled with the previous finding of less favourable labour market conditions in the localities where blacks reside, this finding suggests that blacks and less-educated men are prone to becoming 'trapped' in local labour markets with relatively poor employment opportunities. This pattern is especially important during periods of rapid economic deterioration and change in local labour markets, such as occurred in the United States during the 1970s and 1980s.

Third, we found that when black men do change counties of residence, they tend to relocate to counties with higher unemployment rates than those to which white migrants move. This may partly be due to the fact that most intercounty migrants move to nearby counties, which are likely to have similar unemployment rates. Since blacks reside in counties with higher unemployment rates than whites, one would expect more blacks to move to (nearby) counties with higher unemployment rates. However, the results show that the unemployment rate of the destination county is less dependent on the unemployment rate of the origin county for blacks than for whites. The quality of the labour market in destination counties may also, then, be limited by the more restricted relocation options open to blacks as compared to whites.

These findings lead us to two principal conclusions. It is clear that black Americans have geographical disadvantages in addition to the other disadvantages they experience in contemporary American society. A complex set of historical circumstances has led to a situation in which blacks are more likely than whites to reside in local labour markets with relatively few employment opportunities. The geographical disadvantages of blacks are factors that have largely been ignored, or about which claims have been made without supporting evidence. Our results show that the geographical disadvantages of blacks involve not only concentration in central cities of large metropolitan areas, but also concentration in local labour markets with relatively high unemployment rates.

Second, migration works less effectively for blacks than for whites as a means of improving available job opportunities. The results regarding this issue are consistent with the implications of our theoretical model: black Americans are unable to use migration as successfully as whites because they have fewer alternative locations available to them. Less-educated blacks are doubly disadvantaged because they also have less information about alternative opportunities elsewhere and are more likely to have nonprofessional occupations, which are less mobile. These findings clearly suggest that black/white differences in migration in response to local employment conditions act to exacerbate rather than to reduce existing geographical disparities.

Chapter 12

The analysis of housing and migration careers*

Richard Davies

12.1 Introduction

The notion of a housing or migration career is an ill-defined concept but it is intuitively appealing and proves useful in synthesising disparate theories and ideas. At its simplest, it is merely a description of the residential history of an individual or household. At its most complex, it involves assumptions about dynamic optimisation behaviour including evaluation of alternatives in terms of expected future benefits, appropriately discounted. However, a dominant theme is that moves are purposeful not just with respect to short-term equilibrating behaviour whereby, for example, a household may seek a larger house when family size increases, but also with respect to longer-term ambitions or objectives. Thus a household may accept a period in low-quality rented occupation while saving for a deposit which will permit entry into the owner-occupied sector.

The main appeal of the notion of a career lies in this explicit emphasis upon long-term dynamics; there is concern for the whole trajectory of movements and the usual implication is that individual residences or locations may be valued as 'stepping stones' towards some more desirable outcome in addition to any valuation on their own merits. Much of the micro-level empirical research into residential mobility and migration has been based upon short segments of mobility histories and has been directed at specific themes such as life-cycle characteristics, housing classes, and internal job markets. By focusing attention on the long-term dynamics of behaviour, housing and migration careers provide an organisational framework which appears to facilitate both the integration of results from these diverse approaches and the design of more

* Data from the Michigan Panel Study of Income Dynamics was used in the development of Table 12.1 and Figure 12.3. The author thanks the Inter-University Consortium for Political and Social Research for the provision of these data. The data used for Tables 12.2 and 12.3 and Figures 12.1 and 12.2 were collected within the ESRC-funded project number G13250011: 'Social Change and Economic Life in Rochdale'; the data used for Table 12.4 were collected within the ESRC-funded project HR6578. Neither the ICPSR, the ESRC, nor the original collectors of the data are, of course, responsible for the analyses and conclusions presented.

comprehensive empirical studies using longer mobility history records. It is argued elsewhere (Pickles and Davies 1991) than an important attraction is the generality of this framework and that it is untainted by association with any particular theoretical perspective.

The primary objective of this chapter is to review, with examples, the methodological implications of housing and migration careers for micro-level research into individual and household mobility. Given the inevitable complexity of any attempts to disentangle interrelated factors operating over time, the focus of interest is upon statistical modelling. This provides an integrated approach to statistical inference within which systematic relationships in the data may be distinguished from the obscuring random variation. The statistical modelling theme is reflected in the organisation of the chapter which covers, in turn, model specification, model calibration, and the interpretation of results. However, these methodological sections are preceded by a brief review of the relevant substantive issues.

12.2 The substantive context

Most of the methodological approaches used in micro-level empirical studies of residential mobility are based upon the assumption that moves are equilibrium seeking adjustments to changing requirements and aspirations. Indeed, equilibrating adjustment is often implicit in the terminology used, such as a recent birth 'triggering' (Clark *et al.* 1984) a residential move. Some of this emphasis is attributable to the seminal study by Rossi who concluded that the major function of residential mobility is 'the process by which families adjust their housing to the housing needs that are generated by shifts in family composition that accompany life-cycle changes' (Rossi 1955, p.9). Comparatively modest data requirements will have also contributed to the attractiveness of this approach; empirical research into equilibrium-seeking adjustments only requires short segments of residential histories and, with bold assumptions, some progress is even possible from surveys confined to recent movers.

Following Rossi (1955), there has been a particular interest in space consumption effects (e.g. Goodman 1976; Coupe and Morgan 1981; Davies and Pickles 1985a). It is evident that either surplus or shortage of space resulting from life-cycle changes may increase the probability of a residential move, perhaps enabling a reduction in expenditure on housing services in the case of a surplus and the elimination of overcrowding in the case of a shortage. Much of the research into disequilibrium between housing costs and income also emphasises the changes brought about by progression through the life cycle and consequent adjustment by moving (e.g. Goodman 1976; Hanushek and Quigley 1978; Onaka 1983), although income is more likely to have an impact upon tenure choice than decisions to move (Deurloo *et al.* 1987).

The much discussed notion of cumulative inertia (e.g. McGinnis 1968; Clark and Huff 1977; Davies and Pickles 1983) may appear to suggest an opposing mechanism by which housing consumption is maintained in disequilibrium. The basic idea is that accumulating social, community, and other ties progressively reduce the probability of moving as the length of residence increases. As discussed in a later section of this chapter, the empirical evidence about cumulative inertia is difficult to interpret from conventional analyses. Nevertheless, it is conceptually straightforward to incorporate inertial influences within a model of short-term adjustment; it is only necessary to take a more general view than life-cycle factors of the various sources of a household's satisfaction and dissatisfaction with its dwelling. Following Wolpert (1966) and Brown and Moore (1970), some behavioural geographers adopt a similar broad view, recognising many counter-acting pressures to move and to stay (e.g. Phipps and Carter 1984; Phipps and Holden 1985) while retaining an emphasis on moves as an equilibrating process.

The equilibrium-seeking approach has therefore played an extensive role in residential mobility research and has undoubtedly provided many insights into the factors involved. However, by assuming that moves are responses to changes in household and perhaps neighbourhood characteristics, these insights are necessarily partial. One criticism is that the approach fails to recognise the severe constraints imposed on the housing decision of households by institutions and, more abstractly, by the operation of capitalist class relations. This is probably a less pertinent criticism than is sometimes claimed because constraints may be, and have been, incorporated into conventional statistical models of revealed preference in a variety of ways, including segmentation of the analysis, random effects specifications, interaction terms, or simply the inclusion of appropriate explanatory variables (see Pickles and Davies 1991 for further discussion). Of more concern is the clear evidence from Clark and Onaka (1985) and others that residential mobility is not driven solely by housing dissatisfaction; housing decisions for a household are not a sequence of independent adjustments to changing circumstances. We will outline two possible reasons for this in order to highlight some of the complex issues involved.

First, it is evident that most households have a long-term trajectory in mind, or at least some ideal to which they aspire (see, for example, Lansing 1966; Wilkinson 1976; Morris and Winter 1978), and it is difficult to refute the proposition that this ideal has a profound influence upon residential mobility decision-making. For example, for many working-class households, low-cost furnished rented accommodation is a transitory phase until they can achieve entry into the public rental sector, perhaps after the birth of children (Ineichen 1981); for the professional socioeconomic groups, occupation of this type of accommodation tends to be a transitory phase in the progress to owner-occupation. In both cases, therefore, entry into and continuing occupation of low-quality accommodation is motivated by longer-term strategy. Moreover, the strong over-representation of professional socioeconomic groups (Forrest and Kemeny 1982) could not be explained by short-term equilibrating behaviour. Michelson (1977) argues that long-term aspirations affect residential mobility by determining the criteria used for assessing options although the relative importance of these criteria may change over time, being modified by growing experience of different housing and neighbourhood areas. Within this theoretical framework, the short-term considerations which have dominated residential mobility research are seen as just 'fine-tuning'.

Second, the unusual price/quantity relationships in the housing market, such as the low elasticity of demand with respect to the mortgage rate, alert us to the inadequacy of conventional static theories of consumer behaviour in this context. Housing is an extremely durable commodity and 'it is possible to argue that households will have a long-term horizon in making decisions about housing expenditure' (MacLennan 1982, p. 38). Moreover, housing choice involves not just consumption of housing services or 'use value' (see Merrett and Gray 1982, p. 65), but also investment decisions which may affect future housing opportunities. Quite apart from the challenge to static theory by the compounding of consumption and investment solutions, the household's evaluation of a property may therefore involve the discounting of benefits from beyond the anticipated length of tenure and introduce complex dynamics into housing choice.

The notion of a trajectory or purposeful sequence of moves is far more common in micro-level research into longer distance migration. Migration is sometimes seen as an equilibrating adjustment. 'Most households decide on strategies which are predominantly short-term and responsive to immediate events' (Johnson and Salt 1990, p. 11). However, in contrast to residential mobility research, there is general acknowledgement that long-term strategic considerations, particularly those associated with career development, may play an important role. For example, Goss (1985) argues that the highly skilled advance their careers by changing employers and that this often entails a change of location, while Edstom and Galbraith (1977) note that some employers rotate potential managers between plants or offices to provide them with a variety of experience. The main weakness of micro-level migration research is that, to minimise the complexities of the issues arising from the adoption of a long-term perspective, there is a strong thematic emphasis with individual features of migration behaviour often studied in isolation. Thus migration through internal promotion or transfer tends to be seen as a process isolated from that of migration following a change of employer. This obscures the fact that individuals, at least in principle, may face a choice between these alternatives and the alternative of staying in the same location through foregoing promotion or seeking other employment locally. A simultaneous analysis focusing upon migration careers rather than a particular type or sequence of moves is necessary to distinguish the factors underlying these different choices.

12.3 Model specification

It will be evident from the discussion of the previous section that any formal model of housing careers must allow households to search for alternative properties with varying intensity depending upon current circumstances and aspirations. Such a model must also allow for alternatives to be evaluated not just on their own attributes but also on their potential effectiveness in facilitating the achievement of longer-term housing objectives. These are demanding requirements, particularly that of modelling the 'stepping stone' value of properties within a longer housing career. However, similar problems have been addressed in the context of labour market behaviour (Lippman and McCall 1976; Burdett *et al*. 1984 and, as originally suggested by Flowerdew (1976), this methodology is readily adapted for application to housing choice).

In this approach, the model is formulated in terms of discounted net utility flows and assumes households behave optimally. Extremely complex algebra is required to understand precisely how the 'stepping stone' component of net present value is attributed to any alternative. The iterative, 'recursive reduction', method used is an example of Bellman's optimality equation (Whittle 1982), 'allowing the determination of optimal behaviour over a period of time from a consideration of what is optimal over the next short interval of time, given that future intervals will be examined and acted upon in the same and therefore optimal way' (Pickles and Davies 1991). The method is very general and allows for uncertainty and random variation in costs. Moreover, although formal derivations have assumed utility-maximising behaviour, the resulting model is consistent with a variety of dynamic optimisation assumptions; no one particular formalised representation of decision-making is necessarily implied.

The solution to the recursive reduction problem may be written as a reservation policy model whereby a household moves if the net utility flow associated with an evaluated alternative dwelling exceeds some pre-defined minimum (reservation) level, giving:

$$\lambda_{hij}(t) = \rho_{hij}(t) \int_{U^*_{hij}(t)}^{\infty} dG_{jt}(U) \tag{12.1}$$

where $\lambda_{hij}(t)$ is the instantaneous rate of movement, $\rho_{hij}(t)$ is the search rate for an alternative dwelling, and $U_{hij}(t)$ is the minimum acceptable (reservation) net utility flow, for each household h from dwelling type i to type j at time t, while $G_{jt}(U)$ is the distribution function for the net utility flow of dwellings of type j at time t. More details of this derivation are given by Pickles and Davies (1991). For migration, the subscripts i and j would refer to locations rather than dwelling types.

The use of 'revealed preference' data on actual residential mobility or migration outcomes precludes any attempt to distinguish between the effect of different factors on the search rate and reservation utilities. In practice, therefore, the above model is approximated by the statistically convenient formulation:

$$\lambda_{hij}(t) = \lambda_{ij}^*(\tau_{ht}) \exp(\beta_{ij}'X_{hit}) \tag{12.2}$$

where τ_{ht} is the duration-of-residence of household h at time t, X_{hit} is a vector of explanatory variables describing relevant characteristics of the household, current dwelling, and the external environment, and β_{ij} is a vector of unknown parameters. In statistical terminology this is a proportional hazard, competing risk model. Its main features are readily deduced from equation (12.2).

The first part of the model, $\lambda_{ij}(\tau_{ht})$, is a baseline hazard showing how the instantaneous rate of movement to type j dwellings varies with duration-of-residence in a type i dwelling. The Weibull given by:

$$\lambda_{ij}^*(\tau_{ht}) = \gamma_{ij} \tau_{ht}^{\gamma_{ij}-1} \exp(\beta_{ijo}) \tag{12.3}$$

and the Gompertz given by:

$$\lambda_{ij}^*(\tau_{ht}) = \exp(\beta_{ijo} + \theta_{ij}\tau_{ht}) \tag{12.4}$$

are common and parsimonious parameterisations of the baseline hazard in proportional hazard models. They are sufficiently flexible to allow the instantaneous rate of movement either to increase or decline with duration-of-residence, corresponding to a situation of cumulative stress or cumulative inertia, respectively.

The second part of the model allows explanatory variables to influence the rate of movement to type j dwellings. Transforming the kth explanatory variable to $Z_{hitk} = \exp(X_{hitk})$ and rewriting equation (12.2) as:

$$\lambda_{hij}(t) = \lambda_{ij}(\tau_{ht}) \times (Z_{hit1})^{\beta_{ij1}} \times (Z_{hit2})^{\beta_{ij2}} \times \ldots \tag{12.5}$$

shows that each explanatory variable has a multiplicative effect on the baseline hazard; the explanatory variables are assumed not to alter the basic shape of the hazard but to scale it up or down. A simple but important technical detail is that the linear predictor $\beta_{ij}'X_{hit}$ does not include a constant term because this is incorporated into the baseline hazard. This is made explicit by use of the β_{ijo} for the constant term in equations (12.3) and (12.4).

The competing risk nature of the model arises from the provision for simultaneous risks of movement to competing dwelling types. The instantaneous rate of movement to all possible dwelling types is given by:

$$\lambda_{hi}(t) = \sum_j \lambda_{hij}(t) = \sum_j \lambda_{ij}^*(Z_{ht})\exp(\beta_{ij}X_{hit}) \tag{12.6}$$

The probability of moving to a specific type J at time t if a move occurs is therefore:

$$\rho_{hiJ}(t) = \frac{\lambda_{iJ}(\tau_{ht})\exp(\beta_{iJ}'X_{hit})}{\sum \lambda_{ij}(\tau_{ht})\exp(\beta_{ij}'X_{hit})} \tag{12.7}$$

As the baseline hazards and the β parameters are destination-dependent, both the timing of moves governed by equation (12.6) and the choices between alternatives governed by equation (12.7) are determined not just by 'push' factors included in the vector of explanatory variables, but also by the general characteristics of alternative dwelling types; both origin and destination characteristics are important. It is this feature which provides the directed or 'purposive action' (Coleman 1973) component of the competing risk model.

It was emphasised earlier that the competing risk formulation of equation (12.1) was statistically convenient. This is because competing risk models have been widely used in different areas of scientific enquiry and their statistical and computational characteristics are well researched (see, for example, Kalbfleisch and Prentice 1980, Chapter 7). The derivation has similarities to the random utility derivation of the logistic regression model (e.g. Dhrymes 1978, Chapter 7); a formal representation of discrete choice in terms of utility-maximising behaviour results, with some fairly bold assumptions about random component, is just the probability model that most statisticians would have advocated for analysing discrete choice in the first case. An obvious question arises: what is the scientific status of such derivations?

The writer's view is that they do include an element of tautology, making the assumptions necessary to achieve a familiar probability model. They cannot, therefore, be seen as providing a sound and rigorous theoretical justification for the resulting model. Moreover, the emasculation of the reservation policy formulation by equation (12.1) makes it difficult, if not impossible, to interpret any empirical results in terms of the original theoretical precepts about search rates and reservation utilities. A more general problem is that a model may be consistent with a number of quite different theoretical derivations. For example, Ioannides (1987) also characterised housing decisions as the outcome of lifetime utility maximising processes but used deterministic dynamic programming methods to justify a similar competing risk model.

At the very least, however, formal theoretical derivations help to establish the plausibility of a model. They provide means of ensuring that the models used for empirical analysis have the flexibility to encompass theoretical concerns. They may also provide a framework for assessing the statistical features of the model against substantive interests. Thus the discussion above of the competing risk model revealed that it had a forward-looking, or directed character which, in the light of the earlier derivation, may be interpreted as consistent with the notion of a long-term strategy.

Finally, in this section, we turn to the internal structure of the model. To operationalise the model of equation (12.2), the parameterisation of the baseline hazard must be specified and decisions made about what explanatory variables are to be included and in what form. These considerations do not generally require great theoretical sophistication as the main concern is just to allow sufficient flexibility to approximate anticipated relationships. Nevertheless, there has been a tendency to be rather cavalier over the specifications adopted. For example, various measures of household size and changes in household size have been used as explanatory variables in models of residential mobility with little thought given to their theoretical relevance. The primary theoretical importance of household size lies in its relationship to under- or over-crowding. An increase in household size may result in pressure on space and therefore prompt a move to more spacious accommodation. On the other hand, an increase may result in the utilisation of previously surplus space and therefore reduce the probability of a move; the household is now precluded from trading the surplus space for cash or a more desirable location. Thus it should be a shortage or a surplus of space not household size changes *per se* which increases the probability of a residential move. This has two implications for the internal structure of the model. First, a measure of space consumption should be constructed. Second, this measure should be included in the model at least as a quadratic (i.e. the measure and the measure squared used as explanatory variables) to enable move probabilities to increase with both a shortage and surplus of space.

12.4 Model calibration

Model calibration is just the process of using the data to estimate the unknown parameters in the model. Maximum likelihood methods of model calibration have some desirable statistical properties and, in any case, provide the only realistic approach to calibration for the complex nonlinear models discussed in this chapter. Estimation is based upon the likelihood function. This function shows how the likelihood (proportional to probability) of the observed outcomes varies depending upon the values of the unknown parameters. The maximum likelihood parameter estimates are those for which this likelihood function (or, equivalently, the logarithm of the likelihood function) is a maximum. Loosely speaking, the maximum likelihood estimates are the values of the parameters for which the observed outcomes are the most likely to have occurred, assuming that the model is correct. For an introduction to maximum likelihood methods, the reader is referred to Pickles (1985).

Calculating maximum likelihood estimates usually requires an iterative numerical optimisation procedure although this and other computational issues may not have to concern the analyst if a statistical modelling computer package such as GLIM is appropriate. However, calibration of housing and migration careers is complicated by two problems: time-varying explanatory variables and residual heterogeneity. We will consider these in turn.

12.4.1 Time-varying explanatory variables

Conventional analyses using proportional hazard models assume that explanatory variables are constant over durations to 'failure' (where 'failure' in this context is a household move). This is clearly inappropriate for housing and migration careers where, as discussed above, decisions may at least in part be responses to recent changes. Assuming, for example, that space consumption remains constant throughout a family's tenure in a property precludes any attempt to assess the effects of changing space consumption demands as families progress through the life cycle. The usual solution to this problem is to discretise the data, assuming that explanatory variables are constant over intervals of a month, three months, or even a year. The continuous-time formulation is altered to a discrete-time formulation and the outcome of interest becomes the absence or presence of a move in each interval instead of the precise timing of each move. Preferably, the intervals will be sufficiently short for more than one move to be very unlikely.

To simplify the notation in the remainder of this chapter, we will assume that different types of destination are not differentiated; we will concentrate upon the modelling of move incidence without considering the choice of destination. This is sufficient to illustrate the main methodological issues that arise in modelling housing and migration careers and the move incidence formulations are readily extended to allow for the 'competing risks' of alternative destinations. The notation will be further simplified by assuming that the discrete-time intervals are of unit length.

Let p_{ht} be the probability of household h moving (at least once) during the time interval t. A standard result (see, for example, Kalbfleisch and Prentice 1980, Chapter 1) is that the probability of 'surviving' or staying during a time interval from t_1 to t_2 without 'failure' (i.e. without moving) is given by:

$$\exp\left[-\int_{t_1}^{t_2} \lambda(r)dr\right]$$

where $\lambda(\cdot)$ is the hazard function for the process. It directly follows from equation (12.2), dropping the i and j subscripts because of the focus on move incidence, that:

$$p_{ht} = 1 - \exp\left[-\int_{t-1}^{t} \lambda_h(r)dr\right] \tag{12.8}$$

$$= 1 - \exp\left[-\exp(\beta' X_{ht}) \int_{t-1}^{t} \lambda^*(\tau_{hr})dr\right] \tag{12.9}$$

The likelihood of the whole sequence of stay and move outcomes for household h is just the product of the probabilities of the observed outcome for each time interval and is given by:

$$L_h = \prod_{t=1}^{T_h} (p_{ht})^{y_{ht}}(1 - p_{ht})^{1-y_{ht}} \tag{12.10}$$

where T_h is the number of time intervals and y_{ht} equals one if there is a move during time interval t, zero otherwise. The sample log-likelihood function is simply:

$$\ell = \sum_{h=1}^{H} \log L_h \tag{12.11}$$

where H is the sample size.

Some pragmatism is necessary in operationalising this formulation because, with outcomes occurring anywhere within an interval, a precise measure is not available for the duration-of-residence τ_{ht}. However, alternative ways of resolving this uncertainty, such as assuming that outcomes occur at the centre or at the end of intervals, are likely to lead to very similar results unless the time intervals are unreasonably long.

The integral in equation (12.9) is, in general, readily evaluated. For example, the Gompertz model of equation (12.4) (again suppressing the i and j subscripts) gives:

$$\int_{t-1}^{t} \lambda^*(\tau_{hr})dr = \int_{\tau_{ht}-1}^{\tau_{ht}} \lambda^*(u)du$$

$$= \theta^{-1}[1 - \exp(-\theta)] \exp(\theta\tau_{ht}) \exp(\beta_o) \qquad (12.12)$$

with:

$$p_{ht} = 1 - \exp\{-\theta^{-1}[1 - \exp(-\theta)]\exp(\beta'X_{ht} + \beta_o + \theta\tau_{ht})\} \qquad (12.13)$$

Substituting:

$$\psi = \beta_o + \ln\{\theta^{-1}[1 - \exp(-\theta)]\} \qquad (12.14)$$

gives:

$$p_{ht} = 1 - \exp[-\exp(\psi + \theta\tau_{ht} + \beta'X_{ht})] \qquad (12.15)$$

which is a standard 'complementary log-log' model specification for binary outcomes, a useful result enabling GLIM to be used to calibrate simple models (see Aitkin *et al.* 1989, p. 313). In this specification, the duration-of-residence endogenous variable is included in the linear predictor in exactly the same way as the explanatory variables. It is therefore computationally and conceptually straightforward to extend the flexibility of the Gompertz baseline hazard by including polynomial terms in τ_{ht}. Davies and Pickles (1991) include a quadratic term with:

$$p_{ht} = 1 - \exp[-\exp(\psi + \theta_1\tau_{ht} + \theta_2\tau_{ht}^2 + \beta X_{ht})] \qquad (12.16)$$

to allow a non-monotonic relationship between duration-of-residence and probability of a residential move.

A more common specification for binary outcomes is the logistic model which, in the notation of equation (12.10) would be written as:

$$p_{ht} = \exp(\psi + \theta\tau_{ht} + \beta'X_{ht})/[1 + \exp(\psi + \theta\tau_{ht} + \beta'X_{ht})] \qquad (12.17)$$

Although not derivable directly from the earlier proportional hazard specification, the logistic model clearly provides a similar degree of flexibility in allowing for duration-of-residence effects and the impact of explanatory variables. The question again arises as to the theoretical status of formally derived models. The writer's contention is that the relative merits of similar alternative specifications are better considered as empirical issues; substantive theory in the social sciences is not sufficiently developed to allow precise mathematical specifications to be

Table 12.1 Analysis of residential mobility

Variable	Logistic analysis		With explicit modelling of residual heterogeneity		True parameter	Scaled parameter
	Parameter estimate	Standard error	Parameter estimate	Standard error	Value	Value
Constant	−0.81		−1.09		−1.05	−0.93
Space consumption	0.01	0.13	−0.36	0.17	−0.43	−0.38
(Space consumption)^2	0.05	0.05	0.19	0.06	0.18	0.16
(Age−40)$\times 10^{-2}$	−4.46	0.35	−5.69	0.51	−5.49	−4.89
(Age−40)$^2 \times 10^{-4}$	5.21	1.33	6.97	1.72	8.91	7.93
Owner-occupier	−1.39	0.07	−1.71	0.09	−1.72	−1.53
(Duration-of-residence)$\times 10^{-1}$	−0.96	0.12	0.00	0.23	0.00	0.00
Variance			−0.82		0.86	
Log-likelihood	−3522.19		−3462.13			

justified on a priori grounds. To the writer's knowledge, no empirical comparison has been undertaken of the complementary log-log and the logistic specifications in the context of housing and migration careers, although both have been used in different studies.

12.4.2 Residual heterogeneity

The second problem to be discussed in this section, that of residual heterogeneity, has more severe computational implications and, although now well documented, is still not widely understood. We will therefore illustrate the problem with two examples. Table 12.1 shows the results of calibrating the logistic model of equation (12.10) using annual data on residential mobility for 1073 American households over 12 years. The space consumption variable is the ratio of actual number of rooms to a normative measure of the number of rooms required given the family size and composition, age is the age of the head-of-household, and the owner-occupier variable is a dummy variable for owner-occupier as opposed to rental tenure. The results are generally plausible, being consistent with residential mobility declining steeply with age for younger heads-of-household and then levelling off, declining with duration-of-residence (cumulative inertia), and being appreciably lower for owner-occupiers than renters. These are well-documented phenomena in the literature (see, for example, Weinberg 1977). The only surprise would be that there is no evidence of any significant relationship between space consumption and residential moves.

In fact, although the data used for this analysis were based on real families, the residential moves were entirely hypothetical, generated by computer (simulated) using an assumed logistic model in order that the parameter estimates may be compared with known values in an assessment of the success of the model calibration. The parameter values used in the simulation are shown in the penultimate column of Table 12.1 and it will be evident that there are some serious discrepancies in the estimates obtained. In particular, the cumulative inertia result is entirely spurious as no duration-of-residence effects were included in the simulation. The parameter estimates for all the other explanatory variables are also more than two standard errors from the correct values. These discrepancies arise because random variation between households in their propensity to move was included in the simulation to represent, we would claim not unreasonably, the effect of omitted variables.

This has two consequences. The first is a quite innocuous consequence of the fixed variance of the logistic function; even if the extra-variation is independent of the included variables, ignoring the variation due to omitted variables will reduce the magnitude of the estimated parameters. The effect is innocuous because the same multiplicative reduction applies to all the parameters and their standard errors and is just one facet of a general property of the logistic model, namely that parameters are only estimable up to a multiplicative constant (see, for example, Anas 1982, p. 64). Knowing the variance of the omitted variables effect, the size of the reduction may be calculated and is shown in the final column of Table 12.1; four of the six parameter estimates are still more than two standard errors from these scaled values.

The second consequence of allowing for omitted variables in the simulation is far from innocuous and arises because this random variation is *not* independent of the explanatory variables included in the model. The main difficulty is over duration-of-residence: households with low propensity to move over and above the effects of the explanatory variables will tend to have longer than expected duration-of-residence while those with high propensity to move will tend to have shorter than expected durations. Hence duration-of-residence has a spurious negative relationship with the level of residential mobility due to its correlation with omitted variables. The distorting effects on the other parameter estimates are due to a combination of similar but less obvious endogeneity and the fact that correlation between one explanatory variable and the error term in a regression analysis prejudices consistent estimation of the parameters for any other explanatory variables. This is discussed in more detail by Davies and Pickles (1985b) in a paper devoted to similarly alarming simulation results.

To confirm that extra-variation is the source of the identified problems, Table 12.1 includes the results of a more sophisticated calibration which allowed explicitly for variation between households due to omitted variables. It will be noted that all the parameter estimates obtained in this calibration are well within two standard deviations of their true values. One of the difficulties with simulation studies is establishing the relevance of the results for 'real-life' situations. The relevance of these results was maximised by the unusual expedient of basing the simulation upon an actual empirical study and making every effort to replicate observed characteristics. Moreover, empirical experience tends to confirm that the highlighted effects commonly occur in practice and may result in seriously misleading conclusions if conventional model calibration methods are used. This is illustrated in Table 12.2 which shows the results of calibrating a model of migration behaviour using both a conventional logistic approach and an allowance for residual heterogeneity. The sample consisted of 357 males living in Rochdale in 1986 and the data covered all inter-county moves from the start of first job to the date of survey, an average of about 20 years. The conventional calibration suggests that migration increases with age, has decreased over calendar time, and is characterised by strong cumulative inertia. Allowing for extra-variation does not, in this case, eliminate the cumulative inertia effect but it is considerably attenuated. In addition, the age effect disappears.

The explicit modelling of residual heterogeneity is usually achieved by

Table 12.2 Illustrative analysis of migration data

	Logistic analysis		With explicit modelling of residual heterogeneity	
	Parameter estimate	Standard error	Parameter estimate	Standard error
Constant	− 0.174		0.712	
Duration-of-residence	− 0.203	0.017	− 0.120	0.021
Age	0.045	0.010	0.001	0.015
Calendar year — 1990	− 0.037	0.007	− 0.037	0.011
Log-likelihood	− 1178.88		− 1153.60	

adopting a marginal likelihood approach and this was used for the results in Tables 12.1 and 12.2. The alternative is a conditional likelihood approach (Andersen 1970). In both cases the residual heterogeneity is represented by individual specific error terms in the likelihood function. The conditional likelihood approach relies upon ingenious and generally complex algebraic manipulations which take some features of the outcomes as fixed so that the (conditional) likelihood of the remaining outcome features does not include the error terms. The approach is only appropriate for a limited range of model formulations and inference is restricted to the effects of time-varying explanatory variables. In the marginal likelihood approach the 'nuisance' parameters are eliminated from the analysis by integrating them out of the individual likelihoods, making the implicit but familiar assumption that the error terms are independent of the explanatory variables included in the model. Crouchley and Pickles (1990) provide some comparisons of marginal and conditional likelihood methods in the context of residential mobility.

As an example of the marginal likelihood approach, the logistic model of equation (12.17) may be written as:

$$p_{ht} = \exp(\psi + \theta\tau_{ht} + \beta'X_{ht} + \epsilon_h)/[1 + \exp(\psi + \theta\tau_{ht} + \beta'X_{ht} + \epsilon_h)] \qquad (12.18)$$

where ϵ_h is the individual specific error term. The individual sequence likelihood L_h (see equation (12.10)) is now a function of ϵ_h and the marginal likelihood is given by:

$$L_h^* = \int_{-\infty}^{\infty} L_h f(\epsilon_h) d \qquad (12.19)$$

where $f(\epsilon_h)$ is the probability density function of the error terms in the population. The likelihood is unknown because of the error. It may be helpful to interpret this integration as averaging the likelihood over all its possible values. Inference is then based upon the sample log-likelihood function:

$$\ell^* = \sum_{h=1}^{H} \log L_h^*$$
(12.20)

which does not include the individual specific error terms. This is sometimes referred to as an 'internal' heterogeneity specification (Allison 1987); alternatively, the marginal likelihood may be based upon 'external' heterogeneity (e.g. Heckman and Willis 1977) with, in this case, p_{ht} assumed to have a distribution with mean given by equation (12.17).

The integration involved in the marginal likelihood approach, as exemplified in equation (12.19), introduces several statistical and computational problems and generally (but see Wood and Hinde 1987 for an exception) precludes the use of standard statistical modelling software. The problems are reviewed elsewhere and a full account is not attempted here. One problem that has caused some concern is the apparent sensitivity of marginal likelihood results to alternative specifications of the error distribution and this has given impetus to nonparametric methods of calibration which do not require any distributional form to be assumed for the error terms (e.g. Heckman and Singer 1984; Davies and Pickles 1991). Unfortunately, marginal likelihood calibration with a nonparametric characterisation of the error distribution can be extremely demanding computationally and software development remains at the research stage. For example, MIXTURE (Ezzet and Davies 1988) lacks comprehensive error checking routines and users have to guide the calibration through a series of stages. Software packages enabling marginal likelihood calibration with parametric error distributions, usually assumed to be Normal, appear to be more robust. These include EGRET (1989) and SABRE (Barry *et al*. 1990).

12.5 Interpretation of results

Statistical texts tend to neglect the problems of interpreting the results of statistical modelling analyses and it is often assumed that analysis is completed by the calibration of a preferred model. However, a set of parameter estimates can be quite uninformative without further computation and this is very much the case for the complex, nonlinear models that may be used for housing and migration careers. The issues that arise are not technically difficult but common sense and attention to detail are necessary at this stage if the full insights provided by a modelling approach are to be realised and appreciated. Some of these issues are illustrated in this section by means of a series of examples.

Table 12.3 shows the results of a modelling exercise which was concerned with distinguishing between duration-of-residence, age, and year effects in inter-county migration. It is a more thorough analysis of the Rochdale data used for Table 12.2. The basic model is the logistic

Table 12.3 Duration-of-residence, age, and year effects in inter-county migration

Variable	Parameter estimate	Likelihood ratio (X^2) (p-value)
Constant	−28.042	
Duration-of-residence	−0.243	42.97
(Duration-of-residence)$^2 \times 10^2$	0.598	(<0.001)
Age	3.564	
(Age)^2	−0.165	28.57
(Age)$^3 \times 10^{-2}$	0.325	(<0.001)
(Age)$^4 \times 10^{-4}$	−0.231	
(Year — 1900) $\times 10^{-1}$	0.216	18.42
(Year — 1900)$^2 \times 10^{-3}$	−0.449	(<0.001)
Scale parameter	0.418	
'Stayer' proportion	0.361	
Log-likelihood	−1133.97	

of equation (12.18) for the annual probability of migrating, extended to include a quadratic in duration-of-stay. It will be noted that polynomials were also required to capture the effects of age and year. The error distribution was assumed to be Normal with unknown standard deviation (the scale parameter) but the calibration using SABRE (Barry *et al.* 1990) included provision for an estimable proportion of the population to be 'stayers'. In effect, the Normal probability density function for the error terms is augmented by a 'spike' at minus infinity to allow a finite proportion of the population to have zero, or at least a very low, probability of migrating at any time. This corrects a well-known tendency for parametric error distributions to inadequately represent extreme behaviours and is a compromise between the parametric and nonparametric approaches discussed in the previous section.

The obvious method for interpreting polynomial relationships is to plot graphs. Figure 12.1 shows the modelled relationship between age and the probability of migrating. Clearly, an infinite number of curves could be plotted, depending upon the values of the other variables and the individual-specific error term. For Figure 12.1, the duration-of-residence was specified as 5 years, the year taken to be 1980, and the error term was set at its median value taking into account both the estimated proportion of stayers and the Normal distribution with standard deviation 0.418. As there are no interaction terms in the model, these precise settings do not affect the general shape of the relationship and, in particular, the location of maxima and minima would be unchanged. The model therefore reveals that, controlling for duration-of-residence and year effects, migration probabilities are at a maximum for men aged in their twenties but have a second, subsidiary peak during later middle age. As Rochdale is not a retirement area and the maximum age for men in the sample was 60, this second peak is not associated with retirement

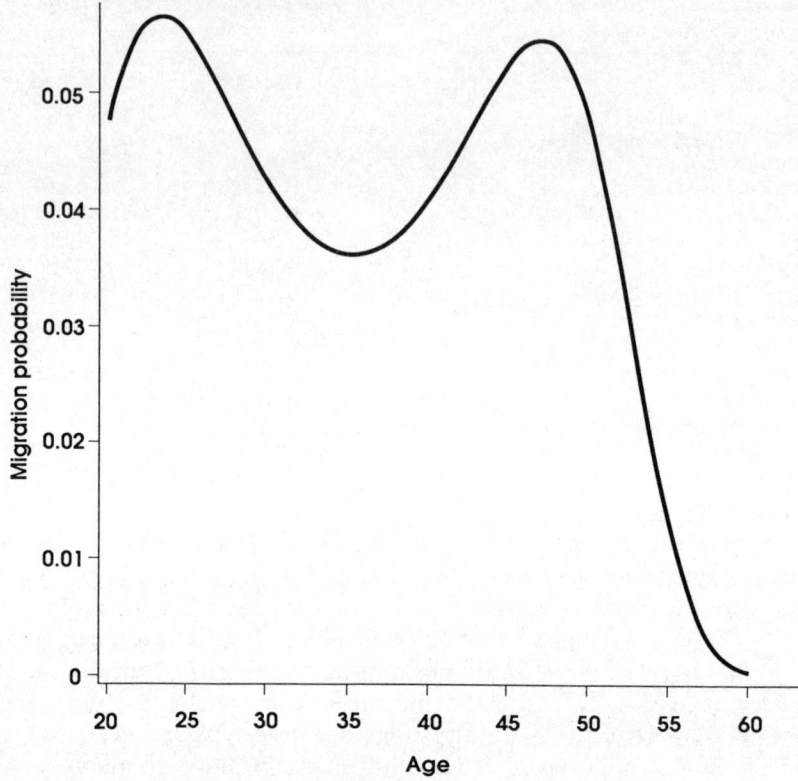

Figure 12.1   A typical relationship between age and migration probability

migration and is presumably a late career phenomenon.

Figure 12.2 provides an alternative representation of the modelled relationship between age and migration, showing the multiplicative effect of age on migration probability. This plot has the advantage that it is independent of other variables and the residual heterogeneity error term. It is made possible by the approximation:

$$p = \exp(z)/[1 + \exp(z)] \simeq \exp(z) \qquad (12.21)$$

for small p. Because $\exp(a + b + c + \ldots) = \exp(a)\exp(b)\exp(c)\ldots$, this permits the logistic regression model to be decomposed into multiplicative components when the outcome probability, as in this application, is small. Figure 12.2 shows the same peaks as Figure 12.1 but also enables some general conclusions about the size of the age effect. For example, the model suggests that, other factors being equal, the probability of migration decreases by a factor of about 0.6 between ages 25 and 35.

The results for dummy variables are often presentable as multiplicative

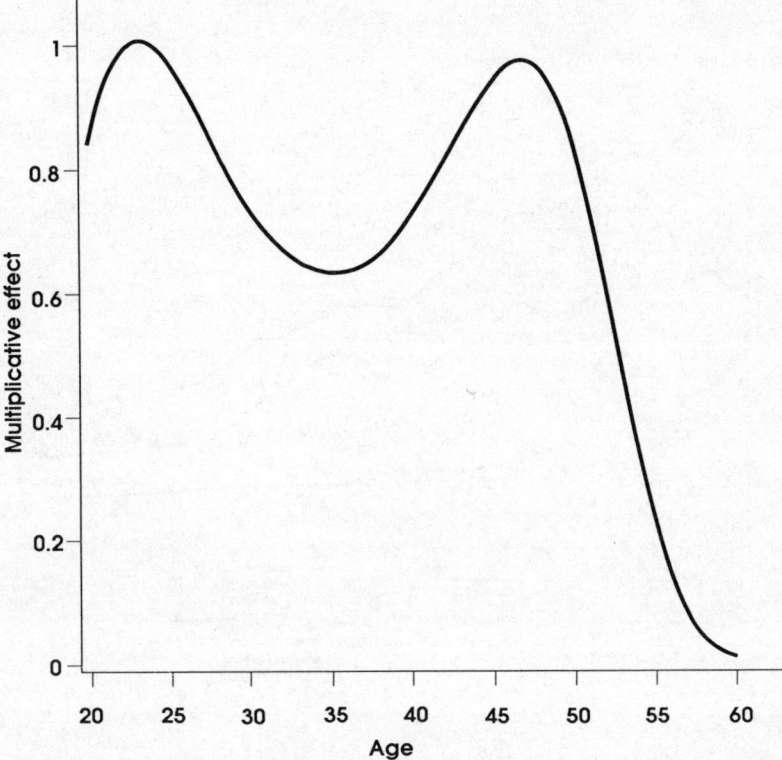

Figure 12.2 The multiplicative effect of age on migration probability

Table 12.4 Results for dummy variables in a competing risk analysis of residential mobility in Cardiff

	Renter–renter hazard			Renter–owner hazard		
	Parameter estimate	p-value	Relative risk	Parameter estimate	p-value	Relative risk
Gender (female)	−0.055	~0.09	0.95	−0.903	0.05	0.41
Single person	0.629	0.02	1.88	−0.353	~0.5	0.70
Social class						
Managerial/prof.	0.805		2.24	1.373		3.95
Skilled	0.079	0.002	1.08	0.668	<0.001	1.95
Unskilled	0.433		1.54	0.754		2.13

effects and this does not require graphical presentation. Table 12.4 shows some of the parameter estimates obtained in a competing risk model of residential mobility in Cardiff. A wide range of other variables was included in the model but the calibration details have been omitted for simplicity. The basic form of the model is in equation (12.2) with

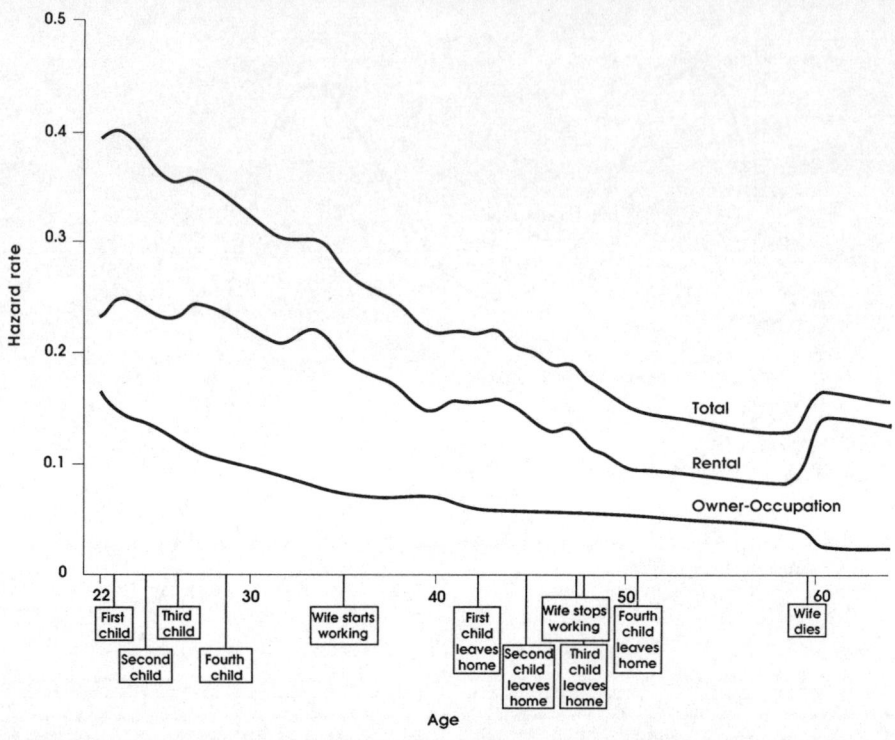

Figure 12.3   Variation over time in residential mobility hazard rates for a
specific household

individual specific error terms added to both the renter–renter and
renter–owner hazard. Further details are given in Davies and Pickles
(1991). The main point of interest here is that exponentiating the
parameter estimates gives the multiplicative effects of the dummy
variables. This is referred to as the 'relative risk' in Table 12.4 because
the multiplicative effect is relative to the reference group. Thus the rate
of mobility of female-headed households to other rental accommodation
is similar to that of the reference group (households with male heads).
However, female-headed households appear to have less than half the
rate of mobility to owner-occupation. On the other hand, single-person
households have nearly twice the rate of mobility of larger households
within the rental sector but do not differ significantly with respect to
moves to owner-occupation. All these results are, of course *ceteris
paribus*. Interpretation of the social class block of dummy variables is
left to the reader. The reference group in this case was 'unclassified'.

A particular challenge in interpreting analyses of housing and migration careers is to summarise the combined effects of all the variables and
the implications for behaviour over time. Pickles and Davies (1985)
addressed this challenge by 'running' the calibrated model for specific

families. One result, for an American family in rental accommodation, is shown in Figure 12.3. The residential mobility model included competing risks to rental and owner-occupation and allowed for age, income, and space factors. The main conclusion from this and other plots is that life-cycle changes in income and family composition have a comparatively modest impact on residential mobility, tending to generate just small disturbances from the dominant effect of declining mobility with age.

12.6 Concluding comments

This chapter has attempted to provide some insights into the empirical research opportunities and prospects generated by the notion of housing or migration careers. The account is necessarily partial and decisions about the precise topics to include were not readily resolved; this is a field in its infancy and the relative importance of different problems and issues are likely to change over the next few years with developments in substantive theory, methodology, and software. In these circumstances, it is not unreasonable, if not inevitable, that the orientation and contents of the chapter should be strongly influenced by the author's own research experience and interests. However, the emphasis upon statistical concerns should stand the test of time.

Social scientists undertaking empirical analysis are accustomed to working to large margins of error, only having rough and ready methods for operationalising many variables, typically unsure of what control variables to include in any analysis (and sometimes even including none), and often having to resort to data of questionable quality because of sampling, nonresponse, or other survey problems. Much data may therefore seem unworthy of sophisticated statistical analysis. Moreover, such an attitude is reinforced by the well-known robustness of many simple statistical analysis methods to quite extreme assumption violation. This is undoubtedly a rational view in some social science empirical research but there are many situations in which such pragmatism is demonstrably misplaced. The clearest example is the analysis of individual-level longitudinal data such as housing and migration careers. For these types of data, conventional and basic methods of statistical analysis do not just risk minor bias in estimating the size of systematic effects or the size of confidence intervals; they may result in seriously misleading conclusions. The overcoming of complex statistical modelling problems is critical to the successful analysis of housing and migration careers.

Chapter 13

Incorporating migration into simulation models

Chrisopher Duley and Philip Rees

> Had we but world enough, and time,
> This coyness lady were no crime . . .
> But at my back I always hear
> Time's winged chariot hurrying near.
>
> (Andrew Marvell, *To His Coy Mistress*, 1650)

13.1 The updating problem and solutions

13.1.1 The updating problem

We wait ten years between censuses for new information about the socioeconomic geography of our country. Writing in 1990, the last firm and reliable picture of the population size and character of our regions, counties, cities and neighbourhoods derives from the 1981 Census of Population.

There are a number of partial sources of information which are tapped by geographers, local government analysts and market analysis firms to update the populations of districts and wards in the United Kingdom. These include the following:

(i)   Surveys are carried out each year or every other year, such as the General Household Survey, the Labour Force Survey and the Family Expenditure Survey, which make enquiries of national samples of households.

(ii) Partial registers can be used, such as the Electoral Register, which counts all those eligible to vote and willing to register or the National Health Service Central Register (NHSCR), from which counts are made of persons transferring between Family Practitioner Committee (FPC) areas (soon to be called Family Health Service Authorities).

(iii) Vital statistics registers yield useful information on new additions to and subtractions from the population. The Office of Population Censuses and Surveys (OPCS) regularly publishes annual counts of births and deaths (with some age disaggregation) for areas down to ward and parish level.

(iv) Information on the number of new housing units completed each year in each local government unit is reported to the Department of the Environment to make up national tabulations.

There is a clear need to develop methods which utilize both the more detailed but less timely Census data for small areas and the less detailed but more timely survey and register data for larger areas to produce up-to-date estimates of the numbers of people living in small areas and their socioeconomic characteristics.

13.1.2 Existing methods

Several attempts have been made to accomplish this updating:

(i) OPCS produces each year estimates of the mid-year population of each local authority (county district, metropolitan district, London borough and health authority area), broken down by age and sex. The method involves simple cohort-component calculations: 'This involves ageing-on the population to make it a year older, subtracting deaths classified by sex and age, adding new births, and making allowances for migration' (Rowntree 1990, p. 33).
(ii) The market analysis firm, CACI, has produced estimates at ward level using the census counts, annual births and deaths for wards and net migration estimates based on changes in electoral register counts from year to year.
(iii) At the University of Leeds, several researchers (Rees *et al.* 1990) have used iterative proportional fitting to produce estimates of ward populations based on census counts for wards, OPCS mid-year population estimates for districts and electoral register counts for wards.

These updating exercises have a number of drawbacks, if the analyst desires as full a picture of the socioeconomic character of the population as possible, and wishes to derive estimates for geographies other than electoral wards. The methods produce counts of persons by gender and five–year age group (0–4 to 80–84 and 85 and over), but no more. OPCS provides estimates only down to county district scale. The CACI estimates and the University of Leeds work are specific to electoral wards, though Rees *et al.* (1990) successfully handle a mid-decade revision in ward boundaries. All the methods face difficulties in estimating the components of change at small geographical scales and, in particular, in incorporating migration into the estimation methodology.

13.1.3 A microsimulation method

Duley (1989), building on Rees, Clarke and Duley (1987), Duley, Rees and Clarke (1988) and Clarke, Duley and Rees (1989), has constructed an alternative method which produces post-censal estimates of the population, broken down not only by age and gender but by household position, living arrangement, marital status and ethnic group and which produces estimates of the number and character of households as well. The method involves microsimulation.

Briefly, lists of households and the constituent individuals in the population of a small area are produced by random sampling of cumulative probability distributions of characteristics. The probability distributions are computed from small area, regional and national census data and other sources. Wherever possible, interdependencies between characteristics are incorporated. The result of the first, *reconstruction*, phase of the model is a partial reproduction of the census at household and individual level. Then, in the second, *updating*, phase, both individuals and households are subjected to a series of demographic and social processes: mortality, fertility, union/breakup, migration and socioeconomic change. In the third, *projection*, phase, households and individuals continue to experience these processes but the probability distributions used are forecast rather than estimated, using contemporary information. The methods in this third phase are the same as those in the second; it is just the nature of the input information that is different.

13.1.4 The structure of the UPDATE simulation system

Figure 13.1 sets out the general structure of the UPDATE model. The area level for which updated lists of households and individuals are produced is the postcode sector. The model processes the population of each postcode sector in turn. For convenience, the postcode sectors corresponding to a local authority district are processed as a set. Information for a postcode sector (PCS) is normally derived by adding up or averaging the information for the Census enumeration districts (EDs) which it covers. The matching of EDs with a PCS can only be approximate for 1981 Census data. Where the relevant information is available only at ward level, it is assumed to apply to all constituent EDs from which a postcode aggregate or average can be obtained (see Duley 1989, Sections 8.2.4 and 8.2.5 for details).

A key feature of the population estimation and projection systems is the extent to which the spatial unit populations interact. In OPCS's subnational projections (Armitage 1986; Rees and Willekens 1989) and in the projections of the population of Swansea wards carried out by Rees *et al.* (1990), migration is allowed between all areas in adapted forms of the multiregional population projection model (see Rees 1989 for a

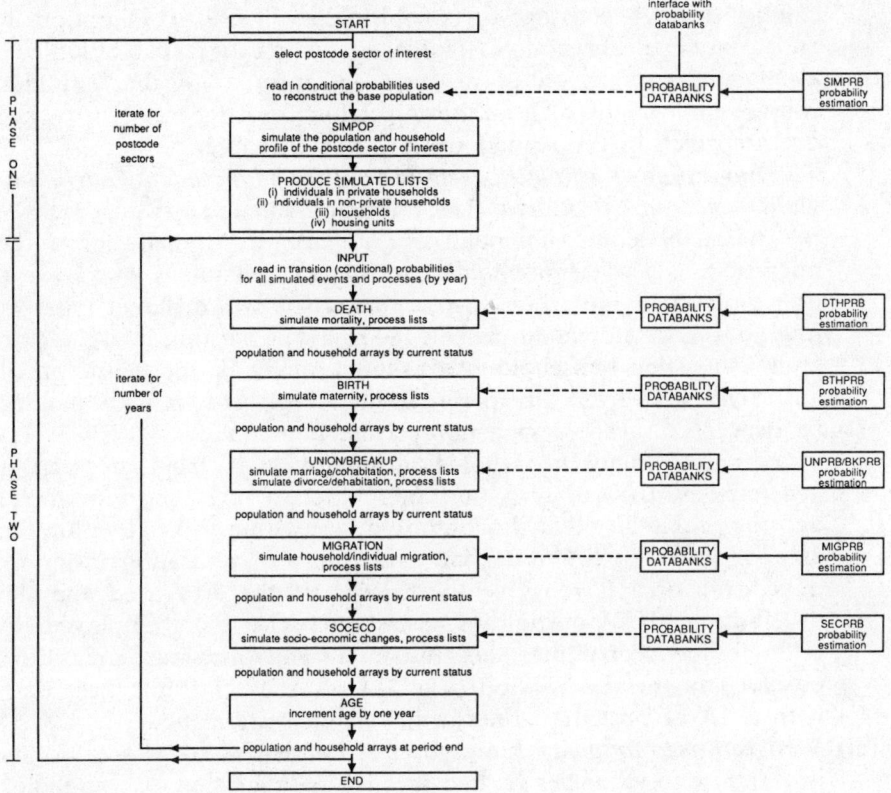

Figure 13.1 The structure of the UPDATE simulation system

review of the current state of this model). However, in the UPDATE system each postcode sector is treated as a single, isolated system receiving inmigrants and sending outmigrants. The number of inmigrants is dependent on events within the postcode sector only, and not elsewhere as in the multiregional model. This simplification made it feasible to produce an operational model and to incorporate a number of interesting innovations.

13.1.5 The migration framework used in the UPDATE model

To incorporate migration into the UPDATE microsimulation model involved eclectic use of a variety of data sources, of a variety of observations and associated models long recognized in descriptive research and of some new concepts.

(i) *Migration associated with pair formation and dissolution.* It is recognized that the process of formal or informal formation of couples through marriage or cohabitation will lead to migration by at least one of the couple. Similarly, divorce or dehabitation will also lead to migration of at least one member of the fissioning couple. Full details of how the migration consequences are worked out are given in the second section of the chapter.

(ii) *The migration of whole households and of independent individuals within and out of an area.* The migration submodel (which follows the union/breakup submodel) is designed to simulate both the migration of whole households and that of individuals who leave a household. It is important to recognize these two different types of migration. An individual can move from one existing household to another existing household. An example might be the migration of an 18-year-old from the parental home to a room in a hall of residence (i.e. a space in a non-private household).

Outmigration by households and individuals from an area is generated by the sampling of probabilities of migrating (anywhere) and the probability that the migration destination will fall within the area or outside it. This second probability of relocation inside or outside an area is sensitive to the size of the area used and the distribution of opportunities elsewhere. The data employed to estimate the probabilities are the inter- and intra-ward migration observed in the year prior to the 1981 Census. To link these data with a set of postcode zones a spatial interaction model is used.

(iii) *Inmigration to an area.* Inmigration of households to an area occurs in response to vacancies created through outmigration of households or as a result of the construction of new housing. Some of the vacancies are taken up by households moving within the area, and some by households moving from outside. Characteristics of these new households and their individual members must be reconstructed through application of the same methods used to reconstruct the starting population.

In the body of the chapter, flesh is added to this skeletal outline of the ways migration processes can be incorporated into simulation models of small area populations. The second section of the chapter deals with migration consequent on pair formation and pair dissolution. The third section of the chapter considers the spatial and temporal features of the push migration models employed to estimate needed mobility and destination selection probabilities. The fourth section of the chapter shows how a pull perspective can be used to model inmigrants to an area. The final section shows how the migration processes are implemented in the microsimulation model.

13.2 Migration associated with pair formation and dissolution

The coupling and uncoupling of individuals has important implications for household dynamics. New households may be formed or existing households may be transformed or even dissolved. Frequently associated with these marital transitions is migration, either within the local area or to/from other areas.

In the UPDATE model two types of living arrangement were identified and modelled, the formal institution of marriage and the informal alternative, cohabitation. Registration requirements ensure that statistics on marriage and divorce are available (in Series FM2, published by OPCS). By contrast, the informal nature of cohabitation means that statistics on this increasingly popular contemporary living arrangement are sparse. No data are currently available on numbers of cohabitation events, formations or terminations, but estimates can be made from survey data on female cohabitation reported in the General Household Survey (GHS). From an amalgam of data sources probabilities are estimated for input to the marital submodels (see Duley 1989 for a detailed exposition), the main features of which will now be described.

13.2.1 The marriage and cohabitation model

The model adopted to handle pair formation at the micro level is an extension of that developed by Clarke (1986), and adopts an open market, whereby migration is directly incorporated: individuals are free to migrate to find their spouse or cohabitee, with the result that individuals are added to or deleted from the population depending on the direction of the flow. The algorithm for marriage and cohabitation and its consequent events is set out in Figure 13.2. There are three stages: (i) testing each individual in the population for eligibility, with different criteria enabling different nuptial paths to be tracked; (ii) testing the eligible individuals for marriage or cohabitation, with different events tested to cater for the different eligibility groups; and (iii) matching selected individuals with partners and working out the consequent location decisions for both partners. Having decided prospective partners by sex, this step models the search for suitable partners in the local marriage and cohabitation market. The matching algorithm is based on the age combination of the potential partners at union.

Based on a five-year age group of a base partner, whose gender is selected at random, an imaginary partner (spouse or cohabitee) is generated with a given age. Then a match of this imaginary person with a locally available person from the relevant partner pool is attempted. If a local partner fitting the age–sex requirement is found, a match is made and the two individuals are united and removed from their respective partner pools. If there is no suitable partner locally available then an

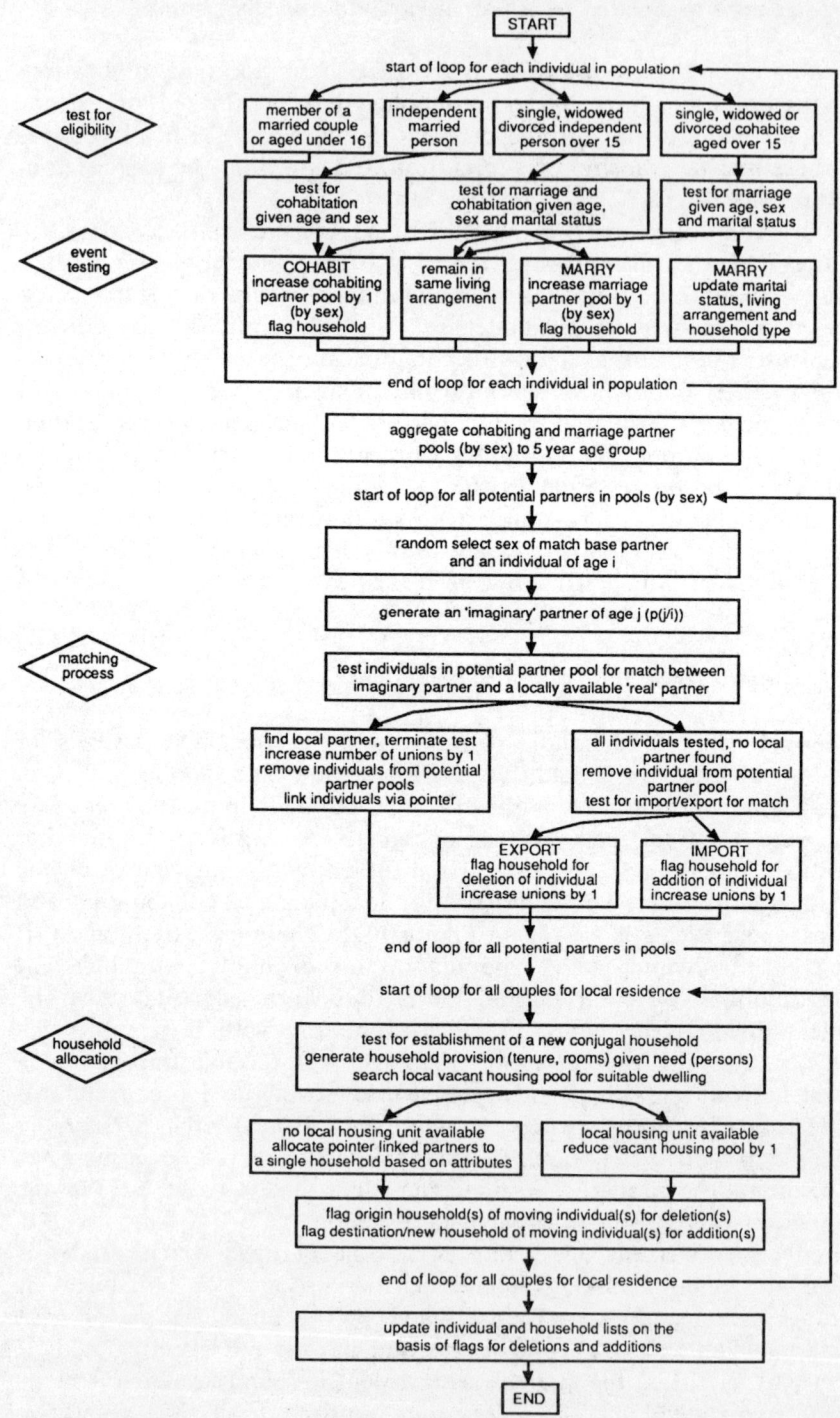

Figure 13.2   Stages in the simulation of marriage and cohabitation

interface with the wider marriage/cohabitation market outside the small area is necessary. This interface results in either the export of the local individual and their removal from the pool, or the import of an 'exotic' partner of the required age and sex. The decision to import or export individuals to satisfy the partner search is based on the annually adjusted local in- and outmigration propensities of individuals by age and sex. Gross figures are used so that there will be a combination of in- and outmigration motivated by marital transitions, although their ratio will reflect the dominant flow.

When the match has been completed, the newly formed couple must then be allocated to a house. The procedure adopted depends on the involvement of migration in the matching process. Outmigration of a local partner or inmigration of an 'exotic' partner requires straightforward accounting. When both partners are locally resident the match will result in movement, unless it is the marriage of an already cohabiting couple. Either one partner or both partners can move. One would expect most newly formed couples to want to set up a new household, unless one or other is already living in a suitable household, taken as a single-person household or lone-parent household without other adults. In some cases this may not be possible, in which event they locate in one or other of their existing households.

We sought to combine these choices and restrictions into a two-stage algorithm. In stage one, couples are given the opportunity to set up in a new conjugal household; that is, to move to a vacant housing unit in the area. This is determined on the basis of housing requirement (number of persons, new couple plus dependent(s) where applicable), from which suitable housing provision is set (tenure and number of rooms). Local vacant housing stocks are then searched and if a suitable dwelling is found the new couple is assigned to it. If no suitable vacant housing unit is available, in stage two movement is restricted to one of the two partners so that the couple or family is formed in an existing household, with no new household being established.

13.2.2 The divorce and dehabitation model

The modelling of pair dissolution is more straightforward than that of marriage, in that no matching algorithm is required since it is this match that is split through the divorce or dehabitation process. However, the implications of pair dissolution are equally complex. Breakup is sampled on the basis of age, sex and ethnic group of the base partner, with sex having been first set at random to avoid gender bias. Certain assumptions concerning the outcome of the divorce/dehabitation transition were made. The first was that the male former partner invariably departs from the existing household and having left is deemed to set up a new single-person household. Given the small area approach, the location of this new household is dependent on the availability of suitable vacant housing (cf. marriage and cohabitation model), with outmigration following an unsuccessful search. The second assumption is that the female former partner and any child(ren) remain in their present dwelling unit with updated attributes reflecting their new circumstances. Both former partners become eligible for remarriage.

13.3 The migration of whole households and independent individuals within and out of an area

In this section of the chapter, the methods used to estimate the various migration probabilities used in the microsimulation model are described. In order, we discuss

(i)   the estimation of mobility probabilities for wholly moving households;
(ii) the estimation of mobility probabilities for independently moving individuals;
(iii) the estimation of the probabilities of staying in an area or outmigrating.

13.3.1 Mobility probabilities for wholly moving households

The target variable to be estimated is as follows:

$\text{ph}_s^{ka}(t)$ = probability that a household of type k with a head in age group a living in postal sector s migrates in year t.

By 'migrates' is meant 'makes a migration of the transition type over a single year'. The term 'mobility' indicates that no spatial boundaries are placed on the migrations involved: they can be moves within the area or out of it. The double classification by household type and age of head is used to capture two important influences on household mobility. Table 13.1 lists the age groups and household types employed in the UPDATE model.

The steps undertaken to estimate household mobility probabilities are as follows:

(i)   *Initial district estimate.* The mobility probabilities for households in 1980–81 (the year prior to the Census), classified by type of household and age of head, are estimated for the district containing the postcode sector of interest.
(ii) *Spatial adjustment factor.* This mobility probability is adjusted up or down to reflect mobility in the particular postcode sector of interest.

Table 13.1 The household mobility variable and associated classifications

Variable	Definition
Target variable $ph_s^{ka}(t)$	mobility probability for households of type k with heads in age group a in postcode sector s in year t
Superscript/subscript classification	
k	(1) 1 adult 60/65 + with no children under 16
	(2) 1 adult under 60/65 with no children under 16
	(3) 1 adult any age with child(ren) under 16
	(4) 2 adults (married male with married female) with no children under 16
	(5) 2 adults (married male with married female) with children under 16
	(6) 3 + adults (married male(s) with married female(s) with or without others) with no children under 16
	(7) 3 + adults (married male(s) with married female(s) with or without others) with children under 16
	(8) other adults (2 +) with no children under 16
	(9) other adults (2 +) with children under 16
a	16–29, 30–44, 45–64, 65 +
s	111 postcode sectors of Leeds metropolitan district
t	1980–81, 1981–82, 1982–83, 1983–84, 1984–85, 1985–86 (mid-year to mid-year annual periods)

(iii) *Temporal adjustment factor*. This adjusted mobility probability is further adjusted up or down to reflect changes in mobility between 1980–81 and the current year of interest.

(iv) *Mobility probability due to demolition*. To this adjusted mobility probability is added an additional mobility probability reflecting moves forced on households as a result of housing demolitions in the particular postcode sector of interest.

In other words:

$$ph_s^{ka}(t) = \text{initial district estimate}$$
$$\times \text{ spatial adjustment factor}$$
$$\times \text{ temporal adjustment factor}$$
$$+ \text{ mobility probability due to demolition} \qquad (13.1)$$

How estimates of each of these elements are achieved is now described.

THE INITIAL DISTRICT ESTIMATE

The target variable to be estimated is:

ph_d^{ka} (81) = the probability that a household of type k with a head in age group a living in district d migrates in the year prior to the 1981 Census,

which may be approximated as:

$$ph_d^{ka} (81) = MH_d^{ka} (81) / H_d^{ka} (81) \qquad (13.2)$$

where

MH_d^{ka} (81) = households of type k and head's age a in district d who moves in the census year 1980–81; and;

H_d^{ka} (81) = all households of type k and head's age a in district d.

Neither of these variables is directly available from published sources, but single classifications of households by type and by head's age are available at the district level from Migration Regional Reports and the MATPAC system for migrant households, and from County Reports for all households. A national table cross-classifying households by type and head's age is also available.

To estimate the variables on the right-hand side of the equation (13.2), the widely used technique of Iterative Proportional Fitting (IPF) is employed (see Fienburg 1970 and Birkin 1987 for more details).

Table 13.2 lays out the IPF computations for all households. A joint probability matrix for Great Britain in Table 13.2(a) is adjusted bi-proportionally to fit row and column marginal totals in Table 13.2(b) and 13.2(c) to yield a best estimate in Table 13.2(d) for the number of households in Leeds district by household type and age group of head.

Table 13.3 shows the IPF computations for estimating the number of mobile (and stayer) households, using the results of the previous estimation (Table 13.3c) and two district marginals classifying households by mobility status (mobile/stayer) and head's age (Table 13.3a) and household type (Table 13.3b). In this case tri-proportional fitting is needed to yield a best-estimate array in Table 13.3(d) from which the requisite mobility probabilities can be computed.

Table 13.3(e) presents the household mobility probabilities for Leeds district. The most mobile households are those with younger heads (16–29 years) with a gradient of declining mobility with age (roughly a 50 per cent reduction in mobility between each age group), with very low rates in pensioner households. The age gradient is strongly apparent for all household types. However, there are noticeable differences in mobility rates between types. Mobility is highest amongst single-person households (types 1 and 2), with one-third of lone adults aged 16–29 moving the previous year. Of family households, those with lone parents are most

Table 13.2 The estimation of household numbers by age group of head and household type for Leeds district

(a) National data: households by age of head and type[1]

Household type	Age group of head				All ages
	16–29	30–44	45–64	65 +	
1	0.0000	0.0000	0.0000	0.1416	0.1416
2	0.0167	0.0203	0.0387	0.0000	0.0757
3	0.0075	0.0109	0.0024	0.0003	0.0211
4	0.0275	0.0277	0.0944	0.0954	0.2450
5	0.0572	0.1278	0.0241	0.0007	0.2098
6	0.0013	0.0110	0.0856	0.0192	0.1171
7	0.0030	0.0341	0.0413	0.0025	0.0809
8	0.0129	0.0130	0.0257	0.0343	0.0859
9	0.0045	0.0111	0.0062	0.0012	0.0230
All types	0.1306	0.2559	0.3183	0.2952	1.0000

(b) District marginal 1: households by type[2]
(c) District marginal 2: households by age of head[3]

Household type	Age group of head				All ages	Probability
	16–29	30–44	45–64	65 +		
1					41 288	0.1571
2					22 791	0.0867
3					6 436	0.0245
4					63 941	0.2433
5					51 463	0.1958
6					28 265	0.1075
7					19 758	0.0752
8					22 143	0.0843
9					6 721	0.0256
All types	33 531	67 048	95 069	67 158	262 806	1.0000
Probability	0.1276	0.2551	0.3618	0.2555	1.0000	—

(d) District estimate: households by age of head and type

Household type	Age group of head				All ages	Probability
	16–29	30–44	45–64	65 +		
1	0	0	0	41 288	41 288	0.1571
2	4 532	5 874	12 384	0	22 790	0.0867
3	2 182	3 384	822	48	6 436	0.0245
4	7 735	8 333	31 302	16 571	63 941	0.2433
5	13 230	31 560	6 566	106	51 462	0.1958
6	281	2 634	22 682	2 668	28 265	0.1075
7	663	8 026	10 733	336	19 758	0.0752
8	3 649	3 943	8 566	5 985	22 143	0.0843
9	1 247	3 267	1 997	210	6 721	0.0256
All types	33 519	67 021	95 052	67 212	262 804	1.0000
Probability	0.1275	0.2550	0.3617	0.2558	1.0000	—

Sources: [1] Adjusted OPCS (1983b) Table 26 (HH); [2] OPCS (1983a) Table 39 (CR 45); [3] OPCS (1983a) Table 35 (CR 45).

Table 13.3 The estimation of mobile and stayer household numbers by age group and household type for Leeds district

Input

(a) District marginal 1: mobile/stayer households by age of head[1]

Household status	Age group of head			
	16–29	30–44	45–64	65+
Mobile	6 174	5 092	3 341	2 110
Stayer	27 357	61 956	91 728	65 048

(b) District marginal 2: mobile/stayer households by type[2]

Household status	Household type								
	1	2	3	4	5	6	7	8	9
Mobile	1 606	3 390	892	3 319	4 407	751	758	1 072	522
Stayer	39 682	19 401	5 544	60 622	47 056	27 514	19 000	21 071	6 199

(c) District marginal 3: households by age of head and type[3]

Household type	Age group of head			
	16–29	30–44	45–64	65+
1	0	0	0	41 288
2	4 532	5 874	12 384	0
3	2 182	3 384	822	48
4	7 735	8 333	31 302	16 571
5	13 230	31 560	6 566	106
6	281	2 634	22 682	2 668
7	663	8 026	10 733	336
8	3 649	3 943	8 566	5 985
9	1 247	3 267	1 997	210

Output

(d) District estimate: mobile/stayer households by age of head and type

Household type	Age group of head							
	16–29		30–44		45–64		65+	
	move	stay	move	stay	move	stay	move	stay
1	0	0	0	0	0	0	1 606	39 682
2	1 484	3 048	947	4 928	959	11 426	0	0
3	498	1 685	353	3 031	40	782	1	47
4	1 299	6 436	615	7 718	1 052	30 250	353	16 219
5	2 061	11 169	2 142	29 419	202	6 364	2	104
6	35	247	139	2 495	538	22 145	40	2 628
7	81	582	419	7 607	252	10 480	5	331
8	505	3 144	235	3 708	231	8 336	102	5 883
9	209	1 038	241	3 026	67	1 929	4	205

Table 13.3 contd
(e) probability of a household residence in Leeds District in 1981 'wholly moving' by age of head and type

Household status	Age group of head			
	16–29	30–44	45–64	65 +
1	0.0000	0.0000	0.0000	0.0389
2	0.3275	0.1612	0.0774	0.0000
3	0.2280	0.1044	0.0484	0.0309
4	0.1679	0.0738	0.0336	0.0213
5	0.1558	0.0679	0.0308	0.0195
6	0.1235	0.0527	0.0237	0.0150
7	0.1226	0.0522	0.0235	0.0148
8	0.1383	0.0596	0.0269	0.0170
9	0.1679	0.0738	0.0336	0.0213

Sources: [1] MATPAC Table 1.5 (DT 6924U); OPCS (1983a) Table 35 (CR); [2] OPCS (1984a) Table 6 (RM 7); [3] Estimate, see Table 13.2.

mobile (type 3). Of married couple family households (types 4, 5, 6 and 7) those with no children under 16 are most migratory, with mobility declining with increased household size. Of the remaining types (types 8 and 9) multi-adult, non- or lone-parent-family households, mobility corresponds more to that of married couples, suggesting the stabilizing effect of larger household size.

THE SPATIAL ADJUSTMENT FACTOR

The district estimates need adjustment when used for individual postcode sectors. Mobility rates for households and for the whole population can be computed from data in the Small Area Statistics of the 1981 Census:

$$mh_s \ (81) = \sum_e (MH_e \ (81)/H_e \ (81)) \qquad (13.3)$$

where

mh_s (81) = the mobility rate for postcode sector s in 1980–81;
mh_e (81) = the number of wholly moving households (i.e. with a different address at the 1981 Census than one year earlier) in enumeration district e;
H_e (81) = the total number of households in enumeration district e.

The summation in equation (13.3) is over all enumeration districts which have been assigned to a postal sector. Enumeration districts were allocated to postal sectors by centroid matching checked by map inspection. The adjustment factor applied to the district mobility probabilities

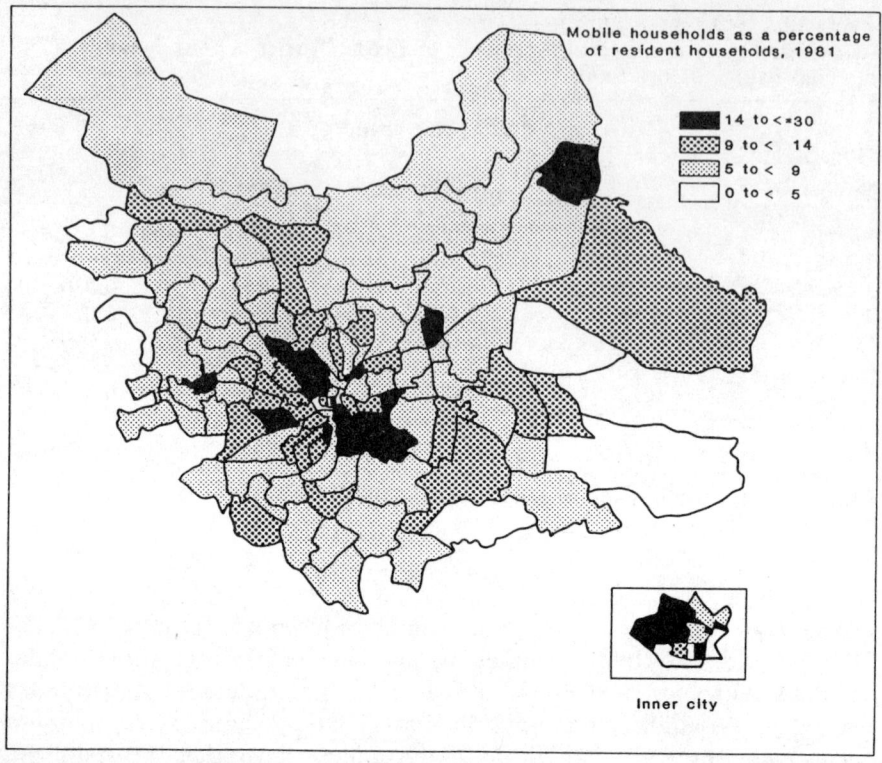

Figure 13.3   Household mobility rates by postcode sector, Leeds, 1981

is the ratio of the sector mobility rate to that for the district d:

spatial adjustment
factor for postal $= mh_s\ (81)/mh_d(81)$ (13.4)
sector s

   To obtain a better understanding of the geography of mobility in
Leeds, Figure 13.3 maps out these mobility rates. The district wide figure
is just over 9 per cent, yet sector figures range from over 25 per cent to
less than 5 per cent. To ignore such small area variation is to disregard
intra-urban relocation, a fundamental element of small area migrant
flows. The highest mobility rates are found in the inner city, apart from
one or two outlying areas where new housing estates were developed in
the year prior to the Census.

THE TEMPORAL ADJUSTMENT FACTOR

Recent research using patient re-registration data from the NHSCR
published by OPCS (Stillwell, Boden and Rees 1988) has established that

migration rates in Britain have varied very substantially over time, rising in the 1980s from low values from 1980–81 to 1982–83 to a peak in 1987–88, with some recession since then. From the NHSCR-derived migration data series can be computed outmigration rates for annual periods for Family Practitioner Committee (FPC) areas (which correspond in general to the former metropolitan districts, shire counties and grouped London boroughs):

$$o_f(t) = O_f(t)/PAR_f(t) \qquad\qquad (13.5)$$

where

$o_f(t)$ = outmigration rate for FPC area f in year t;
$O_f(t)$ = total outflows of patients from FPC area f in year t; and
$PAR_f(t)$ = population at risk for FPC area f in year t.

The temporal adjustment factor is defined as the ratio of the outmigration rate for year t of interest to that in the year prior to the Census in 1981:

$$o_f(t)/o_f(81)$$

THE MOBILITY PROBABILITY DUE TO DEMOLITION

At the small area scale, migration levels are determined not only by attribute-based mobility propensities (the mobility component) but also by changes in local housing stock, that is, by the number of new dwellings constructed and existing dwellings demolished. Clearly, the construction of a new housing estate or the demolition of a 1960s flat complex will have a sudden and major impact of movement into and out of a small area. Data on housing unit dynamics are available quarterly at local government level (Local Housing Statistics, England and Wales produced by the Department of the Environment). Although this is a valuable total constraint, the UPDATE model requires housing unit constructions and demolitions at the more detailed spatial scale of the postal sector.

Table 13.4 presents estimated postal sector housing unit demolitions and constructions for the period April 1981 to September 1986, computed from Leeds City Planning Department ward figures. An annual figure can be estimated by the simple deconsolidation of the six-year aggregate. Not only has there been a small but significant increase in Leeds housing stocks, but more importantly, there has been considerable local variation in stock changes, ranging from large-scale demolitions to equally large-scale new housing constructions. Broadly, there has been a net reduction in stocks in inner urban areas and net expansion in suburban housing stocks.

Table 13.4 Housing unit accounts for postcode sectors, Leeds, 1981–86

Sector label	1981 Housing stock	4/1981–9/1986 Housing unit +	−	net	Sector label	1981 Housing stock	4/1981–9/1986 Housing unit +	−	net
LS1 2	49	2	1	1	LS22 4	3 481	271	0	271
LS1 3	46	3	4	−1	LS22 5	879	68	0	68
LS1 4	157	9	12	−3	LS23 6	2 575	200	0	200
LS1 5	0	0	0	0	LS23 7	292	23	0	23
LS1 6	27	1	0	1	LS24 9	136	11	0	11
LS10 1	1 060	95	169	−74	LS25 1	3 094	102	28	74
LS10 2	2 263	236	415	−179	LS25 2	2 663	88	24	64
LS10 3	5 166	464	681	−217	LS25 3	521	24	0	24
LS10 4	4 424	227	2	225	LS25 4	700	32	0	32
LS11 0	1 996	51	10	41	LS25 5	67	3	0	3
LS11 5	2 651	74	17	57	LS25 7	3 550	162	0	162
LS11 6	2 315	81	25	56	LS26 0	4 895	54	0	54
LS11 7	3 626	80	11	69	LS26 8	4 435	87	17	70
LS11 8	3 223	101	27	74	LS26 9	1 416	42	11	31
LS11 9	1 443	59	21	38	LS27 0	2 693	149	9	140
LS12 1	1 984	65	68	−3	LS27 7	3 283	107	2	105
LS12 2	2 482	61	135	−74	LS27 8	3 050	176	11	165
LS12 3	3 362	91	123	−32	LS27 9	2 435	91	3	88
LS12 4	3 325	110	7	103	LS28 5	4 297	81	0	81
LS12 5	3 588	115	2	113	LS28 6	1 748	61	11	50
LS12 6	872	29	2	27	LS28 7	3 656	55	0	55
LS13 1	2 480	89	17	72	LS28 8	2 986	39	0	39
LS13 2	4 777	212	137	75	LS28 9	2 084	23	0	23
LS13 3	3 671	198	60	138	LS29 6	149	6	0	6
LS13 4	4 249	88	81	7	LS3 1	948	55	73	−18
LS14 1	3 427	58	0	58	LS4 2	3 848	192	45	147
LS14 2	1 451	105	0	105	LS5 3	3 193	153	48	105
LS14 3	966	51	0	51	LS6 1	5 285	142	130	12
LS14 5	3 627	262	0	262	LS6 2	2 977	123	152	−29
LS14 6	5 626	4	9	−5	LS6 3	4 257	120	71	49
LS15 0	3 687	179	72	107	LS6 4	3 534	57	1	56
LS15 4	2 043	118	0	118	LS7 1	1 382	80	106	−26
LS15 7	3 878	253	9	244	LS7 2	3 432	110	45	65
LS15 8	3 724	402	0	402	LS7 3	4 074	152	21	131
LS15 9	337	37	0	37	LS7 4	2 842	109	24	85
LS16 5	2 812	61	7	54	LS8 1	3 754	94	8	86
LS16 6	4 007	258	1	257	LS8 2	4 599	126	15	111
LS16 7	4 437	422	0	422	LS8 3	4 506	46	2	44
LS16 8	1 267	120	0	120	LS8 4	2 409	56	6	50
LS16 9	1 227	20	0	20	LS8 5	3 885	110	111	−1
LS17 5	3 848	196	0	196	LS9 0	3 288	34	100	−66
LS17 6	3 850	97	0	97	LS9 6	5 489	17	47	−30
LS17 7	3 688	279	0	279	LS9 7	4 100	106	144	−38
LS17 8	3 662	223	4	219	LS9 8	1 703	17	44	−27
LS17 9	1 210	94	0	94	LS9 9	2 257	24	71	−47
LS18 4	3 635	70	0	70	BD10 0	0	0	0	0
LS18 5	3 540	69	0	69	BD11 1	1 780	54	1	53
LS19 6	2 505	58	0	58	BD3 7	340	6	0	6

Table 13.4 contd.

Sector label	1981 Housing stock	4/1981–9/1986 Housing unit			Sector label	1981 Housing stock	4/1981–9/1986 Housing unit		
		+	–	net			+	–	net
LS19 7	4 999	182	0	182	BD4 8	630	7	0	7
LS2 8	320	18	25	– 7	WF10 2	1 679	77	0	77
LS2 9	720	41	55	– 14	WF2 0	192	13	1	12
LS20 8	2 362	93	0	93	WF3 1	2 643	178	12	166
LS20 9	2 008	79	0	79	WF3 2	1 567	106	7	99
LS21 1	2 008	33	0	33	WF3 3	2 125	92	0	92
LS21 2	2 330	38	0	38	WF3 4	207	2	0	2
LS21 3	2 114	34	0	34	All pcs	282 471	10 907	3 608	7 299

The mobility probability due to housing demolitions can be estimated as:

$$DU_s(t)/TU_s(t)$$

where

$DU_s(t)$ = the number of housing units demolished in postcode sector s at the start of year t; and

$TU_s(t)$ = the total number of units in postcode sector s in year t.

13.3.2 The model for estimating mobility probabilities for wholly moving households

We can now bring together the detailed definitions and estimates outlined in the four previous subsections to produce a more precise specification for the model that estimates the mobility probabilities for wholly moving households. Equation (13.1) becomes:

$$\begin{aligned}
ph_s^{ka}(t) &= ph_d^{ka}(81) \\
&\times (mh_s(81)/mh_d(81)) \\
&\times (o_f(t)/o_f(81)) \\
&+ (DU_s(t)/TU_s(t))
\end{aligned} \tag{13.6}$$

where postal sector s is contained within local government district d, which is either coincident with or contained within FPC area f.

This formulation can be applied to any postal sector in England and Wales, and with a little modification to any postal sector in Scotland (where Area Health Boards are the equivalent of English or Welsh FPCs).

Table 13.5 illustrates the result of the spatial, temporal and stock adjustment for postcode sector LS6 1. Rates are considerably higher than

Table 13.5   The probability of a household 'wholly moving' from a small area, 1981–86, the example of Leeds postal sector LS6 1

Age of head	Household type*								
	1	2	3	4	5	6	7	8	9
1 16–29	0.000	0.807	0.563	0.416	0.386	0.307	0.305	0.343	0.416
9 30–44	0.000	0.399	0.260	0.185	0.171	0.133	0.132	0.150	0.185
8 45–64	0.000	0.194	0.123	0.087	0.080	0.062	0.062	0.070	0.087
1 65 +	0.100	0.000	0.080	0.056	0.052	0.041	0.041	0.046	0.056
1 16–29	0.000	0.760	0.530	0.392	0.0364	0.289	0.287	0.323	0.392
9 30–44	0.000	0.376	0.245	0.174	0.161	0.126	0.125	0.142	0.174
8 45–64	0.000	0.183	0.116	0.082	0.075	0.059	0.058	0.066	0.082
2 65 +	0.094	0.000	0.075	0.053	0.049	0.039	0.038	0.043	0.053
1 16–29	0.000	0.742	0.518	0.383	0.355	0.282	0.280	0.316	0.383
9 30–44	0.000	0.367	0.239	0.170	0.157	0.123	0.122	0.138	0.170
8 45–64	0.000	0.179	0.113	0.080	0.074	0.058	0.057	0.065	0.080
3 65 +	0.092	0.000	0.074	0.052	0.048	0.038	0.038	0.042	0.052
1 16–29	0.000	0.818	0.570	0.421	0.391	0.311	0.309	0.348	0.421
9 30–44	0.000	0.404	0.263	0.187	0.173	0.135	0.134	0.152	0.187
8 45–64	0.000	0.196	0.124	0.088	0.081	0.063	0.062	0.071	0.088
4 65 +	0.101	0.000	0.081	0.057	0.053	0.041	0.041	0.046	0.057
1 16–29	0.000	0.840	0.586	0.432	0.401	0.319	0.317	0.357	0.432
9 30–44	0.000	0.415	0.270	0.192	0.177	0.138	0.137	0.156	0.192
8 45–64	0.000	0.201	0.127	0.090	0.083	0.064	0.064	0.073	0.090
5 65 +	0.103	0.000	0.083	0.058	0.054	0.042	0.042	0.047	0.058
1 16–29	0.000	0.830	0.579	0.428	0.397	0.315	0.313	0.353	0.428
9 30–44	0.000	0.410	0.267	0.190	0.175	0.137	0.136	0.154	0.190
8 45–64	0.000	0.199	0.126	0.089	0.082	0.064	0.063	0.072	0.089
6 65 +	0.102	0.000	0.082	0.058	0.053	0.042	0.041	0.047	0.058

* For classification of household type, see Table 13.1.

those for the district, which is in line with the picture provided in the Census in Figure 13.3. Mobility rates fall slightly from their 1981 level in 1982 and 1983 but then pick up again from 1984. From Table 13.4, one can see that the impact of housing stock dynamics is very minor, with only 130 housing units out of a 1981 stock total of 5285 demolished over the six-year period (2.5 per cent) and a net change in housing stocks of +12 (less than 0.25 per cent).

13.3.3 Mobility probabilities for independent individuals

For each household that does not move as a whole, each eligible house-hold member is exposed to a rate of moving as an individual or as part of a unit smaller than a household. Eligibility for 'independent' mobility excludes children under 16 and members of formal and informal couples, whose migration related to pair dissolution is modelled separately in the BREAKUP module.

Similar steps to those employed for wholly moving households are used to estimate individual mobility probabilities, with the exclusion of the housing stock component. The target variable to be estimated is as follows:

$pi_s^{agm}(t)$ = probability that an independent individual of age a, gender g, marital status m in postal sector s migrates in year t.

This probability is estimated as follows:

$pi_s^{agm}(t)$ = initial district estimate
× spatial adjustment factor
× temporal adjustment factor
× reduction factor to reflect prior migration in the pair formation and dissolution process   (13.7)

THE INITIAL DISTRICT ESTIMATE

An estimate of the probability of migration for independent individuals at district level involves the subtraction of non-eligible individuals from both the migrant count of individuals and from the population divisor. All household heads and their *de facto* spouses were deleted. Full details are given in Duley (1989, Chapter 7, Section 7.2.5). The initial district estimate was adjusted downwards by the ratio of reported 'independent' or 'lone' migrants to the reduced number of migrants:

$$pi_d^{agm}(81) = (MiR_d^{agm}(81)/PiR_d^{agm}(81))$$
$$\times \text{(total lone migrants}/\sum_a\sum_g\sum_m MiR_d^{agm}(81)) \qquad (13.8)$$

where

$pi_d^{agm}(81)$ = the probability that independent individuals of age a, gender g and marital status m in district d migrate in 1980–81;

$MiR_d^{agm}(81)$ = an estimate of the reduced number of individuals of age a, gender g and marital status m in district d who carried out 'independent' migration in 1980–81; and

$PiR_d^{agm}(81)$ = an estimate of the reduced number of individuals of age a, gender g and marital status m in district d eligible for 'independent' migration in 1980–81.

THE SPATIAL ADJUSTMENT FACTOR

The district probability was adjusted to reflect postcode sector mobility rates by multiplication by the ratio of sector to district migration rates for persons

$$(mi_s^{bgn} (81)/mi_d^{bgn} (81))$$

where mi_s^{bgn} (81) is the rate of migration of age b, gender g, marital status n in sector s in 1980–81. The age classification available, signified by use of the letter b, was an aggregated one (16–24, 25–34, 35–44, 45–59, 60–64, 65 +), as was the marital status classification, signified by the use of the letter n (married, single and widowed/divorced).

THE TEMPORAL ADJUSTMENT FACTOR

The same factors were used as described for wholly migrating households. It is necessary to specify the method for estimating mobility probabilities at this stage as follows:

$$
\begin{aligned}
pi_s^{agm}(t) = {}& pi_d^{agm} (81) \\
& \times (mi_s^{agm} (81)/mi_d^{agm} (81)) \\
& \times (o_f(t)/o_f (81))
\end{aligned}
\tag{13.8}
$$

Table 13.6 shows the results of this estimation for the Leeds postal sector LS6 1.

THE REDUCTION FACTOR TO ALLOW FOR PRIOR MIGRATION IN THE PAIR FORMATION AND DISSOLUTION PROCESS

Account must be taken of 'independent' individual migration already modelled in the pair formation and dissolution process. The number of such migrants is counted as the model runs and expressed as a ratio to the total number of persons migrating, and this is subtracted from unity:

$$\text{reduction factor} = [1 - (PM_s^{agm}(t)/TM_s^{agm}(t))] \tag{13.9}$$

where

$PM_s^{agm}(t)$ = the number of 'pair' migrants of age a, gender g and marital status m simulated during pair formation and dissolution who move from postcode sector s in year t; and

$TM_s^{agm}(t)$ = total number of migrants of age a, gender g and marital status m expected to migrate in postcode sector s in year t.

13.3.4 *The model for estimating mobility probabilities for independent individuals*

The total number of migrants is estimated by multiplication of the probabilities defined in equation (13.9) by the local, small-area population at risk. Using the reduction factor defined in equation (13.9) produces the final estimate of the mobility probabilities for 'independent' individuals:

$$
\begin{aligned}
\text{pi}_s^{agm}(t) = \ & \text{pi}_d^{agm}\ (81) \\
& \times\ (\text{mi}_s^{agm}\ (81)/\text{mi}_d^{agm}\ (81)) \\
& \times\ (o_f(t)/o_f\ (81)) \\
& \times\ [1 - (\text{PM}_s^{agm}(t)/\text{TM}_s^{agm}(t)]
\end{aligned}
\tag{13.10}
$$

13.3.5 *The probabilities of relocation within an area and of outmigration*

THE MOBILITY POOL

The first pass through the list of simulated households generates a pool of moving households and fissioned part of households (mainly individuals), which will search for suitable housing vacancies in the local housing market. To allocate migrants to housing units it is necessary to distinguish between moves within the area and moves to the outside world. The within-area movers compete for housing units in the small area, but movers out of the area release units for occupation by inmigrants.

THE PROBABILITIES OF STAYING AND LEAVING

Households and independent individuals for whom a migration has been simulated must therefore be allocated a destination inside or outside the small area of interest by sampling the appropriate probabilities of staying and leaving. If a matrix of intra- and inter-area flows is known, probabilities of relocation within an area or outside it given mobility can be computed:

$$
\text{pr(staying)} = M_{ii}/\sum_j M_{ij}
\tag{13.11}
$$

and

$$
\text{pr(leaving)} = \sum_{j/i} M_{ij}/\sum_j M_{ij}
\tag{13.12}
$$

where M_{ij} = the number of migrants from origin i to destination j. However, such a matrix of inter-area flows exists only for one set of areas, namely within district wards. We need therefore to develop a

Table 13.6 The probability of an 'independent' person migrating from a small area, 1981–86, the example of Leeds postal sector LS6 1

Age	married	Male single	wid/div	married	Female single	wid/div
16–20	0.0136	0.0071	0.0069	0.0328	0.0082	0.0278
21–24	0.0096	0.0136	0.0298	0.0190	0.0159	0.0320
25–29	0.0049	0.0144	0.0281	0.0098	0.0145	0.0204
30–34	0.0030	0.0073	0.0148	0.0049	0.0032	0.0045
35–39	0.0020	0.0046	0.0119	0.0034	0.0021	0.0035
40–44	0.0015	0.0045	0.0089	0.0025	0.0018	0.0026
45–49	0.0001	0.0020	0.0044	0.0030	0.0019	0.0030
50–54	0.0001	0.0017	0.0033	0.0027	0.0017	0.0029
55–59	0.0001	0.0018	0.0020	0.0026	0.0018	0.0025
60–64	0.0001	0.0016	0.0019	0.0025	0.0014	0.0022
65–69	0.0015	0.0019	0.0021	0.0012	0.0011	0.0017
70–74	0.0014	0.0022	0.0021	0.0010	0.0011	0.0017
75+	0.0013	0.0019	0.0026	0.0011	0.0017	0.0021

Age	married	Male single	wid/div	married	Female single	wid/div
16–20	0.0157	0.0081	0.0080	0.0342	0.0086	0.0290
21–24	0.0092	0.0131	0.0285	0.0174	0.0145	0.0293
25–29	0.0039	0.0116	0.0226	0.0090	0.0133	0.0188
30–34	0.0025	0.0061	0.0123	0.0044	0.0029	0.0041
35–39	0.0020	0.0046	0.0119	0.0027	0.0017	0.0028
40–44	0.0019	0.0055	0.0109	0.0030	0.0022	0.0031
45–49	0.0001	0.0021	0.0047	0.0022	0.0014	0.0023
50–54	0.0001	0.0014	0.0027	0.0024	0.0015	0.0026
55–59	0.0001	0.0026	0.0028	0.0034	0.0023	0.0032
60–64	0.0001	0.0018	0.0021	0.0034	0.0020	0.0031
65–69	0.0010	0.0013	0.0015	0.0006	0.0005	0.0007
70–74	0.0010	0.0016	0.0015	0.0008	0.0009	0.0014
75+	0.0012	0.0017	0.0022	0.0013	0.0021	0.0026

Age	married	Male single	wid/div	married	Female single	wid/div
16–20	0.0119	0.0062	0.0061	0.0265	0.0066	0.0225
21–24	0.0098	0.0139	0.0304	0.0178	0.0149	0.0300
25–29	0.0049	0.0144	0.0282	0.0101	0.0150	0.0212
30–34	0.0027	0.0067	0.0135	0.0047	0.0031	0.0043
35–39	0.0025	0.0059	0.0154	0.0048	0.0030	0.0050
40–44	0.0017	0.0051	0.0101	0.0036	0.0026	0.0037
45–49	0.0001	0.0019	0.0041	0.0028	0.0017	0.0028
50–54	0.0001	0.0021	0.0040	0.0027	0.0017	0.0029
55–59	0.0001	0.0025	0.0028	0.0032	0.0021	0.0030
60–64	0.0001	0.0018	0.0020	0.0032	0.0018	0.0028
65–69	0.0019	0.0024	0.0027	0.0013	0.0011	0.0017
70–74	0.0019	0.0029	0.0028	0.0010	0.0011	0.0017
75+	0.0014	0.0021	0.0028	0.0019	0.0030	0.0036

Age	married	Male single	wid/div	married	Female single	wid/div
16–20	0.0130	0.0067	0.0066	0.0271	0.0068	0.0230
21–24	0.0098	0.0140	0.0306	0.0190	0.0159	0.0320
25–29	0.0049	0.0144	0.0281	0.0103	0.0153	0.0215
30–34	0.0027	0.0067	0.0136	0.0053	0.0035	0.0049
35–39	0.0027	0.0062	0.0163	0.0044	0.0027	0.0046
40–44	0.0019	0.0058	0.0114	0.0037	0.0027	0.0038
45–49	0.0002	0.0022	0.0049	0.0035	0.0021	0.0035
50–54	0.0001	0.0020	0.0038	0.0026	0.0016	0.0027
55–59	0.0001	0.0027	0.0030	0.0030	0.0021	0.0028
60–64	0.0001	0.0019	0.0022	0.0033	0.0019	0.0029
65–69	0.0014	0.0017	0.0020	0.0013	0.0011	0.0017
70–74	0.0017	0.0026	0.0025	0.0009	0.0009	0.0015
75+	0.0014	0.0020	0.0028	0.0019	0.0031	0.0037

Table 13.6 contd

Age	married	Male single	wid/div	married	Female single	wid/div
16–20	0.0117	0.0060	0.0059	0.0244	0.0061	0.0206
21–24	0.0096	0.0136	0.0298	0.0194	0.0162	0.0326
25–29	0.0051	0.0151	0.0296	0.0113	0.0168	0.0237
30–34	0.0027	0.0066	0.0132	0.0050	0.0033	0.0046
35–39	0.0025	0.0058	0.0152	0.0045	0.0028	0.0047
40–44	0.0020	0.0059	0.0117	0.0037	0.0026	0.0037
45–49	0.0002	0.0025	0.0055	0.0030	0.0018	0.0030
50–54	0.0001	0.0019	0.0037	0.0025	0.0016	0.0027
55–59	0.0001	0.0027	0.0029	0.0033	0.0023	0.0031
60–64	0.0001	0.0016	0.0019	0.0028	0.0016	0.0025
65–69	0.0012	0.0015	0.0017	0.0014	0.0013	0.0019
70–74	0.0016	0.0025	0.0024	0.0007	0.0007	0.0012
75+	0.0016	0.0023	0.0031	0.0019	0.0030	0.0036

Age	married	Male single	wid/div	married	Female single	wid/div
16–20	0.0142	0.0074	0.0072	0.0319	0.0080	0.0270
21–24	0.0089	0.0126	0.0275	0.0167	0.0139	0.0281
25–29	0.0038	0.0111	0.0217	0.0091	0.0135	0.0191
30–34	0.0022	0.0054	0.0109	0.0044	0.0029	0.0041
35–39	0.0024	0.0054	0.0142	0.0027	0.0017	0.0028
40–44	0.0014	0.0043	0.0084	0.0030	0.0022	0.0031
45–49	0.0001	0.0018	0.0040	0.0028	0.0017	0.0028
50–54	0.0001	0.0016	0.0030	0.0023	0.0015	0.0025
55–59	0.0001	0.0026	0.0028	0.0023	0.0016	0.0022
60–64	0.0000	0.0008	0.0009	0.0031	0.0018	0.0027
65–69	0.0010	0.0013	0.0015	0.0010	0.0009	0.0014
70–74	0.0010	0.0016	0.0015	0.0009	0.0010	0.0015
75+	0.0013	0.0019	0.0026	0.0016	0.0025	0.0030

Source: Computed in UPDATE.

method using this information to make an estimate at an alternative spatial scale. The effect of spatial scale on gravity model parameters has been thoroughly explored in a series of papers by Batty and Sikdar (1982a, 1982b, 1982c, 1982d, 1984). The methods proposed in the last-cited paper seem promising, but need adaptation for the estimation problem faced in the UPDATE model. The simpler assumption is made that the friction-of-distance parameters calibrated at ward scale (33 units) can be applied at postal sector scale (111 units).

A PRODUCTION-CONSTRAINED SPATIAL INTERACTION MODEL

The method comprises the following steps:

(i)   An origin-specific, production-constrained spatial interaction model (SIM) is fitted to the observed inter-ward migration matrix (derived from OPCS's Special Migration Statistics from the 1981 Census using the MATPAC program). The model takes the form:

$$M_{ij} = A_i \, O_i \, W_j \, \exp(-\text{beta}_i \, d_{ij}) \tag{13.13}$$

where

$O_i = \sum_j M_{ij}$ = total migrants originating in ward i;

$W_j = \sum_i M_{ij}$ = attractiveness of ward j to migrants;

beta_i = distance decay parameter for ward i;

d_{ij} = the distance between ward i and ward j; and

$A_i = 1/\sum_j W_j \, \exp(-\text{beta}_i \, d_{ij})$ = balancing factor for ward i.

The IMP program of Stillwell (1984) was used to estimate the beta_i values. The values for Leeds wards are shown in Table 13.7(a).

(ii) These ward beta parameters are used to estimate the equivalent parameters for postcode sectors by inputting the ward values to constituent enumeration districts and then computing a weighted average for enumeration districts lying within a postal sector, employing enumeration district populations as weights. These imputed beta values for postcode sectors are given in Table 13.7(b).

(iii) An inter-sector distance matrix is computed from knowledge of sector centroids and Pythagoras' theorem. Intra-sector distance is assumed to be:

$$d_{ii} = (A_i/\text{pi})^{0.5} \tag{13.14}$$

where A_i is the area of postal sector i.

(iv) The production-constrained SIM is used to predict the share of outmigration from each sector to itself:

Table 13.7 Best-fit origin-specific beta values for Leeds wards, and weighted estimates of corresponding betas for postal sectors

(a) Wards

Ward label	Beta value	Ward label	Beta value	Ward label	Beta value
Aireborough	0.50470	Harehills	0.42681	Pudsey Nth	0.50175
Armley	0.43945	Headingley	0.41754	Pudsey Sth	0.53856
Barwk & Kipx	0.48386	Horsforth	0.46395	Richmond H	0.51260
Beeston	0.53033	Hunslet	0.76208	Rothwell	0.71714
Bramley	0.54200	Kirkstall	0.28774	Roundhay	0.26449
Burmantofts	0.35914	Middleton	0.72415	Seacroft	0.34526
Chap Allrtn	0.33196	Moortown	0.29405	University	0.35889
City & Holb	0.42565	Morley Nth	0.53837	Weetwood	0.29387
Cookridge	0.33437	Morley Sth	0.65828	Wetherby	0.61252
Garf & Swill	0.47769	North	0.53048	Whinmoor	0.36583
Halton	0.39596	Otley & Whf	0.74272	Wortley	0.43251

(b) Postcode sectors

Sector label	Beta value	Sector label	Beta value	Sector label	Beta value
LS1 2	0.42565	LS16 7	0.33437	LS28 5	0.50175
LS1 3	0.35889	LS16 8	0.34915	LS28 6	0.52797
LS1 4	0.35889	LS16 9	0.74272	LS28 7	0.52047
LS1 5	0.00000	LS17 5	0.38080	LS28 8	0.53184
LS1 6	0.42565	LS17 6	0.30987	LS28 9	0.53856
LS10 1	0.74815	LS17 7	0.53048	LS29 6	0.50470
LS10 2	0.76208	LS17 8	0.43515	LS3 1	0.35889
LS10 3	0.75065	LS17 9	0.60457	LS4 2	0.28774
LS10 4	0.70087	LS18 4	0.46395	LS5 3	0.30098
LS11 0	0.49309	LS18 5	0.46395	LS6 1	0.40345
LS11 5	0.48461	LS19 6	0.55153	LS6 2	0.38501
LS11 6	0.44248	LS19 7	0.53310	LS6 3	0.38646
LS11 7	0.49353	LS2 8	0.35889	LS6 4	0.29389
LS11 8	0.46869	LS2 9	0.35889	LS7 1	0.35889
LS11 9	0.42565	LS20 8	0.50470	LS7 2	0.34078
LS12 1	0.43318	LS20 9	0.50470	LS7 3	0.33196
LS12 2	0.43945	LS21 1	0.74272	LS7 4	0.33291
LS12 3	0.43660	LS21 2	0.74272	LS8 1	0.27160
LS12 4	0.43135	LS21 3	0.74272	LS8 2	0.26756
LS12 5	0.43251	LS22 4	0.61252	LS8 3	0.42318
LS12 6	0.43184	LS22 5	0.61252	LS8 4	0.36523
LS13 1	0.51688	LS23 6	0.61252	LS8 5	0.40159
LS13 2	0.51071	LS23 7	0.61252	LS9 0	0.50568
LS13 3	0.53951	LS24 9	0.61252	LS9 6	0.36936
LS13 4	0.47738	LS25 1	0.47769	LS9 7	0.37365
LS14 1	0.35063	LS25 2	0.47769	LS9 8	0.47195
LS14 2	0.36583	LS25 3	0.48386	LS9 9	0.51260
LS14 3	0.49714	LS25 4	0.48386	BD10 0	0.00000
LS14 5	0.36583	LS25 5	0.48386	BD11 1	0.53837

Table 13.7 contd

Sector label	Beta value	Sector label	Beta value	Sector label	Beta value
LS14 6	0.34718	LS25 7	0.48386	BD3 7	0.50175
LS15 0	0.47991	LS26 0	0.71844	BD4 8	0.53856
LS15 4	0.43124	LS26 8	0.61331	WF10 2	0.48386
LS15 7	0.37740	LS26 9	0.51190	WF2 0	0.65828
LS15 8	0.39462	LS27 0	0.62643	WF3 1	0.65828
LS15 9	0.39596	LS27 7	0.54489	WF3 2	0.65828
LS16 5	0.29340	LS27 8	0.62705	WF3 3	0.72238
LS16 6	0.32213	LS27 9	0.55339	WF3 4	0.71714

Source: Computed using IMP package (Stillwell 1984).

$$M_{ii} \, / \, O_i \, = \, W_i \, \exp(-\text{beta}_i \, d_{ii})/\sum_j W_j \, \exp(-\text{beta}_i \, d_{ij}) \qquad (13.15)$$

where W_i and W_j are the attractiveness variables for postal sectors i and j which are set as equal to the migration within or into the sector estimated by summing that variable available for enumeration districts.

(v) So the probability of staying in an area given mobility is computed by the left-hand side of equation (13.15), while the probability of leaving the area is 1 minus the probability of staying. Table 13.8 presents the within/without dichotomy for Leeds postal sectors. The variation is considerable, ranging from near-negligible intra-area flows within LS1 to large and in some cases dominant flows within peripheral postal sectors, those in LS21 and LS22, for example. Such a distribution can be explained broadly on the basis that migrants have further to travel to cross boundaries in the larger peripheral postal sectors. However, this relationship is constrained somewhat by local housing stock that increases the attractiveness of the destination sector, and intervening opportunities that reduce the distance of moves.

Within-area movers are then matched to vacant dwellings in the housing pool of the small area. Their successful matching is based on a probabilistic matching of their respective attributes: housing provision versus housing requirement (size of household–size of unit; disposable household income–purchase price/rental value). The mechanisms for such matching, the links between housing units, households and/or individuals are provided by pointers or common reference numbers.

Table 13.8 Destination selection: the division of movement within and without the small-area, postal sectors in Leeds

Sector	Within	Without	Sector	Within	Without	Sector	Within	Without
LS1 2	0.003	0.997	LS1 3	0.001	0.999	LS1 4	0.001	0.999
LS1 5	0.000	0.000	LS1 6	0.001	0.999	LS10 1	0.103	0.897
LS10 2	0.250	0.750	LS10 3	0.185	0.815	LS10 4	0.283	0.717
LS11 0	0.050	0.950	LS11 5	0.042	0.958	LS11 6	0.088	0.912
LS11 7	0.103	0.897	LS11 8	0.079	0.921	LS11 9	0.024	0.976
LS12 1	0.042	0.958	LS12 2	0.046	0.954	LS12 3	0.068	0.932
LS12 4	0.091	0.909	LS12 5	0.076	0.924	LS12 6	0.013	0.987
LS13 1	0.063	0.937	LS13 2	0.134	0.866	LS13 3	0.112	0.888
LS13 4	0.093	0.907	LS14 1	0.052	0.948	LS14 2	0.084	0.916
LS14 3	0.048	0.952	LS14 5	0.083	0.917	LS14 6	0.094	0.906
LS15 0	0.097	0.903	LS15 4	0.056	0.944	LS15 7	0.076	0.924
LS15 8	0.090	0.910	LS15 9	0.012	0.988	LS16 5	0.031	0.969
LS16 6	0.069	0.931	LS16 7	0.095	0.905	LS16 8	0.032	0.968
LS16 9	0.146	0.854	LS17 5	0.046	0.954	LS17 6	0.051	0.949
LS17 7	0.123	0.877	LS17 8	0.092	0.908	LS17 9	0.077	0.923
LS18 4	0.071	0.929	LS18 5	0.092	0.908	LS19 6	0.115	0.885
LS19 7	0.266	0.734	LS2 8	0.003	0.997	LS2 9	0.019	0.981
LS20 8	0.325	0.675	LS20 9	0.163	0.837	LS21 1	0.277	0.723
LS21 2	0.424	0.576	LS21 3	0.314	0.686	LS22 4	0.715	0.285
LS22 5	0.152	0.848	LS23 6	0.546	0.454	LS23 7	0.398	0.602
LS24 9	0.111	0.889	LS25 1	0.128	0.872	LS25 2	0.145	0.855
LS25 3	0.037	0.963	LS25 4	0.132	0.868	LS25 5	0.011	0.989
LS25 7	0.337	0.663	LS26 0	0.220	0.780	LS26 8	0.292	0.708
LS26 9	0.075	0.925	LS27 0	0.225	0.775	LS27 7	0.077	0.923
LS27 8	0.108	0.892	LS27 9	0.109	0.891	LS28 5	0.164	0.836
LS28 6	0.129	0.871	LS28 7	0.122	0.878	LS28 8	0.116	0.884
LS28 9	0.058	0.942	LS29 6	0.014	0.986	LS3 1	0.018	0.982
LS4 2	0.047	0.952	LS5 3	0.043	0.957	LS6 1	0.135	0.865
LS6 2	0.050	0.950	LS6 3	0.076	0.924	LS6 4	0.049	0.951
LS7 1	0.017	0.983	LS7 2	0.040	0.960	LS7 3	0.067	0.933
LS8 1	0.051	0.949	LS8 2	0.048	0.952	LS8 3	0.057	0.943
LS8 4	0.087	0.913	LS8 5	0.058	0.942	LS9 0	0.115	0.885
LS9 6	0.073	0.927	LS9 7	0.083	0.917	LS9 8	0.068	0.932
LS9 9	0.035	0.965	LS7 4	0.042	0.958	BD10 0	0.000	0.000
BD11 1	0.110	0.890	BD3 7	0.029	0.971	BD4 8	0.073	0.927
WF10 2	0.202	0.798	WF2 0	0.034	0.966	WF3 1	0.144	0.856
WF3 2	0.127	0.873	WF3 3	0.167	0.833	WF3 4	0.054	0.946

13.4 The estimation and reconstruction of inmigrant households and individuals

13.4.1 The estimation of inmigrant numbers

The units in the housing pool not taken up by moving households, and housing spaces within existing households not taken up by moving individuals resident at the start of the time interval are then available for occupation by new, inmigrating households and individuals.

Table 13.9 Migrant household accounts: the composition of inmigrant
households numbers
An example of Leeds postcode sector LS6 1

Description	Code	Count
Households migrating within area	a	265
Households outmigrating from area	b	874
Total 'wholly moving' households	a + b = c	1 139
Total housing unit demolitions	d	22
Total housing units contructions	e	24
Total vacated housing units available to inmigrant households	b − d = f	852
Total inmigrant households	e + f = g	876

Source: UPDATE simulation run.

Central to the modelling of migration at the small-area scale is the role
of the 'pull' of vacant housing stock. Very simply, migrants can only
move into an area if there are housing spaces for them to occupy (ignoring the migration of the homeless). It follows that the most significant
changes in household and population counts will be caused by changes
in housing stock.

To estimate inmigrant numbers one again distinguishes between
mobility and housing stock components. Due to the total absence of
small-area migration data for years after 1981 and the effect of boundary
definition and spatial scale on mobility levels, simplifications that no net
migration effect on household numbers is induced by the mobility
component. That is, all housing units left vacant by outmigrating
households will be filled by inmigrant households. To this total must be
added the new housing component. Assuming that all new housing completions are occupied within one year of construction, this additional
annual sum corresponds to the number of housing completions. The
annual inmigrant household sum is of the form:

Total number of inmigrant households
= number of mobile   + number of new   − number of old
  inmigrant   housing units   housing units
  households   constructed   demolished

(13.16)

Table 13.9 illustrates the form that the migrant household accounts take.

13.4.2 *Assigning personal and relational attributes to inmigrants*

Finally, the characteristics of inmigrant households and individuals must be determined. In part this is dependent on the particular nature of migrants and in part on the particular nature of the small-area population. The size and composition of inmigrants' households is determined in part by those of the housing units and in part by the collective demographic and socioeconomic character of the small area. The detailed reconstruction of the inmigrant population is carried out using modified versions of the techniques used to construct the starting stock of households and individuals in the small area. Full details are given in Duley (1989, Section 7.2.8).

13.5 Implementing migration in the microsimulation model

How are the probability distributions described in the third section of the chapter and the inmigrant numbers described in the fourth section handled in the microsimulation? Two figures show how the results of the estimation work are used. Figure 13.4 highlights stages in the modelling of the mobility and destination processes, while Figure 13.5 sets out the stages involved in adding inmigrants to the small-area population.

13.5.1 *The testing of existing households and eligible individuals for mobility*

Each household in the small area is tested for migration as a whole, using the standard Monte Carlo sampling technique. Testing is carried out on the basis of the age of the head and the type of household comprising the 'whole'. If movement is deemed to occur, the household is placed in a pool of migrant households. The associated housing unit, previously occupied, is added to the vacant housing pool becoming eligible for reoccupation. The next household is then processed and so on. If the household is deemed to stay, and is not a single-person household, eligible individuals within it are tested for independent migration on the basis of their age, sex and marital status. Such individuals are confined to non-family adults and non-dependent children. Members of formal and informal unions are excluded due to the separate modelling of their migration associated with pair dissolution in the BREAKUP module. It follows that new non-family adults generated due to couple breakup are also excluded. If the eligible individual is deemed to move, he or she is placed in an individual migrant pool, with the household size and composition updated to reflect new household conditions.

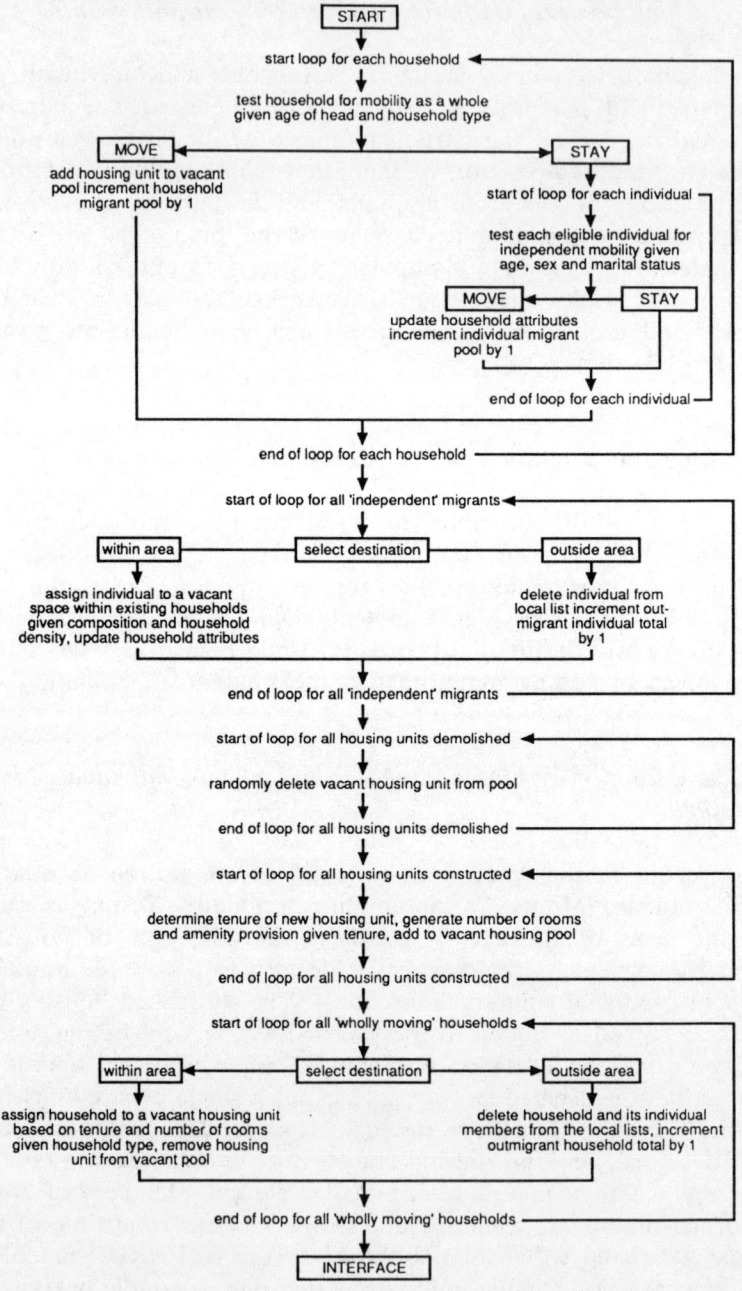

Figure 13.4   Stages in the simulation of within and outmigration households and individuals

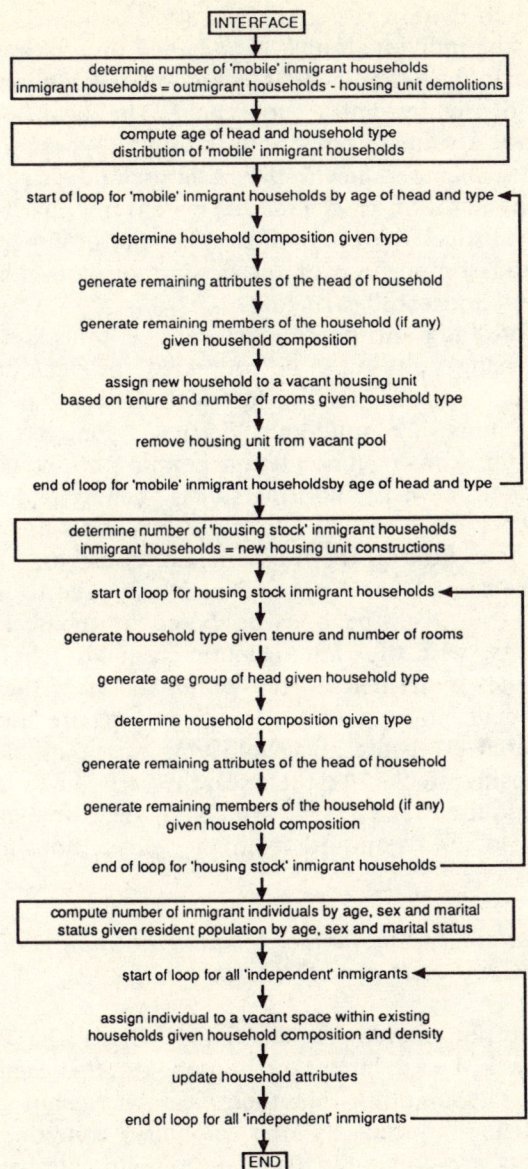

Figure 13.5 Stages in the simulation of inmigration of households and individuals

13.5.2 *The destination selection of migrant households and individuals*

Firstly, each individual in the 'independent' migrant pool is assigned a destination, sampling from a local distance function. If deemed to migrate to a destination outside the small area, the individual is deleted.

If deemed to remain within the small area (destination zone the same as the origin zone), the individual must be assigned to a vacant space within an existing household. Assignment is based on the random selection of the composition of the destination household. The local household list is then searched until a suitable household is found. Where the addition of another household member means that a household density criterion is exceeded, then the addition is excluded. This ensures that households do not become unrealistically overcrowded. Like the origin household, the household size and composition of the destination household is updated to match the new household structure.

Secondly, before migrant households can be processed, existing or newly vacant housing units must be processed for demolition and new units added through construction. In line with the relevant count for the period, housing units are randomly deleted from the vacant pool. Similarly, given the known construction count, new housing units are generated and added to vacant housing stocks. Tenure is determined first from which number of rooms and amenity provision are assigned.

Thirdly, each household in the migrant pool is assigned a destination, sampling from the same local distance function applied to individuals. If deemed to leave the area, the household and its members are deleted from the local lists, with the running outmigrant household total being incremented by one. If deemed to stay within the area, the household is assigned to a vacant housing unit. 'Imaginary' tenure and number of rooms are generated given the household type of the mobile household. Local vacant housing stocks are then searched to find a 'real' housing unit with the required attributes, which is then matched with the homeless household, and removed from the vacant housing pool.

13.5.3 The simulation of the number of inmigrant households and individuals and their characteristics

Firstly, inmigrant households are simulated. Given the distinction of 'mobile'- and 'stock'-based inmigrant households, this task is split into two. Adopting the assumption that there is no net migration effect on household numbers induced by the mobility component, 'mobile' inmigrant numbers are computed from outmigrant numbers reduced in line with demolitions of existing housing units (stock push effect). The migrant character of these households is established next. The inmigrant households are distributed amongst the type and age of head groups using local estimates. Proceeding through each age-type combination, each household assigned to it is then fully reconstructed (cf. population reconstruction). First, household type is converted to a corresponding broad household composition category (summing with/without others) for parity with the household classification adopted in the UPDATE model. The remaining attributes of the head are generated next. Then in all but single-person households, remaining member(s) of the household are generated on the basis of the household composition set, which predefines the path of household membership simulation. Finally, each new household is assigned to a vacant housing unit. As with internal migrant households, assignment is carried out by matching 'imaginary' and 'real' units with suitable tenure and unit size given household type, the unit being removed from the vacant housing pool.

'Stock'-based inmigrant households are processed next, equal to new unit construction. The household simulated must fit the housing unit. In this case, household type is determined first given tenure and size of the new unit, from which the age group of the head is ascribed. The household type is then converted to its respective compositional group, with the detailed membership simulation continuing in the same manner as for 'mobile' inmigrant households.

Then, inmigrant individuals are simulated. Given that we are unable to model the link between spaces within existing households (supply) and 'independent' migrants searching for accommodation (demand), simulation is performed on the basis of local inmigration estimates applied to current small-area population (at risk) by age, size and marital status. Each 'independent' inmigrant so generated is assigned to vacant spaces within existing households following the mechanism of internal migration updating the attributes of the destination household accordingly.

13.6 Conclusions

There is a strong tradition of using microsimulation models to study the changing geography of population (Hagerstrand 1957; Morrill 1965; Woods 1981). The focus in previous work has been on migration occurring in a fine network of areas to a simply classified population of individuals. The focus of this work has been on tracing the migration behaviour of a richly classified set of households and associated individuals in a rather simple set of areas. In so doing migration has been regarded as the outcome of several important processes which interface intimately with both the marriage and housing markets. In common with the earlier geographic tradition, we have had to think imaginatively of ways in which the probabilities and numbers required in the microsimulation process can be estimated. The estimation procedures have been presented in some detail. The results of the estimation have considerable interest in themselves, but in the case of the present work are seen only as a means to a more ambitious end, that of updating the population of small areas within cities or counties between Censuses, while retaining a good proportion of the richness of character available in those decennial, national endeavours.

Chapter 14

Internal migration projection in England: the OPCS/DOE model examined*

Peter Boden, John Stillwell and Philip Rees

14.1 Introduction

The Office of Population Censuses and Surveys (OPCS) is responsible for the production of subnational population projections in England using a demographic component methodology (Armitage 1986). Base-year population estimates are available for five-year age groups which can be approximately disaggregated to single year of age using the national age profile. Age-specific mortality rates are applied to these population estimates to generate the number of persons surviving to be one year older. Fertility rates are then applied to the female population aged 15–44 during the year to calculate the number of live births. Finally, the number of persons entering or leaving each subnational area during the year are taken into account in order to allow for population change due to migration.

In this chapter, we are concerned to outline the submodel that is used by OPCS, in collaboration with the Department of the Environment (DOE), for generating estimates of internal migration between local authority areas. Prior to 1981, the net migration assumptions used within the projection procedure were derived in a hierarchical manner with initial totals for the standard regions being used to constrain the assumptions for local authority areas (metropolitan districts, non-metropolitan counties, London boroughs). The DOE, with its close links with planning authorities, was responsible for the initial regional estimates. Lengthy consultation between the DOE and the individual local authorities was then necessary in order to establish appropriate net totals for each local area, taking account of the possible effect of local factors upon net migration. Decision-making was not made any easier by the dearth of available migration statistics. Once the DOE had decided the net figures, an age and sex structure was allocated to the migration flows. The whole projection process was deemed to be too costly in terms of time spent in consultation with the planning authorities and in the considerable

* The authors are very grateful for comments on an earlier version of this chapter by colleagues from OPCS. We remain, nevertheless, entirely responsible for the contents.

effort required by OPCS to produce the age breakdown of net migration flows by sex for each individual local authority. OPCS and DOE consequently sought to improve the migration projections by making better use of existing data and producing a first estimate of net migration which could be input to the consultation process.

In 1981, Martin and Voorhees Associates and John Bates Services were contracted by the DOE to develop an improved model for generating the net migration assumptions for the 108 English local authority areas concerned; the 36 metropolitan districts, 39 shire counties and 33 London boroughs. The procedure which they proposed for the production of net migration estimates disaggregated by sex and single year of age is documented in Martin, Voorhees and Bates (1981), and has been used to produce sets of projections from base years 1981, 1983 and 1985 (OPCS 1983, 1986, 1988). The methodology for producing projections for local authority areas (not the recent extension to health authority areas) is described in detail in Section 14.2 of the chapter. In Section 14.3, certain features of the model are investigated using data from the National Health Service Central Register (NHSCR) on patient re-registrations between Family Practitioner Committee (FPC) areas in England and Wales. Firstly, a clustering procedure is used to show how the definition of the broad age groups adopted by OPCS in their modelling procedures might be improved. Secondly, changes in the distribution pattern of migration since 1980–81 are identified which call into question that part of the modelling procedure which uses probabilities based on 1981 Census data to assign projected outmigrants to destinations. Finally, a different method of grouping local authority areas is proposed which generates clusters that differ from those currently used in the OPCS/DOE methodology. Conclusions are drawn in the final section of the chapter.

14.2 The OPCS/DOE migration projection methodology

The starting point for each round of projections is the set of mid-year population estimates for males and females by five-year age group. These estimates, prepared by OPCS (1982, 1984, 1986) for each local authority area, include all persons usually resident in local government areas of England, together with Armed Forces personnel stationed in each area and students counted as residents at their term-time addresses.

There are four main stages in the methodology for generating internal migration estimates:

(i) the projection of migration flows out of each local authority area by age and sex;
(ii) the assignment of these outflows by broad age group to individual destinations;

(iii) the aggregation of these flows to provide area inmigration totals and their disaggregation by age and sex; and

(iv) the calculation of net migration assumptions from age-specific outflow and inflow totals for males and females.

We can explain the methodology in more detail by setting out the equations associated with each stage, following Rees and Willekens (1989).

14.2.1 Outmigration projection

The first stage of the migration projection procedure involves projecting age-specific outflows from each individual area for males and females for a given time period as the product of the mid-year population estimate or projection for the area, the area's gross migraproduction rate (gmr_i) and the proportion of this rate accounted for by a particular age and sex group. The model equation takes the form:

$$M_{i\bullet}^{as}(t) = gmr_i(t) \cdot om_I^{as}(r) \cdot P_i^{as}(t_o) \tag{14.1}$$

where:

$M_{i\bullet}^{as}(t)$ = the total number of outmigrations from area i by single year of age a and sex s for year t;

$gmr_i(t)$ = the gross migraproduction rate from area i in year t;

$om_I^{as}(r)$ = the proportion of the migraproduction rate in single year age group a and sex s (derived from modelled, standardized migration rates for area cluster I for a standard period r, 1980–81); and

$P_i^{as}(t_o)$ = the population of area i at single year of age a and sex s at t_o, the beginning of year t.

Current projections adopt 1981 Census gross migraproduction rates adjusted for under-enumeration and modified in the light of changes evident from NHSCR movement data. The Census gmr for a local authority area is simply trended parallel to that of an NHSCR total outmigration rate using the slope of a linear regression through an annual time series of NHSCR patient re-registration data for each sex. The outmigration proportions have been derived from the age-specific profiles of clusters of areas. To reduce the data requirements of the model (i.e. to avoid having to use and store male and female age-specific outmigration rates for each area), a classification of area outmigration profiles was derived based on similarities between individual model migration schedules calibrated initially on 1971 Census data (Martin, Voorhees and Bates 1981; Bates and Bracken 1982; Bracken and Bates 1983) and subsequently on 1981 Census data (Bates 1984; Bates and

Table 14.1 Summary of English local authority groupings based on 1981 male outmigration profiles

Group	Area type	Number of areas
1A	Shire counties (most)	27
1B	Shire counties (remainder)	4
2	London boroughs (most)	28
3	Metropolitan districts (most)	34
4A	Home counties A	4
4B	Home counties B (remainder)	3
5	Outer London boroughs (remainder)	4
6	Lancashire and Bradford	2
7	Liverpool	1

Source: Bates (1984).

Bracken 1987). Using the techniques developed by Rogers *et al.* (1978), model migration schedules were fitted to observed outmigration rate profiles for each area. The parameters describing the model schedules were used to compare areas and group them into categories based on profile similarities. A classification of seven groups emerged with the majority of English local authorities falling into one of three main groups containing respectively, most of the shire counties, the London boroughs and the metropolitan districts (Table 14.1). Subdivisions of groups 1 (shire counties) and 4 (home counties) were suggested in order to distinguish areas where a retirement effect was evident in the migration profile from areas where this effect was not present. The same grouping was used for females.

14.2.2 Assignment

The second stage of the projection procedure involves the assignment of the estimated outmigration totals to individual destination areas. Because of the problem of handling matrices containing large numbers of small or zero flows, single year of age outmigrants are grouped into three broad age bands (0–16/29–59, 17–28 and 60+), which corresponds with different types of migratory movement. The first age group is composed of migrant families; the second involves moves about the time of entry to the labour force when young people frequently leave home; and the third group is associated with retirement and elderly migration. Assignment probabilities are then used to allocate outmigrants to destinations. The assignment submodel can be written as:

$$M_{ij}^{As}(t) = M_{i*}^{As}(t) \cdot k_{ij}^{As}(r) \qquad (14.2)$$

where:

$M_{ij}^{As}(t)$ = migration flows from area i to area j in broad age group A and sex s during year t;

$$M_{i*}^{As}(t) = \sum_{a \varepsilon A} M_{i*}^{as}(t) \qquad (14.3)$$

= total out migration from area i in broad age group A and sex s during year t; and

$k_{ij}^{As}(r)$ = the proportion of outmigrants from area i in broad age group A and of sex s which moved to destination area j in a standard period r.

1981 Census data are currently used as the basis for assigning outflows to destinations and so the period r refers to the 12 months before the Census (1980–81). No updating of the inter-area probability information has been undertaken and therefore the distribution patterns of migration are assumed to have remained constant since 1980–81.

14.2.3 Inmigration projection

The product of the second stage in the procedure is a series of migration inflows to individual areas disaggregated by broad age group and sex. The third component of the projection model aggregates these flows to produce total migration and then disaggregates the totals to provide flows by single year of age and sex. The inflow model can be written as:

$$M_{*j}^{as}(t) = \sum_{A} \sum_{i} M_{ij}^{As}(t) \cdot im_j^{as}(r) \qquad (14.4)$$

where

$M_{*j}^{as}(t)$ = the total number of inmigrants to area j by single year of age a and sex s in year t;

$\sum_{A} \sum_{i} M_{ij}^{As}(t)$ = the aggregation of inter-area flows by broad age group and sex to provide total inmigration to area j by sex in year t; and

$im_j^{as}(r)$ = the proportion of inmigration gmr in single year age group a and sex s (derived from modelled, standardized migration rates for area cluster J for a standard period r).

The im values are derived from area clusters based on inmigration data from the 1981 Census. The classification of areas on the basis of their inmigration profiles in 1980–81 is more complex than the outmigration grouping illustrated earlier: 11 groupings with distinctive profiles are identified by Bates (1984). Since each area is associated with a particular group profile, area inflow totals are disaggregated into single years of age according to proportions evident from the standardized profiles of the cluster to which that area belongs.

14.2.4 Net migration calculation

At this stage of the procedure, gross outflows and inflows disaggregated by single year of age and sex have been projected for each area. From these it is possible to compute net migration assumptions as:

$$N_i^{as}(t) = M_{*i}^{as}(t) - M_{i*}^{as}(t) \qquad\qquad (14.5)$$

where

$N_i^{as}(t)$ = net migration for area i by single year of age a and sex s in year t;

$M_{*i}^{as}(t)$ = projected gross inmigration to area i by age a and sex s in year t; and

$M_{i*}^{as}(t)$ = projected gross outmigration from area i by age a and sex s in year t.

These net migration assumptions form part of the OPCS model to produce subnational population projections. This model has certain facilities to amend gross migraproduction rates and to input maximum or minimum values of net migration as constraints for a few specified individual areas or groups of areas.

14.2.5 Consultation

The generation of projections by OPCS is followed by an exercise in which the DOE consults the local authorities over the in-, out- and net migration projections and local authorities are able to respond by stating the factors that they believe will result in figures different from the trend-based assumptions (e.g. house-building or clearance programmes). As a result of these consultations, changes are made to the migration assumptions and the population projections before the procedure is finalized.

14.3 Three features of the model examined

There is little doubt that the procedure developed by Martin, Voorhees and Bates has provided a much improved framework for generating projections. The derivation of migration assumptions is based essentially on outmigration and inmigration age profiles and inter-area assignment matrices for the 1980–81 pre-Census period, with the Census gross migraproduction rate trended using more recent NHSCR mid-year to mid-year movement data. However, as the length of time since 1981 increases, there is inevitably a growing concern about the changes in age structure and spatial distribution of migration that may have occurred during the last decade. There is no mechanism for their incorporation in the existing OPCS/DOE model structure, other than through the gross migraproduction rate.

In the remainder of this chapter, we therefore use data from the NHSCR to examine three selected questions relating to the OPCS/DOE model. It should be recognized that the FPC areas do not fully correspond with the local authority areas for which the OPCS makes its projections although this inconsistency is only important in Greater London. Furthermore, despite OPCS projections only being generated for England, the ready availability of NHSCR data on movements involving Welsh FPC areas suggests that Wales be included in the analysis, as it was in the earlier work of Martin, Voorhees and Bates (1981), Bates and Bracken (1982) and Bracken and Bates (1983). The reliability of the NHSCR data and its precise relationship with Census transition data for 1980–81 is discussed in Devis and Mills (1986) and in Boden *et al.* (1987, 1988).

The first of three questions concerns the validity of the broad age groups defined for use in the model. Whilst the broad age groups that are used in the assignment stage are deemed to encapsulate the major components of migration — family movement, entry to the labour force and retirement migration — little justification is given by OPCS/DOE for adopting these precise age-group boundaries. An alternative broad age-group classification is therefore derived which is based on age-specific, inter-area movement occurring between FPC areas in England and Wales between 1984 and 1986.

The second question we address is concerned with what changes in the spatial patterns of migration have taken place since 1980–81, given the implicit assumption of the OPCS/DOE model that the distribution of migrants has remained constant. Mid-year to mid-year NHSCR data for 1985–86 is used to explore the extent of change since 1980–81 in gross and net migration for aggregate and selected age-specific groups of movers.

The third question focuses on the classification of local authority areas into groupings on the basis of their age profiles. An alternative categorization of outmigration and inmigration areas to that of Bates and Bracken (1987) is proposed which uses a clustering technique based on each area's profile of observed age-specific rates rather than the parameters of each area's model migration schedule.

14.3.1 Systematic derivation of broad age groups

The three broad age categories used in the assignment stage of the OPCS/DOE model have been chosen to reflect the major components of migration. No systematic methodology is provided for the precise definition of the broad age-group boundaries. However, cluster analysis procedures are available in several statistical packages which can be used to derive optimum groupings from age-disaggregated information. In this context, a clustering procedure in SPSSX (Norusis 1985) is used to generate optimum broad age groups. The analysis should be conducted, ideally, using single year of age data, but the size of the array presents severe storage problems and consequently five-year age group inter-FPC area movement matrices for 1984–85 and 1985–86 are used.

The initial step is to compute 'distances' between the values in corresponding cells of the origin–destination matrices for each age group. In order to remove the effect of the level of migration upon the clustering process, the flows are standardized by expressing each value as a proportion of the total movement between the two 'areas'. The Squared Euclidian Distance (SED) between two 'cases' (age groups a and b) is defined as:

$$\text{SED}^{ab} = \sum_t \sum_i \sum_j (M_{ij}^a(t)/M_{ij}^*(t) - M_{ij}^b(t)/M_{ij}^*(t))^2 \tag{14.6}$$

where

$M_{ij}^a(t)$, $M_{ij}^b(t)$ = the number of moves between origin area i and destination area j in age group a (b) in year t; and

$M_{ij}^*(t)$ = the total number of moves between origin area i and destination area j in year t.

The computation of the distance array is a precursor to the actual clustering procedure which is based on the 'average linkage between groups' method. The distance between two clusters is the average of the distance between all pairs of age groups in which one member of the pair is from each of the clusters. Thus the average linkage value or the 'distance coefficient' (D) between clusters A and B is defined as:

$$D^{AB} = \sum_{a \epsilon A} \sum_{b \epsilon B} \text{SED}^{ab}/n^A n^B \tag{14.7}$$

where

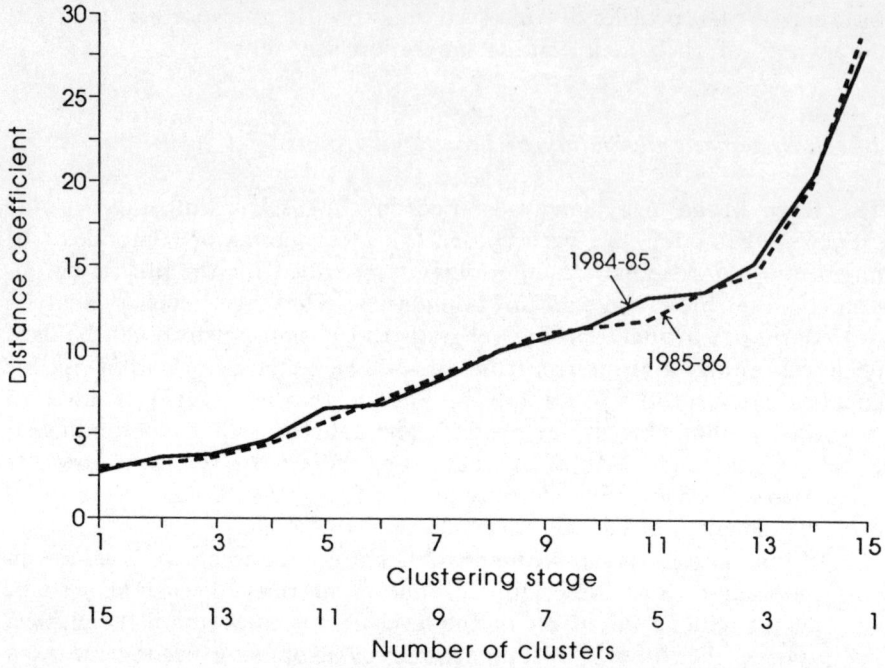

Figure 14.1   Agglomeration schedules from the clustering of five-year age groups based on NHSCR inter-area migration data

n^A, n^B = the number of age groups in clusters A and B respectively.

The process is agglomerative, commencing with the maximum number of clusters (16 age groups), and then combining those cases where the distance coefficient is smallest on each iteration, until all cases are classified in one cluster. The agglomeration schedules for the two mid-year to mid-year periods (Figure 14.1) indicate how the distance coefficient increases as the number of clusters decreases. The D value increases steadily until the point at which four clusters become three (stage 13), whereupon the distance coefficient increases more significantly. In Table 14.2, the three- and four-cluster solutions, which are the same for both time periods, are compared with the broad age categories used by OPCS/DOE. Although this comparison is complicated by the use of five-year age groups and the variation by age which occurs in the ratio of Census to NHSCR migration data as reported in Boden *et al.* (1988), two important differences can be identified. Firstly, the results show that the inclusion of moves by persons in their late 20s with those in their late teens and early 20s is not appropriate. Although it is not feasible to suggest that 15 is a better break point than 17, the results do indicate that 29 is too high a break point for the category defined by OPCS to

Table 14.2 OPCS/DOE broad age groups compared with classifications derived from clustering of five-year age groups

OPCS/DOE group	3-cluster solution	4-cluster solution
0–16/29–59	0–14/25–54	0–14/25–54
17–28	15–24	15–24
60+	55+	55–69
		70+

Table 14.3 Goodness-of-fit statistics comparing inter-FPC area movement by age group, 1980–81 with 1985–86

Age group	Index of dissimilarity	Correlation coefficient
0–14	20.1	0.950
15–19	24.7	0.908
20–24	19.1	0.953
25–54	14.0	0.977
55–69	27.2	0.926
70+	33.5	0.891
All ages	10.5	0.982

Note: The index of dissimilarity compares the two distributions by calculating the sum of the deviations between cell proportions in the two matrices.

include moves around the time of entry to the labour force, when young people frequently leave the parental home. The 25–29 age group combines readily (i.e. at the second stage) with the 30–34 age group in the clustering procedure and therefore 24 is a more appropriate upper age limit for this most highly mobile group. Secondly, the inclusion of moves by persons in their late 50s with retirement moves and post-retirement moves is more appropriate than combining them with the 'family' moves of those aged 25–54. The 55–59 age group combines most readily with the 60–69 age group, and then subsequently with the 70+ age groups at the next stage. More research is clearly required in this context using migration data disaggregated by single year of age and by sex to establish the boundaries precisely.

14.3.2 Changing migration patterns

In the assignment stage of the OPCS/DOE model, it is assumed that the distribution pattern of migration by broad age group in 1980–81 has been continued in subsequent years. The validity of this assumption can be assessed by comparing the NHSCR matrix of moves between FPC areas in England and Wales for the 12-month period which most closely approximates to the year before the 1981 Census (1 April 1980 to 31 March 1981) with the corresponding matrix for mid-year 1985 to mid-

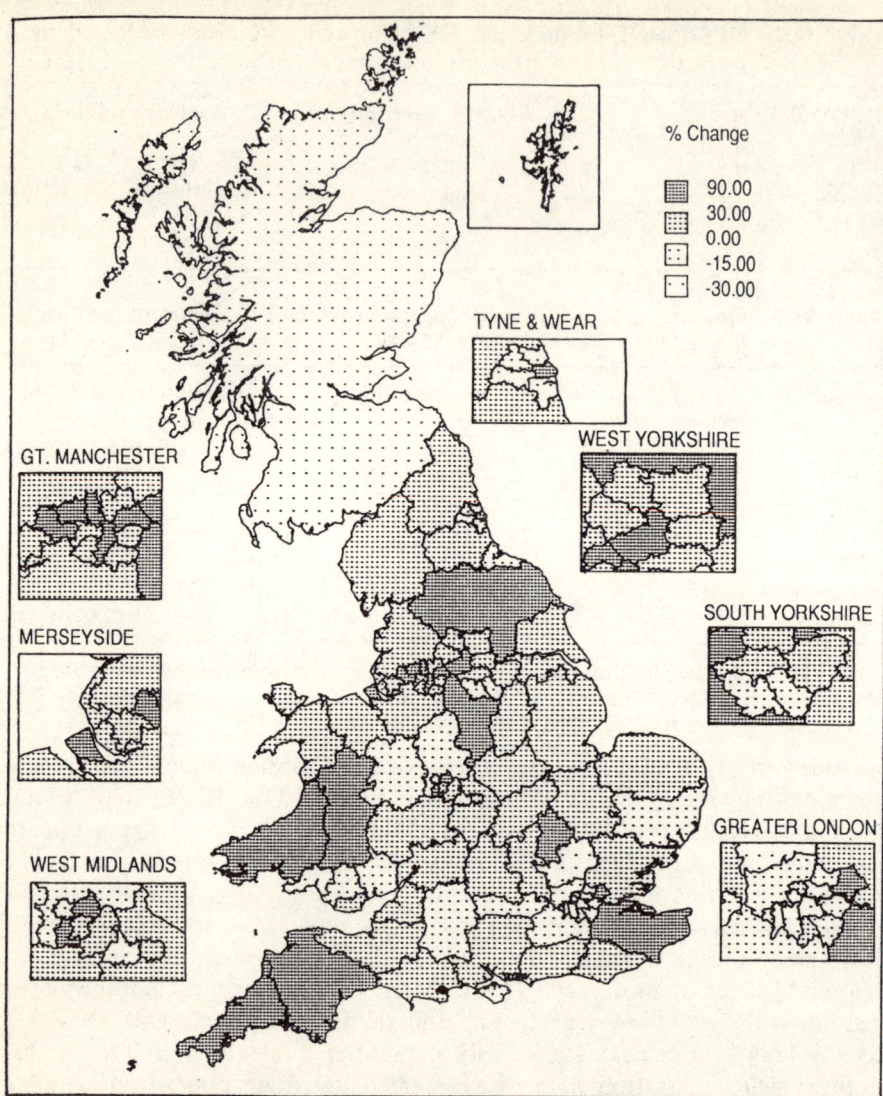

Figure 14.2   Percentage change in inmigration rates of 70+ age group, 1980–81 to 1985–86

year 1986. Two goodness-of-fit statistics, the index of dissimilarity and the correlation coefficient, provide measures of association between the patterns of inter-FPC area migration for six age groups (Table 14.3) in addition to the aggregate flows.

Dissimilarity is most significant and correlation weakest for the post-retirement age group, suggesting a quite substantial alteration in their pattern of movement. The highest rates of gross inmigration for the 70+ group are found in the FPC areas which constitute the South East

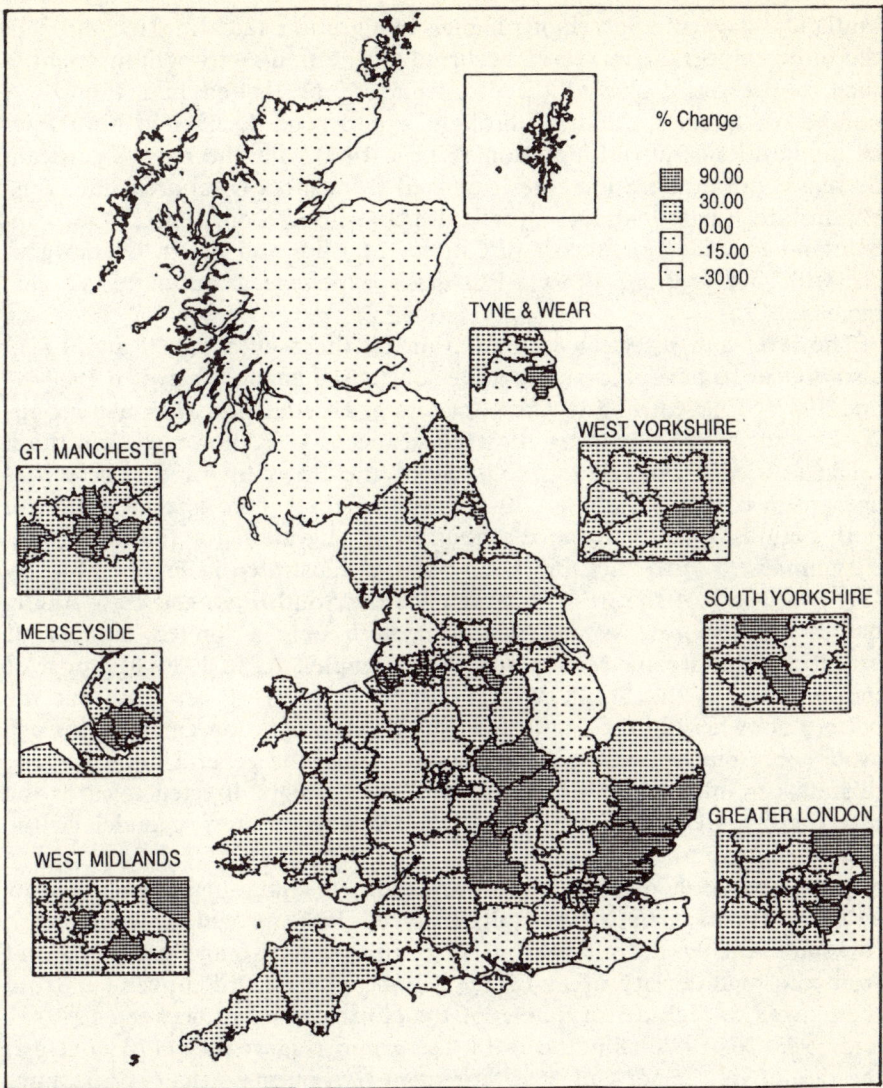

Figure 14.3 Percentage change in outmigration rates of 70+ age group, 1980–81 to 1985–86

(outside Greater London), the South West and East Anglia, whereas the highest gross outmigration rates are found to occur from Greater London boroughs. The observed rates for this age group are relatively small in comparison with other age groups and so their percentage change between 1980–81 and 1985–86 is more marked. The map of changing inmigration rates (Figure 14.2) shows the majority of FPC areas experiencing increased rates during the period. A number of metropolitan FPC areas in Greater Manchester, Merseyside and the West

Midlands showed appreciably higher inmigration rates in 1985–86, but the more important increases occurred in the non-metropolitan counties such as Devon, Cornwall, Bedfordshire, Kent, Dyfed and Powys. A number of Greater London boroughs experienced declines in both rates of inmigration and outmigration (Figure 14.3), but the most significant decreases in outmigration rates occurred from more rural areas including Hampshire, East Sussex, Kent, Lincolnshire, Lancashire, Durham, Scotland and the two Welsh FPC areas of Mid- and South Glamorgan. As with inmigration, most FPC areas experienced outmigration rate increases.

The level and direction of migration by those aged 55–69 and 15–19 also appear to have undergone quite substantial changes between 1980–81 and 1985–86, according to the goodness-of-fit statistics, with age groups 20–24 and 25–54 exhibiting most consistency. It is, however, important to acknowledge the relative volumes of the flows involved. The 20–24 age group comprised almost 20 per cent of total inter-area migration in both periods. The changing distribution of migration for this age group is summarized in the net migration patterns illustrated in Figure 14.4. By 1985–86, most of the FPC areas outside the South East and East Anglia had a negative rate of net migration with only a limited number of exceptions (in Greater Manchester, for example). As in 1980–81, most of the counties in the South West experienced rates of net loss, but the pattern elsewhere in the South was one of net migration gains in this age group, in Greater London in particular. Thus, the general movement of this most mobile age group has become increasingly directed towards the high-density areas of the South at the expense of the remainder of the United Kingdom.

A classification of FPC areas into high-, medium–high, medium–low and low-density groups (see Stillwell *et al.* 1990) provides a framework for summarizing the changes in migration rates by age group to and from the high-density areas of the South. The rate of movement from these areas to high-density areas of the North increased between 1980–81 and 1985–86 for all but the 0–14 age group (Figure 14.5). In contrast, the rate of retirement and post-retirement movement to the two medium-density area categories of the North decreased, whilst, at the same time, low-density areas in the North became more attractive to migrants from Greater London in these two age groups. The importance of family moves and retirement and post-retirement moves out of Greater London to the more rural areas of the South East, East Anglia, South West and East Midlands increased, emphasizing the preference of these groups for residence away from Greater London. This contrasts with the patterns of the 15–19 and 20–24 age groups whose rate of movement out of high-density to lower-density FPC areas decreased significantly up to 1985–86. Figure 14.6 illustrates the changes in rates of outmigration from other areas to the high-density FPC areas of Greater London. Movement rates from Northern high-density areas increased in all age groups: there was

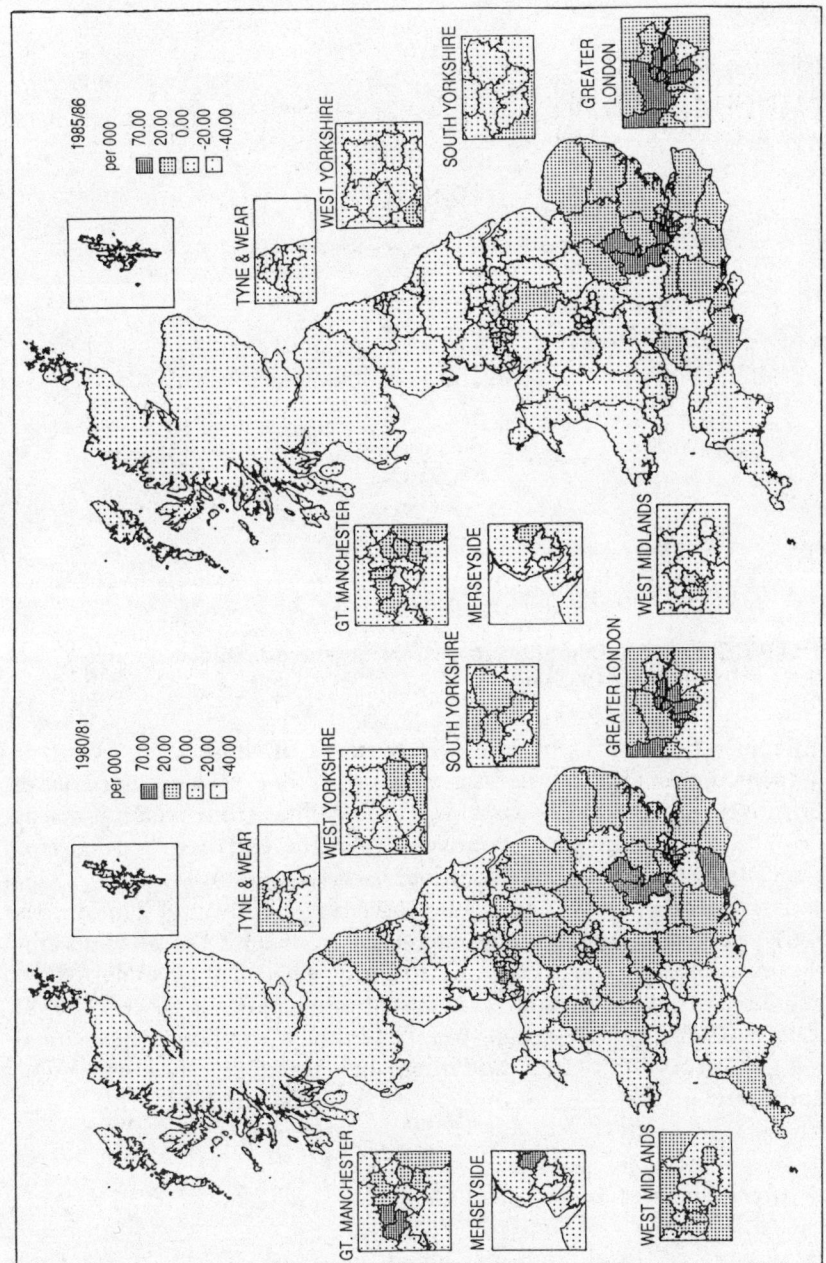

Figure 14.4 Net migration rates of 20–24 age group for 1980–81 and 1985–86

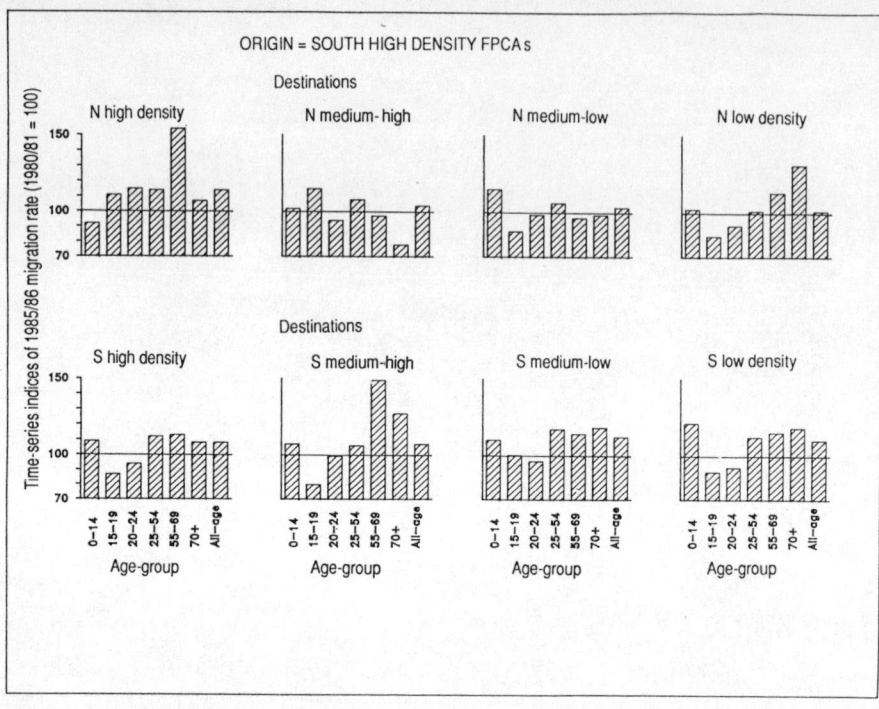

Figure 14.5   Changes in migration rates from Southern high-density areas, 1980–81 to 1985–86

a significant reduction in the rate of movement of those aged 70+ from Northern medium- and low-density areas; a decline also occurred in the rate of movement of 15–19-year-olds to the capital from medium-density areas of the North; the rate of movement in the early age groups from lower-density areas in the South declined, whereas inmovement by 25–54-year-olds from low-density areas increased marginally and inmovement by 55–69-year-olds, paradoxically, increased from both the medium–high and the low-density areas. These illustrations suggest that some marked changes have occurred in migration distribution patterns since 1980–81. The OPCS/DOE model would benefit from a method which incorporated a procedure for updating or trending the assignment probabilities.

14.3.3 Migrating profile classification

The groupings of local authority areas in stages (i) and (iii) of the OPCS/DOE model outlined in Section 14.2 are determined on the basis of the similarity of the parameters of model schedules. The methodology requires the calibration of model migration schedules for the

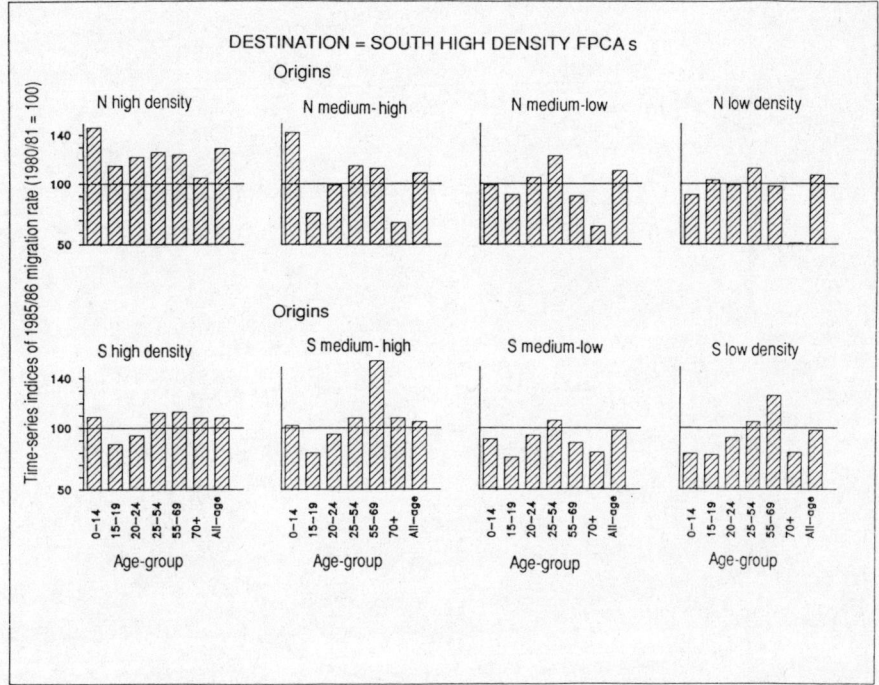

Figure 14.6 Changes in migration rates to Southern high-density areas, 1980–81 to 1985–86

standardized outmigration and inmigration rate profiles of each area in 1980–81 (Bates and Bracken 1987), and therefore requires prior selection of a model for each area with or without a retirement component. An alternative classification method is suggested here which derives groupings of areas on the basis of observed single year of age migration rate schedules. Using the observed schedules removes the difficulty of identifying whether or not a retirement component is present, and retains more information than that based on smoothed profiles. Age-specific rates within each cluster are then aggregated and a single cluster model migration schedule is calibrated.

The clustering technique used to group the standardized migration rates is similar in principle to that outlined in a previous section. NHSCR data on gross outmigration and inmigration by single year of age for FPC areas in England and Wales in 1985–86 are used, and an age range of 1–79 is adopted because small numbers beyond age 79 lead to large fluctuations in rates. The initial step in the process is the computation of the Squared Euclidian Distance (SED) between two FPC areas i and j by direction d (out or in) as:

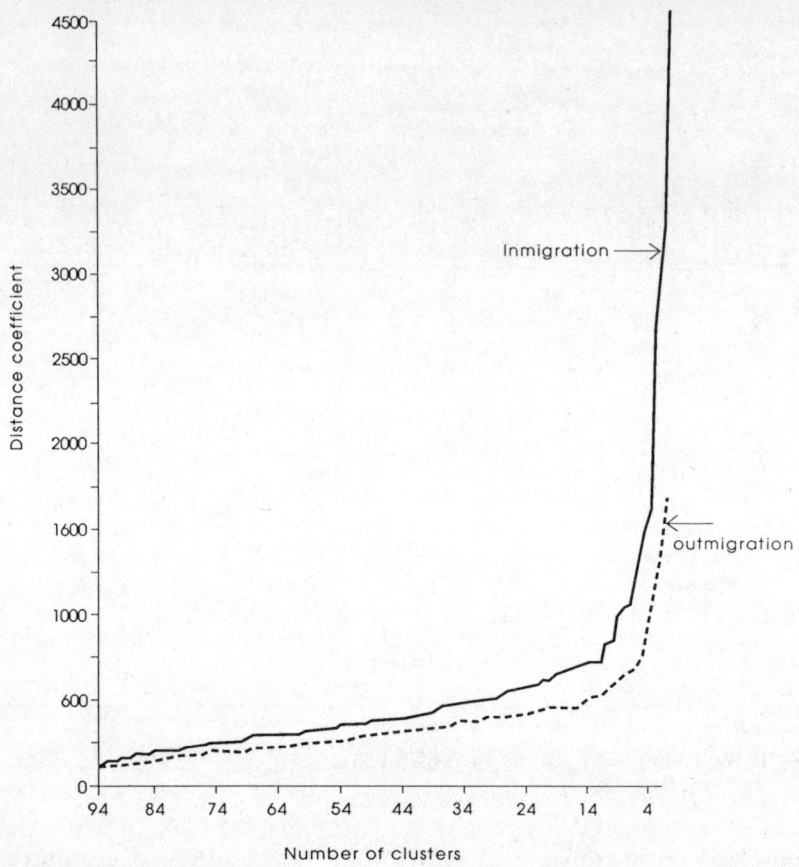

Figure 14.7 Agglomeration schedules from clustering out- and inmigration rate schedules, 1985–86

$$\text{SED}^d_{ij} = \sum_a (m^{ad}_i - m^{ad}_j)^2 \tag{14.8}$$

where

m^{ad}_i, m^{ad}_j = the standardized out or inmigration rates for areas i and j by single year of age a.

The 'average linkage between groups' method is again used where the distance (D) between clusters, I and J, is the average distance between all pairs of FPC areas in which one member of the pair is from each of the clusters:

$$D_{IJ} = \sum_{i \epsilon I} \sum_{j \epsilon J} \text{SED}_{ij}/n_I n_J \tag{14.9}$$

where

Table 14.4 15-cluster stage of FPC area classification process for 1985–86 inmigration

1. Camden and Islington; Kensington, Chelsea and Westminster
2. Redbridge and Waltham Forest; Croydon; Greenwich and Bexley
3. City and East London; Kingston and Richmond; Merton, Sutton and Wandsworth; Lambeth, Southwark and Lewisham; Middlesex
4. Lincolnshire; Suffolk; Isle of Wight; W. Sussex; Cornwall; Dorset; Somerset; Hereford; Salop; Clwyd; Powys
5. Humberside; Norfolk; E. Sussex; Devon; Lancashire; Dyfed; Gwynedd
6. Cumbria; Northumberland; Rotherham; Calderdale; Wakefield; Derbyshire; Northamptonshire; Buckinghamshire; Essex; Kent; Gloucestershire; Wiltshire; Warwickshire; Bolton; Oldham; Rochdale; Tameside; Sefton; Wirral; Cheshire; Gwent
7. Gateshead; N. Tyneside; Barnsley; Bedfordshire; Hertfordshire; Berkshire; Barking and Havering; Bromley; Dudley; Sandwell; Walsall; Bury; Stockport; Trafford; Wigan; St. Helens
8. Durham; Leicestershire; Nottinghamshire; Oxfordshire; Avon; Birmingham; Wolverhampton; Manchester; Salford; S. Glamorgan
9. Newcastle; Sheffield; Coventry
10. Leeds; Liverpool
11. Sunderland; Cleveland; Bradford; Kirklees; Cambridgeshire; Staffordshire; Mid-Glamorgan
12. Scotland; Doncaster; N. Yorkshire; Hampshire
13. S. Tyneside
14. Solihull
15. W. Glamorgan

Note: Middlesex represents a group of five FPC areas.

n_I and n_J = the number of areas in clusters I and J respectively.

The agglomeration schedules produced in the clustering of outmigration and inmigration profiles (Figure 14.7) indicate that the increase in the distance coefficient is fairly constant until around stages 75–80 of the procedure (15–20 clusters). After this point, increases become larger and less uniform, indicating that the association of areas becomes more irregular. A 'break' in the series can be identified as a point at which an optimum number of clusters has been reached and Tables 14.4. and 14.5 outline the FPC area composition of 15 clusters for inmigration and outmigration respectively. The age-specific migration rates for areas within each cluster are aggregated to form a 'cluster profile'. Finally, characteristic features of profiles can be quantified by calibrating a model migration schedule for each cluster using a version of the MODEL package developed by Rogers and Planck (1984) and operationalized at Leeds by Stillwell *et al.* (1987). The MODEL package requires preselection of a schedule for each cluster with either (i) a retirement peak, (ii) a retirement slope or (iii) no retirement component. The full model schedule with a retirement component is defined as:

Table 14.5   15-cluster stage of FPc area classification process for 1985–86 outmigration

1. City and East London; Redbridge and Waltham Forest; Barking and Havering; Merton, Sutton and Wandsworth; Croydon; Lambeth, Southwark and Lewisham; Bromley; Greenwich and Bexley; Middlesex
2. Newcastle; Sheffield; Leeds; Coventry; Wolverhampton; S. Glamorgan
3. Cambridgeshire; Oxfordshire; Surrey; Kingston and Richmond; Birmingham; Manchester; Salford; Liverpool; E. Sussex
4. Bradford; Bedfordshire; Buckinghamshire; Essex; Hertfordshire; Berkshire; Hampshire; Rochdale; Tameside
5. Durham; Leicestershire; Nottinghamshire; Avon; Devon; Dyfed; W. Glamorgan
6. Northumberland; Barnsley; Doncaster; Rotherham; Calderdale; Wakefield; Lincolnshire; Northants; Suffolk; W. Sussex; Dudley; Solihull; Warwickshire; Bolton; Bury; Oldham; Stockport; Trafford; Wigan; Wiltshire
7. Cleveland; Cumbria; Kirklees; N. Yorkshire; Derbyshire; Norfolk; Cornwall; Dorset; Gloucestershire; Somerset; Hereford; Salop; Staffordshire; Sefton; Wirral; Cheshire; Lancashire; Clwyd; Gwent; Mid-Glamorgan
8. N. Tyneside; Walsall; St. Helens; Sunderland
9. Scotland; Gateshead
10. Camden & Islington; Kensington; Chelsea & Westminster
11. S. Tyneside
12. Isle of Wight
13. Sandwell
14. Gwynedd
15. Powys

Note: Middlesex represents a group of five FPC areas.

$$m_I^a = b_1 \exp(-\alpha_1 a)$$
$$+ b_2 \exp\{-\alpha_2(a - \mu_2) - \exp(-\lambda_2(a - \mu_2))\}$$
$$+ b_3 \exp\{-\alpha_3(a - \mu_3) - \exp(-\lambda_3(a - \mu_3))\} + c \qquad (14.10)$$

where m_I^a is the rate of migration into or out of one cluster I of those aged a, and where the profile of the schedule is defined by seven of the eleven parameters (α_1, α_2, μ_2, λ_2, α_3, μ_3, λ_3) and the level of the schedule is determined by the remaining parameters (b_1, b_2, b_3, c). This model is similar to that used by OPCS. A complete model schedule was only fitted to certain profiles (Figures 14.8 and 14.9) after careful inspection of the observed rates. A seven-parameter model was fitted in other cases. The goodness-of-fit of each model schedule is measured using the E statistic following Rogers and Castro (1981) which is the mean of the absolute difference between the predicted and observed rates expressed as a percentage of the observed mean, or:

$$E = 100\{(\sum_a |m_I^a(\text{mod}) - m_I^a(\text{obs})|/n)/(\sum_a m_I^a(\text{obs})/n)\} \qquad (14.11)$$

where

Table 14.6 Parameters and parameter ratios for inmigration clusters

Parameter	Cluster							
	1	2	3	4	5	6	7	8
b_1	0.007	0.013	0.010	0.010	0.010	0.014	0.016	0.012
α_1	0.039	0.108	0.091	0.031	0.046	0.066	0.058	0.059
b_2	0.055	0.087	0.088	0.026	0.027	0.043	0.058	0.050
μ_2	18.319	22.028	20.434	20.899	18.186	20.949	21.024	18.129
α_2	0.087	0.148	0.123	0.096	0.071	0.096	0.104	0.098
λ_2	1.514	0.289	0.404	0.403	1.580	0.352	0.335	1.978
b_3	—	—	—	0.000	0.000	0.004	0.002	—
μ_3	—	—	—	81.157	80.985	60.257	0.000	—
α_3	—	—	—	0.545	0.557	0.047	0.051	—
λ_3	—	—	—	0.099	0.101	0.384	0.000	—
c	0.003	0.005	0.003	0.005	0.005	0.004	0.002	0.004
γ	0.132	0.155	0.119	0.383	0.389	0.332	0.280	0.246
β	0.447	0.729	0.735	0.325	0.650	0.686	0.553	0.610
ϵ	17.492	1.960	3.275	4.195	22.114	3.655	3.214	20.280

Parameter	Cluster						
	9	10	11	12	13	14	15
b_1	0.014	0.014	0.013	0.015	0.024	0.018	0.011
α_1	0.091	0.081	0.077	0.064	0.105	0.095	0.078
b_2	0.076	0.064	0.042	0.029	0.067	0.050	0.054
μ_2	17.949	18.081	18.539	18.771	24.210	23.300	17.900
α_2	0.121	0.107	0.089	0.070	0.137	0.121	0.105
λ_2	2.745	2.159	1.304	2.512	0.210	0.400	3.060
b_3	—	—	0.003	0.005	—	—	—
μ_3	—	—	70.000	86.825	—	—	—
α_3	—	—	0.500	0.500	—	—	—
λ_3	—	—	0.227	0.623	—	—	—
c	0.003	0.003	0.005	0.005	0.004	0.006	0.005
γ	0.181	0.224	0.306	0.523	0.358	0.360	0.204
β	0.752	0.756	0.863	0.917	0.766	0.785	0.743
ϵ	22.747	20.106	14.594	36.123	1.533	3.306	29.143

$m_i^a(mod)$ = the predicted migration rate for age a; and

$m_i^a(obs)$ = the observed migration rate for age a;

and

n   = the number of age-specific rates.

Apart from where model schedules are fitted to single areas, the E values fall below 10.0 in most cases. The parameter values for each of

Table 14.7 Parameters and parameter ratios for outmigration clusters

	Cluster							
Parameter	1	2	3	4	5	6	7	8
b_1	0.012	0.013	0.010	0.012	0.011	0.012	0.011	0.014
α_1	0.125	0.096	0.074	0.059	0.066	0.058	0.055	0.074
b_2	0.063	0.069	0.054	0.033	0.056	0.032	0.041	0.052
μ_2	23.254	20.055	20.227	18.804	19.046	18.219	18.227	19.524
α_2	0.142	0.119	0.114	0.078	0.113	0.077	0.096	0.099
λ_2	0.247	0.497	0.438	0.781	0.715	1.457	1.353	0.398
b_3	0.000	—	0.000	0.000	—	—	—	—
μ_3	79.905	—	76.001	77.829	—	—	—	—
α_3	0.638	—	0.821	0.640	—	—	—	—
λ_3	0.113	—	0.157	0.126	—	—	—	—
c	0.006	0.004	0.005	0.005	0.005	0.005	0.005	0.004
γ	0.192	0.196	0.178	0.368	0.205	0.389	0.282	0.272
β	0.882	0.805	0.647	0.755	0.581	0.749	0.572	0.743
ϵ	1.748	4.166	3.839	10.047	6.316	18.875	14.052	4.010

	Cluster						
Parameter	9	10	11	12	13	14	15
b_1	0.019	0.011	0.016	0.012	0.019	0.008	0.011
α_1	0.070	0.083	0.105	0.008	0.111	0.104	0.045
b_2	0.059	0.058	0.053	0.076	0.070	0.067	0.036
μ_2	20.893	22.386	19.200	19.800	24.010	19.100	17.900
α_2	0.108	0.116	0.099	0.215	0.142	0.134	0.102
λ_2	0.331	0.351	0.500	0.400	0.190	0.410	2.340
c	0.003	0.006	0.005	0.005	0.005	0.006	0.005
γ	0.316	0.183	0.302	0.158	0.271	0.119	0.306
β	0.650	0.717	1.061	0.037	0.782	0.776	0.441
ϵ	3.063	3.038	5.051	1.861	1.338	3.060	22.941

the 15 cluster profiles are presented in Tables 14.6 and 14.7 together with three further measures:

(i)   the child dependency index

$$\gamma = b_1/b_2 \qquad (14.12)$$

which measures the rate at which children migrate with their parents by comparing the level parameters of the pre-labour force and labour force components;

(ii)   the parental-shift regularity

$$\beta = \alpha_1/\alpha_2 \qquad (14.13)$$

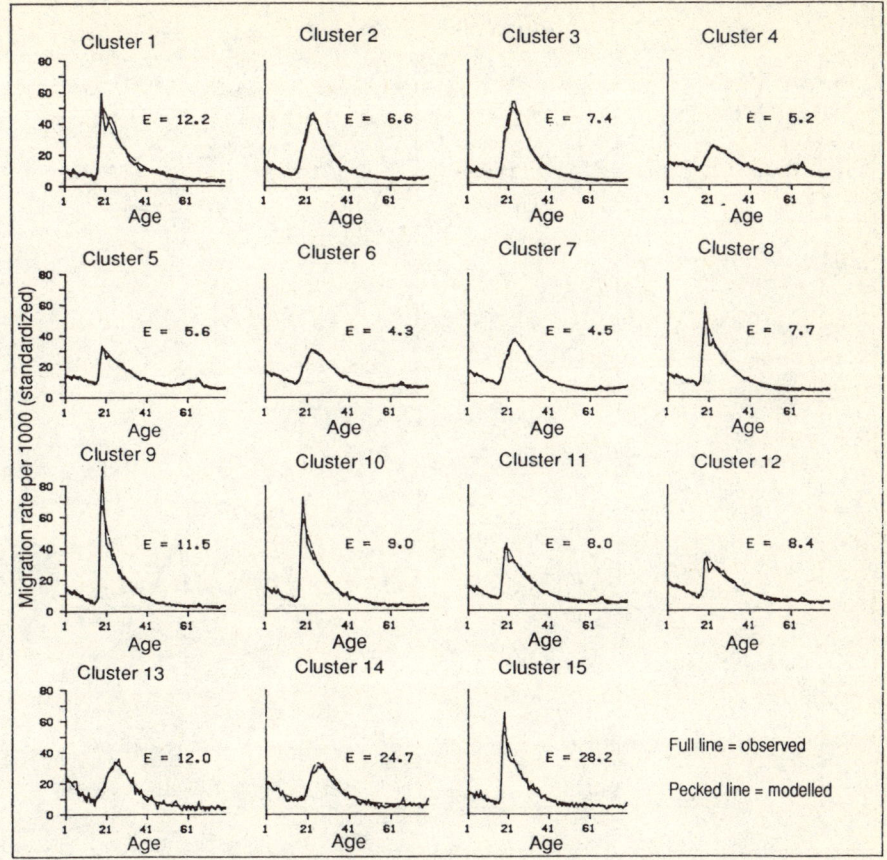

Figure 14.8 Observed and estimated schedules for inmigration clusters, 1985–86

which measures the ratio between the rates of descent of the pre-labour force and labour force curves; and

(iii) the labour asymmetry index

$$\epsilon = \lambda_2/\alpha_2 \tag{14.14}$$

which involves the relationship between the rates of ascent and descent of the labour force curve.

These parameter ratios assist in describing differences between the model schedules for inmigration and outmigration. The London FPC areas are divided into three distinct groups on the basis of the inmigration data. Camden, Islington, Kensington, Chelsea and Westminster, with a double-peaking evident in the observed labour force curve, form the first group. The model schedule smooths the curve and produces a relatively low μ_2 parameter, illustrating the importance of inmigration

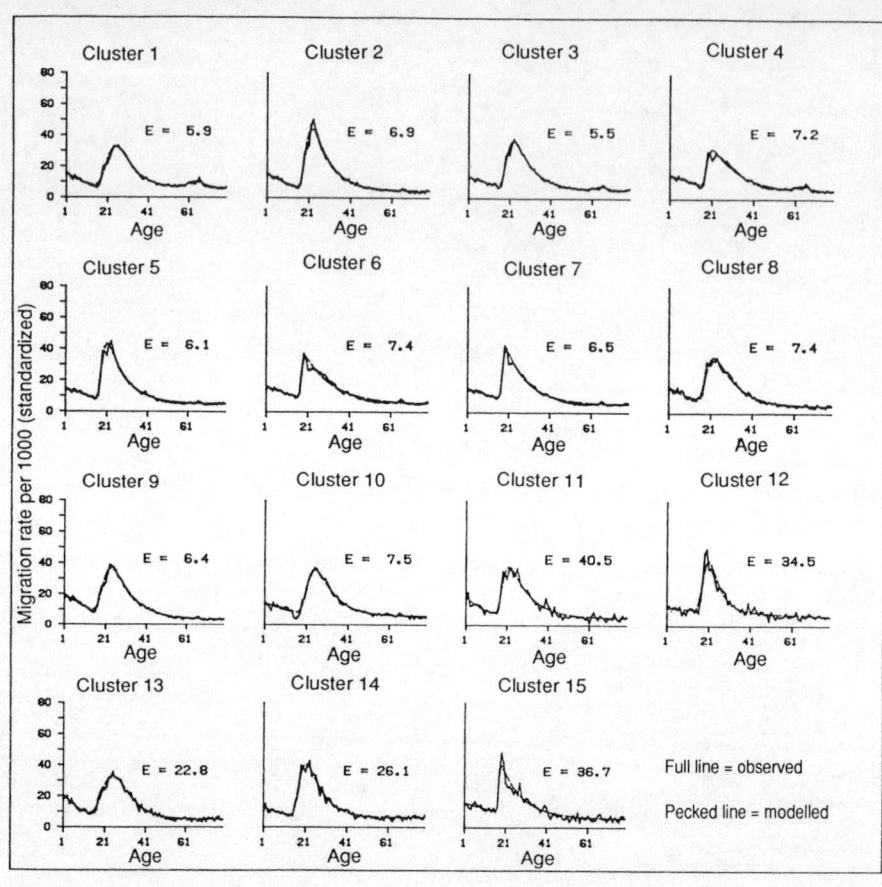

Figure 14.9 Observed and estimated schedules for outmigration clusters, 1985–86

of those in their late teens. The high ϵ value emphasizes the sharp increase in the rate of migration at age 18. The other two groups of London FPC areas have profiles with a high but later labour force peak. The labour force curves are rather more symmetrical with a less emphatic jump in the rate of migration on the upward slope. Clusters 4, 5 and 6 contain many of the rural counties and all show some evidence of a small peak in retirement inmigration. The labour force peaks for these groups are generally at a lower level than for the London groups, and significantly, these clusters exhibit a considerably higher child dependency index than the London groups. In cluster 7, a number of constituent areas show clear evidence of an upward retirement slope: Bedfordshire, Hertfordshire, Berkshire, Surrey, St. Helens, Trafford and Barking/Havering.

The schedules of clusters 8, 9 and 10 are dominated by very high peaks in their labour force curves at an early age and no retirement component.

The sharp increase in the rate of inmovement around age 18 is emphasized by the relatively high λ_2 values giving significant asymmetry. The student factor may be important in determining the shape of the schedule for these three clusters which are all major university cities or counties. Clusters 11 and 12 contain rather unusual combinations of areas. Cambridgeshire stands out as having a unique profile which contains a labour force curve with a sharp peak at age 19 (student factor again) and quite a significant retirement component. Areas of group 12 show evidence of a relatively flat labour force curve but Scotland, North Yorkshire and Hampshire have a localized peak at age 19. The only three areas failing to combine were South Tyneside, which had a very late labour force-peak; Solihull, having a unique profile shape for a metropolitan area with a rounded labour-force curve and a retirement peak; and West Glamorgan.

At the 15-cluster stage of the outmigration classification, 10 distinct groups were formed with five individual areas failing to combine. The majority of London FPC areas make up the first cluster. The peak in outmigration is much lower and later than in clusters 2 and 3, and there is a significant retirement component. The labour force curve is more symmetrical and the correspondence between child and parent migration is high. The high-density FPC areas in London of Camden, Islington, Kensington, Chelsea and Westminster make up cluster 10 where the labour-force peak is earlier and more skewed and where migration activity around retirement age is less significant. Clusters 2 and 3 contain the majority of high-density metropolitan areas outside Greater London, together with in cluster 3, a number of counties in the South. Both schedules have a peak at age 20 with that of cluster 2 at a higher level. The β value is greatest for the metropolitan districts in cluster 2, indicating the importance of family movement away from these high density areas. Clusters 3 and 4 have a significant retirement component although cluster 4 is distinguished by a double peak in its labour-force curve. Cluster 5 is also non-metropolitan in area composition but has no retirement component. It has a slightly later modelled peak in labour force movement but the observed schedule has a double peak indicating higher levels of outmovement around the age of leaving school and after higher education.

Clusters 6 and 7 are two much larger groups and their model schedules stand out in Figure 14.9 as having the greatest degree of labour asymmetry. The peak in labour force migration occurs around age 18 and although observed rates do rise to age 65 in each case, the cluster schedules were modelled without a retirement component. Cluster 8 contains four metropolitan areas whose schedules are characterized by a labour-force curve with a relatively late peak, whereas cluster 9 combines Scotland with the metropolitan district of Gateshead. Those areas failing to combine at this 15-cluster stage are Gwynedd; Sandwell; South Tyneside with a multi-peaked labour force component; Isle of Wight with a high labour-force peak but large fluctuations in age-specific rates after age 40; and Powys, with its labour-force decline curve interrupted by a small peak at age 30.

14.4 Conclusion

This chapter has attempted to outline the framework of the OPCS/DOE migration projection methodology, to set out the equations associated with different stages in a transparent form, and to examine three selected features of the model in more detail using data from the NHSCR. Three recommendations emerge. Firstly, a careful and systematic specification of the broad age group boundaries of the migrant streams defined in the assignment stage is required. Secondly, changes have taken place in the age-specific distributions of migration since the beginning of the 1980s which cast doubts on the assumption of constant 1981 Census-based assignment probabilities. It would therefore be appropriate to consider a mechanism for trending or updating the assignment probabilities based on the information provided by the NHSCR data for more recent years, particularly as the interval between the Census and the base period of projection increases. Such a mechanism would need to accommodate the conceptual and definitional differences in the two measures of migration identified by Devis and Mills (1986) and by Boden *et al*. (1987, 1988). An alternative solution, given the availability of the continuous time series of NHSCR data, would be to adopt a movement-based migration projection model (Rees 1984) as suggested by Boden (1989), rather than attempting to modify further the existing Census-based transition procedure for grouping local authority areas which is based on observed rates rather than model parameters. Model migration schedules can then be used to identify the different characteristics of particular groups of areas. Once again, there is the opportunity of using NHSCR Primary Unit Data to take into account the shifts occurring in the level and age structure of migration.

Chapter 15

Migration projection in Norway: a regional demographic-economic model

Lasse Stambøl

15.1 Introduction

The Central Bureau of Statistics in Norway has traditionally produced regional population projections in which migration is projected using fixed rates of gross outmigration and a fixed distribution of inmigrants among regions. However, in recent years a model called DREM (Demographic Regional Economic Model) has been completed which incorporates migration assumptions that take into account changes in regional labour markets, measured through balances between demand and supply of labour. This chapter is primarily concerned with the migration submodel of the DREM model. A short presentation of the whole model is given together with a description of how the migration submodel is estimated. The chapter also presents some results of the model's explanatory power of time variation in migration rates and includes some measures showing the relationship between regional labour markets and cross-sectional variation in gross migration rates. Finally, some proposals for further work with the migration submodel are discussed.

15.2 The DREM model

The aims of the DREM model are twofold. On the one hand, it projects the balance between demand and supply of labour in regional labour markets; on the other, it acts as a model for migration and population projections at the county level. Counties in Norway are the administrative divisions that exist between the national and municipal levels and have important planning responsibilities. Altogether, Norway is divided into 19 counties although in the DREM migration submodel, the capital and the surrounding county, Oslo and Akershus, are treated as one region, so that the model is based on a spatial system of 18 counties.

The DREM migration submodel is based on migration assumptions different from those made in traditional population projections since it takes into consideration labour market variables. Migration totals projected by fixed rates of migration observed in a base period may be

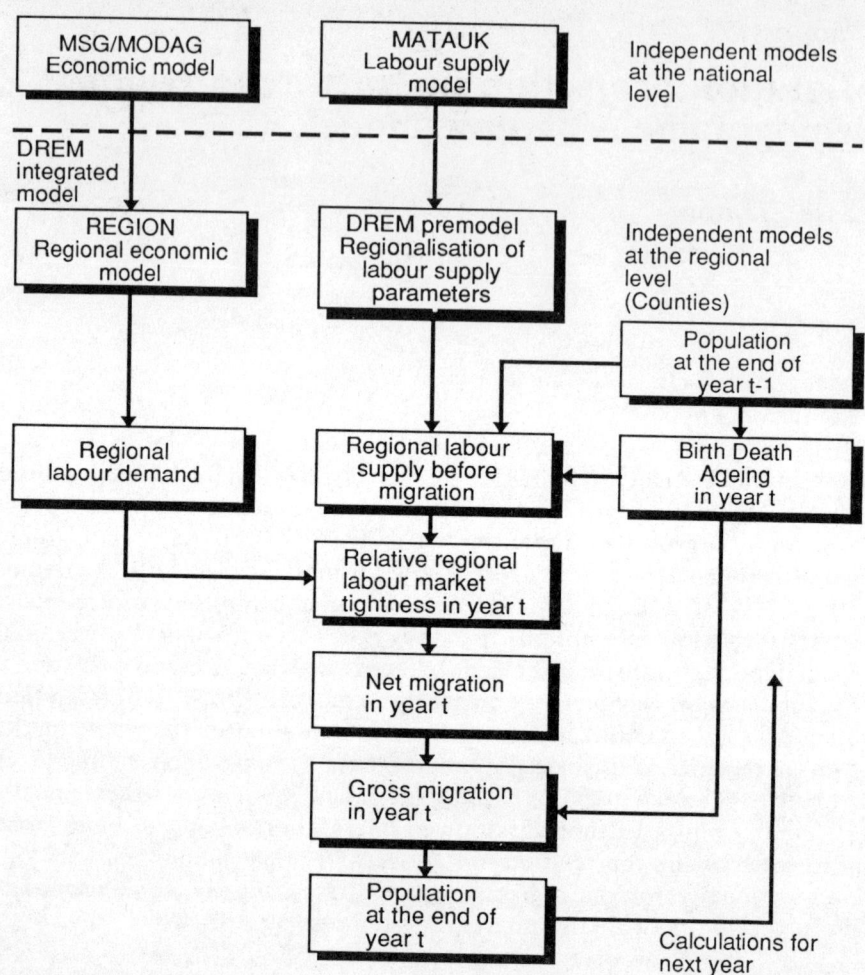

Figure 15.1 The DREM model

helpful to users, but they give no deep insight into the driving forces behind migration patterns.

The whole DREM model may be seen in the tradition of models that include input–output economic and demographic forecasts as components in an integrated regional modelling system. Madden and Batey (1980), for example, suggest that the problem of achieving forecasts of population and economic activity can be tackled by setting a variety of individual models within a single forecasting framework. The DREM model represents to a certain degree such a framework of separate but interlinked models.

One of the main problems is to link the economic and demographic components. So far the relationship between economic and demographic changes in DREM is limited to the description of the regional labour markets influencing migration. The DREM migration submodel may thus be classified to a certain degree as demand-driven, in so far as the demand side of the regional economic component functions as a predetermined factor in the migration submodel. The feedback effects that may arise from the population totals projected by the model have, however, an effect (albeit minor) on the projected demand for labour by the regional input–output model.

An outline of the main elements in the DREM model is given in Figure 15.1 (in Norwegian, the model is called DRØM). The labour market projections of DREM are designed to give regional breakdowns of results from projections made by the use of national models. Projections of labour demand resulting from computations with a national economic planning model are broken down to county level by means of a regional input–output model called REGION. This is a separate model that has been operative for some years.

The REGION model comprises about 30 industries and gives a rather disaggregated description of the regional economy. The basic theoretical approach used in the REGION model consists of regional input–output assumptions within a commodity-by-industry framework. The model contains no price relationships. Constant input coefficients are assumed for each type of commodity flow. The input coefficients are differentiated by commodity, industry and region. The model does not specify interregional commodity flows between pairs of regions, but it is assumed that demand in all regions is met by the same regional pattern of supply. Private consumption and investment are also specified by region and linked to regional production activities. It is furthermore assumed that the labour demand in each regional industry is determined by calculated growth in production and exogenously given growth in labour productivity.

The main empirical basis for estimating the coefficients of the REGION model are the national accounts by county, which have been constructed by the Central Bureau of Statistics for the years 1973, 1976, 1980, 1983 and 1986. For more details see, for example, Schreiner and Skoglund (1985) and Skoglund and Stokka (1988).

There also exists a model of labour supply at the national level (MATAUK). The MATAUK model projects the labour force disaggregated by one-year age group, sex, education, and marital status of women. The model does not specify employed and unemployed persons, but gives a total supply of both groups, expressed as the labour force. Projections obtained from this model are broken down by county in the DREM submodel. Imbalances between demand and supply in regional labour markets are thus projected by REGION and the DREM labour supply submodel.

The labour market balances are used to project net migration for each of the two age groups 16–24 years and 25–49 years. Gross outmigration, specified by one-year age group and sex, is calculated assuming fixed rates of outmigration. Gross inmigration to each region for each of the broader age groups is projected residually and distributed by sex and one-year age group on the same proportions as in the base period. Gross inmigration of children is assumed to depend on inmigration of adults (25–49 years). The migration rates for persons 50 years or more are the same as in the ordinary population projections with fixed migration assumptions.

The net migration submodel in DREM is estimated for the period 1973–86 by using regression methods. The model is estimated applying an iterative non-linear least squares routine to data of a combined time series–cross-section type. In our migration analysis, corresponding computations are also made for gross in- and gross outmigration.

15.3 The DREM migration submodel: theoretical perspectives

Several theories and models have been developed to explain the migration process. They are all more or less selective in their way of handling explanatory variables, and none of them represents a comprehensive representation of the various factors influencing migration. Most attempts to model internal migration at an aggregate level have assumed the labour market to be a key factor. This may be for theoretical reasons, or due to problems connected with forecasting regional trends of other factors. The DREM model falls into the category of such 'partial models' by focusing just on the relationship between migration and labour market development.

However, studies at micro level, like the Norwegian Survey of Migration Motives 1972 (Central Bureau of Statistics 1977), show the complexity of motivations behind migration flows. Factors such as migration distance and direction, and personal characteristics of the migrants like age, education and family type are all important. The complexity of migration motives makes it natural to question the utility of crude studies at an aggregate level in gaining insights into migration processes. On the other hand, answers to surveys of individual motives might have an 'egocentric bias'. Respondents often mention the last personal argument in a chain of causes, and take political or economic conditions that may affect migration decisions for granted. In many cases the macrostructures will be more or less 'invisible', so that subjective reports of migration motives often may represent rationalisations inside a frame of a more complex reality.

In many cases surveys may indicate factors which are worth modelling at an aggregate level. The Norwegian Survey of Migration Motives 1972 pointed out the following major motives for migration between munici-palities: labour market conditions (35 per cent), housing and environment (27 per cent), family (12 per cent), and education (9 per cent). At the higher county level, migration motives relating to labour market conditions and education increased in importance to 38 per cent and 11 per cent respectively, while housing and environment reasons decreased to 21 per cent. Migration motives related to housing tend to be more important for short-distance moves, while motives related to labour market and education tend to be more important for moves over longer distances.

An earlier empirical migration analysis of the DREM migration sub-model also included proxies for regional housing markets and educational opportunities. The results showed that house-building and educational opportunities seem to affect only inmigration, and that the explanatory power in regard to net migration rates was very low; beyond that caused by the regional labour market change (Lian 1986).

In the international literature we find several attempts to model the relationship between labour market change and internal migration. The DREM migration submodel is basically a macro model of migration, since net migration is related to regional labour market change. This connects the model to migration theories grounded more on macro than micro relations. Regional imbalances between the demand and supply of labour are traditionally associated with so-called equilibrium theories grounded in classical economic theory. These theories consider migration as a mechanism contributing to produce equilibrium between regions with unequal income levels. The more affluent regions will gradually lower their income level as a result of high inmigration. However, these theories do not explain why migration takes place in the opposite direction to that expected, and why migration does not correct for continued decline in labour demand in some regions.

As an alternative to equilibrium theories, there are theories that assume a more cumulative development in the migration process. It is maintained that spiral effects often arise, so that differences between regions with positive and negative net migration may increase. Long-term outmigration will have cumulative negative feedback effects on the labour market and reduce the demand for services. This pattern of development will give new incentives to migrate and the whole outmigration process will become cumulative (Lian 1986).

The DREM migration submodel is mainly guided by the assumptions of tendencies towards equilibrium. Unlike the traditional equilibrium theories, the model is more directly related to the demand and supply of labour, and not to regional differences in income level. The migration pattern in DREM is modelled so that outmigration from a region reduces the supply of labour, which means that an excess of supply over demand for labour will be reduced. From this follows, in the next period, a reduction in projected net outmigration. In the same way the model will, after some time, reduce net inmigration to regions with surplus demand for labour, as the supply of labour increases through the net inmigration.

The model thus places heavier weight on the demand side of the labour market, and only to a lesser degree takes into account the feedback effects of the supply side. The existing migration model has constant terms and lagged variables that to a certain degree give cumulative effects, but the labour market indicator (discussed below) might partially counteract this. We have, however, in the REGION model recently introduced feedback effects from population change in the projections of certain public service activities, which can partially give rise to more cumulative effects in the migration projections of the model.

The DREM migration submodel reflects so-called pull–push theories of migration (Lee 1969) in the way it postulates decreasing net inmigration to regions with strong push factors in the labour market, and increasing net inmigration to regions with strong pull factors in the labour market. On the other hand, the model is less adapted to migration analyses that aim to explain the migration processes according to more individually-based migration theories. Nevertheless, even micro-based migration theories, such as the human capital-investment and career/life-cycle approaches, expect regions with the largest and most diversified labour market and with the best employment possibilities to be net receivers of migrants.

Ideally, we should have constructed a migration model that included some micro and macro relations simultaneously. Trønnes (1983) and Lian (1986) in their migration analyses connect regional labour market changes to time variation in both net and gross migration rates. The results showed that such models give better explanations of time variation in net migration rates.

The empirical migration analysis presented in this chapter is an attempt to update earlier migration analyses in the DREM model. Both the net and gross migration rates are related to data on labour market change. The regional labour market data are extended to the period 1972–86, while the earlier migration analyses were based on the period 1967–79. The regression analysis is now disaggregated by estimating specific parameters for each county. The hypothetical expectations are that counties with a negative labour market indicator (see below) will have decreasing net inmigration rates, while counties with a positive labour market indicator with have increasing net inmigration rates. With regard to gross migration, we expect the rate of gross outmigration to decrease with increasing demand pressure on the regional labour market. For inmigration the expectations will be the opposite.

15.4 The data and the labour market indicator

In our empirical migration analysis, relevant data are needed for the development of migration between counties and for measuring demand and supply of labour in regional labour markets. The migration rates are derived from annual counts from the population register, which is of good quality. Persons living in different counties at the beginning and end of a year are defined as migrants. In this way migration is counted as the number of migrants and not as the number of migrations, as some migrants move several times during a year. A migration rate is calculated as the number of migrants per thousand inhabitants. The population at the beginning of each year is used as the denominator to compute rates both of net and gross migration.

It has been more difficult to find relevant data on regional labour markets. The statistical base for regional labour market data is rather weak, and we have used different methods to construct regional time series by combining various statistical sources (see Stambøl 1989).

There is, as indicated in the previous section, an extensive international literature on how the relative tightness of regional labour markets affects both the extent and the direction of migration. Brun (1982) has, on the basis of such hypotheses, defined an indicator of the tightness in the labour market as the relation between demand for and supply of labour. This measure is used as a regional labour market indicator. In order to rule out general variations in economic activity, it is calculated as the difference between the tightness in a regional and national labour market:

$$X_j(t) = \frac{D_j(t)}{S_j(t)} - \frac{\sum_j D_j(t)}{\sum_j S_j(t)} \qquad (15.1)$$

where $X_j(t)$ is the labour market indicator for region j in year t and D and S are the demand and supply of labour, respectively. The demand for labour in a county is defined by:

$$D = ER + V \qquad (15.2)$$

where

ER = the number of employed persons by county of residence; and
V = reported vacancies in the county.

Correspondingly the supply of labour is given as:

$$S = ER + U \qquad (15.3)$$

where U = the number of unemployed in the county. Equation (15.1) is used as one alternative for expressing regional labour market status, and in this chapter is named alternative A. This labour market indicator is, however, very sensitive to the registration of vacancies and unemployment. One problem is the data quality of each of these variables, which may vary both over time and between regions.

Another problem is the focus on this variable as a labour market indicator. Fields (1976) suggests that the probability of getting a job and keeping it should be the preferred indicator for the potentiality of migration rather than unemployment. He thinks that 'turnover' in the labour market gives a better explanation for migration rates than unemployment. There are also several types of unemployment that do not necessarily result in migration (e.g. social unemployment, seasonal unemployment, etc.). In the case of structural unemployment caused by changes in industrial and occupational structure, the unemployed will not necessarily find convenient jobs either in the home region or in another region.

We have constructed an alternative measure of regional labour market change by counting the number of employed according to the county of employment (as opposed to the county of residence). This is referred to as alternative B. This alternative is more in accordance with the REGION model, which projects regional labour demand according to the county of employment. It also includes a one-year lag on the labour supply side, with the intention of measuring better year-to-year changes in the labour force of different regional labour markets. The labour market indicator B is formulated as follows:

$$X_j(t) = \frac{D_j(t)}{S_j(t-1)} - \frac{\sum\limits_j D_j(t)}{\sum\limits_j S_j(t-1)} \tag{15.4}$$

where the symbols D, S, j and t represent the same variables as in equation (15.1), but their definitions are different. The demand of labour in a county (D) is defined as:

$$D = EE + V \tag{15.5}$$

where EE = the employed persons by county of employment. The supply of labour (S) is defined as:

$$S = (ER + U)C \tag{15.6}$$

where

C = a measure of net commuting between counties (calculated as employed persons by county of employment divided by employed persons by county of residence).

In the calculation of the supply of labour we have, then, made the assumption that the unemployed will apply for jobs outside their counties according to each county's level of net commuting.

The employment data used in the empirical analysis include 12 groups of persons according to sex, age (16–24 years, 25–49 years and 50–74 years) and hours worked (full-time/part-time). In this chapter we restrict attention to the two age groups 16–24 years (young adults) and 25–49 years (middle-aged adults). This is a natural age specification, since migration patterns of young adults differ from other age groups. In addition, migration motives also differ between young and older adults as a reflection of different life-cycle phases (Stambøl 1987). The labour market figures are used to calculate aggregate labour market balances, where demand and supply of labour are counted for each sex and age group separately.

15.5 The regression model

In generating population projections, we primarily need to project the time series of migration rates. Ideally we should have constructed a model explaining simultaneously cross-sectional variation in migration rates between counties at the beginning of the period. It is, however, difficult both to measure and to project cross-section variables. Factors explaining time series variation in migration rates may differ from factors explaining differences in average migration rates between counties. In the model, there are incorporated estimates of county-specific constant terms, which should capture most of the differences in the average level of migration rates between counties. We have, however, made an *ad hoc* analysis of cross-section variation of migration rates in relation to regional labour market change. The findings may establish some basis for later extensions of the migration model.

Previous analyses for the DREM project developed a regression model of migration rates. In Trønnes (1983), it is shown how assumptions about unobserved variables may lead to a model with county-specific constant terms and autocorrelated residuals. These assumptions give a model with a one-year lag on both the migration rates and the regional labour market indicator. A special measure was defined to calculate the specific explanatory power of labour market indicators on variation in migration rates. With some minor adjustments we have used the same model in our present migration analysis. To simplify the formal presentation, only the simplest version is presented here:

$$m_j(t) = a_j + b_j X_j(t) + u_j(t) \tag{15.7}$$

where j and t are indexes for county and year respectively; and

$m_j(t)$ = the migration rate;
$X_j(t)$ = the labour market indicator;
a_j = a county-specific constant term;
b_j = a county-specific parameter for the labour market indicator; and
$u_j(t)$ = a residual term.

Equation (15.7) gives the relationship between the observed variables. It is, however, reasonable to expect the residuals to be correlated. It is possible to get consistent estimates of the coefficients by using a standard least squares method, but the variance of the estimates becomes higher than by taking into consideration the structure of correlation in the residuals. The variance of the residuals will not be consistently estimated by the least squares method if the residuals are correlated.

There are reasons to expect the unobserved variables in the residuals to change slowly through time and show dependencies between the counties. The correlation of the residuals is then expected to have both a time and a space dimension. In the DREM migration submodel, we have assumed that the residuals follow a first-order autoregressive process, which means that the correlation between two points of time decreases exponentially when the time interval increases. Unlike the earlier migration analyses in DREM, we operate with county-specific parameters of both the labour market and the autocorrelation. We get:

$$u_j(t) = k_j u_j(t-1) + d_j(t) \qquad (15.8)$$

where

k_j = county-specific autocorrelation coefficient; and
$d_j(t)$ = independent normally distributed residuals with constant variance and expectation zero.

The spatial correlation of the residuals between the counties is much more difficult to model. One possible way to describe this dependence is to let it be a function of the distance between counties. So far we have disregarded the spatial autocorrelation in the model.

Multiplying equation (15.7) for time $t-1$ by k_j and subtracting the results from (15.8) we get:

$$m_j(t) = c_j + k_j m_j(t-1) + b_j X_j(t) - b_j k_j X_j(t-1) + d_j(t) \qquad (15.9)$$

where c_j = a county-specific constant term.

Model (15.9) is non-linear in the parameters, owing to our assumptions of the correlation structure of the residuals of the model (15.7). Regressions using (15.9) give consistent estimates of both the parameters and variance of the residuals in model (15.7). The formulation (15.9) is also convenient for our projection purposes. Current migration rates will then be 'explained' by the current labour market indicator, and by the labour market indicator and the migration rate lagged one year. We assume that the county-specific constant term of the model captures cross-sectional differences in the average level of county migration rates. Model (15.9) is estimated by applying an iterative least squares method.

To help in evaluating the results, we use a special measure, expressing the reduction in residual variance achieved by going from a simple model, disregarding explanatory variables, to a full model (15.9), including labour market indicators. The simple model is:

$$m_j(t) = e_j + v_j(t) \tag{15.10}$$

e_j = a county-specific constant term; and
$v_j(t)$ = a residual term.

We also here assume that the residuals follow a first-order autoregressive process, and in the same way as under (15.8) we get:

$$v_j(t) = l_j v_j(t-1) + g_j(t) \tag{15.11}$$

where

l_j = a county-specific autocorrelation coefficient; and
$g_j(t)$ = the independent normally distributed residuals with constant variance and expectations zero.

In the same way as under (15.9) we get:

$$m_j(t) = h_j + l_j m_j(t-1) + g_j(t) \tag{15.12}$$

where h_j = a county-specific constant term.

Unlike model (15.9), the model (15.12) is linear in the parameters. The expression (15.12) may be seen as a special case of (15.9), setting the coefficients for the labour market to zero. In model (15.12) the possible effect of the labour market variable is instead unobserved, i.e. it is included in the residuals. The regressions are based on (15.12) given consistent estimates on both the parameters and the variance of residuals in model (15.10).

We suppose that the residuals, $v_j(t)$, of the simple model will have a structure similar to the residuals, $u_j(t)$, of the full model. The variance reduction in the residuals achieved by turning from model (15.10) to model (15.7) should then give a measure of the ability of labour market indicators to account for the evolution over time in migration rates. This variance reduction in the residuals is expressed in terms of the parameters of (15.9) and (15.12), and we get an expression, R_x^2, which shows the proportion of the variance in migration rates explained by labour market indicators:

$$R_x^2 = \frac{\text{Var } (v_j(t)) - \text{Var } (u_j(t))}{\text{Var } (v_j(t))} = 1 - \frac{(1-l^2)\ (1-R_f^2)}{(1-k^2)\ (1-R_s^2)} \tag{15.13}$$

where

$$l^2 = \frac{1}{N} \sum_j l_j^2 \tag{15.14}$$

and

$$k^2 = \frac{1}{N} \sum_j k_j^2 \tag{15.15}$$

where

R_f^2 = explained proportion of the variance in model (15.9) (full model);

R_s^2 = explained proportion of the variance in model (15.12) (simple model); and

N = number of areas (18 for Norwegian counties).

When the migration submodel is used for a population projection, the model (15.9) should give a somewhat better explanation than model (15.12), provided that our measure of regional labour market demand gives some explanation of migration rates. The measure R_x^2 in equation (15.13) gives the necessary information. The second equality shows how the variance of residuals of the underlying models (15.8) and (15.11) may be expressed in terms of the usual R^2 and estimates of the actually estimated equations (15.9) and (15.12), taking account of the assumed equality of the variance of the residuals $d_j(t)$ and $g_j(t)$ over each county. From equation (15.13), if follows that the labour market's explanation of time variation in migration rates increases with increasing explained variance and with decreasing autocorrelation coefficient by turning from a simple model (15.12) to a full model (15.9). By intuition, the latter seems reasonable because it indicates that the lagged variable is losing importance, while the labour market indicator gains in importance. Our model makes it possible to include other explanatory variables in the analysis in the same way as we have handled the regional labour market indicator.

15.6 Empirical results

In this section of the chapter we present some of the results from our migration analysis. First, we have chosen some results showing the effects of the labour market indicator on time variation in both net and gross migration rates. Second, we show some results from an analysis measuring the relationship between the regional labour market indicator and cross-sectional differences in the average level of migration rates. All the results reported here are based on alternative A as labour market indicator. We did not obtain complete regressions based on alternative B

Table 15.1 Explained variance in models with and without the regional labour market indicator, 1973–1986, alternative A

Age group	16–24 years			25–49 years		
Model	R_s^2	R_f^2	R_x^2	R_s^2	R_f^2	R_x^2
Net migration						
Total	0.89	0.91	0.15	0.84	0.85	0.11
Male	0.84	0.87	0.14	0.79	0.80	0.04
Female	0.88	0.89	0.06	0.84	0.86	0.14
Outmigration						
Total	0.94	0.94	0.19	0.95	0.96	0.16
Male	0.89	0.90	0.16	0.93	0.94	0.17
Female	0.94	0.95	0.12	0.95	0.96	0.17
Inmigration						
Total	0.93	0.93	0.07	0.87	0.88	0.09
Male	0.91	0.92	0.06	0.86	0.87	0.10
Female	0.91	0.92	0.09	0.85	0.86	0.08

Notes:
(i) R_s^2 = explained proportion of the variance in model without the regional labour market indicator.
(ii) R_f^2 = explained proportion of the variance in model with the regional labour market indicator.
(iii) R_x^2 = the regional labour market's explanatory power of time variation in migration rates.

because the estimation routine did not converge for some of the person groups involved.

15.6.1 Time series regressions

The results of the time series regressions are shown for each sex and for the age groups 16–24 years and 25–49 years. In Table 15.1 are shown the models' level of explanation for both net and gross migration rates. R_x^2 shows the proportion of the variance in migration rates explained by the labour market indicator. The total explained variance in the simple model (R_s^2) and the full model (R_f^2) is high due to a model formulation with county-specific constant terms, capturing most of the differences in the average level of the migration rates between counties.

In general, the migration rates vary more between counties than they do over time (Lian and Sørensen 1984). The most surprising result is that the labour market indicator seems to have a stronger effect on time variation in gross migration rates than on that in net migration rates. The effect is particularly strong on gross outmigration for both age groups. We also notice that the explained variance in both the simple and the full model is stronger for gross migration than for net migration in all the person groups. This implies that fluctuation in net migration rates

Table 15.2   Explained variance in models with and without the regional labour market indicator, 1973–79 and 1980–86, alternative A

Age group	16–24 years			25–49 years		
Model	R_s^2	R_f^2	R_x^2	R_s^2	R_f^2	F_x^2
1973–79: net migration	0.90	0.92	0.15	0.85	0.87	0.08
Outmigration	0.95	0.97	0.49	0.95	0.97	0.17
Inmigration	0.94	0.95	0.25	0.87	na	na
1980–1986: net migration	0.93	0.94	0.07	0.88	0.90	0.14
Outmigration	0.91	0.93	0.23	0.96	0.96	0.01
Inmigration	0.93	0.95	0.16	0.89	0.91	0.14

Notes:
(i) na = not available, i.e. estimation routine did not converge.
(ii) See Table 15.1 for definition of R_s^2, R_f^2 and R_x^2

has been stronger than in gross migration rates. The results in Table 15.1 show considerable differences between the sexes, in particular in the explanation for the net migration rates. The results might reflect the fact that females have a tendency to migrate earlier than males, so the migration structure between sexes become different in the two age groups.

In order to test the stability in the model estimates over time, we have performed regressions for both the periods 1973–79 and 1980–86 separately. The results for both sexes are shown in Table 15.2. The model gives considerable differences in the explanation between the 1970s and the 1980s. Except for net migration among the older age group, the labour market's explanation of time variation in migration rates decreases. In the older age group this coincides with increasing explained variance in the simple model (R_s^2), which means that year-to-year changes in migration rates are smaller in the 1980s than in the 1970s. In the younger age group there is an increase in fluctuations in gross migration rates. This should partially increase the potential of the labour market's explanation of time variation in gross migration rates. When it does not, it is due to changes in autocorrelation in going from the simple model to the full model.

In any case, the results for each of the two subperiods separately also show that the labour market's explanation is strongest for outmigration, except for the oldest age group in the 1980s. It is, however, important to note that in the former migration analyses, one parameter common to all counties indicated a strongly significant influence of the labour market indicator at a 5 per cent level of significance. In our new analysis, several of the estimated county-specific parameters are not significant at this level, so the interpretation of the results must be done very carefully.

Among other regression results, it is noteworthy that when the estimation routine did converge, the labour market's explanation of time

Table 15.3 County-specific parameters for the labour market indicator, 1973–86, alternative A

County	Code	Age group 16–24 years			Age group 25–49 years		
		Out	In	Net	Out	In	Net
Østfold	Ø	0.01	0.02	0.06	0.04	0.04	−0.02
Oslo/Akershus	O/A	−0.36	−0.48	−0.04	−0.45*	−0.09	0.31
Hedmark	He	−0.07	−0.06	−0.01	−0.07	0.03	0.11
Oppland	O	−0.27	−0.26	0.11	−0.05	0.14	0.21
Buskerud	B	−0.08	0.04	0.26	0.21	0.22	−0.10
Vestfold	V	0.06	−0.02	−0.13	−0.03	0.04	−0.07
Telemark	Te	0.08	0.12	0.22	$0.12^†$	$0.15^†$	0.01
Aust-Agder	AA	0.02	0.14	0.40*	0.14	−0.21	−0.24
Vest-Agder	VA	0.02	0.06	0.13	0.26*	−0.13	0.14
Rogaland	R	−0.01	0.05	0.11	0.00	0.23	0.24
Hordaland	Ho	−0.01	−0.01	−0.13	−0.06	−0.07	−0.02
Sogn og Fjordane	SF	−0.38*	$0.37^†$	0.75*	−0.21*	−0.04	0.15
Møre og Romsdal	MR	0.11	0.25	0.02	$0.10^†$	−0.02	0.02
Sør-Trøndelag	ST	0.18	0.22	0.24	0.26*	0.04	−0.08
Nord-Trøndelag	NT	−0.06	0.14	0.18	0.00	0.11	0.12
Nordland	N	0.07	−0.11	−0.20	−0.10	0.18	$0.29^†$
Troms	Tr	0.05	0.21	−0.28*	0.08	0.14	0.05
Finnmark	F	−0.64*	0.60*	−0.38*	0.18*	−0.36*	−0.51*
All counties		−0.07	0.07	0.07	0.02	0.02	0.03

Notes:
(i) * = significantly different from zero at a 5% level.
(ii) † = significantly different from zero at a 10% level.

variation in migration rates based on the labour market indicator alternative B showed a somewhat stronger explanation of net migration rates and a somewhat weaker explanation of gross migration rates. Regression performed on different segments of the labour market showed some differences in explanatory power going from models including complete labour markets to models including sex and age-specific labour markets. It seemed that for males the labour market's explanatory power of migration rates was reduced for more disaggregated labour markets, while the situation for females seemed to be the opposite. The results might reflect the fact that males have access to a greater part of the labour market, while female employment opportunities are concentrated within fewer occupations.

According to our expectations concerning the influence of the regional labour market indicator on net and gross migration rates, the hypothesis concerning time variation in migration rates can be tested using the estimated county-specific parameters for the labour market indicator (see equation (15.7) and Table 15.3). For the age group 16–24 years, the average (all-county) tendency seems to follow the expected one, with negative parameters on outmigration and positive parameters on both in- and net migration. For the age group 25–49 years, the average tendency fits well with that expected for in- and net migration, but not for outmigration. For the younger age group, 11 out of 18 counties follow the expected tendency for net migration, while 12 and 9 counties follow the expected tendency for inmigration and outmigration respectively. For the older age group, the number of counties following the expected tendency are 11 counties for in- and net migration and only 7 counties for outmigration.

In a population projection, high values on the parameter estimates for the regional labour market indicator mean that year-to-year changes in the projected regional labour market indicator will cause considerable changes in projected migration rates (see equation (15.9)). Counties with unexpected signs on the parameter estimates will produce more unfavourable net migration rates in the case of a more favourable labour market indicator, and more favourable net migration rates in the case of a negative developing labour market indicator. To avoid this problem, we suggest putting the value of the parameter estimate for the labour market indicator in these counties to zero in a population projection.

15.6.2 Cross-sectional analysis

So far we have discussed the estimation results stressing the time variation in migration rates. It is also of great interest to consider cross-sectional variation in migration rates in relation to the regional labour market indicator. In the model the county-specific constant terms are expected to capture cross-sectional variation in migration rates. Accordingly, we have looked into the relationship between the regional labour market indicator and cross-sectional variation in gross migration rates using relative measures for both data sets. The relative level of the gross migration rates in each county is calculated in the same way as we calculated the regional labour market indicator (see equation (15.1)). The average level of the gross migration rates for the whole country is a weighted average over all the counties. When both the regional labour market indicator and the relative level of each county's gross migration rate are measured per thousand, it is possible to plot the relative level of each county's labour market indicator and gross migration rates in the coordinate system shown in Figures 15.2 and 15.3. The figures show average measures for the periods 1973–79 and 1980–86 respectively.

The figures show eight different possible combinations of the relative regional labour market indicators and the relative gross migration rates. Counties with index values along the diagonal — where the ratios between the relative labour market indicator and relative gross inmigration rates are 1.0 — have a level of gross inmigration rate that fits well with their labour market indicator (Figure 15.2). Counties with index

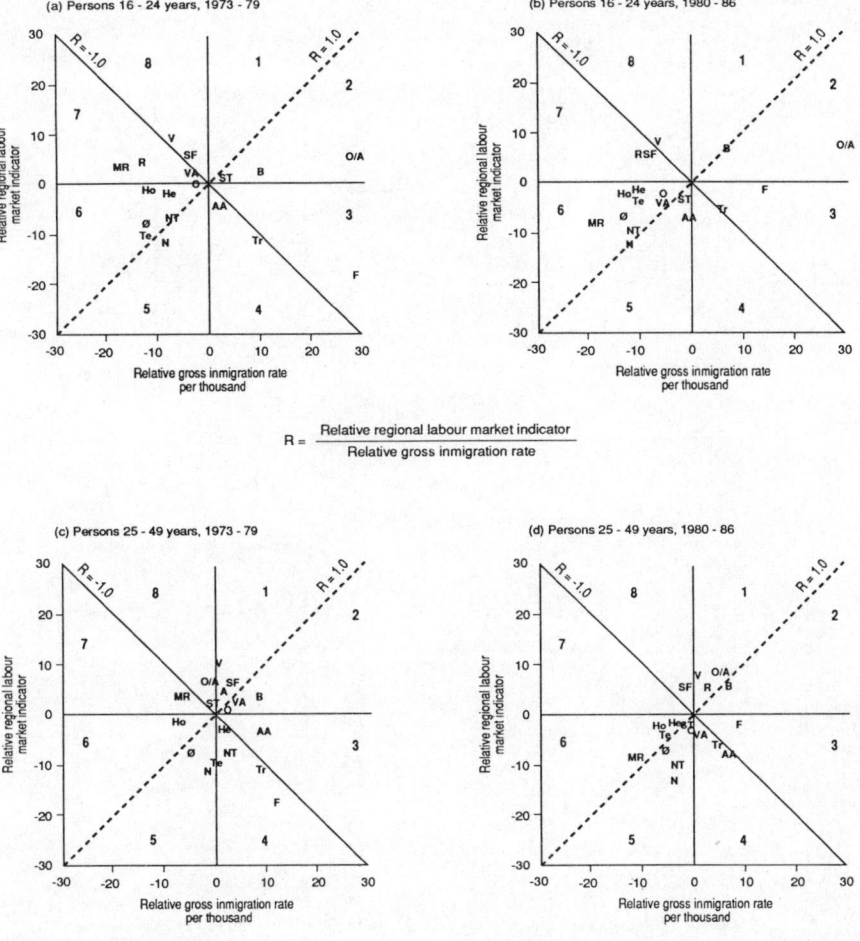

Figure 15.2 Relationships between relative regional labour market conditions and gross inmigration rates

values in sectors 2, 3, 4 and 5 will have a relative level of gross inmigration rates which is higher than the labour market indicator would suggest, while the situation is opposite in the counties with index values in the other sectors. Correspondingly, in the case of relative gross outmigration (Figure 15.3), counties with index values along the diagonal where the ratio is − 1.0 have a level of gross outmigration rates that fits well with their labour market indicator. Counties with index values in sectors 1, 2, 3 and 8 all have a relative level of gross outmigration rates which is higher than the labour market indicator would suggest, while the situation is opposite in the counties with index values in the other sectors.

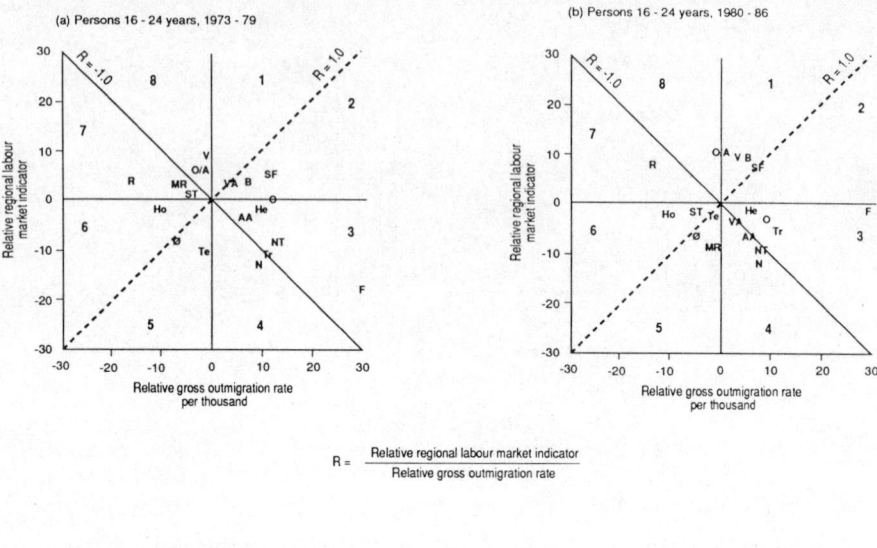

$$R = \frac{\text{Relative regional labour market indicator}}{\text{Relative gross outmigration rate}}$$

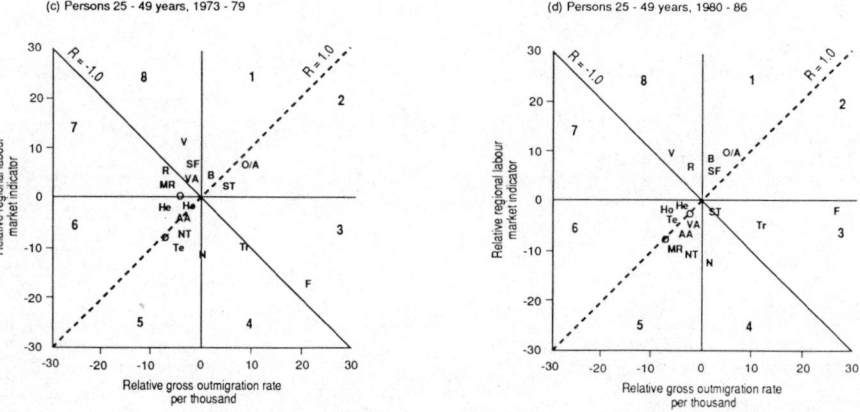

Figure 15.3   Relationships between relative regional labour market conditions and gross outmigration rates

Using pull–push theories, counties with index values in sectors 7 and 8 in the case of gross outmigrations, and in sectors 1 and 2 in the case of gross inmigrations, show a strong pull influence on migration by the regional labour market indicator. Correspondingly, the push explanation appears to be strong in counties with index values in sectors 3 and 4 in the case of gross outmigration and in sectors 5 and 6 in the case of gross inmigration. According to our hypothesis concerning the relationship between the regional labour market indicator and gross inmigration rates, we should expect to find the counties' index values either along the expected diagonals or in sectors 1, 2, 5 and 6 in the case of gross inmigration and in sectors 3, 4, 7 and 8 in the case of gross outmigration.

Our analysis is carried out separately for the 1970s and the 1980s, and performed for the age groups 16–24 years and 25–49 years. Some of the results indicate a tendency for counties' relative level of gross outmigration rates in relation to the labour market indicator to be lower in the 1980s than in the 1970s. Correspondingly, the relative level of gross inmigration rates also seems to be somewhat lower in the 1980s than in the 1970s according to the regional labour market indicator. An immediate interpretation of these results might be that both the push and pull factors have decreased their explanatory power of the migration rates from the 1970s to the 1980s. It is, however, important to note that employment is geographically more concentrated in the 1980s than in the 1970s. About half of the counties had a labour market indicator above the national average in the 1970s, while this share is reduced to about one-quarter in the 1980s. The results indicate that migration rates, particularly in the case of gross outmigration, have not changed as much as would be expected from these changes towards more concentration in regional labour demand. In spite of a stronger tendency to migrate in the direction of more centrally localized counties in the 1980s, this shift seems to be rather weaker than we would expect from changes in the regional labour market indicator.

The results for gross inmigration show that 9 counties follow the expected pattern for the young age group in the 1970s, while 11 counties follow the expected pattern for the older age group. This number increases to 13 counties for both age groups in the 1980s. As to gross outmigration, 11 counties follow the expected pattern for the younger age group in the 1970s, and 9 for the older age group. This number decreases to 10 counties for the younger age group and to only 6 counties for the older age group in the 1980s. These results show that the changes in the relative level of gross inmigration rates seem to be somewhat more in accordance with the regional labour market indicator, while changes in the relative level of gross outmigration rates seem to diverge somewhat from the regional labour market indicator.

15.7 Concluding remarks

Migration is a major source of uncertainty in the projection of regional population development. The DREM model is meant to be a functional model, exploring some alternative assumptions about migration in addition to the fixed rates (stationarity) assumption used in traditional population projections. The explicit link between migration and the regional labour market indicator in DREM opens up possibilities for more satisfactory specifications of non-stationary migration assumptions. Many of our central users appreciate an attempt to link regional population and labour markets in relation to national long-term economic and demographic prospects. To some extent, we have achieved this by establishing links to the existing national planning models (see Figure 15.1).

The results of our estimates of the migration model show, however, a weaker tendency for the regional labour market indicator to explain time variation in migration rates than we have found in earlier migration analyses. One of the reasons for this may be a tendency to lower annual fluctuation in migration rates in the 1980s as compared to the 1970s. This does not necessarily mean that recent trends in migration rates fit better with the traditional population projection model, using fixed rates of migration over time.

Of great interest when the model is used in population projections are the differences found between the labour market's power to explain net and gross migration rates within and between the sexes. The DREM migration submodel emphasizes the relationship between changes in the regional labour market indicator and net migration. The results from our empirical migration analysis indicate that we also should consider implementing relations explaining gross migration, especially gross out migration. With the analysis based on gross migration rates, the empirical model should be reformulated, taking into account the stochastic nature of these rates. As earlier migration analyses revealed only small differences in the parameter estimates between sexes, the model was implemented assuming common parameters for both sexes. However, our analysis presented in this chapter indicates that the model ought to have sex-specific parameters.

According to our hypothesis concerning the relationship between the regional labour market indicator and the direction of migration, the results show to some extent a tendency to follow the expected one, both for time variation and cross-sectional variation, in migration rates. Yet this relationship seems to be relatively much stronger in some counties, and on average little more than half of the counties seem to follow the expected tendency.

In our model, no attempt is made to explain the differences between the counties in average migration rates over the time period. As shown, these differences do seem to show some covariation with the labour market indicator. We should need to introduce into the model a better measure of the long-run prospects of labour market development in order to explain more of the long-run differences in migration rates between counties.

15.8 Some further research proposals

Finally, we will discuss some possible changes in the migration submodel which have not been examined in our empirical analysis so far. Up to now, calculations of the relationship between migration rates and changes in labour market demand have been made on the basis of a regional labour market indicator measured relative to the labour market situation in the whole country. The model does not consider where inmigrants are coming from or where outmigrants are going to. A change in one county's relative labour market indicator might affect the migration flows between some counties more than between others. An alternative hypothesis is that a change in the relative labour market indicator in one county will primarily affect the migration flows between this county and other counties with which in the past it has shown a high degree of migration interaction. We might take up such an analysis, based on interaction theories, comparing each county's relative labour market indicator (relative to the national average) to each of the other county's relative labour market indicators separately. It would be necessary to calculate parameters for the probabilities for a migrant moving from one particular county to another. The Norwegian migration data give the necessary detail for a county-to-county approach like this.

Another problem with the regional labour market indicator is its weak sensitivity to the level of changes in the labour market in the nation as a whole. The migration process might differ between years with increasing or decreasing employment at the national level. With decreasing national employment, some counties may have positive indicators of relative labour market demand despite generally decreasing employment. Correspondingly, with increasing national employment, some counties may have negative labour market indicators even though their employment is increasing. Thus we should like to investigate how regional migration processes respond to different employment changes at the national level.

In defining our regional labour market indicators we would find it most appropriate for our model to use the alternative which is based on county of employment (alternative B). As we have mentioned earlier, this alternative did not give parameter estimates for all the person groups involved, and for this reason we cannot use it in a complete population projection. We should then need to project commuting. This in turn raises the problem of a partial migration analysis in the more general context of labour market adjustment. In principle, the analysis should be extended to cover other modes of labour market adjustment simultaneously. Data of forms of regional labour market adjustments in Norway (apart from migration) are, however, weak.

Yet another problem is related to the aggregation level of the labour market indicator. Measuring the regional labour market balances through total demand and supply of labour, we have no information on the mismatches between the regional industrial structures and the qualifications of the labour force. To measure adjustment processes in regional labour markets we need data showing the industrial structure, or even better the occupational structure, on the demand side as against the qualifications of the supply of labour. At the moment the regional economic model, REGION, projects the regional demand of labour for about 30 production sectors, but gives no further classifications showing occupational structures. On the supply side we have no data projecting the qualifications of the regional supply of labour. Furthermore, we would need migration rates giving migrants by occupation or qualification. Accordingly, we have not found it possible to disaggregate the labour market indicator further than by sex and age. Our data problems might, however, be more manageable, if we aggregated the counties into a smaller number of regions.

International inmigration represents another problem in the DREM migration submodel. Today inmigration is projected in the same way as in traditional population projections, which means the number of net migrants is set exogenously, while the projections of regional distributions of inmigrants follows the same procedure as for the interregional migrants. One possible improvement is to see whether net inmigration is related to changes in the labour market indicator at the national level. The character of recent inmigration to Norway has indeed changed from labour migration more in the direction of refugees and asylum-seekers, but we still hypothesize that net inmigration may be sensitive to the situation at the national labour market. Second, it might be of interest to project the internal distribution of inmigrants separately because the regional pattern of settlement by international immigrants is quite different from that of internal migrants.

In our empirical analysis, we have so far used crude age intervals. As the migration rate varies markedly over age, unchanged individual behaviour gives rise to changing average rates if the age composition of the group changes. As the necessary demographic detail is available, we could take this effect into account in our analysis of gross migration rates by the usual demographic standardization techniques. This method might be of special relevance if we chose to use a longer period than just a one-year lag on the migration rate and the regional labour market indicator. As the model operates now, the base year in the population projection will have a strong effect on the projected migration rate because of this choice of a one-year lag only.

References

Abu-Lughod, J., Foley, M. and Winnick, L. (1960) *Housing choice and housing constraints*, Prentice-Hall, Englewood Cliffs, NJ.

Aitkin, M., Anderson, D., Francis, B. and Hinde, J. (1989) *Statistical modelling in GLIM*, Clarendon Press, Oxford.

Allison, P.D. (1982) 'Discrete-time methods for the analysis of event histories', in Leinhardt, S. (ed.), *Sociological methodology*, Jossey-Bass, San Francisco, pp. 61–98.

Allison, P.D. (1987) 'Introducing a disturbance into logit and probit regression models', *Sociological Methods and Research*, **15**, 335–74.

Amrhein, C.G. and Flowerdew, R. (1989) 'The effect of data aggregation on a Poisson model of Canadian migration', in Goodchild, M. and Gopal, S. (eds), *Accuracy of spatial databases*, Taylor and Francis, London, pp. 229–38.

Anas, A. (1982) *Residential location markets and urban transportation: economic theory, econometrics, and policy analysis with discrete choice models*, Academic Press, New York.

Andersen, E.B. (1970) 'Asymptotic properties of conditional maximum likelihood estimators', *Journal of the Royal Statistical Society B*, **32**, 283–301.

Armitage, R. (1986) 'Population projections for English local authority areas', *Population Trends*, **43**, 31–40.

Aufhauser, E. and Fischer, M.M. (1985) 'Log-linear modelling and spatial analysis', *Environment and Planning A*, **17**, 7, 931–51.

Bailey, A.J. (1989) 'Getting on your bike: what difference does a migration history make?', *Tijdschrift voor Economische en Sociale Geografie*, **80**, 5, 312–17.

Barlow, J. (1989) 'Regionalisation or geographic segmentation? Developments in London and South East housing markets', in Breheny, M. and Congdon, P. (eds), *Growth and change in a core region*, Pion, London, pp. 182–202.

Barry, J.T., Francis, B.J. and Davies, R.B. (1990) *SABRE: a guide for users, version 2.0*, Centre for Applied Statistics, Lancaster University, England.

Bates, J.J. (1984) 'Migration age profiles from the 1981 Census', report prepared for RPD2 Division of the DOE, London.

Bates, J.J. and Bracken, I. (1982) 'Estimation of migration profiles in England and Wales', *Environment and Planning A*, **14**, 889–900.

Bates, J.J. and Bracken, I. (1987) 'Migration age profiles for local authority areas in England, 1917–1981', *Environment and Planning A*, **19**, 521–35.

Batty, M. and Mackie, S. (1972) 'The calibration of gravity, entropy, and related models of spatial interaction', *Environment and Planning A*, **4**, 205–33.

Batty, M. and Sikdar, P.K. (1982a) 'Spatial aggregation in gravity models. 1. An information-theoretic framework', *Environment and Planning A*, **14**, 377–405.

Batty, M. and Sikdar, P.K. (1982b) 'Spatial aggregation in gravity models. 2. One-dimensional population density framework', *Environment and Planning A*, **14**, 525–53.

Batty, M. and Sikdar, P.K. (1982c) 'Spatial aggregation in gravity models. 3. Two-dimensional trip distribution and location models', *Environment and Planning A*, **14**, 629–58.

Batty, M. and Sikdar, P.K. (1982d) 'Spatial aggregation in gravity models. 4. Generalisations and large-scale applications', *Environment and Planning A*, **14**, 795–822.

Batty, M. and Sikdar, P.K. (1984) 'Proximate aggregation estimation of spatial interaction models', *Environment and Planning A*, **16**, 467–86.

Baxter, M. (1982) 'Similarities in methods of estimating spatial interaction models', *Geographical Analysis*, **14**, 267–72.

Baxter, M. (1983) 'Estimation and inference in spatial interaction models', *Progress in Human Geography*, **7**, 1, 40–59.

Baxter, M. (1984) 'A note on the estimation of a nonlinear migration model using GLIM', *Geographical Analysis*, **16**, 282–6.

Baxter, M. (1985) 'Quasi-likelihood estimation and diagnostic statistics for spatial interaction models', *Environment and Planning A*, **17**, 627–35.

Baydar, N. (1983) 'Analysis of the temporal stability of migration patterns in the context of multiregional forecasting', *Working Paper 38*, Netherlands Interuniversity Demographic Institute, Voorburg.

Becker, G.S. (1964) *Human capital*, Columbia University Press, New York.

Ben-Akiva, M. and Lerman, S.R. (1985) *Discrete choice analysis: theory and application to travel demand*, MIT Press, Cambridge, Mass.

Bettman, J.R. (1979) *An information processing theory of consumer choice*, Addison-Wesley, Reading, Mass.

Birkin, M. (1987) 'Iterative proportional fitting (IPF): theory, method and examples', *Computer Manual 26*, School of Geography, University of Leeds.

Black, J.A. and Salter, R.J. (1975) 'A statistical evaluation of the accuracy of a family of gravity models', *Proceedings, Institution of Civil Engineers: Part 2, Research and Theory*, **59**, 1–20.

Blattner, N. (1981) 'Zur berucksichtigung von anpassungsprozessen in des-aggregierten arbeitsmarktmodellen mit prognoseanspruch', in Blattner, N., Maillat, D. and Ratti, R. (eds), *Regionale Arbeitsmarktprozesse*, Diessenhofen.

Boadway, R. and Flatters, F. (1982) 'Efficiency and equalisation payments in a federal government: a synthesis and extension of recent results', *Canadian Journal of Economics* **XV**, 613–33.

Boden, P. (1989) 'The analysis of internal migration in the United Kingdom using Census and National Health Service Central Register data', unpublished Ph.D. thesis, School of Geography, University of Leeds.

Boden, P., Stillwell, J.C.H. and Rees, P.H. (1987) 'Migration data from the National Health Service Central Register and the 1981 Census: further comparative analysis', *Working Paper 495*, School of Geography, University of Leeds.

Boden, P., Stillwell, J.C.H. and Rees, P.H. (1988) 'Linking Census and NHSCR migration data', *Working Paper 511*, School of Geography, University of Leeds.

Boden, P., Stillwell, J.C.H. and Rees, P.H. (1991) 'NHS Central Register data: how good is it?', Chapter 1 in Stillwell, J.C.H., Rees, P.H. and Boden, P. (eds), *Migration processes and patterns Volume 2: Population redistribution in the 1980s*, Belhaven, London.

Bogue, D.J. (1977) 'A migrant's eye-view of the costs and benefits of migration to a metropolis', in Brown, A.A. and Neuberger, E. (eds), *Internal migration, a comparative perspective*, Academic Press, New York, pp. 167–82.

Boots, B.N. and Kanaroglou, P.S. (1987) 'Incorporating the effects of spatial structure in discrete choice models of migration', paper presented at the Annual Meeting of the Canadian Regional Science Association, Hamilton, Ontario (May).

Börsch-Supan, A. (1987) *Econometric analysis of discrete choice, with applications on the demand for housing in the US and West Germany*, Springer, Berlin.

Bracken, I. and Bates, J.J. (1983) 'Analysis of gross migration profiles in England and Wales: some developments in classification', *Environment and Planning A*, **15**, 343–55.

Breslow, N. (1984) 'Extra-Poisson variations in log-linear models', *Applied Statistics*, **33**, 1, 38–44.

Brown, C.C. (1975) 'On the use of indicator variables for studying the time dependence of parameters in a response-time model', *Biometrics*, **31**, 863–72.

Brown, L.A. and Moore, E.G. (1970) 'The intra-urban migration process: a perspective', *Geografiska Annaler*, Series B52, 1–13.

Brun, S.E. (1982) 'Nettoflytting oq arbeidsmarked i fylkene', *Rapporter 82/6*, Central Bureau of Statistics, Oslo.

Buck, N., Gordon, I. and Young, K. (1985) *The London employment problem*, Clarendon Press, Oxford.

Burdett, K., Kiefer, N.M., Mortensen, D.T. and Neumann, G.R. (1984) 'Earnings of unemployment and the allocation of time over time', *Review of Economic Studies*, **51**, 559–78.

Cadwallader, M. (1985) 'Structural-equation models of migration: an example from the upper midwest USA', *Environment and Planning A*, **17**, 101–13.

Cadwallader, M. (1989) 'A conceptual framework for analysing migration behaviour in the developed world', *Progress in Human Geography*, **13**, 4, 494–511.

Carpenter, C., Glassner, B., Johnson, B.D. and Loughlin, J. (1988) *Kids, drugs, and crime*, Lexington Books, Lexington, Mass.

Cebula, R. (1979) 'A survey of the literature on the migration impact of state and local government policies', *Public Finance*, **34**, 69–84.

Central Bureau of Statistics (1977) *Flyttemotivundersokelsen 1972*, Samfunn-sokonomiske studier, **35**.

Center for Human Resource Research (1988) *NLS handbook*, Ohio State University, Columbus.

Chalmers, J.A. and Greenwood, M.J. (1985) 'The regional labor market adjustment process: determinants of changes in rates of labor force participation, unemployment and migration', *Annals of Regional Science*, **19**.

Champion, A.G., Green, A.E., Owen, D.W., Ellin, D.J. and Coombes, M.G. (1987) *Changing places: Britain's demographic, economic and social complexion*, Arnold, London.

Chisholm, M. and O'Sullivan, P. (1973) *Freight flows and spatial aspects of the British economy*, Cambridge University Press, Cambridge.

Clark, G.L. and Ballard, K.P. (1980) 'Modelling out-migration from depressed regions: the significance of origin and destination characteristics', *Environment and Planning A*, **12**, 799–812.

Clark, W.A.V. and Huff, J.O. (1977) 'Some empirical tests of duration-of-stay effects in intraurban migration', *Environment and Planning A*, **9**, 1357–74.

Clark, W.A.V. and Onaka, J.L. (1985) 'An empirical test of a joint model of residential mobility and housing choice', *Environment and Planning A*, **17**, 915–30.

Clark, W.A.V. Deurloo, M.C. and Dielemen, F.M. (1984) 'Housing consumption and residential mobility', *Annals of the Association of American Geographers*, **74**, 29–43.

Clarke, M.C. (1986) 'Demographic processes and household dynamics: a microsimulation approach', Chapter 10 in Woods, R.I. and Rees, P.H. (eds), *Population structures and models: developments in spatial demography*, Allen and Unwin, London, pp. 245–72.

Clarke, M.C., Duley, C.J. and Rees, P.H. (1989) 'Microsimulation models for updating household and individual characteristics in small areas between censuses: demographics and mobility', paper presented at the International

Migration Seminar, Galve, Sweden (30–31 January).

Cliff, A.D., Martin, R.L. and Ord, J.K. (1974) 'Evaluating the friction of distance parameters in gravity models', *Regional Studies*, **8**, 281–6.

Cliff, A.D., Martin, R.L. and Ord, J.K. (1975) 'Map pattern and friction of distance parameters: reply to comments by R.J. Johnston, and by L. Curry, D.A. Griffith, and E.S. Sheppard', *Regional Studies*, **9**, 285–88.

Cliff, A.D., Martin, R.L. and Ord, J.K. (1976) 'A reply to the final comment', *Regional Studies*, **10**, 341–2.

Coleman, J.S. (1973) *The mathematics of collective action*, Heinemann, London.

Congdon, P.D. (1983) 'A model for the interaction of migration and commuting', *Urban Studies*, **20**.

Congdon, P.D. (1989a) 'Trends and patterns in London migration in the 1980s', *Reviews and Studies*, **37**, London Research Centre, London.

Congdon, P.D. (1989b) 'Modelling migration flows between areas: an analysis for London using the Census and the OPCS Longitudinal Study', *Regional Studies*, **23**, 87–103.

Congdon, P.D. and Champion, A.G. (1989a) 'Trends and structure in London's migration and their relation to employment and housing markets', in Congdon P. and Batey, P. (eds), *Advances in regional demography*, Belhaven Press, London.

Congdon, P.D. and Champion, A.G. (1989b) 'Recent population shifts in South East England and their relevance to the counterurbanisation debate', in Breheny, M. and Congdon, P. (eds), *Growth and change in a core region*, Pion, London, pp. 106–29.

Coombes, M., Dixon, J., Goddard, J., Openshaw, S. and Taylor P. (1982) 'Functional regions for the population census of Great Britain', in Herbert D. and Johnston R. (eds), *Geography and the urban environment*, Volume 5, Wiley, Chichester, pp. 63–112.

Coupe, R.T. and Morgan, B.S. (1981) 'Towards a fuller understanding of residential mobility: a case study in Northampton, England', *Environment and Planning A*, **13**, 201–15.

Courgeau, D. (1970) *Les champs migratoires en France*, Institut National D'Etudes Démographiques, Travaux et documents, Cahier No. 58, Presses Universitaires de France, Paris.

Courgeau, D. (1973) 'Migrants and migrations', *Population*, **28**, 1, 95–129.

Courgeau, D. (1980) *Analyse quantitative des migrations humaines*, Masson, Paris.

Culp, J. and Dunson, B.H. (1986) 'Brothers of a different color: a preliminary look at employer treatment of white and black youth', in Freeman, R.B. and Holzer, H.J. (eds), *The black youth employment crisis*, University of Chicago Press, Chicago.

Crouchley, R. and Pickles, A.R. (1990) 'An empirical comparison of conditional and marginal likelihood methods', Chapter 5 in Clogg, C. (ed.), *Sociological methodology*, Jossey Bass, San Francisco.

Curry, L. (1972) 'A spatial analysis of gravity flows', *Regional Studies*, **6**, 131–47.

Curry, L., Griffith, D.A. and Sheppard, E.S. (1975) 'Those gravity parameters again', *Regional Studies*, **9**, 289–96.

Cushing, B. (1989) 'Use and misuse of the allocation rate in models of population migration', *Annals of Regional Science*, **23**, 51–8.

DaVanzo, J.S. (1978) 'Does unemployment affect migration? The evidence from the micro-data', *Review of Economics and Statistics*, **60**, 504–14.

DaVanzo, J.S. and Morrison, P.A. (1981) 'Return and other sequences of migration in the United States', *Demography*, **18**, 1, 85–101.

Davies, R.B. (1989) 'A reappraisal of some simple statistical models', in Uncles,

M. (ed.), *Longitudinal data analysis: methods and applications*, Pion, London, pp. 103–15.

Davies, R.B. and Guy, C.M. (1987) 'The statistical modeling of flow data when the Poisson assumption is violated', *Geographical Analysis*, **19**, 4, 300–14.

Davies, R.B. and Pickles, A.R. (1983) 'The estimation of duration-of-residence effects: a stochastic modelling approach'. *Geographical Analysis*, **15**, 305–17.

Davies, R.B. and Pickles, A.R. (1985a) 'A panel study of life-cycle effects in residential mobility', *Geographical Analysis*, **17**, 199–216.

Davies, R.B. and Pickles, A.R. (1985b) 'Longitudinal versus cross-sectional methods of behavioural research: a first round knockout', *Environment and Planning A*, **17**, 1315–29.

Davies, R.B. and Pickles, A.R. (1991) 'An analysis of housing careers in Cardiff', *Environment and Planning A*, forthcoming.

De Jong, G.F. and Fawcett, J.T. (1981) 'Motivations for migration: an assessment and a value-expectancy research model', in De Jong, G.F. and Gardner, R.W. (eds), *Migration decision making: multidisciplinary approaches to microlevel studies in developed and developing countries*, Pergamon Press, New York, pp. 13–58.

Deurloo, M.C., Dieleman, F.M. and Clark, W.A.V. (1987) 'Tenure choice in the Dutch housing market', *Environment and Planning A*, **19**, 763–81.

Devis, T.L.F. and Mills, I. (1986) 'A comparison of migration data from the National Health Service Central Register and the 1981 Census', *OPCS Occasional Paper 35*, OPCS, London.

Dhrymes, P.J. (1978) *Introductory econometrics*, Springer-Verlag, New York.

Domencich, T.A. and McFadden, D. (1975) *Urban travel demand: a behavioural analysis*, North Holland, Amsterdam.

Duley, C.J. (1989) 'A model for updating census-based household and population information for inter-censal years', unpublished Ph.D. thesis, School of Geography, University of Leeds.

Duley, C.J., Rees, P.H. and Clarke, M.C. (1988) 'A microsimulation model for updating households in small areas between censuses, *Working Paper 515*, School of Geography, University of Leeds.

Edstom, A. and Galbraith, J.R. (1977) 'Transfer of managers as a co-ordination and control strategy in multinational organisations', *Administrative Science Quarterly*, **22**, 248–63.

Egle, F. and Apfelthaler, G. (1979) 'Die regionalen unterschiede in der struktur der arbeitslosen- und offenen-stellen-quoten', *Mitteilungen aus der Arbeitsmarkt- und Berufsforschung*, **12**.

EGRET (1989) *The EGRET manual*, Statistics and Epidemiology Research Corporation, Seattle.

Evers, G.H.M. (1989) 'Simultaneous models for migration and commuting: macro and micro economic approaches', in van Dijk, J.H., Folmer, H.W., Herzog, H.W., Jr, and Schlottmann, A.M. (eds), *Migration and labor market adjustment*, Kluwer, Dordrecht, pp. 177–97.

Evers, G.H.M. and van der Veen, A. (1985) 'A simultaneous non-linear model for labor migration and commuting', *Regional Studies*, **19**, 217–29.

Ezzet, F.L. and Davies, R.B. (1988) *A manual for mixture*, Centre for Applied Statistics, Lancaster University.

Falaris, E.M. (1987) 'A nested logit migration model with selectivity', *International Economic Review*, **28**, 2, 429–43.

Falaris, E.M. (1989) 'Migration and wages of young men', *Journal of Human Resources*, **23**, 4, 514–34.

Feder, G. (1979) 'Alternative opportunities and migration: an exposition', *Annals of Regional Science*, **13**, 57–67.

Feder, G. (1980) 'Alternative opportunities and migration: evidence from Korea', *Annals of Regional Science*, **14**, 1–11.

Fields, G.S. (1976) 'Labour force migration, unemployment and job turnover', *The Review of Economics and Statistics*, **4**, 407–15.

Fields, G.S. (1982) 'Place-to-place migration in Columbia', *Economic Development and Cultural Change*, **90**, 539–58.

Fienburg, S.E. (1970) 'An iterative procedure for estimation in contingency tables', *The Annals of Mathematical Statistics*, **41**, 907–17.

Fischer, M.M. and Nijkamp, R. (eds) (1987) *Regional labour markets, analytical contributions and cross-national comparison*, Elsevier, Amsterdam.

Flowerdew, R.T. (1976) 'Search strategies and stopping rules in residential mobility', *Transactions of the Institute of British Geographers*, **1**, 47–57.

Flowerdew, R. and Aitkin, M. (1982) 'A method of fitting the gravity model based on the Poisson distribution', *Journal of Regional Science*, **22**, 191–202.

Flowerdew, R. and Lovett, A. (1988) 'Fitting constrained Poisson regression models to inter-urban migration flows', *Geographical Analysis*, **20**, 297–307.

Flowerdew, R. and Lovett, A. (1989) 'Compound and generalised Poisson models for inter-urban migration', in Congdon P. and Batey, P. (eds), *Advances in regional demography: information, forecasts, models*, Belhaven Press, London, pp. 246–56.

Flowerdew, R. and Salt, J. (1979) 'Migration between labour market areas in Great Britain, 1970–1971', *Regional Studies*, **13**, 2, 211–31.

Foot, D.K. and Milne, W.J. (1984) 'Net migration estimation in an extended multi-regional gravity model', *Journal of Regional Science*, **24**, 119–33.

Foot, D.K. and Milne, W.J. (1989) 'Multiregional estimation of gross internal migration flows', *International Regional Science Review*, **12**, 29–43.

Foot, D.K. and Milne, W.J. (1990) 'Serial correlation in multiregional migration models', *Journal of Regional Science*.

Forrest, R. and Kemeny, J. (1982) 'Middle-class housing careers: the relationship between furnished renting and home ownership', *Sociological Review*, **30**, 208–21.

Fotheringham, A.S. (1981) 'Spatial structure and distance-decay parameters', *Annals of the Association of American Geographers*, **71**, 425–36.

Fotheringham, A.S. (1983) 'A new set of spatial interaction models: the theory of competing destinations', *Environment and Planning A*, **15**, 15–36.

Fotheringham, A.S. (1984) 'Spatial flows and spatial patterns', *Environment and Planning A*, **16**, 529–43.

Fotheringham, A.S. (1986) 'Modelling hierarchical destination choice', *Environment and Planning A*, **18**, 401–18.

Fotheringham, A.S. (1987) 'Hierarchical destination choice: discussion with evidence from migration in The Netherlands', *Working Paper 69*, Netherlands InterUniversity Demographic Institute, The Hague.

Fotheringham, A.S. (1988) 'Consumer store choice and choice set definition', *Marketing Science*, **7**, 299–310.

Fotheringham, A.S. and O'Kelly, M.E. (1989) *Spatial interaction models: formulations and applications*, Kluwer, Dordrecht.

Fotheringham, A.S. and Webber, M.J. (1980) 'Spatial structure and the parameters of spatial interaction models', *Geographical Analysis*, **12**, 33–46.

Friedman, M. (1968) 'The role of monetary policy', *American Economic Review*, **58**.

Gabriel, S.A., Justman, M. and Levy, A. (1987) 'Place-to-place migration in Israel, estimates of a logit model', *Regional Science and Urban Economics* **17**, 595–606.

Genosko, J. (1979) 'Die arbeitslosenquote: ein konzept mit mangeln', *Dargestellt am Beispiel Ostbayers*, Konjunkturpolitik, **25**.

Genosko, J. (1980) 'Zur selektivitat raumlicher mobilitat', *Kölner Zeitschrift fur Soziologie und Sozialpsychologie*, **32**.

Genosko, J. (1987) 'The interregional technology transfer: some sceptical remarks', *Regensburger Diskussionsbeitrage zur Wirtschaftswissenschaft No. 191*.

Genosko, J. (1988a) 'Zur konjunkturellen reagibilitat von arbeitslosigkeit und beschaftigung: eine regionalisierte zeitreihenbetrachtung', *Raumforschung und Raumordnung*, **46**.

Genosko, J. (1988b) 'The impact of regional policy on location decisions of firms: an evaluation of the German case', *Diskussionsbeitrage aus dem Institut fur Volkswirtschaftslehre der Universitat Hohenheim No. 37*.

Genosko, J. (1989) 'Regional labour market adjustment processes', *Diskussionsbeitrage aus dem Institut fur Volkswirtschaftslehre der Universitat Hohenheim No. 43*.

Ginsberg, R. (1978) 'The relationship between timing of moves and choice of destination in stochastic models of migration', *Environment and Planning A*, **10**, 667–79.

Gleave, D. and Cordey-Hayes, M. (1977) 'Migration dynamics and labour market turnover', *Progress in Planning*, **8**, 1, Pergamon Press, Oxford.

Goldstein, S. (1964) 'The extent of repeated migration: an analysis based on the Danish population register', *Journal of the American Statistical Association*, **59**, 1121–32.

Goodman, J.L. (1976) 'Housing consumption disequilibrium and local residential mobility', *Environment and Planning A*, **8**, 855–74.

Goodman, J.L. (1981) 'Information, uncertainty, and the microeconomics model of migration decision-making', in De Jong, G.F. and Gardner, R.W. (eds), *Migration decision making: multidisciplinary approaches to microlevel studies in developed and developing countries*, Pergamon Press, New York, pp. 130–48.

Gordon, I.R. (1975) 'Employment and housing streams in British interregional migration', *Scottish Journal of Political Economy*, **22**, 161–77.

Gordon, I.R. (1982) 'The analysis of motivation-specific migration streams', *Environment and Planning A*, **14**, 5–20.

Gordon, I.R. (1985a) 'The cyclical sensitivity of regional employment and unemployment differentials', *Regional Studies*, **19**.

Gordon, I.R. (1985b) 'Economic explanations of spatial variation in distance deterrence', *Environment and Planning A*, **17**, 59–72.

Gordon, I.R. (1988a) 'Interdistrict migration in Great Britain 1980/81: a multistream model with a commuting option', *Environment and Planning A*, **20**, 907–24.

Gordon, I.R. (1988b) 'Resurrecting counter-urbanisation; housing market influences on migration fluctuations from London', *Built Environment*, 212–22.

Gordon, I.R. and Lamont, D.W. (1982) 'A model of labour market interdependencies in the London region', *Environment and Planning A*, **14**, 237–64.

Gordon, I.R. and Molho, I.I. (1985) 'Women in the labour markets of the London region: a model of dependence and constraint', *Urban Studies*, **22**, 367–86.

Gordon, I.R. and Molho, I.I. (1987) 'The changing pattern on interregional migration in Great Britain 1960–86', paper presented to the Annual Conference of the British section of the Regional Science Association, University of Sterling.

Gordon, I.R. and Pitfield, D.E. (1982) 'A multi-stream approach to the analysis of hierarchically differentiated spatial interactions', *Papers of the Regional Science Association*, **49**, 23–5.

Gordon, I.R. and Vickerman, R.W. (1982) 'Opportunities, preferences and constraints: an approach to the analysis of metropolitan migration', *Urban Studies*, **19**, 247–61.

Gordon, I.R., Vickerman, R.W., Lamont, D.W. and Thomas, A.M. (1983) 'Opportunities, preferences and constraints on population movement in the London region', Urban and Regional Studies, Unit, University of Kent at Canterbury, Canterbury.

Gordon, P., Richardson, H. and Wong, H. (1986) 'The distribution of population and employment in a polycentric city: the case of Los Angeles', *Environment and Planning A*, **18**, 161–73.

Goss, E.P. (1985) 'General Skills, specific skills, and the migration decision', *Regional Science Perspective*, **15**, 17–26.

Goss, E.P. and Schoening, N.C. (1984) 'Search time, unemployment and the migration decision', *Journal of Human Resources*, **19**, 4, 570–81.

Gould, P. (1975) 'Acquiring spatial information', *Economic Geography*, **15**, 87–9.

Gould, P. and White, R. (1974) *Mental maps*, Allen and Unwin, Boston.

Gourieroux, C., Monfort, A. and Trognon, A. (1984) 'Pseudo maximum likelihood methods: theory', *Econometrica*, **52**, 681–700.

Goux, J.M. (1962) 'Structure de l'espace et migration', in Sutter, J. (ed.), *Human displacements* (Entretiens de Monaco en Science Humaines, Première Session), Hachette, Paris, pp. 167–72.

Graves, P.E. (1980) 'Migration and climate', *Journal of Regional Science*, **20**, 227–37.

Graves, P.E. (1983) 'Migration with a composite amenity: the role of rents', *Journal of Regional Science*, **23**, 541–6.

Greenwood, M.J. (1975) 'Research on internal migration in the United States: a survey', *Journal of Economic Literature*, **13**, 2, 397–433.

Greenwood, M.J. (1985) 'Human migration: theory, models and empirical studies', *Journal of Regional Science*, **25**, 521–44.

Greenwood, M.J. and Hunt, G. (1984a) 'Econometrically accounting for identities and restrictions in models of interregional migration', *Regional Science and Urban Economics*, **14**, 113–28.

Greenwood, M.J. and Hunt, G. (1984b) 'Migration and interregional employment distribution in the United States', *American Economic Review*, **17**, 957–69.

Greenwood, M.J. and Sweetland, D. (1972) 'The determinants of migration between Standard Metropolitan Statistical Areas, *Demography*, **9**, 665–81.

Griffith, D.A. (1987) *Spatial autocorrelation: a primer*, Association of American Geographers, Washington, DC.

Hagerstrand, T. (1957) 'Migration and area', in Hannerberg, D. (ed.), *Migration in Sweden: a symposium*, Lund Studies in Geography, Series B, Human Geography, No. 13, Lund, pp. 27–158.

Hamnett, C. (1984) 'Gentrification and residential location theory: a review and assessment', Chapter 8 in Herbert, D. and Johnston, R. (eds), *Geography and the urban environment: progress in research and applications*, Volume VI, Wiley, London.

Hanushek, E.A. and Quigley, J.M. (1978) 'The dynamics of the housing market: a stock adjustment model of housing construction', *Journal of Urban Economics*, **5**, 411–29.

Harkman, A. (1989) 'Migration behaviour among the unemployed and the role of unemployment benefits', *Papers of the Regional Science Association*, **66**, 143–50.

Harris, A.I. and Clausen, R. (1967) *Labour mobility in Great Britain 1953-63*, HMSO, London.

Hart, R. (1973) 'Economic expectations and the decision to migrate: an analysis by socio-economic group', *Regional Studies*, **7**, 271–85.

Hart, R. (1975) 'Inter-regional migration: some theoretical considerations (Part 2)', *Journal of Regional Science*, **15**, 3, 289–305.

Haurin, D.R. (1980) 'The regional distribution of population, migration, and climate', *Quarterly Journal of Economics*, **95**, 3, 293–308.

Haurin, D.R. and Haurin, R.J. (1988) 'Net migration, unemployment and the business cycle', *Journal of Regional Science*, **28**, 2, 239–53.

Haworth, J. and Vincent, P. (1979) 'The stochastic disturbance specification and its implications for log-linear regression', *Environment and Planning A*, **11**, 781–90.

Heckman, J.J. (1976) 'The common structure of statistical models of truncation: sample selection and limited dependent variables and a simple estimator for such models', *The Annals of Economic and Social Measurement*, **5**, 475–92.

Heckman, J.J. (1979) 'Sample selection bias as a specification error', *Econometrica*, **47**, 153–61.

Heckman, J.J. (1981) 'Statistical models for discrete panel data', in Manski, C.F. and McFadden, D. (eds), *Structural analysis of discrete data with econometric applications*, MIT Press, Cambridge, Mass., pp. 114–78.

Heckman, J.J. and Singer, B. (1982) 'The identification problem in econometric models for duration data', in Hildenbrand, W. (ed.), *Advances in Econometrics*, **III**, 37–77.

Heckman, J.J. and Singer, B. (1984) 'A method for minimising the impact of distributional assumptions in econometric models of duration', *Econometrica*, **52**, 271–320.

Heckman, J.J. and Willis, R.J. (1977) 'A beta-logical model for the analysis of sequential labor force participation by married women', *Journal of Political Economy*, **85**, 27–58.

Henretta, J.C. (1987) 'Family transitions, housing market context, and first home purchase by young married households', *Social Forces*, **66**, 2, 520–36.

Herzog, H.W. and Schlottmann, A.M. (1983) 'Migrant information, job search and the remigration decision', *Southern Economic Journal*, **50**, 1, 43–56.

Hinde, J. (1982) 'Compound regression models', in Gilchrist, R. (ed.), *GLIM82, Proceedings of the international conference on generalised linear models*, Springer, New York, pp. 109–21.

Hsiao, C. (1986) *Analysis of panel data*, Cambridge University Press, Cambridge.

Hughes, G. and McCormick, B. (1987) 'Does migration reduce differentials in regional unemployment rates?', Department of Economics, University of Edinburgh (MS).

Hughes, G. and McCormick, B. (1989) 'Does migration reduce differentials in regional unemployment rates?', in van Dijk, J., Folmer, H., Herzog, Jr, H.W. and Schlottmann, A.M. (eds), *Migration and labor market adjustment*, Kluwer, Dordrecht, pp. 85–108.

Hyman, G.M. (1969) 'The calibration of trip distribution models', *Environment and Planning*, **1**, 105–12.

Hyman, G.M. and Gleave, D. (1976) 'A reasonable theory of migration', *RP-22*, Centre for Environmental Studies, London.

Ineichen, B. (1981) 'The housing decisions of young people', *British Journal of Sociology*, **32**, 252–8.

Ioannides, Y.M. (1987) 'Residential mobility and housing tenure choice', *Journal of Urban Economics*, **17**, 265–87.

Isard, W. (1975) *Introduction to regional science*, Prentice-Hall, Englewood Cliffs, NJ.

Ishikawa, Y. (1989) 'Explorations into the two-stage destination choice', *Geographical Review of Japan*, **62**, 75–85.

Isserman, A.M. Taylor, C., Gerking, S. and Schubert, U. (1986) 'Regional labour market analysis', in Nijkamp, P. (ed.), *Handbook of regional and urban economics, Volume 1: Regional economics*, North Holland, Amsterdam.

Johnson, J.H. and Salt, J. (eds), (1990) *Labour migration*, David Fulton, London.

Johnson, J.H., Salt, J. and Wood, P.A. (1974) *Housing and the migration of labour in England and Wales*, Saxon House, Farnborough.

Johnson, J.H., Salt, J. and Wood, P.A. (1975) 'Housing and the geographical mobility of labour in England and Wales: some theoretical considerations', in Kosinski, L. and Prothero, R. (eds), *People on the move: studies on internal migration*, Methuen, London, pp. 91–101.

Johnston, R.J. (1973) 'On frictions of distance and regression and coefficients', *Area*, **5**, 187–91.

Johnston, R.J. (1975) 'Map pattern and friction of distance parameters: a comment', *Regional Studies*, **9**, 281–3.

Jüttner, D.J. (1972) 'Arbeitspotential, arbeitsmarktreserven und vollbeschaftigung', *Zeitschrift fur die Gesamte Staatswissenschaft (JITE) 128*.

Kalbfleisch, J.D. and Prentice, R.L. (1980) *The statistical analysis of failure time date*, Wiley, New York.

Kasarda, J.D. (1985) 'Urban change and minority opportunities', in Peterson, P.E. (ed.), *The new urban reality*, The Brookings Institution, Washington, DC.

Kasarda, D. (1988) 'Jobs, migration, and emerging urban mismatches', in McGeary, M.G.H. and Lynn, L.E., Jr, (eds), *Urban change and poverty*, National Academy Press, Washington, DC, pp. 148–98.

Kasarda, D. (1989) 'Urban industrial transition and the underclass', *Annals of the American Academy of Political and Social Science*.

Kau, J.R. and Sirmans, C.F. (1977) 'The influence of information costs of uncertainty on migration: a comparison of migrant types', *Journal of Regional Science*, **17**, 89–96.

Kau, J.R. and Sirmans, C.F. (1979) 'A recursive model of the spatial allocation of migrants', *Journal of Regional Science*, **19**, 47–56.

Kephart, G. (1989) 'The effects of local economic restructuring on out-migration from US counties', Ph.D. thesis, University of Wisconsin, Madison.

Kish, L. (1965) *Survey sampling*, John Wiley, New York.

Knudsen, D.C. and Fotheringham, A.S. (1986) 'Matrix comparison, goodness of fit, and spatial interaction modelling', *International Regional Science Review*, **10**, 2, 127–47.

Lansing, J.B. (1966) *Residential location and urban mobility: the second wave of interviews*, Survey Research Centre, Institute for Social Research, University of Michigan.

Lawless, J. (1987) 'Negative binomial and mixed Poisson regression', *Canadian Journal of Statistics*, **15**, 3, 209–25.

Ledent, J. (1980) 'Multistate life tables: movement versus transition perspectives', *Environment and Planning A*, **12**, 533–62.

Ledent, J. (1986a) 'Forecasting interregional migration using longitudinal data', in Isserman, A.M. (ed.), *Population change and the economy*, Kluwer-Nijhoff, Boston.

Ledent, J. (1986b) 'Forecasting interregional migration: an economic demographic approach', in Isserman, A.M. (ed.), *Population change and the economy*, Kluwer-Nijhoff, Boston.

Ledent, J. and Rees, P.H. (1980) 'Choices in the construction of multiregional life tables', *Working Paper 289*, School of Geography, University of Leeds (also *Working Paper 80–173*, International Institute of Applied Systems Analysis, Luxenburg).

Lee, E.S. (1966) 'Theory of migration', in Hauser, P.H. and Duncan, O.D. (eds), *The study of population*, University of Chicago Press, Chicago.

Lee, E.S. (1969) 'A theory of migration', in Jackson, J.A. (ed.), *Migration*, Cambridge University Press, Cambridge, pp. 282–97.

Lee, E.T. (1980) *Statistical methods for survival data analysis*, Lifetime Learning Publications, Belmont.

Lee, L.F. (1976) 'Estimation of limited dependent variable models by two stage methods', Ph.D. thesis, University of Rochester.

Leinbach, T.R. (1973) 'Distance information flows and modernisation: some observations from West Malaysia', *The Professional Geographer*, **25**, 7–11.

Levy, M. and Wadycki, W. (1974) 'What is the opportunity cost of moving? Reconsideration of the effect of distance on migration', *Economic Development and Cultural Change*, **22**, 198–214.

Lian, J.I. (1986) 'Flytting over fylkesgrensene 1967–79', *Rapporter*, **86**, 19, Central Bureau of Statistics, Oslo.

Lian, J.I. and Sørensen, K.O. (1985) 'Migration analysis and regional population projections', *Scandinavian Population Studies 7*, The Scandinavian Demographic Society, Helsinki.

Liaw, K.-L. and Ledent, J. (1987) 'Nested logit model and maximum quasi-likelihood method: a flexible methodology for analysing interregional migration patterns', *Regional Science and Urban Economics*, **17**, 67–88.

Lindsay, P.H. and Norman, D.A. (1972) *Human information processing*, Academic Press, New York.

Lippman, S.A. and McCall, J.J. (1976) 'The economics of job search: a survey', *Economic Inquiry*, **14**, 2, 155–89, and **14**, 3, 347–68.

Lippman, S.A. and McCall, J.J. (1979) *Studies in the economics of search*, North Holland, Amsterdam.

Long, L. (1988) *Migration and residential mobility in the United States*, Russell Sage Foundation, New York.

Lovett, A. and Flowerdew, R. (1989) 'Analysis of count data using Poisson regression', *Professional Geographer*, **41**, 2, 190–8.

Lovett, A.A., Whyte, I.D. and Whyte, K.A. (1985) 'Poisson regression analysis and migration fields: the example of the apprenticeship records of Edinburgh in the seventeenth and eighteenth centuries', *Transactions of the Institute of British Geographers*, **10**, 317–32.

Lowry, I. (1966) *Migration and metropolitan growth: two analytical reports*, Chandler, San Francisco.

McCullagh, P. and Nelder, J.A. (1983) *Generalised linear models*, Chapman and Hall, London.

McCullagh, P. and Nelder, J.A. (1989) *Generalised linear models*, 2nd edition, Chapman and Hall, London.

McDevitt, T.M., Hawley, A.H., Udry, J.R., Gadalla, S., Leoprapai, B. and Cardona, R. (1986) 'Migration plans of the rural population of Third World countries: a probit analysis of micro-level data from Asia, Africa, and Latin America', *Journal of Developing Areas* **20**, 473–90.

McFadden, D. (1973) 'Conditional logit analysis of qualitative choice behaviour', in Zarembka, P. (ed.), *Frontiers in econometrics*, Academic Press, London, pp. 105–42.

McFadden, D. (1978) 'Modelling the choice of residential location', in Karlqvist, A., Lundqvist, L., Snickars, F. and Weibull, J.W. (eds), *Spatial interaction theory and residential location*, North Holland, Amsterdam, pp. 75–96.

McFadden, D. (1981) 'Econometric models of probabilistic choice', in Manski, C.F. and McFadden, D. (eds), *Structural analysis of discrete data with econometric applications*, MIT Press, Cambridge, Mass., pp. 198–272.

McGinnis, R. (1968) 'A stochastic model of social mobility', *American Sociological Review*, **23**, 712–22.

McKenna, C.J. (1987) 'Theories of individual search behaviour', in Hey, J.D. and Lambert, P.J. (eds), *Surveys in the economics of uncertainty*, Blackwell, Oxford, pp. 91–109.

McMahon, W.W. and Melton, C. (1978) 'Measuring cost of living variation', *Industrial Relations*, **17**, 3, 324–32.

MacLennan, D. (1982) *Housing economics*, Longman, London.

Maddala, G.S. (1977) 'Self-selectivity problems in econometric models', in Krishnaiah, P.R. (ed.), *Applications of statistics*, North Holland, Amsterdam.

Maddala, G.S. (1986) *Limited dependent and qualitative variables in econometrics*, Cambridge University Press, Cambridge.

Madden, M. and Batey, P.W.J. (1980) 'Achieving consistency in demographic economic forecasting', *Papers of the Regional Science Association*, 91–106.

Maier, G. (1985) 'Cumulative causation and selectivity in labour market oriented migration caused by imperfect information', *Regional Studies*, **19**, 231–41.

Maier, G. (1986) 'The impact of optimal job search models on the modelling of migration behaviour', *IIR-Discussion No. 29*, Interdisciplinary Institute for Urban and Regional Studies, University of Economics and Business Administration, Vienna.

Maier, G. (1987) 'Job search and migration', in Fischer, M.M. and Nijkamp, P. (eds), *Regional labour markets*, North Holland, Amsterdam, pp. 189–204.

Maier, G. (1990a) 'The economics of information in the context of migration', in Johnson, J.H. and Salt, J. (eds), *Labour migration*, Fulton, London, pp. 115–36.

Maier, G. (1990b) 'Modelling search processes in space', paper presented at the 30th European Congress of the Regional Science Association, Istanbul (August).

Maier, G. and Fischer, M.M. (1985) 'Random utility modelling and labour supply mobility analysis', *Papers of the Regional Science Association*, **58**, 21–33.

Maier, G. and Rogerson, P. (1986) 'Discrete choice, optimal search and spatial interaction models: some fundamental relationships', *IIR-Discussion No. 31*, Interdisciplinary Institute for Urban and Regional Studies, University of Economics and Business Administration, Vienna, Austria.

Maier, G. and Weiss, P. (1990a) *Modelle diskreter entscheidungen, theorie und anwendung in den sozial- und wirtschaftswissenschaften*, Springer, Vienna.

Maier, G. and Weiss, P. (1990b) 'Segmentation mobility, and the spatial distribution of activities', paper presented at the 29th European Congress of the Regional Science Association, Cambridge (August).

Martin and Voorhees Associates and John Bates Services (1981) 'Developing the migration component of the official subnational population projections', Final Report prepared for DPRP3 Division, Department of the Environment, London.

Massey, S. and Denton, N.A. (1989) 'Hypersegregation in US metropolitan areas: black and hispanic segregation along five dimensions', *Demography*, **26**, 3, 373–92.

Merrett, S. and Gray, F. (1982) *Owner-occupation in Britain*, Routledge and Kegan Paul, London.

Michelson, W. (1977) *Environment choice, human behaviour and residential satisfaction*, Oxford University Press, New York.

Mieth, W. and Genosko, J. (1982) 'Qualitative polarisierung der regionen als folge der raumlichen selektion der wanderung und der arbeitsplatze, in Qualitat von Arbeitsmarkten und regionale Entwicklung', *Forschungs- und Sitzungsberichte der Akademie fur Raumforschung und Landesplanung No. 143*, Hannover.

Miller, E. (1973) 'Is out-migration affected by economic conditions?', *Southern Economic Journal*, **39**, 396–405.

Milne, W.J. (1981) 'Migration in an interregional macroeconometric model of the United States: will net outmigration from the Northeast continue?', *International Regional Science Review*, **6**, 71–83.

Mincer, J. (1966) 'Labor force participation and unemployment: a review of recent evidence', in Gordon, R.A. and Gordon, M.S. (eds), *Prosperity and unemployment*, New York.

Mincer, J. (1974) *School experience and earnings*, Columbian University Press, New York.

Molho, I.I. (1982) 'Contiguity and inter-regional migration flows in Great Britain', *Scottish Journal of Political Economy*, **29**, 283–97.

Molho, I.I. (1984a) 'Distance deterrence relationships in multi-stream migration models', *The Manchester School*, **52**, 49–69.

Molho, I.I. (1984b) 'A dynamic model of inter-regional migration in Great Britain', *Journal of Regional Science*, **24**, 317–27.

Molho, I.I. (1986) 'Theories of migration: a review', *Scottish Journal of Political Economy*, **33**, 396–419.

Molho, I.I. (1990) 'A behavioural map of commuting distances in the London region', *Environment and Planning A*, **22**, 779–92.

Morgan, J.N. (1986) 'Panel study of income dynamics 1968–1984 (Waves I–XVII), machine-readable data file produced by the Survey Research Center, Ann Arbor, Michigan, and distributed by the Inter-university Consortium for Political and Social Research, Ann Arbor, Michigan.

Morgan, J.N. and Robb, E.H. (1981) 'The impact of age upon interregional migration', *Annals of Regional Science*, **15**, 32–45.

Morrill, R.L. (1965) 'The negro ghetto: problems and alternatives', *Geographical Review*, **55**, 2, 339–61.

Morris, E.W. and Winter, M. (1978) *Housing, family and society*, John Wiley, New York.

Morrison, P.A. (1971) 'Chronic movers and the future redistribution of population', *Demography*, **8**, 171–84.

Morrison, P.A. (1973) 'Theoretical issues in the design of population mobility models', *Environment and Planning*, **5**, 1, 125–34.

Muellbauer, J. and Murphy, A. (1988) *UK house prices and migration: economic and investment implications*, Shearson Lehman Hutton.

Mueser, P. and White, M. (1989) 'Explaining the association between rates of in-migration and out-migration', *Papers of the Regional Science Association*, **67**, 121–34.

Myrdal, G. (1957) *Rich lands and poor*, Harper and Row, New York.

Nakosteen, R. and Zimmer, M. (1980) 'Migration and income: the question of self-selection', *Southern Economic Journal*, **46**, 840–51.

Nam, C.B., Serow, W.J. and Sly, D.F. (1990) *International handbook on internal migration*, Greenwood Press, London.

Nelder, J.A. and Wedderburn, R.W.M. (1972) 'Generalised linear models', *Journal, Royal Statistical Society A*, **135**, 370–84.

Newell, A. and Simon H.A. (1972) *Human problem solving*, Prentice-Hall, Englewood Cliffs, NJ.

Norman, D.A. and Bubrow, D.G. (1975) 'On data-limited and resource-limited process', *Cognitive Psychology*, **7**, 44–64.

Norusis, M. (1985) *SPSSX advanced statistics guide*, McGraw-Hill, London.

Odland, J. and Bailey, A. (1990) 'Regional out-migration rates and migration histories', *Geographical Analysis*, **22**, 2, 158–70.

Odland, J. and Ellis, M. (1988) 'Household organisation and the interregional variation of outmigration rates', *Demography*, **25**, 4, 567–79.

Olsson, G. (1965) *Distance and human interaction: a review and bibliography*, Regional Science Research Institute, Philadelphia.

Onaka, J.L. (1983) 'A multiple-attribute housing disequilibrium model of residential mobility', *Environment and Planning A*, **15**, 751–65.

Onaka, J.L. and Clarke, W.A.V. (1983) 'A disaggregate model of residential mobility and housing choice', *Geographical Analysis*, **15**, 4, 287–304.

OPCS (1982, 1984, 1986) *OPCS Monitor PP1*, Mid-year population estimates for local government and health authority areas of England and Wales, OPCS, London.

OPCS (1983, 1986, 1988) 'Population projections: area population projections by age and sex for standard regions, counties, London boroughs and metropolitan districts of England from mid-1981, mid-1983 and mid-1985', *Series PP3*, HMSO, London.

OPCS (1983a) *Census 1981: county report*, CEN81 CR nn, HMSO, London.

OPCS (1983b) *Census 1981: housing and households, England and Wales*, CEN81 HH, HMSO, London.

OPCS (1984a) *Census 1981: regional migration*, CEN81 RM nn, HMSO, London.

OPCS (1984b) 'National grid references of the centres of population of local authority districts, counties and regions, England and Wales 1981, and movements of centres of population 1971–81', *OPCS Users Guide 214*, HMSO, London.

OPCS, RGS (1983a) *Census 1981 National Migration Great Britain Part 1 (100% tables)*, HMSO, London.

OPCS, RGS (1983b) *Census 1981 Usual Residence Great Britain*, HMSO, London.

Openshaw, S. (1984) *The modifiable areal unit problem*, Geo Abstracts, Norwich.

Op't Veld, A., Bijlsma, E. and Starmans, J. (1984) 'Exploratory analysis of interregional migration in the nineteen-seventies', Chapter 9, in ter Heide H. and Willekens, F.J. (eds), *Demographic research and spatial policy: the Dutch experience*, Academic Press, London.

Payne, C. (ed.) (1987) *The GLIM system, release 3.77, Generalised Linear Interactive Modelling manual*, Royal Statistical Society.

Phipps, A.G. and Carter, J.E. (1984) 'An individual-level analysis of the stress-resistance model of household mobility', *Geographical Analysis*, **16**, 176–89.

Phipps, A.G. and Holden, W.J. (1985) 'Intended-mobility responses to inner-city school closure', *Environment and Planning A*, **17**, 1169–83.

Pickles, A.R. (1985) *An introduction to likelihood*, CATMOG Series, Geo Abstracts, Norwich, England.

Pickles, A.R. and Davies, R.B. (1985) 'The longitudinal analysis of housing careers', *Journal of Regional Science*, **25**, 85–101.

Pickles, A.R. and Davies, R.B. (1991) 'The empirical analysis of housing careers: a review and a general statistical modelling framework', *Environment and Planning A*, forthcoming.

Pitfield, D.E. (1978) 'Freight distribution models compared: a test of hypotheses', *Environment and Planning A*, **10**, 7, 813–36.

Provin, R.W. (1977) 'The perception of numerousness on dot maps', *The American Cartographer*, **4**, 111–25.

Putnam, S.H. and Chung, S.H. (1989) 'Effects of spatial system design on spatial interaction models: 1. The spatial system definition problem', *Environment and Planning A*, **21**, 27–46.

Quigley, J.M. and Weinberg, D.H. (1977) 'Intra-urban residential mobility: a review and synthesis', *International Regional Science Review*, **2**, 41–66.

Ravenstein, E.G. (1885) 'The laws of migration', *Journal of the Royal Statistical Society*, **48**, II, 167–227.

Ravenstein, E.G. (1889) 'The laws of migration', *Journal of the Royal Statistical Society*, **52**, 241–301.

Rees, P.H. (1983) 'Does it really matter which migration data you use in a population model?', Chapter 5 in White, P. and Van der Knaap, B. (eds), *Contemporary studies of migration*, Geo Books, Norwich, pp. 5–77.

Rees, P.H. (1984) 'Spatial population analysis using movement data and accounting methods: theory, models, the MOVE program and examples', *Working Paper 404*, School of Geography, University of Leeds.

Rees, P.H. (1986) 'Developments in the modelling of spatial populations', Chapter 6 in Woods, R. and Rees, P.H. (eds), *Population structures and models*, Allen and Unwin, London, pp. 97–125.

Rees, P.H. (1989) 'Old model faces new challenges: a review of the state of the art in multispace population modelling', *Working Paper 531*, School of Geography, University of Leeds.

Rees, P.H., Clarke, M.C. and Duley, C.J. (1987) 'A model for updating individual and household populations', *Working Paper 486*, School of Geography, University of Leeds.

Rees, P.H., Duley, C., Bristow, M., Patel, I. and Rees, G. (1990) *Swansea project: programmers' documentation*, GMAP Ltd., University of Leeds.

Rees, P.H. and Stillwell, J.C.H. (1984) 'An integrated model of migration flows and population change for a system of UK metropolitan and non-metropolitan regions: a framework', in Boyce, A.J. (ed.), *Migration and mobility*, Taylor and Francis, London, pp. 317–53.

Rees, P.H., Stillwell, J.C.H., Boden, P., Duley, C., Ramsden, C., Bristow, M., Patel, I. and Rees, G. (1990) *SWIS: an information and projection system for ward populations and housing (for the) City of Swansea, Manual and Report*, GMAP Ltd., University of Leeds.

Rees, P.H. and Willekens, F. (1989) 'Population projection: Dutch and English multiregional methods', Chapter 2 in Stillwell, J.C.H. and Scholten, H.J. (eds), *Contemporary Research in Population Geography: A Comparison of the United Kingdom and the Netherlands*, Kluwer, Dordrecht, pp. 19–37.

Rees, P.H. and Wilson, A.G. (1977) *Spatial population analysis*, Edward Arnold, London.

Rees, P.H. and Woods, R.I. (1986) 'Demographic estimation: problems, methods and examples', Chapter 12 in Woods, R.I. and Rees, P.H. (eds), *Population structures and models*, Allen and Unwin, London, pp. 301–43.

Ricketts, E.R. and Sawhill, I.V. (1986) 'Defining and measuring the underclass', *Urban Institute Working Paper*, Washington, DC.

Ricketts, E.R. and Sawhill, I.V. (1986) *Statistical Abstract of the United States: 1986*, 106th edition, US Government Printing Office, Washington, DC.

Robinson, I.M. (1981) *Canadian urban growth trends: implications for a national settlement policy*, University of British Columbia Press, Vancouver.

Robinson, C. and Tomes, N. (1982) 'Self selection and interprovincial migration in Canada', *Canadian Journal of Economics*, **15**, 3, 474–502.

Rogers, A. (1990) 'Requiem for the net migrant', *Geographical Analysis*, **22**, 4, 283–300.

Rogers, A. and Castro, L.J. (1981) 'Model migration schedules', *RR-81-30*, International Institute of Applied Systems Analysis, Laxenburg, Austria.

Rogers, A. and Planck, F. (1984) 'MODEL: a general program for estimation parameterized model schedules of fertility, mortality, migration and marital status and labour force status transitions', *Working Paper 83-102*, IIASA, Laxenburg, Austria.

Rogers, A., Raquillet, R. and Castro, L.J. (1978) 'Model migration schedules and their applications', *Environment and Planning A*, **10**, 475–502.

Rogers, A. and Willekens, F. (eds) (1986) *Migration and settlement: a comparative study*, Reidel, Dordrecht.

Rossi, P. (1955) *Why families move: a study in the social psychology of urban residential mobility*, Free Press, Glencoe, Illinois.

Rothenberg, J. (1977) 'On the microeconomics of internal migration', in Brown, A.A. and Neuberger, E. (eds), *Internal migration: a comparative perspective*, Academic Press, New York, pp. 183–208.

Rouwendal, J. and Nijkamp, P. (1987) 'Regional economic research on labour markets', in Fischer, M.M. and Nijkamp, P. (eds), *Regional labour markets*, Elsevier, Amsterdam.

Rowntree, J.A. (1990) 'Population estimates and projections', *Population Trends*, **60**, 33–4.

Sandefur, G.D. and Scott, W.J. (1981) 'A dynamic analysis of migration: an assessment of the effects of age, family and career variables', *Demography*, **18**, 3, 355–68.

Sandell, S.H. (1977) 'Women and the economics of family migration', *Review of Economics and Statistics*, **59**, 4, 406–14.

Saunders, M.N.K. and Flowerdew, R. (1987) 'Spatial aspects of the provision of job information', in Fischer, M.M. and Nijkamp, P. (eds), *Regional labour markets*, Elsevier, Amsterdam, pp. 206–28.

Schlottmann, A.M. and Herzog, H.W. (1982) 'Home economic condition and the decision to migrate: new evidence for the US labor force', *Southern Economic Journal*, **48**, 4, 950–61.

Schlottmann, A.M. and Herzog, H.W. (1984) 'Career and geographic mobility interactions: implications for the age selectivity of migration', *Journal of Human Resources*, **19**, 72–86.

Schreiner, A. and Skoglund, T. (1985) 'Regional impacts of petroleum activities in Norway', in Bjerkholt, O. and Offerdal, E. (eds), *Macroeconomic prospects for a small oil exporting country*, Martinus Nijhoff Publishers, Dordrecht.

Schubert, U., Gerking, S., Isserman, A.S. and Taylor, C. (1987) 'Regional labour market modelling: a state of the art review', in Fischer, M.M. and Nijkamp, P. (eds), *Regional labour markets*, Elsevier, Amsterdam.

Schultz, T.P. (1982) 'Lifetime migration within educational strata in Venezuela: estimation of a logistic model', *Economic Development and Cultural Change*, **31**, 559–93.

Senior, M.L. (1979) 'From gravity modelling to entropy maximizing: a pedagogic guide', *Progress in Human Geography*, **3**, 2, 175–210.

SERPLAN (1986) 'Regional trends in the South East', *Regional Monitor 1985–86, RPC 535*, London and South East Regional Planning Conference, 50–64 Broadway, London.

SERPLAN (1987) 'Regional trends in the South East', *Regional Monitor 1986–87, RPC 800*, London and South East Regional Planning Conference, 50–64 Broadway, London.

SERPLAN (1988) 'House price differentials in the South East, 1981–86', *Regional Monitor 1987–88 Technical Appendix, (RPC 1062)*, London and South East Regional Planning Conference, 50–64 Broadway, London.

SERPLAN (1989) 'Regional trends in the South East', *ROC 1430*, London and South East Regional Planning Conference, 50–64 Broadway, London.

Shaw, R.P. (1975) *Migration theory and fact*, Regional Science Research Institute, Philadelphia.

Shaw, R.P. (1986) 'Fiscal versus traditional market variables in Canadian migration, *Journal of Political Economy*, **94**, 648–66.

Shields, G.M. and Shields, M.P. (1989) 'Family migration and nonmarket activities in Costa Rica', *Economic Development and Cultural Change*, **38**, 1, 73–88.

Siegel, J.S. and Hamilton, C.H. (1952) 'Some considerations in the use of the residual method of estimating net migration', *Journal of the American Statistical Association*, **XLVII**, 475–500.

Silvers, A.L. (1979) 'Probabilistic income maximising behaviour in regional migration', *International Regional Science Review*, **2**, 1, 29–40.

Simon, H.A. (1969) *The sciences of the artificial*, MIT Press, Cambridge, Mass.

Simon, J.L. (1978) *Basic research methods in social sciences*, Random House, New York.

Sjaastad, L. (1962) 'The costs and returns in human migration', *Journal of Political Economy, Supplement*, **70**, 80–93.

Skoglund, T. and Stokka, A. (1988) 'Problems of linking single-region and multiregional economic models', *Discussion Paper No. 37*, Central Bureau of Statistics, Oslo.

Smart, M. (1974) 'Labour market areas: uses and definitions', *Progress in Planning*, **2**, 4, Pergamon Press, Oxford.

Smart, M. (1981) 'Labour market areas in Great Britain: developments since 1961', *Geoforum*, **12**, 4, 301–18.

Somermeyer, W.H. (1971) 'Multi-polar human flow models', *Regional Science Association Papers*, **XXVI**, 131–44.

Speare, A., Jr, Goldstein, S. and Frey, W.H. (1975) *Residential mobility, migration and metropolitan change*, Ballinger Publishing Co., Cambridge, Mass.

Spitze, G. (1984) 'Black family migration and wives' employment', *Journal of Marriage and the Family*, **46**, 4, 781–90.

Stambøl, L.S. (1987) 'Flytting i modellen DROM, status oq videreforing', *Interne notater 87/48*, Central Bureau of Statistics, Oslo.

Stambøl, L.S. (1989) 'Arbeidsmarkedsutvikling i fylkene 1972–1986', *Interne notater 89/26*, Central Bureau of Statistics, Oslo.

Stevens, S.S. (1957) 'On the psychophysical law', *Psychological Review*, **64**, 153–81.

Stewart, J.Q. (1948) 'Demographic gravitation: evidence and applications', *Sociometry*, **11**, 31–58.

Stillwell, J.C.H. (1978) 'Interzonal migration: some historical tests of spatial interaction models', *Environment and Planning*, **10**, 1187-1200.

Stillwell, J.C.H. (1980) 'An investigation of some alternative model-based approaches to projecting inter-regional migration', *Working Paper 270*, School of Geography, University of Leeds.

Stillwell, J.C.H. (1984) 'IMP: a program for inter-area migration analysis and projection: user's manual (revised)', *Computer Manual 12*, School of Geography, University of Leeds.

Stillwell, J.C.H. (1986) 'The analysis and projection of interregional migration in the United Kingdom', Chapter 8 in Woods, R.I. and Rees, P.H. (eds), *Population structures and models*, Allen and Unwin, London, pp. 160–202.

Stillwell, J.C.H. (1990) 'Migration analysis based on National Health Service Central register data: trends and models', *Working Paper 537*, School of Geography, University of Leeds.

Stillwell, J.C.H., Boden, P. and Rees, P.H. (1987) 'Migration Schedule construction using MODEL and GIMMS, *Computer Manual 2912*, School of Geography, University of Leeds.

Stillwell, J.C.H., Boden, P. and Rees, P.H. (1988) 'Internal migration change in the UK: trends based on NHSCR movement data, 1975-6 to 1985-6', *Working Paper 510*, School of Geography, University of Leeds.

Stillwell, J.C.H., Boden, P. and Rees, P.H. (1990) 'Trends in internal net migration in the UK: 1975 to 1986', *Area*, **22**, 1, 57–65.

Stillwell, J.C.H. and Rees, P.H. (1985) 'Where do British universities get their students from', *Working Paper 435*, School of Geography, University of Leeds.

Stouffer, S.A. (1940) 'Intervening opportunities: a theory relating mobility and distance', *American Sociological Review*, **5**, 845–67.

Stouffer, S.A. (1960) 'Intervening opportunities and competing migrants', *Journal of Regional Science*, **2**, 1–26.

Taylor, P.J. (1975) 'Distance decay in spatial interactions', *Concepts and Techniques in Modern Geography 2*, Geo Abstracts, London.

Thomas, D.S. (1938) *Research memorandum on migration differentials*, Social Science Research Council, New York.

Todaro, M.P. (1969) 'A model of labour migration and urban unemployment in less developed countries', *American Economic Review*, **59**, 138–48.

Trønnes, D.H. (1983) 'Bruttoflytting og arbeidsmarked i fylkene', *Interne notater 83/28*, Central Bureau of Statistics, Oslo.

Tunali, I. (1986) 'A general structure for models of double selection and an application to a joint migration/earnings process with remigration', in Ehrenberg, R.G. (ed.), *Research in labour economics*, **8**, (Part B), 235–83, JAI Press, Greenwich, London.

UCCA (1978–84) *Statistical supplement*, UCCA, Cheltenham.

US Bureau of the Census (1986) 'County Statistics File 2 (CO-STAT 2)', machine-readable data file produced by the US Bureau of the Census, Washington, DC, and distributed by the Inter-university Consortium for Political and Social Research, Ann Arbor, Michigan.

Vanderkamp, J. (1972a) 'Migration flows, their determinants and the effects of return migration', *Journal of Political Economy*, **80**, 1012–31.

Vanderkamp, J. (1972b) 'Return migration: its significance and behaviour', *Western Economic Journal*, **10**, 460–5.

Vanderkamp, J. (1976) 'The role of population size in migration studies', *Canadian Journal of Economics*, **IX**, 308–17.

Vanderkamp, J. (1986) 'On testing the human capital model of migration', *Canadian Journal of Economics*, **IX**, 387–94.

van Dijk, J., Folmer, H., Herzog, H.W., Jr, and Schlottmann, A.M. (1989) 'Labor market institutions and the efficiency of interregional migration: a cross-nation comparison, in van Dijk, J., Folmer, H., Herzog, H.W., Jr, and Schlottmann, A.M. (eds), *Migration and labor market adjustment*, Kluwer, Dordrecht, pp. 61–84.

Varian, H.R. (1984) *Mikrookonomie*, Oldenbourg, Munich.

Viscusi, W.K. (1986) 'Market incentives for criminal behaviour', in Freeman, R.B. and Holzer, H.J. (eds), *The black youth employment crisis*, University of Chicago Press, Chicago.

Wachter, M.L. (1972) 'A labour supply model for secondary workers', *Review of Economics and Statistics*, **54**.

Wadycki, W. (1979) 'Alternative opportunities and United States interstate migration', *Annals of Regional Science*, **13**, 35–41.

Weeden, R. (1973) 'Inter-regional migration models and their application to Great Britain', *National Institute of Economic and Social Research Paper 2*, Cambridge University Press, London.

White, P. and Woods, R. (eds) (1980) *The geographical impact of migration*, Longman, London.

White, S.E. (1980) 'A philosophical dichotomy in migration research', *Professional Geographer*, **32**, 6–13.

Whittle, P. (1982) *Optimization over time: dynamic programming and stochastic control*, John Wiley, New York.

Wilkinson, R.K. (1976) 'How people value their housing: some factors in tenure choice', *Housing Review*, **25**, 11–14.

Willekens, F.J. (1983) 'Specification and calibration of spatial interaction models: a contingency-table perspective and an application to intra-urban migration in Rotterdam', *Tijdschrift voor Economische en Sociale Geografie,* **74**, 4, 239–52.

Willekens, F. and Baydar, N. (1986) 'Forecasting place-to-place migration with generalized linear models', Chapter 9 in Woods, R.I. and Rees, P.H. (eds), *Population structures and models,* Allen and Unwin, London, pp. 203–44.

Willekens, F., Por, A. and Raquillet, R. (1981) 'Entropy, multiproportional and quadratic techniques for inferring detailed migration patterns from aggregate data', in Rogers, A. (ed.), *Advances in multiregional demography,* RR-81-6, International Institute of Applied Systems Analysis, Laxenburg, Austria.

Willis, K.G. (1974) *Problems in migration analysis,* Lexington Books, Lexington, Mass.

Wilson, A.G. (1967) 'A statistical theory of spatial distribution models', *Transportation Research,* 1, 253–69.

Wilson, A.G. (1970) *Entropy in urban and regional modelling,* Pion, London.

Wilson, A.G. (1974) *Urban and regional models in geography and planning,* Wiley, Chichester.

Wilson, A.G. and Kirkby, M.J.K. (1980) *Mathematics for geographers and planners,* Second Edition, Clarendon Press, Oxford.

Wilson, W.J. (1987) *The truly disadvantaged: the inner city, the underclass, and public policy,* University of Chicago Press, Chicago.

Winer, S.L. and Gauthier, D. (1982) *Internal migration and fiscal structure,* Economic Council of Canada, Ottawa.

Wolpert, J. (1966) 'Migration as an adjustment to environmental stress', *Journal of Social Issues,* **22**, 92–102.

Wolpert, J. (1973) 'Behavioural aspects of the decision to migrate', *Papers of the Regional Science Association,* **15**, 159–69.

Woode, A. and Hinde, J. (1987) 'Binomial variance component models with nonparametric mixing distributions: a GLIM approach', in Crouchley, R. (ed.), *Longitudinal data analysis,* Avebury, Aldershot, pp. 110–28.

Woods, R.I. (1981) 'Spatio-temporal models of ethnic segregation and their implications for housing policy', *Environment and Planning A,* **13**, 1415–33.

Wrigley, N. (1985) *Categorical data analysis for geographers and environmental scientists,* Longman, London.

Yezer, A.M. and Thurston, L. (1976) 'Migration patterns and income change: implication for the human capital approach to migration', *Southern Economic Journal,* **42**, 4, 693–702.

Zelinsky, W. (1971) 'The hypothesis of the mobility transition', *Geographical Review,* **61**, 219–49.

Zipf, G.K. (1946) 'The P1P2/D hypothesis: on intercity movement of persons', *American Sociological Review,* **11**, 677–86.

Index